The Olive in California

The Olive in CALIFORNIA

HISTORY OF AN IMMIGRANT TREE

Judith M. Taylor, M.D.

Foreword by Dr. Kevin Starr, State Librarian of California

TEN SPEED PRESS
Berkeley ❧ Toronto

Ten Speed Press
PO Box 7123
Berkeley, California 94707
www.tenspeed.com

Distributed in Australia by Simon and Schuster Australia, in Canada by Ten Speed Press Canada, in New Zealand by Southern Publishers Group, in South Africa by Real Books, in Southeast Asia by Berkeley Books, and in the United Kingdom and Europe by Airlift Book Company.

Cover & Text Design by Jeff Puda

Library of Congress Cataloging-in-Publication Data
Taylor, Judith M.
The olive in California : history of an immigrant tree / Judith M. Taylor.
p. cm.
Includes bibliographical references (pp. 276–295).
ISBN 1-58008-131-2
1. Olive—California—History. 2.Olive industry and trade—California—History. 3. Adventive plants—California—History. I. Title.
SB367.T29   2000
338.1'7463'09794—dc21   99-051302

First printing, 2000
Printed in Hong Kong

1 2 3 4 5 6 7 8 9 10—03 02 01 00

To Irvin, who made it all possible.

ॐ

Contents

Foreword

by DR. KEVIN STARR
STATE LIBRARIAN OF CALIFORNIA

History can be sweeping and grand: the rise and fall of empires, the sweep of vast military campaigns, the ebb and flow of philosophy, science, literature, and the arts. History can also be a matter of something as simple as an olive tree brought to the New World from Spain in the early sixteenth century and later arriving in California, again thanks to Spain, at about the time the American Republic was being established. But when history is concerned with something as fundamental as the olive, as is this extensively researched and graciously written history by Dr. Judith M. Taylor, the particular tends almost immediately towards the universal, and the small becomes important, because the olive in and of itself—like wheat leading to bread, like grapes leading to wine, like the honeycomb of Virgilian memory—bespeaks nature and human cultivation. To suggest the olive tree, the olive, and olive oil, that is, is to suggest something very fundamental about the way, at least in the West, human beings have through the arts of agriculture pressed from the very earth itself an inexhaustible fountain of goodness.

❦ GNARLED TRUNK OF AN ANCIENT
OLIVE TREE IN THE GARDEN OF
THE MUSÉE RENOIR, FORMERLY
THE HOME OF AUGUSTE RENOIR,
CAGNES-SUR-MER, FRANCE.

Already, by ancient times, as Dr. Taylor succinctly chronicles, the Western imagination was beholding in the grain of wheat, in the vines ripening in the sun, in the woodland hives of bees, in the fig tree and the olive, the perfect symbol of the truth that human beings, having found themselves on this planet, were making the best of it. Through cultivation, they were establishing the very premises of civilization itself. Even more powerful, these fundamental gifts of the earth offered as well near-transcendental symbols of nature, time, human care, and, even more subliminally, the sacred. Not surprisingly, these products and symbols—bread, wine, the olive oil of anointment—made their way into the center of classical and Judeo-Christian religious symbolism.

Like its other counterparts in the litany of near-sacred crops—wheat, grapes, honey, figs—the olive was at once a present-tense, near-spontaneous gift of nature arising from the earth itself and the patient work of human husbandry and hence a work of time. Even today, on the hillsides of Corfu and Cyprus, in the orchards of northern Israel, Lebanon, and Syria, or in the orchards of Greece, Italy, and Spain, there stand groves of olive trees which have absorbed unto themselves millennia of sunny days and cool nights, water and minerals from the soil. These hoary trees can frequently seem like the Sybil herself: filled, that is, with age and ancient knowledge and startling complexities.

When the Spanish brought the olive to California, their final colony in the New World, they were bringing nothing less than history itself to these distant shores: meaning, in this instance, the total experience of the Classical world and the Mediterranean Europe which succeeded it. The olive cuttings they brought by ship, then planted in the mission orchards of San Diego, San Jose, Santa Clara, and other places were endowed by many expectations: nourishment of body, anointment of soul, the ordering of landscape, shade from sun. But pervading all these was a sense of time and human cultivation. From this perspective, the olive tree and its fruit, and the oil pressed from olives, was bringing historical time itself—past, present, and future—to a remote Pacific shore whose landscape, climate, and cycle of seasons closely resembled the Mediterranean regions of Europe that had nurtured the olive—and hence nurtured history—in ages past.

Here, then, is the olive as history, more precisely California history; and here also is California history as the olive. It is fascinating to see the olive at once pace the unfolding development of California and be part of its times. In the mission era, the olive came to California, thanks to the Franciscan missionaries who brought the agriculture of Europe to Spain's newest frontier, along with all the other aspects of Hispanic civilization. As in the case of viticulture and winemaking, olive growing was easily taken up by the first generation of residents of California as an American state: men such as John Bidwell of Chico, one of the founders of agriculture in California in the American era. Such a grafting of Anglo-American farming skill onto olive culture, in fact, suggests the basic historical process of this era: the amalgamation of Hispanic with Anglo-American California. So too did the olive, as chronicled by Dr. Taylor, receive its most complete nineteenth-century development in these decades, climaxing in the boom of the 1880s, in which California reentered the imagination of the American East and Midwest following a decade of transcontinental railroad connection and the recovery of the economy. In the late nineteenth century, the olive was not only diversified and strengthened by the influx of new stocks, it also played an important role in the growing perception of that era—beginning with the novel *Ramona* (1884), and the Mission Revival in architecture that followed, and the Spanish Revival that followed the revival of Mission architecture—that began to envision and promote with special intensity the image of California as Mediterranean shores of America.

This was a time when the heedless frontier yielded, sometimes self-consciously, to civility and the genteel tradition. Hence, in terms of the storyline and concerns of Dr. Taylor's history, the frontier era of bonanza wheat, during which entire counties were sown and harvested and sown and harvested all over again without regard to the recuperative powers of the soil, was replaced by the more patient and environmentally sensitive planting of fruit trees, to include the olive. All this pastorale, however, had an industrial base or at least an industrial component; and as California began to develop the beginnings of industry in the San Francisco Bay Area, especially in maritime engineering and construction, it also began to utilize the refrigerated rail car to ship its perishable fruits to the East and to bring the olive, a luxury fruit, to a mass market through canning and railroad distribution. Like the orange, also emerging in California in this era, and the raisin—and wine and walnuts, for that matter—the olive was, to Anglo-American perception at least, an elite commodity that, almost miraculously, California was now making available to ordinary consumers. Thanks to California, Americans were soon eating oranges beyond the one or two of the Christmas season. Raisins and nuts were also becoming available; and a major campaign was gathering strength, thanks to the efforts of such figures as Andrea Sbarboro to fulfill the desire of Thomas Jefferson to make wine an everyday temperance-promoting beverage.

Yet, industrialism, which is to say, a mass society, has its dangers, and an epidemic of botulism, which Dr. Taylor honestly faces and chronicles, cost the lives of many Americans and severely compromised the California olive trade. In botulism carried by canned olives, the sunny possibilities of California, indeed nature itself, revealed its dangerous side, especially when altered through industrial use. Conversely, the canning of olives also caused environmental damage through its vast utilization and discard of salt and other leaching minerals. And this too, over time, emerged as a problem that had to be dealt with—but such challenges offered a paradigm through the olive of California correcting and improving itself. The garden of California, after all, was in so many instances an invented garden, the product of technology and human will. This invented garden was yielding enormous payoffs, but there had to be paybacks as well.

As in the case of the citrus industry, moreover, the cooperative impulse came forth to assist in meeting such challenges: cooperation between the growers themselves, and of equal importance, cooperation with the scientists of the University of California. As Dr. Taylor develops this theme, it soon becomes evident that the University of California played a major role not only in rescuing the California canned olive industry, but also in improving the very nature of olive culture itself. So too did the federal government, especially in the depression-ridden 1930s, play an equally important role in bringing the olive industry back to life: another instance in which the olive reflected larger historical patterns; for it was the federal government that created and governed California in the first place and, later, financed and constructed much of its water system.

In the postwar era, California doubled, almost tripled, its population largely through internal migration, as California became the desired haven for the middle classes. This was the era of the canned pitted olive served as an hors d'oeuvre in an outdoor patio prior to a barbecue, the chopped olive in a deviled egg sandwich sent off to school in a paper bag carried by a freckled-faced kid; and yes, the olive perched majestically on its toothpick in a crystal clear arctic-cold martini which, like the barbecue and the public school, also bespoke the aspirations of the postwar era.

In the 1970s and 1980s, following upon a political revolution that exhausted itself and a social revolution that changed America forever, a revolution in cuisine was ushered onto the historical stage. It began in California when wine and food, always revered in the Golden State, became the fact and symbol *par excellence* of California as private place and personal paradise. As California wine reached new heights in this era, so too did the California olive; and California olive oil, thanks to a new generation of growers and vintners, achieved, then surpassed, world standards. An increasingly health-minded generation, moreover, began to move olive oil farther and farther into the center of food preparation and cooking; and bottles of olive oil began to vie with the butter dish on restaurant and family tables.

Every industry does better when its history, to include its successes and failures, is brought forth into structured statement. This is what Dr. Taylor does so well in this volume: coax to awareness everything we might have suspected or half-known about the olive but were too busy to ask. Now thanks to this book, the great solemn olive trees of our state and the presses that attend them, together with the more prosaic canneries, have their history brought to light. Reading this book, we encounter an important chapter in the history of the olive; but we also encounter a precisely defined but significant dimension of the history of California agriculture, as well as the social and cultural extensions of California as garden of the world. Because the olive, moreover, is so fundamental to our symbolism of human culture, this history does something else as well. It links California to the near-mythic hillsides of ancient times when men and women first looked to the horizon and saw olive trees, or sat beneath them and dreamed of Arcady, or harvested and pressed their fruit. From that harvest, crushed by stone, there has for millennia come forth a joyous liquid, which has become and remained the precious oil of life itself.

MANZANILLO OLIVE

SEVILLANO OLIVE

CALIFORNIA HORTICULTURE

BY
GEO. C. ROEDING.

1909

Preface

It was one of those typical San Francisco mornings, gray, cool, and slightly misty. My husband, Irvin, and I had decided to go to the San Francisco farmers' market that week instead of the one we usually went to in San Rafael. When we arrived, Irvin was very interested in the delicious aroma emanating from the grills set up by a well-known restaurant in the city and began pursuing its source. I was prospecting among the booths with their wonderful selections of fruit, vegetables, homemade breads, honey, cheeses, and all the things that make farmers' markets so attractive. I came across one that had numerous bottles of olive oil bearing odd and unfamiliar names. The legend said "Nick Sciabica and Sons" of Modesto, California.

Many previous experiences led up to that moment. Irvin and I had just moved to California the year before, from Westchester County, New York. The house we bought in Marin County had a very fine view of the city of San Francisco, San Francisco Bay, Belvedere, the Golden Gate Bridge, Oakland, Berkeley, and all the delightful places in between. It also had a garden that had been quite neglected. This gave me a wonderful opportunity to create a new garden and put into practice all the principles I had been learning about California's climate and terrain.

On a previous visit to the Bay Area, we had visited the Strybing Arboretum in Golden Gate Park, and I was struck by the docent's describing much of California's climate as "Mediterranean." The features of this climate are its hot dry summers and cool

❧ COVER OF GEORGE ROEDING'S 1909
  California Horticulture.

wet winters, usually without snow or ice. The Mediterranean climate lies in two bands, one in the Northern Hemisphere and one in the Southern Hemisphere, its mirror image, falling roughly between 30 and 45 degrees latitude. Sections of South Africa, Australia, and South America fit the definition of this climate and not surprisingly, olive trees grow as well there as in the northern belt. Though plants must be able to tolerate six months of desertlike drought and recuperate during the winter rains, many flourish under these circumstances.

We had been told the same thing about the Mediterranean climate of California when we visited the Huntington Library, Art Collections, and Botanical Gardens in San Marino, near Los Angeles. The Huntington's gardens are thrifty in the use of water and drought tolerant, if not fully drought resistant. I fell in love with the delicate "angels' fishing rods," or Dierama, an African desert flower. I was also captivated by the elegant desert plants from South Africa and Australia, which are at home both on the Huntington grounds as well as at the Strybing. Yet the quintessential thing that says "Mediterranean" is the olive tree. Now that I was in California, I could grow many wonderful plants, but most of all I looked forward to growing olive and lemon trees.

When the olive trees arrived in their large wooden tubs, their beauty simply enchanted me. Although the tubs just sat in the rubble that would one day become a garden, the trees still exerted a calm power. Once they were planted, I felt an enormous sense of satisfaction. I had begun to create a garden that both fit the California landscape and was integrated into it.

All this was in my mind when I stumbled on the olive oil stand that day at the farmers' market. Dan Sciabica presided over the olive oil bottles. He is a warm and friendly man, very affable and approachable. He told me about an oil that he had just pressed the day before—green, fruity, and not filtered or blended. It sounded marvelous, and I bought a bottle. It was so new it did not even have a label on it. He explained that it had so much flavor, there was no need to add vinegar to salad dressing when using it.

I told him about my trees. We had bought them in thirty-six-inch containers, so they were already several years old. Some fruit was ripening on them. The berries were not all alike, some being round, others oval, and yet others in between. It seemed that I might have trees of different varieties. He showed me oil that had been pressed from Nevadillo, Sevillano, or Manzanillo olives. These names were all new to me, though I associated Manzanillo with Manzanilla sherry from Spain. He suggested I bring some samples of my olives back the following week, and he would identify them for me.

Since planting the trees, I had tried to find a book that would give me a lot more information about them, but I had not been successful. The library and bookshops had many beautiful horticultural books about roses, camellias, bromeliads, azaleas, and many other plants and trees, as well as the general history of the California garden, but nothing focused on olives. I did find an extensive literature about olives in the Old World later but none devoted solely to the New World. A vague thought began to take shape at the back of my mind. Here was a gap that needed to be filled, and maybe I could fill it. The chief question was how to begin.

I owe a great deal of what happened next to the "kindness of strangers." Dan Sciabica came to my rescue with practical help as he has in so many cases. Many of the people I subsequently spoke to traced much of their knowledge and skill back to his, and his family's, assistance.

The following week I returned to the farmers' market. (Of course the new green oil had been all that Dan had told me it would be, and I was hooked for life.) I took a sample of each kind of olive back with me and showed them to Dan. He offered some possible names but was not convinced that the trees were really all that different. I told him that I was toying with the idea of writing a book about olives and the history of olive trees. It was all very vague. He thought that the best thing I could do would be to call a friend of his in Sacramento, Darrell Corti, a man he referred to as a "walking encyclopedia" of olive lore. He gave me Mr. Corti's phone number and thus helped me to get started in my research.

As I thought more about the idea of such a book, I recognized that anything I constructed would have to be within the framework of California's history as a whole. The growth of a state consists of the sum of all the events that take place within its borders. Immigrants, whether human, animal, or vegetable have defined modern California. Which kind of immigrant, when they arrived, and what happened to them after they arrived are all significant questions. In attempting to answer them, this book took shape.

The whole enterprise turned out to be the most intoxicating adventure. I could never have known how fascinating the search would be. I did not know that I would explore the beginning of the Spanish colonization of California and the efforts to establish agriculture as a means of survival. I did not know that almost three hundred varieties of olive trees were imported into this state from 1874 to 1955. I did not know that I would delve into the fragrant byways of old nurseries with their romantic pictures and excited prose, nor did I know that I would learn how botulism would affect the olive industry and how the challenge it presented would help make all processed foods safer for the consumer. I could not know that one of the most respected and important of the great immigrants, John Bidwell, would turn out to be a pioneer in making olive oil, among other achievements. I also could not know that men whose names were merely on a series of lists could become familiar and alive in my mind.

The condition of almost total ignorance allows one to learn a great deal, something I proceeded to do. To glean material for this book, I went to see for myself how olives are grown and processed in California. Several people had given me names and phone numbers that I used to get started. I began my journeys in the cool spring of 1996, while there was still snow on the Sierras and even a bit on the Coast Range. I drove from one end of the Central Valley to the other. I met many people, and I also encountered agriculture in a very personal way.

With the change of seasons, the road revealed all the beauties of fruit blossoms, wildflowers, and wild descendants of cultivated flowers that had escaped and become naturalized on their own. Great stands of "wild" sunflowers along the borders of Highway 99 were a delightful surprise. Later in the summer, as I returned from Woodlake near Lindsay, driving through narrow country lanes, I found myself surrounded by orchards—cherries, peaches, apricots, plums—and vineyards. In orange and lemon groves, fruit was forming on the trees but not yet ripe. There were no houses or signs of human life for miles until I went through the village of Yettem, which is the Armenian term for "the Garden of Eden." The Hamalian brothers named their colony well.[1]

Now my explorations and this project are over, and I suppose someone will ask why I collected all this information. What difference does it make that all those olive companies and growers struggled to make a living doing something very uncertain a long time ago? It is all gone now and will never return. The short answer is I did it for its own sake—and I enjoyed it immensely. The more formal and academic answer is that there are valuable lessons to be learned, lessons about what contributed to the growth of California and its institutions. Included in this view are the courage, vision, and perseverance of its people.

Now it's time to share much of what I learned about the trajectory of the olive in California with you. It is a fascinating story, a living story that began with a few trees on the inhospitable shore of Alta (Upper) California in the mission period and that grew to hundreds of thousands of trees and dozens or even hundreds of small businesses within a hundred years. Though the olive processing industry has shrunk through consolidation in the 1990s, dozens of eager little olive oil companies are once again getting established. The story of the olive in California thus reflects the cycles of growth, decline, and renewal that are a part of life as a whole. Its roots reach far back into history, which is where our story begins.

🌸 Avenue of olive trees planted by John Wolfskill at his estate at Putah Creek, now Winters.

Introduction

The Olive in Ancient Times

The landscapes of the Mediterranean countries are defined by the olive tree. This definition is mythical, symbolic, and religious as well as physical, historical, and agricultural. Quite apart from their important role as producers of food, olive trees have exercised an inordinate fascination over many people during the six thousand years they have been cultivated. No other food of equal or greater antiquity—with the possible exception of the grape—is surrounded by the same aura of myth and romance.

According to Greek myths, the olive tree was the gift of the goddess Athena. While disputing possession of the province of Attica with the god Poseidon, Athena drove a spear into the ground to stake her claim. An olive tree sprang up at the spot. The city that arose on this land was called Athens in her honor.

With that mythical foundation, the olive tree came to have many symbolic and religious functions in Athenian culture. Athens itself was a living memorial to Athena, and the longevity of the tree was equated with the survival of the city. At all important epochs in each individual's life and in civic affairs, olive branches or olive oil played key roles. An infant received an olive branch at birth. Youths competing in the various religious games received a portion of olive oil as a prize. Young men at the brink of manhood, undergoing ordeal by combat before entering the army,

Avenue of olive trees at the University of California at Davis, by Ansel Adams, circa 1967.

I

planted an olive tree at the periphery of the city after the ordeal was over. The elders, who controlled all these institutions, wore an olive branch on their heads while officiating at the games. In homage to the sacred fruit, those who harvested it had to swear an oath of chastity for the duration of the harvest.

The Greek kings believed that the olive tree was an instrument of their personal, royal magic. Armed with its symbolic strength, the king was supposed to be able to increase crops and livestock, ward off pestilence, and propitiate the gods. This was a crucial power. If the population starved under his rule, a king was obviously much reduced in status: no population, no kingdom. In really dire emergencies, the canny ruler did not rely solely on his magical powers but went out into the open market and bought food wherever he could find it.[1]

The olive tree is also a symbol of strength, though it is not so immediately familiar in that guise to most of us today. A moment's thought, however, provides an explanation. The olive tree survives for hundreds of years and provides food that strengthens the body. Its wood is exceedingly hard and therefore is useful for building as well as for making furniture and tools. The tree is almost indestructible. Only fire and excessive water kill it. Any nation with many such trees will be able to field a large army, because it has sufficient food, both at home and on the march, to feed its soldiers. The olive tree is clearly a warrior's friend—and by extension, it is also the friend of those whom the warrior protects.

We are more familiar with the olive tree (or branch) being a symbol of peace. Yet the roots of that symbolism may not be any more obvious to us than the olive tree as a symbol of strength. The best explanation is that the tree is a recurring metaphor of pastoral virtue. Peace is essential if one is to live from the produce of an olive orchard. It takes a very long time living in one place to wait for the tree to grow and yield fruit, something that is impossible in the constant chaos of war. Separated from its original meaning, the expression "extending an olive branch"—meaning an offer to make peace—has become a cliché.

Echoes of the undying symbolism and traditions surrounding the olive tree can still be found in today's world. Few Americans realize, for example, that they see an olive branch whenever they take out a quarter. The quarter has the impression of the Great Seal of the United States, and an olive branch is a central feature of that seal.

The design of the Great Seal was adopted by the Continental Congress on June 20, 1782. A committee consisting of John Adams, Benjamin Franklin, and Thomas Jefferson had been appointed to select the best design. Their charge was to find an appropriate set of dominant symbols for a new, radically different country. They turned to two reliable sources, the Bible and Greek mythology. The winning design contained an eagle, arrows, and an olive branch. In the seal, which has not changed materially over the past two hundred years, the American bald eagle holds an olive branch and a sheaf of arrows in its talons. This was intended to indicate the power to make war or peace. The eagle has been a symbol of brute force and strength in numerous western civilizations. Although there was some debate over other aspects of the design, the one thing they all agreed was that the olive branch was a dignified and fitting symbol for their new country.

The fact that these early American founders turned to the Bible as a source of appropriate symbols for the fledgling United States again attests to the powerful symbolism of the olive tree: it permeated the religious life of many different peoples. Throughout history, a number of Western religions have regarded the olive tree as sacred. There are several theories about why that should be. One reason is that its extreme longevity inspired awe. Not only that, but pieces of even the most ancient olive tree will develop into a new tree when planted in the ground. Fertility and new growth at great age seemed to be magical. The tree provided shelter and food with almost no effort at all. Surely that betokened a benevolent god somewhere, working in not such mysterious ways.

❀ The First Seal of the United States of America, 1782.

For our purposes, it does not matter where these beliefs originated or which people initially adopted them. What is important for us in this study is recognizing the power of the olive tree symbol to endure and to evoke sacred meaning for peoples through the ages. As different religions succeeded each other, the populace maintained its old beliefs while incorporating new tenets and teachings. The priests recognized this behavior and built on it.

Both Judaism and Christianity incorporate the olive tree as a symbol in scripture and ritual. The olive as a symbol of peace comes from the Old Testament. When Noah reached the end of his voyage, the dove he dispatched to see if they were near land found an olive branch floating in the water. This was taken as a sign that God's wrath was appeased.

Olive oil was critical to Jewish religious practice. It was, for example, used in the sacred act of anointing. In ancient Judaism, the high priests in Jerusalem were anointed, as were kings and other lay people on special occasions. (Although anointment eventually fell into disuse in Judaism, it survived almost intact in Christianity.)

Another use of olive oil was that of providing light—both physical and spiritual. The great seven-branched lamp in the Temple was lit by oil. The miracle story of Hanukkah commemorates the amazing feat of Judas Maccabeus in driving the Syrians out of Israel, while the Temple lamp burned for eight days with only one day's supply of oil. (It is only recently that Hanukkah is celebrated by using candles in the nine-branched menorah, one for each of the eight days the lamp was lit, plus a center candle.) In another story from the Hebrew scriptures, Elijah's miracles for the poor widow and her sick son included the provision of a seemingly endless supply of olive oil in the "widow's cruse."

In the Christian scriptures, all of the specific references to olives in the New Testament are about the Mount of Olives in Jerusalem. There is also an indirect reference: Jesus was arrested in the Garden of Gethsemane by the Roman soldiers after the Last Supper. Gethsemane means "garden of the oil press."

Christians, like Jews, used olive oil as a potent symbol in their rituals. Anointing was a visible reminder that the olive tree's symbolic strength and virtue had been transferred to the anointee. It is hardly surprising that Christians should continue this Jewish practice as part of their rituals. The very word "Christ" is from the Greek for "anointed." "Chrism" is an oil that has been blessed.

The different branches of Christianity vary in the actual rites that call for anointment, but it can be used for confirmation, ordination, the consecration of a church, and for the sick. It is intended to augment a sick person's strength in wrestling with the forces of evil and overcoming them. Also, in England, for example, coronation is a standard, if rarely required, occasion for anointment.

As we have seen, the olive tree has played a deeply significant role mythically, symbolically, and religiously for many peoples from ancient times to the present day. At least one reason for this, as noted earlier, was the olive tree's central role in daily life and sustenance. Let's take a brief look now at the history of the olive tree itself and how it came to be a part of the daily lives of so many people in the ancient world.

Concerning the lineage of the olive tree, the best guess of most scholars is that it was first domesticated by tribes living in the highlands of ancient Iran and Turkistan. The putative ancestor of the modern olive tree is the oleaster, a wild shrub that still grows in much of the Middle East, North Africa, and the Mediterranean countries. (Both the oleaster and the olive tree belong to the genus *Olea,* in the botanical family Oleaceae.)

Grafts between oleaster and the olive tree will succeed. Scions, the detached living portion of a plant joined to another in grafting, from modern, cultivated olive trees are frequently bonded to wild oleasters as a rootstock. Oleasters have fruit that can be pressed to make an oil very similar to that of the cultivated olive tree. Based on pollen studies, there is some evidence that the oil jars found in the palace of Knossos on Crete held oleaster oil, not oil from cultivated olive trees.

Though many scholars place the origin of the olive tree in ancient Iran and Turkestan, others argue that the modern olive tree originated in more than one place. This would explain its apparently simultaneous appearance in southern Anatolia, Jordan, Israel, and Syria, countries that were extremely far from each other in antiquity and almost impossible to reach easily when travel was all on foot or by oxcart. Farmers in peacetime would move small distances, if at all, and then only if they outgrew their land. Such incremental movements could account for large changes but only over long periods of time.

The spread of agriculture and civilization over the Mediterranean basin is attributed to incremental movements of this sort. Evidence for intentional cultivation of the olive tree, dating back to 3500 B.C.E., has been found in the islands off the coast of Greece and Turkey. (One of these islands, Samos, is also known as Elaiophytos, which means "planted with olives.") Olive pits of varying sizes, attesting to the changes attendant on cultivation, have been retrieved at the archeological sites.

Olive trees were already widespread in the eastern Mediterranean, Egypt, and North Africa before the proto-Greeks entered the Greek peninsula from the north in the early Iron Age. This occurred about 1000 B.C.E. Olive trees had begun to move west across the Mediterranean Sea before this period, probably through trading and colonization.

As the new immigrants in the Greek peninsula settled the land and differentiated themselves into cities and *demes* (a unit of local government), they adopted the custom of growing olive trees. It was not a universal activity. As late as the fifth century B.C.E., civic leaders were still exhorting their people to grow more olive trees and explaining the advantages of doing so.

One piece of evidence for the probability that much Greek agriculture was adopted from their predecessors is linguistic. The words for several plants found in ancient Greek are not Greek at all but examples of an early Indo-European language descended from Hittite or Anatolian; almost exactly the same words are found in the older languages. Greek coopted the older words for cherry *(kerassos)*, narcissus *(narkissos)*, mint *(minthos)*, cypress *(cupressos)*, and hyacinth *(huakinthos)*, and these words have passed down into modern times.[2]

The Greek word for olive was *elaia* and their word for olive oil was *elaialadh.* This is quite different from the Semitic word for olive oil, which was *zeit.* Therefore we can assume the Greeks did not receive their word from the Phoenicians, a Semitic people. Greeks had already started to grow olives before Phoenician traders were active in the western Mediterranean in the sixth century B.C.E.

Wherever the Greeks grew olive trees, archeologists have recovered whole pits, not just crushed ones from the presses.[3] The raw, untreated olive is extremely bitter and inedible unless something is done to remove the bitter principle, chemicals known as *amygdalins.* How ancient peoples discovered the way to do this is not recorded, but scholars assume it depended on some form of

SIXTH-CENTURY B.C.E. ATTIC VASE DEPICTING AN OLIVE HARVEST. NOTE THE MEN HITTING THE BRANCHES TO MAKE THE OLIVES FALL, AND THE PERSON KNEELING TO GATHER THE FALLEN FRUIT.

providential serendipity. Charming accounts of a traveler finding an olive branch floating in the sea, tasting the olives, and finding them delicious are the kind of stories that have survived. Other stories tell of finding olives, pleasantly sweet, in a river. Both fresh and salt water will cure olives effectively.

The Greeks wanted the olive for its oil and only later used the fruit for the table. Olive oil began as an external application, an emollient for the skin. It was not used as food until a later epoch. (Athens was ahead of Sparta in feeding the soldiers with olives.)

Once olive oil became a dietary staple, the Athenians were encouraged to grow more olives than they needed for their families and sell them for export. Ancient texts indicate that even in those days, olives were an expensive crop to harvest and that the profit margin was very low. Olives were viewed as a subsistence crop, not a cash producer. This is one of the reasons the citizens had to be prodded to grow olives more often.

By today's standards, the large majority of Athenians would be considered small farmers, generally single family units with a modest amount of land. Such a property could barely support its owners, and almost no one had enough food to feed a slave. The rugged independence and democratic structure of Athenian society had its roots in this fact. Great wealth was required to support enough slaves for a large estate.

Harvest was always a very stressful time, because ripe crops had to be picked in a relatively brief interval. Olives are a perfect example of this dilemma. Even if the branches are beaten with sticks, only the ripe fruit falls and the process has to be repeated several times. Each tree takes a finite period of time. Farmers could not afford to support a slave all year round just to get the extra help during the harvest. Hiring a freelance laborer was another option, but it too cost money, which small farmers could ill afford. (If one puts aside the slavery issue, none of this sounds unfamiliar to today's olive growers. The challenges of harvesting olives spans the centuries. The Romans, too, shared this burden. In fact, Columella, the great Roman agronomist of the second century c.e., commented on this very issue in his own time.)

The Greek cities grew gratifyingly fast, and it soon became apparent that there was insufficient room for everyone. The population grew as a result of the solid foundation of farming and a resulting surplus of food. The more adventurous families began moving out, founding colonies along the Mediterranean littoral. Colonies existed in Sicily, southern France, and the west coast of Spain as early as the eighth century b.c.e. Other émigrés went east to Cyrenaica, Thrace, and the shores of the Black Sea (Euxine) and the Hellespont. In all cases, they took olive trees with them. The olive belt represented the frontier of expansion.

While the Greek diaspora was forming, the Phoenicians were consolidating their trade routes. They sailed from Carthage to buy oil in Philistia. Among other places, they bought oil in the city of Ekron (thought to be modern Khirbet el-Muqanna, located about twenty miles from Jerusalem). Stone troughs to crush the fruit and clay jars to hold the oil have been found at several sites in what is now Israel, but Ekron's olive oil industry seems to have been the largest and most well organized of the cities then extant.

The reports of excavations at Ekron indicate an industrial level of equipment, like modern factories. More than one building con-

🌿 Ancient lever- and screw-press and crushing basin found in excavations at Khirbet Qseir, southern Upper Galilee, Israel.

tained large, rectangular rooms devoted to crushing the olive, with stones, troughs, basins, presses, and vats. Over one hundred such presses have been unearthed to date. One estimate is that these factories could produce more than a thousand tons of olive oil in a year.

Combining knowledge of the arrangement of the presses and related equipment with an outline of the system still used by modern Palestinians to make olive oil allows archeologists to work out how the Philistines in Ekron must have made their oil. This method has remained unchanged for hundreds, if not thousands of years.

❧ RECONSTRUCTED OLIVE MILL IN THE ERETZ ISRAEL MUSEUM, TEL AVIV, SHOWING STORAGE BINS (FOREGROUND) AND A DONKEY WAITING TO TURN THE STONE CRUSHER.

The olives were first crushed in basins. The resulting mash was then transferred to straw baskets for the actual pressing to be done. Several baskets were stacked in a press. Various methods of producing a graduated pressure were developed over the early centuries, chiefly a long, extremely heavy beam counterpoised with weights. The crushed fruit yielded a liquid comprised of water and oil. It had to be allowed to settle before oil could be skimmed off at successive intervals.

This is still an effective method of making olive oil. The Palestinians have continued to do it, and one of the nineteenth-century California innovators, Ellwood Cooper, chose it too. There is evidence at the sites in Ekron that olive oil was made in these rooms for over five hundred years. The only obvious difference with the passage of time was that the presses changed from round to square.

Phoenicia, whose traders bought oil in Ekron, was an aggressive commercial country with an important trading partnership with Egypt. Phoenician traders transported olive trees to Egypt, where they flourished in the oases together with date palms. Traders also spread the tree to Crete and Cyprus, by the fifteenth century B.C.E.

The trading activities of Phoenicia allow us to see what happened to olive culture and some significant changes that affected it in the Mediterranean region. The Phoenicians visited several provinces that grew grain and other foods. These provinces have since become deserts. Until the fall of the Roman Empire, Sicily and much of North Africa were important agricultural centers. Changes in the climate, combined with exploitation of the soil, led to the decline.

Only the olive trees that have been there for centuries remain a reliable source of food. The trees were planted far apart from each other. Their roots are shallow and can spread a long distance to find subterranean water. This renders them independent of the almost nonexistent rainfall. Studies of olive trees in desert sections of California and Arizona bear out this observation.

The cultural requirements of the modern olive tree show that it probably evolved elsewhere, not in the semi-deserts it now inhabits. While it survives in warm and arid places, it gives its best crops when it has water regularly and goes through a sharp winter chilling period.[4] It is thus incorrect to equate the limits of the Mediterranean climate with the olive belt.

For example, in Greece, supposedly its quintessential home, the olive tree did not prosper in all areas. It did quite well in the province of Attica, where myth claims that Athena called it into being at Athens, but in mountainous places like Arkadia, the soil and climate were always unfavorable. Even in Attica, the tree did better when interspersed with other crops. This is probably because the soil that supported grain was more fertile than the marginal sections in which wheat could not be grown.

Just as the olive played a large role in trading in the ancient world, it also played an important part in military conquests and the expansion of empires. By the time olive oil and table olives had become conventional articles of food used for soldiers, Alexander the Great was recognized as the leading exponent of careful logistical planning for long campaigns. It is unclear whether he was in fact the only general to do this, or if his extraordinary reputation led to having everything he did recorded. He set out on his first great campaign in 320 B.C.E., having carefully calculated how much food could be taken with the troops and how much had to be obtained at given stages en route. The quartermasters carried grain and drove cattle for meat, but olive oil is not mentioned. Perhaps it was so banal that they saw no need to write anything about it. It makes sense that he took it with him. Olive oil is easily carried, lasts a long time, and, like all fats, provides a significant number of calories.

The Romans copied many of the Greek practices as they developed their empire. At first they did not cultivate olive trees in Italy itself but relied on the established producers in distant provinces like Baetica in Spain. Baetica resembles Ekron in some ways, though at a later date. Once Rome conquered the rest of the Mediterranean and eliminated the last vestiges of Greek power, it turned to cultivating the olive tree in Italy.

Rome's long war with Carthage provided the next watershed in the spread of the olive tree. For two hundred years, Carthage, the greatest city in that region, challenged the Romans. Cato the Elder recognized that Rome would never be secure until Carthage was leveled. His continual refrain was "Carthago delenda esse" (Carthage *must* be destroyed). When the Romans finally reduced Carthage to rubble and its people to slavery in 148 B.C.E., they plowed the fields of Carthage with salt, preventing its rebirth as a great agricultural center. Some years later, the Romans relented and decided to plant olive trees in the damaged soil over much of North Africa. This was done in enlightened self-interest. Olive oil was still a significant trading commodity, and they could not feed their citizens with the output from Italy alone. (At this same time, the Romans also expanded the former Greek olive orchards in southern France and parts of Spain.)

The trees the Romans planted in Carthage were very productive at first, but as the rainfall diminished seriously, the desert gradually encroached. Today there are still extensive olive orchards all over North Africa with a low but steady unit yield. The oil can be sold very cheaply because so little money is spent on the ancient trees.

The olive oil of Roman days was horrid. Contemporary writers sneered at it because it smelled bad. For a long time, it was only used to feed slaves. The slaves also ate the preserved olives. Spoiled, wealthy Romans would not touch such foods. Imperial Rome reeked of cabbage and oil. The hot Mediterranean summers meant that most of the oil became rancid quickly. While this is unpleasant for the taste buds, it does have one advantage in an economy that uses olive oil for lighting: rancid oil burns more brightly and clearly than fresh, because much of the water has evaporated. Olive oil was a significant staple for these reasons and continued to be an article of commerce for the next few centuries.

The inertia and steadfastness of rural life depending on olive cultivation was such that it even survived the onset of the later barbarian invasions. It was only after Rome fell in the fifth century c.e. that even the best established farmers in Italy succumbed to the chaos of this cataclysm. Rome entered the Dark Ages, but olive growing still persisted in the Eastern empire, Byzantium. With numerous invasions by various Christian armies (the "Franks") and later the Ottoman conquests, Byzantium was hardly a stable place over the years, but olive growing remained an important feature of the land that is now Turkey.

As we have seen, the influence and movement of the olive tree (and its products) was quite extensive. The words used for olives and olive oil in modern languages still give a hint of these ancient movements. If the trees went with the Greeks, olives were *elaia,* or a derivative of this word. The Latin word *olea* is a corruption of *elaia. Olea* in turn has passed into Romance languages, so that even the English word *oil* reflects that linguistic descent.

Where the olive followed the Phoenician trails, words that stem from the Semitic *zeit* are common: *sait, tait,* even *tat* in Egypt. Further west, in Morocco, the olive is also known by one of these Semitic variants. Across the Strait of Gibraltar, the Phoenicians were said to be the first to plant olive trees on the Iberian peninsula. The Romans greatly expanded the orchards, but the Moors were so thorough in their seventh-century conquest that almost all traces of Rome were expunged. Today, traces of Arabic in modern Spanish—olive oil is *aceite*—bear testimony to the power of the Saracen (Moorish) invasion and their centuries-long occupation of Spain.

Our exploration of the olive in the ancient world ends in Spain. This is a fitting place to close, for Spain would ultimately play an important role in bringing the olive to California, as we will see in the next chapter.

1

How the Olive Came to California

The olive tree, *Olea europaea L.*, is not native to the Americas. The trees look as if they have always belonged in California and Arizona, their principal North American habitat, but that is not the case. Olive trees originally came to the Western Hemisphere from Spain, and it is the story of this journey that I want to tell in this chapter. The principal events leading up to the transmission of the olive tree began in the late fifteenth and early sixteenth centuries. The path led from the Old World to the New World—from Spain to the Caribbean settlements, then to the mainland of South America, New Spain (Mexico), and finally to what is now the state of California.

A very few attempts to get olive trees to take hold in the eastern half of the United States as a valuable commercial crop failed. The olive trees in that instance were chiefly from Italy, not Spain. Thomas Jefferson was the most well known of the amateur horticulturists who tried to do this. He worked with his friend and neighbor, Philip Mazzei, but they were both defeated by the Virginia climate. Colonists in Georgia, South Carolina, and Florida also attempted to develop the olive industry, with orchards in South Carolina being the most successful, lasting until the mid–nineteenth century. But generally the trees did not succeed in the American South, and after those tentative beginnings, commercial olive growing in the United States was confined to the uniquely well-suited ecosystems of California and Arizona.

❦ Mission Santa Barbara, pre-
restoration, circa 1902.

The history of the New World seems to have been solely one of conquest, wars, pestilence, and violence of many sorts. It is easy to lose sight of the fact that ordinary people, seeking opportunity, also ventured there. The king and queen of Spain, Ferdinand and Isabella, initially restricted Spanish settlement in the New World because they had given sole rights for this to Columbus, but by 1495, any Spaniard in good standing was allowed to go. Columbus was a poor administrator and those in power wanted to see their new possessions populated and producing wealth. Precious metals and trade were the chief goals, but the authorities disguised this naked greed with a pious gloss about converting and civilizing the poor benighted savages.

By 1498, nearly 2,000 colonists had sailed from Spain to the New World. At first, none of the Spanish colonists settled on the mainland. They lived on the islands of Hispaniola and Cuba—the "West Indies." Agriculture was specifically encouraged by the crown. The king had even started a "public farm" in Spain in 1497 for prospective colonists to obtain plants and seed more easily.

Alonso Ojeda opened up the next phase by exploring the coast of Venezuela in 1499, showing that there was space for further expansion. As the number of colonists and traders increased, Spain started an agency called the Casa de Contratacion in 1503 to keep track of everything and everyone.[1] (In 1524, this agency became the Council of the Indies. The Council's meticulous records have largely survived and form an indispensable archive.) The Board of the Casa maintained warehouses both for goods going to the Indies and for the valuable cargo coming from them. The staff of the Casa also assembled the items requested by the colonies.

Among the essential plants the Casa staff provided for the settlers were olive trees. They bought living trees from well-known olive orchards near Seville in Spain. Nothing is recorded about which variety of olive tree was originally exported to the colonies, though it is logical to assume they sent the most popular and prolific trees. The fruit of what is now known as the "Mission" variety was a good source of oil, but it also made quite good pickles. Whatever the variety, it is clear that actual trees were sent. Entries in the archives note that 250 living plants and 1,200 slips were sent in 1520 from Olivares near Seville in the Aljarafe district to Hispaniola and Cuba. Considering how slowly everything moved in those days and that there were many other more important needs, this establishment of olive orchards in the New World within only thirty years is astonishing.

The colonists pursued agriculture as they had been encouraged to do, but things did not work out as intended. Disease, the lack of adequate labor, and Spanish policy itself prevented them from succeeding. The last straw was the need to trade solely with the Spanish government. Spanish economic policy hewed to the mercantilist line, just as the English and other maritime powers were to do for so long. Colonies were to be exploited for raw materials but not allowed to manufacture anything, for fear of diluting the monopoly of the merchants back home. This approach led to slow decay and reduced initiative. By the

✺ OLIVE ORCHARD AT MISSION SAN FERNANDO REY DE ESPANA, CIRCA 1913.

end of twenty-five years, the Caribbean settlements were in decay. Puerto Rico was actually abandoned for a short time. It soon became apparent that more money could be made on the mainland of South America. Only Cuba, particularly Havana, remained important as the point of departure for all future journeys into Central and South America.

The church was active during this early, formative period. The Reverend Juan Diaz, a secular priest (that is, a priest who is not a member of an order such as the Franciscans), and the Reverend Bartolome de Olmeda, a priest of the Order of the Holy Trinity, went with Hernán Cortés to the Valley of Mexico in 1519. Once the Aztec Mexicans were overcome two years later, Cortés asked the Pope for missionaries to convert the natives and civilize them. The Franciscans responded and became very deeply involved, creating a foundation for later activity.

The movement of priests and ordinary people with their foodstuffs shadowed the voyages of explorers and, later, conquistadors. Missionaries would be the ones to take olive trees to Baja California (the long western peninsula of New Spain) and, later, Alta California (the old Spanish name for the modern state of California). Some lay people carried olives to New Spain and Peru, but priests did most of the plant introductions. Without the cultivation of the mission orchards of New Spain, there would have been no olive trees to go to Alta California.

In 1522, three Franciscan missionaries came to New Spain: Father Juan de Aora, Father Juan Tecto, and Brother Pedro de Mura. They were the vanguard, but the real work began when the so-called "twelve apostles" arrived in 1524 with Father Martin de Valencia. Father de Valencia planted olive trees when he arrived, possibly obtained from the Casa de Contratacion.[2] The Franciscans would also eventually contribute significantly to the settlement of Alta California.

Continued exploration revealed more territory for conquest and colonization on the western shores of the mainland. In 1528, Francisco Pizarro was following a lead he had been given for a place called "Viru," south of Ecuador, when he landed in a bay on the west coast of South America. The place he found was to become the country now called Peru, and he played a major role in its early formation, from the battles to win it to the building of its society. Starting in 1535, Pizarro laid out the city of Lima. He built his own house at the corner of the main square, surrounding it with gardens. He too pursued horticulture and would later encourage agriculture.

The story of how olive trees got started in Peru has an almost legendary quality, but it is attested to in different sources. It had to do with the marriages of the first Spanish lady who ever landed in Peru, Doña Inez Muñoz. The trees are generally believed to have been taken to Peru in 1560. Clements Markham, a senior English civil servant and dedicated amateur historian, tells the story in *A History of Peru*.[3]

Doña Inez's first husband was a Señor Alcantara. Señora Alcantara was praised for her skill as a thrifty housekeeper. A shipment of rice she had ordered contained a few grains of wheat by mistake. Instead of throwing them away, she put the wheat aside, planted it, and gradually built up enough seed to share it with other colonists.

Early Lima was a violent place, and not long after their marriage, Señor Alcantara was murdered. Doña Inez then married a new arrival, the procurator Don Antonio de Ribera. Don Antonio had taken a number of young olive plants with him on his journey to Lima, but very few survived the voyage. He planted them in Doña Inez's garden and set slaves with dogs to guard the trees. In spite of these precautions, one of the trees was stolen and supposedly taken to Chile. It is said that this tree became the parent of all the olive trees in Chile.

The one left to the Riberas did survive, and it became the "parent of all the subsequent olive trees growing in Peru." Even more astonishing, the tree that had been stolen was returned to Don Antonio's garden anonymously three years later. This is a delightful story—and part of it may even be true.

Meanwhile, further discoveries elsewhere seemed to confirm Cortés's longheld belief that there was a northwest passage to the Indies. He thought that they were close to it and its associated islands. In 1510, Garci Ordonez de Montalvo's fantasy novel *Las Sergas de Esplandian* (sometimes titled *Las Ergas de Esplandian*) had propagated the notion that the Pacific had several islands ruled by the mythical Queen Calafia, who resembled an Amazon.[4] "Calafia" eventually provided the root for the name "California."

Jesuit missionaries came to New Spain in 1571, fifty years after the Franciscans. The Spanish government did not want to spend any more money on uncertain missionary projects, but the Society of Jesus managed to support their work privately by means of a "Pious Fund" solicited from wealthy merchants. (The merchants wanted to be sure that they would merit a seat in heaven when they died and believed that paying to convert heathens was a good way to do it.) Once the Jesuits could support themselves, the Crown gave them a license and permitted them to "convert and settle" Baja California. This royal protection also gave them secular and military authority under the Crown.

With these assurances, the Jesuit Father Juan Maria Salvatierra founded a mission at Loreto on the eastern shore of Baja California in 1697. An Italian from Milan, Father Salvatierra quickly learned the native language and eventually founded six missions during his tenure. The immediate source of the olive trees introduced in Alta California in the eighteenth century was to be these Baja California missions. The missions lasted until 1762 but were defeated by drought and lack of money.

The missionaries decided that they needed more fertile soil. In 1701, Father Juan de Ugarte, who later succeeded Father Salvatierra, was sent across the mountain to an old settlement at Vigge Biaundo, west of Loreto, with a group of other men. They rebuilt an old mission that had been destroyed by the natives and began the first phase of what became very successful agriculture throughout Baja California. Father Ugarte created irrigation ditches and planted fruit trees and vines. The subsequent success of all agriculture in the Californias can be traced in part to the skill and legendary strength of Father Ugarte.

Later in the eighteenth century, other Jesuits continued the work. In 1728, Father Luyando built San Ignacio in northern Baja California. The nineteenth-century California historian, Alexander Forbes recorded comments by early travelers. By 1759, many "exotic" fruits—meaning fruit from Europe, not native plants—were flourishing in San Ignacio's orchards. Olive trees were clearly mentioned.[5]

The olive trees in Baja California initially came from Mexico City. Jesuits, Franciscans, and Dominicans all had to pass through the capital en route to their assignments. When they were preparing to take supplies to start the new missions in northern New Spain and Baja California, they had only to pot cuttings or olive slips from the existing orchards and take with them to the remote outposts. The College of San Fernando in Mexico City had olive trees in its orchard. (A "college" at that time meant a monastery or convent.)

In the end, there were twenty missions in Baja California: fifteen founded by the Jesuits, four by the Dominicans in the northern province, and one by the Franciscans. The soil and climate did not support prosperous agriculture, but they were able to survive. Each one had its livestock and staple crops such as wheat, corn, and beans. Five of them had vineyards. A number of the missions also had enclosed orchards and kitchen gardens nearer to the central house. The fathers planted familiar trees—such as pears, pomegranates, figs, peaches, dates, nuts, and olives—in their orchards.

During all that time, the Spanish government did nothing about the huge, "empty" land to their north described by Portuguese navigator Juan Rodríguez Cabrillo in 1542 and again by the Spaniard Sebastián Vizcaíno in 1602. San Diego was known and one port further north had already been named Monterey. Other sea captains explored too and filed reports describing great natural harbors and magnificent country. The reports gathered dust in the Escorial, Spain's royal palace and seat of government, for almost two hundred years.

By the mid–eighteenth century King Carlos III of Spain decided that the Jesuits were becoming too powerful and "disestablished" them in 1767. (This was the result of complicated political problems, including an ancient struggle between the Catholic monarchy and the Papacy about who had the ultimate power.) At very short notice, the Jesuit priests were informed that they were persona non grata and should leave New Spain almost immediately. The Jesuits left and would not return to the New World until 1851, after California had become part of the United States.

This expulsion occurred at almost the same time that King Carlos recognized that he had to take action in his northern territory in the New World. As a result, the king instructed the Franciscans to take over all the clerical activities at the former Jesuit missions in Baja California. Temporal affairs (primarily finance and defense) were to be assigned to the military. The Franciscans were stretched quite thin and would have preferred not to take on this additional responsibility, but they were in no position to refuse such an order. They were aware that the chain of missions was to be extended northward and that they would have to find the manpower to participate.

Clearly, the Spanish had finally noticed that other nations were paying great attention to the nominally Spanish areas on the west coast of North America. The French and English sailed in and out seeking trade, and the Russians looked as if they might even invade. When a small party of Russians from Sitka in Alaska actually settled at Bodega Bay (about sixty miles north of San Francisco) to capitalize on the fur trade, it was time to act.

The Spanish Foreign Minister instructed the Viceroy of New Spain that Governor Gaspar de Portolá and Don José de Galvez, newly appointed Visitor-General of New Spain, should move to protect the Spanish claims. The government agreed that the Spanish already in the New World should take possession of the land by sending troops and priests to settle on it. Galvez had to organize all this.

Don José was an unusual grandee. He had risen from humble origins because of skill and hard work. The task he had been given suited him very well. In a very short time, he picked Father Junípero Serra to be the leading missionary. Galvez recognized that the success of the enterprise depended heavily on the character of his agents in the new land. He himself was not destined to go to Alta California, but he knew that the right leader would make everything work. It was a true inspiration to choose Father Junípero Serra.

Galvez divided the initial colonizing party into four units, two to travel north over land to Alta California and the others to go by sea. They would meet at San Diego. This was a very good idea because of the perils facing them on both routes. It meant that at least some portion of the party would get through, one way or another.

Governor Portolá and Father Serra reached San Diego in July 1769, three months after two other priests, Father Juan Crespi and Captain Rivera y Moncada, had arrived. They had to build themselves some shelter and explore the new territory in detail to find sites for missions and presidios. Harrowing accounts of their struggles have been preserved.

One of the principal factors in the precarious situation the missionaries faced initially was the difficulty encountered by the ships that were to bring them supplies. The ships first sailed from San Blas on the mainland of New Spain to La Paz or Cape San Lucas in Baja California. After taking on supplies there, they then continued round the tip of the Baja peninsula to San Diego. This often took far longer than anyone expected because of the perversity of the prevailing winds and bad weather in the Pacific.

Another problem was that the officials in Mexico City who controlled the expenses from the Pious Fund, which financed the new missions, frequently underestimated how much food the missions needed. Grains—mainly wheat, rice, barley, and millet—together with corn (maize) were the largest part of the cargo. Salted meat and dried fish were important. Sweet things were included, such as figs, raisins, and even candy. In each load, smaller quantities of hams, olive oil, and spices or seasonings, together with a little wine and brandy were also sent. Specific amounts of the latter were not noted.

There were almost no margins for error in calculating the rations and need for food at the beginning. For the first five years the missionaries were in Alta California, they were always at the brink of starvation. For many weeks in 1773, they subsisted on milk from their cows and a few vegetables from their gardens because they had nothing else left to eat. The herds of cattle had not yet increased substantially in size, and new plantings were constantly ravaged by pests of many sorts. Until 1774, their very survival was in doubt. It was not till then, when a good harvest at San Gabriel set the tone for the next phase, that they were free of the fear of actual starvation.

After a mission site had been selected, the principal crops to be sown were grains and legumes. The cattle thrived with very little effort because of extensive pasturage. Milk was an important food, but the priests seldom indiscriminately killed the cows for meat. They were too valuable as draft animals. The padres were not so hesitant about killing sheep. Mutton was often added to the daily stew that the natives were given. Chickens were not listed in the inventories but are said to have been numerous. The eggs were a great help. A few pigs accompanied the early expeditions. Small quantities of pork and lard could be prepared. Though this all sounds plentiful, whatever there was had to be shared with too many and simply did not go far enough in the early days.

When the padres had finished the core buildings for each mission—the chapel, the private quarters, dairies, laundries, cookhouses, tanneries, smithies, barns, granaries, and dormitories for the neophytes (newly converted native peoples)—they could turn their attention to gardens and orchards surrounding their quarters. They needed vegetables to supplement their diet. Fruit would also help their nutrition, but putting in the trees was not an early priority. It is commonly thought that fruit trees, including olives, were planted in that first year they arrived. Because the early missions struggled so painfully to survive, logic suggests that it could not possibly have been before the late 1770s, if not later.

❧ Father Testa, S.J., with
Monsignor Mulligan, S.J., in
the old garden at Mission
Santa Clara. Note vines in the
foreground and olive trees
in the background. Date
uncertain.

The likelihood of this later introduction of trees is borne out by surviving letters from Father Serra. He wrote to Viceroy Antonio Maria Bucareli y Ursua in 1777 that he and the then-governor of Alta California, Felipe Neve, had had some discussions about improving the prosperity of Alta California. They had concluded that "some improvements could easily be introduced from [Baja] California, such as obtaining additional livestock, grafts from fruit trees, for instance fig and pomegranate trees and grapevines."[6]

Bucareli y Ursua must have accepted Father Serra's suggestion and Governor Neve got busy. Vine cuttings were sent from Baja California, and vineyards were reported by 1779. Peaches too were started early in 1779 at Mission San Gabriel and possibly other missions. They chose peaches because the trees mature quickly.

As if there were not enough uncertainty about the way in which California's original olive trees were imported, whether as seeds or cuttings (see sidebar), there is an equivalent problem in finding out exactly when they were introduced. In order to come up with the best approximation, one has to sift through and judiciously compare the various sources and make an educated guess. These sources include such of the original documents as are still available, the Bancroft Library's reduction and compilation of many of these documents, and the work of two other reliable scholars, Edith Webb and Father Zephyrin Engelhardt.

There are three principal accounts of the California coast from the period shortly after the missions began. Among the earliest non-Spanish visitors to the newly colonized Alta California: Jean-François Galaup, the Comte de la Perouse, who arrived at Monterey in 1786, paid particular attention to the fruit and vegetables growing in the mission gardens. Alejandro Malaspina, the captain of the Spanish exploring vessel colloquially known as *Sutil*, followed in 1791 and again in 1792. The English sea captain George Vancouver, also visited the coast of California in 1792. Each of these intelligent and observant men noted different fruit trees in the orchards of the missions they visited.

A Question Unanswered: **Seeds or Cuttings?**

One significant question remains unanswered concerning the introduction of the olive in Alta California: were the olive trees at the first missions grown from seeds or cuttings? Unfortunately, there is probably no way of definitely knowing, but it may be helpful to look briefly at some of the issues and opinions surrounding this question.

First, some arguments concerning seed: Because of the long journey, sending seed would make sense. It could stand delays, bad conditions, and neglect better than cuttings or live trees. The disadvantages of seed are that germination is slow and difficult, the trees grow from seed very slowly, and they develop a long, fragile taproot that does not survive transplanting well. The seedlings need to be grafted for the best results. Such trees are also subject to the vagaries of genetic variability, and the type of fruit produced cannot always be predicted or relied upon for consistency.

Second, some arguments concerning cuttings: Almost any olive shoot can be used to propagate new trees in several ways. Slips and cuttings can be made to grow easily, and sections of limb wood known as "truncheons" can develop vigorous new trees. A truncheon is a section of a branch, about eighteen inches long and two to three inches thick. It will sprout roots and shoots when kept in moist sand. Today when one visits an olive orchard, boxes of sprouting truncheons are frequently seen. The branches cut during pruning are another source of the new trees. Inert truncheons or rooted cuttings in small pots could have been used to take the olive tree to the missions. Once the early missions were stable, the missionaries transferred new orchard trees by cuttings or slips, taking them the relatively short distance to the next site.

Next, some differing opinions from authorities:

☙ Harry M. Butterfield, an agriculturist with the University of California's Agricultural Extension Service in the mid–twentieth century and a student of the history of California horticulture, believed that seeds were brought from San Blas (in New Spain).

☙ Another proponent of seed was Edith Webb, author of the standard monograph on Indian life at the missions published in 1953. She believed that seed was the most likely, because it was easy to carry and resistant to bad conditions.

☙ In an 1898 report to the governor of California by the State Board of Horticulture, the board's secretary, B. M. Lelong, suggested that seeds may have been the way olive trees first came to the state.

☙ Current experts, such as George Martin (recently retired from the Pomology Department of the University of California at Davis and a noted authority on olive growing), lean toward the theory that the trees came in as cuttings or small trees.

☙ Joseph Connell, the University of California Farm Advisor for Butte County, shares the opinion that olive trees came to the missions as cuttings or small trees. Mr. Connell also believes that the missions imported more than one type of olive tree, not just the variety that has become known as the "Mission" olive.

Galaup's ships, *L'Astrolabe* and *La Boussole*, were the most elaborate of their kind at the time. They had been fitted up as floating horticultural laboratories, with fruit and vegetable plants from many countries. Each one was properly tended so that the plants would survive the very long voyages. There were fifty living trees on the decks, including olive trees. A master gardener, M. Collignon, was attached to the ship's company to supervise the plants. He had appropriate gardening tools with him, both to use on the voyage and to give away if necessary.

The king of France, Louis XIV, sent Galaup to gather a detailed report about conditions in the north Pacific, and to determine where France could seize an advantage, if any. Because of Galaup's prudence and foresight, a journal of his voyages reached France, though he himself was fated never to do so; the French Revolution intervened and the king was executed. Nothing was known about what happened to Galaup for forty years. Then a report from the Southern Hemisphere to the French government revealed that he had been murdered off the coast of New Zealand many years before.

The relevant pages of his journal indicate that Galaup noticed some fruit trees in the mission orchards, though he thought they were not in good condition, and that the climate and land should support many more. Based on the correspondence between Serra and Bucareli y Ursua quoted above, the trees he saw were probably peaches or figs and maybe pomegranates. There was no mention of olive trees in Serra's letters. Similarly, Galaup did not comment on any olive trees being present during his visit, something he is likely to have done if they had been there.

The missionaries were very generous to visitors, and Galaup decided to give them some of his plants in return. His diary notes that he gave them Chilean potatoes, as well as some different types of grain. He did not leave any of his fruit or olive trees in California.

This makes it clear that any fruit or olive trees subsequently seen did not come from Galaup. What has clouded the issue is a note attributed to the next visitor, Alejandro Malaspina. He is said to have commented that the fruit trees left behind by the Comte de la Perouse were doing very well. Malaspina was a careful observer, but his report, originally filed in Madrid and recently translated and published in English, does not contain this statement.

The third keen witness of the period, Captain George Vancouver of His Britannic Majesty's Navy, anchored in Monterey in 1792, and was taken to see eight missions. The orchard at San Buenaventura contained peach, apricot, apple, pear, and fig trees. He also noticed grapevines, as well as orange, plum, pomegranate, and banana trees. He did not mention olive trees at this or any other mission in his list.

Because it seems to be clear that all the initial fruit trees in Alta California came from well-established mission orchards in Baja California, and because observant visitors in 1786, 1791, and 1792 did not remark on the presence of olive trees at the missions they visited, we have to conclude that olive trees were introduced into Alta California at some time between 1792 and 1803, the time Father Fermín Lasuén, successor to Father Serra, first informed his superiors that the missionaries had pressed their own olive oil.

The amount of time for the trees to mature and bear an adequate crop appears to be about right. In those days, young olive trees did not bear a significant amount of fruit for at least six or seven years. Modern horticultural methods have speeded this process a little—a grower nowadays can begin harvesting a useful crop from three- or four-year-old trees.

Ultimately, all the trees in that first period came from Spain. A seminal article in 1934 by George Hendry, Professor of Archeology at the University of California at Berkeley, traced the sources of the olive trees in fourteen different references, starting with the first one from the Casa de Contratacion in 1503.

After Viceroy Bucareli agreed with Father Serra that it was time to expand the crops at the missions, fruit trees were very carefully set out and tended. In spite of the very primitive way in which cuttings were transported and the difficulty in keeping them properly watered once planted, the orchards and vineyards thrived.

The olive trees served the dual function of shade as well as fruit production. Each tree was lovingly watered by hand with water from a gourd. The men from Baja California, sent from the well-established missions to help in the new ones, made double yokes for their shoulders and carried heavy buckets of water on each side, dipping the gourds as they went through the fields. The fathers grew the gourds specifically to be used as cups once the vegetable gardens were established. At the more successful missions, where ample water could be brought in by irrigation systems, watering could be done more efficiently.

After the terrible first five years, mission agriculture began to pick up speed. Father Serra lived long enough to see it start, but the real expansion came during the tenure of Father Fermín Francísco Lasuén. He took over as Father President after Serra died in 1784. When Lasuén died in 1803, the crops had increased sevenfold. One reason was that the Franciscans had completed nine new missions in that time, each one on good land and capable of superior performance. The reports sent to Madrid, reports whose format Lasuén had improved by including crop production, clearly show this. Olive oil was first mentioned in them in 1803. It had been pressed at Mission San Diego.

In everyday life, olive oil was used for cooking and lighting. Much later, once cattle herds were established in Alta California and the hide and tallow trade solidified, the missions could use tallow for lighting. Until then, olive oil was essential. The oil was also needed for making soap. This can be made with very low-grade oil, even the "pomace" (the residue after all the edible fluids have been expressed from the mash). In addition, olive oil was used in the preparation of wool for spinning and to lubricate machinery.

One of the milestones in the course of the missions' existence was when they pressed enough of their own oil to replenish the holy oils. Once this independence was established, they still had to send each season's oil to Mexico City to be blessed by a bishop. Only then could it be called holy oil and be used in services.

The Franciscans were not professional farmers. In an analysis of the 142 friars who would eventually serve at the Alta California missions, very few were from farming families. We don't know exactly how the Franciscans learned their agricultural methods, but the mission libraries did contain some agriculture treatises. At least

❧ WALKWAY AT MISSION SANTA CLARA, WITH OLD OLIVE TREES IN THE BACKGROUND, CIRCA 1922.

two distinct manuals have survived. Both of them have the same title, *Agricultura General*. One is now in the library at the Mission Santa Barbara. It was attributed to Alonso de Herrera and published in Madrid in 1777. Herrera must have been the editor, for he lists four authors who each wrote a specific section. One assumes that Herrera wrote much of the rest of it as it is a very thorough compendium. The copy at Santa Barbara is a fine tall copy, quarto, bound in fine white vellum and in quite good condition.

Herrera devoted ten pages to the olive and gave careful instructions for planting olive trees. He explained that they can be grown by planting seed or by rooting the suckers, branches, pieces of the old root, or indeed any part that has bark on it. He thought that the best ways were to use the "barbados," shoots that come up at the base of the tree, or the large pieces of the wood that are now called "truncheons." Vegetative propagation avoids the need for transplanting and grafting. The cuttings can be put in the ground where they are to remain. If the padres wished to graft, Herrera gave clear instructions for that procedure too.

The other text, *Agricultura General, y Gobierno de la Casa de Campo*, was written by Joseph Antonio Valcarcel. Its eight volumes appeared over about a twenty-year period, starting in 1763. Only three of these volumes have survived. They are in the library at Santa Clara University, the mission which became a university. The table of contents shows that Valcarcel wrote about olive trees, but unfortunately, these pages are missing.

🌿 Old olive orchard at Mission San Diego de Alcala.

The missions continued to flourish for almost forty more years. From the beginning of their tenure in California, the Franciscans had held all the land and personal property in the name of the Spanish Crown. After Mexico's emancipation from Spanish control in 1822, the government of Mexico officially took over all the public lands in California, formerly in the possession of Spain, by a colonization act of 1828. Five years later, in August 1833, the Mexican government passed an act to "secularize" the missions, that is, to take the land away from the church and attach it to the colony of California.

In November of that same year, the Mexican government passed another act to bring the missions under the colonization laws covering the rest of California. To confirm the process, a last law to take the land was passed in 1834. The process of secularizing the missions took over a year but was really completed by the end of 1835.

The Franciscans were forced to leave the missions and abandon the fields. The gardens and orchards deteriorated badly because no one tended them consistently. They were not irrigated anymore, cattle were turned loose into them to graze, and fires were started in them. All that the missionaries were allowed to keep were the actual church buildings and a few pieces of land for schools. Priests who formerly managed great estates were reduced to starvation and abject poverty.

Later descriptions by Californians and others, plus inventories for the secularization, however, clearly state the continued presence of olive trees. Edwin Bryant, a journalist from Kentucky who succeeded Lt. Bartlett of the U.S. Navy as Alcalde of San Francisco briefly in 1846, noticed olive trees together with oranges, figs, palms, and grapes at San Luis Obispo.[7] General Vallejo's (see page 33) niece, Guadalupe, wrote about them in a memoir in 1890. She commented that five hundred or so well-established old olive trees at Mission San Diego were destroyed by fire. American squatters camped in the groves and either cut them for firewood or lit their fires too close to the trees.[8]

Other early visitors to the missions in the nineteenth century commented both directly and in passing on the olive trees in the orchards. Edith Webb, author of the standard monograph on Indian life at the missions, quoted from Waseurtz, a Swedish aristocrat traveling through California in 1842. Waseurtz wrote that the mission at San Luis Obispo was in ruins, but although the gardens were badly kept, "there was a splendid olive grove and the crop for the season was abundant."[9] Webb also cited Henry Chapman Ford's remarks that the orchard at Mission San Fernando probably had the largest olive trees in the state. He visited the mission in the 1880s and thought that these were a variety different from the usual Mission olive.

One of the best observers was William Brewer, a botanist attached to the state's geological survey.[10] By the late 1850s, the state of California recognized that the haphazard way in which the state's mineral wealth and other resources had been exploited could not continue. Judge Stephen Field lobbied the legislature to have a formal survey performed, and Professor Josiah Dwight Whitney was appointed to carry it out. He chose Brewer to assist him. (Brewer was a rising star in the scientific world and would go on to become Silliman Professor of Agriculture at Yale.)

AGRICULTURA GENERAL, Y

GOBIERNO DE LA CASA DE CAMPO:

EN QUE

POR ESTENSO SE TRATA DE TODOS LOS BIEnes del Campo, con los nuevos defcubrimientos, y metodos de cultivo para la multiplicacion de los granos; del aumento en la cria de Ganados, y en lo demàs dependiente de una Cafa de Campo:

CON EL CULTIVO DE PRADOS, Y PASTOS NATUrales, y artificiales: de los arboles de Bofque, y Monte : de las Viñas, de los Olivares, de los Morerales, con la cria de la Seda; y de otros frutos utiles mui fingulares.

Y con los Tratados de Huerta, y de Jardineria: todo con efpeciales avifos, è inftrucciones.

COMPUESTA DEL NOBLE AGRICULTOR DE M. DUPUY, DE LOS AUtores, que mejor han tratado de efta Arte, y de otras varias obfervaciones particulares.

CON DIVERSAS ESTAMPAS.

POR DON JOSEPH ANTONIO VALCARCEL.

TOMO II.

EN VALENCIA:

Por Jofeph Eftevan Dolz, Impreffor del Santo Oficio. Año 1765.

🙵 TITLE PAGE OF *Agricultura General, y Gobieron de la Casa de Campo* BY DON JOSEPH ANTONIO VALCARCEL, 1765.

Brewer visited several of the missions in late 1860 and early 1861. At San Buenaventura, he noted that, in spite of ruined buildings, the fig and olive trees were still flourishing. It was different at Santa Barbara: ". . . the olive and fig trees were dilapidated and broken." The mission at San Gabriel, which was "now a ruin and cut up into ranches," still had quite a good orchard left: "Olives abound. . . ." It was much the same as San Buenaventura. The buildings had collapsed, but the fig and olive trees still bore fruit. As a general comment, Brewer noted the healthy growth of semitropical fruits in the places he visited. He was enchanted by the oranges, lemons, limes, and olives. The date palms looked handsome, but he commented that the fruit did not ripen.

MISSION SAN DIEGO DE ALCALA IN A VERY DILAPIDATED STATE BEFORE RESTORATION BEGAN IN 1931.

Today there are only a few remnants of the original trees left. Mission San Jose has a few, and they still produce fruit. Some trees survived at Mission San Diego until twenty years ago, but they were rather sad looking. The oldest trees at Mission Santa Clara probably date back to 1805, not before. There are six of the original trees remaining along the old adobe wall adjacent to the church and another five or six nearby. The entire garden, not just these old trees, is beautifully kept. When I saw the olive trees in January 1996, they were full of fruit.

Most of the trees at the restored missions have been planted recently to re-create the old effect. In the original plantings, olive trees were grown in several parts of the missions. There would be, by itself, a principal small orchard, or what Frances Calderon, American wife of the first Spanish Ambassador to Mexico, called the "olive ground." The missionaries also put the trees, primarily for shade, by the sides of the ditches, along paths by the cloisters, around the edges of fields and lining the roads to and from the mission.

The trees did quite well in the warmer, more southerly missions but, with the exception of San Jose and Sonoma, were not so successful in the northern ones. They were seldom watered, unless a particularly prolonged drought was in effect. The missionaries managed to keep them going with whatever care they could.

A generation after the secularization of the missions, enough trees had survived in quite improbable ways to provide the foundation of the next stage in California olive history. During that interval, a few ranchers and farmers took cuttings to grow olive trees on their property, largely for their ornamental and shade-giving qualities. Some of them may have learned how to cure the fruit from old Mexican or Indian workers, because there is the occasional reference in literature and correspondence to table olives. Nothing resembling an industry had yet developed.

The signs of continuity between the Hispanic era and the American one are interesting. The rapidly expanding American group had only a marginal taste for olive products. The Hispanic population, descended from the earlier settlers as well as newer arrivals, was accustomed to eating olives and using the oil. In the years from 1835 to 1875, when olive culture was restricted to these localized endeavors, this population obtained its supplies from several possible sources. Olive oil was imported from Mexico with many other staples but may have been too expensive for a poor family. People could prepare their own cured olives or

❧ OLD OLIVE TREES AT MISSION SANTA CLARA, NEXT TO THE COVERED WALKWAY BY THE OLD ADOBE WALL.

oil from old mission trees that still bore fruit, even if at a reduced rate. The fruit was there for the picking, but it required some energy and initiative.

The old mission trees were not the only source of fruit. The main avenue at John Wolfskill's Winters estate, for example, had serried rows of tall old olive trees—trees that still exist today. (The Wolfskill brothers—John and William—were pioneer settlers in California in the 1830s.) At her death in 1934, John Wolfskill's granddaughter bequeathed the estate to the University of California at Davis. Now the property of the UC Davis Pomology Department, it is known as the Wolfskill Experimental Orchard. The USDA's National Clonal Germplasm Repository occupies about seventy acres of the orchard as a guest.

Such old trees can also be seen in many of the old farming towns up and down the Central Valley and in other places where the townspeople took pride in their communities. All these trees had the dual functions of shade and fruit bearing. One of the most impressive arrays is at Cairns' Corner in Lindsay.

Laborers on the farms and ranches could pick the fruit and prepare enough olives and oil for their own families, if their employers allowed it. In 1916, Mr. William B. Bourn II, enriched by the proceeds of the Empire Gold Mine in Nevada City, encouraged this activity at his magnificent new estate, Filoli (in present-day Woodside). His mansion had exquisite stone work and plastering, and the work was done almost entirely by Italian craftsmen. The landscape designer, Bruce Porter, used olive trees to create an Italian aesthetic. The design called for a large grove to the east of the garden, a small orchard in the northwest section of the garden, and a single row of olive trees near the yew allée. The trees still stand and are well maintained. The grove has since become the parking lot, and the olive trees provide the first glimpse of the superb gardens, now part of the National Trust.

The source of these trees is currently unknown. The director of horticulture at Filoli, Lucy Tolmach, cannot find any record at the estate. The construction and landscaping took place over many years. Mrs. Tolmach reported that the owners' cook used to go up to the Italian bachelors' quarters and get the olives they had picked and preserved. I had hoped that the owner and managers would have kept such things as receipts or invoices giving the name of the nursery, but they did not. By that late date, more than thirty nurseries, possibly even more, were selling olive trees.

Olive trees are now found over much of California, in large and small stands of many origins. The trees are grown both for their beauty and their usefulness. For some Californians, they are a business and a way of life. For others, they are lovely reminders of the mild Mediterranean climate. For all, they are an echo of the past as well as a living testament to the courage and perseverance of the early Spanish padres and settlers who brought their beloved olive trees with them from homes far away.

2

Development of a Market and an Industry

The story of the olive in California is more than the story of olive oil alone. An outsider, charmed by the "romance of the tree," may think only of olive oil when considering olives. Although olive oil looms large in the general imagination, it is not the principal product of the California olive companies. Prosaic and unromantic, canned table olives currently account for about 99 percent of the industry; oil absorbs only a fraction of the crop. In spite of that, olive oil has a glamour that continues to exert great fascination, propelling the most unexpected people into growing olive trees and turning themselves into merchants.

The original purpose in growing the olive in California was to make oil. Curing some of the fruit to make table olives had always gone hand in hand with this function, but as a subsidiary activity. Olive oil became a commercial enterprise long before the table, or preserved, olive caught up with it, making the division into two separate industries a modern phenomenon. The great expansion in olive growing toward the end of the nineteenth century was intended to make olive oil on a hitherto unprecedented scale. As that phase peaked, circumstances changed so that olive oil was no longer the principal reason to grow the fruit, and the table olive overtook it, but that was not the end of the story.

❧ THE OLD BIDWELL MANSION AT
CHICO, CALIFORNIA.

The popularity of olive oil in California seems to have followed great cycles. After the downturn in the early 1900s, sales of olive oil languished for some years. Demand returned three decades later, only to slip back once again after the Second World War. At present, we are seeing another upswing, the demand this time fueled by the fairly well-documented medical benefits of the oil. California olive oil will probably never rival the high output or low cost of the Mediterranean countries, but its proponents' main goal is quality.

Commercial olive growing in California owes its beginnings to the development of large-scale agriculture in the state. This agriculture grew from foundations forged by the Franciscans. There were three clear stages from that start to the present. Though there was considerable overlap, especially in the second and third periods, a brief look at the stages is helpful for understanding the development of California agriculture.

Cattle raising was the first stage of large-scale agriculture in California. The cattle, originally brought in by the Franciscans at the end of the eighteenth century, thrived with relatively little care and for many years were profitable as well. However, unprecedented bad weather would lead to the demise of cattle's hegemony. In 1861 and 1862, terrible floods struck the Sacramento Valley where most of the cattle ranches were situated. The floods were followed by several years of drought, so that the herds never regained their original numbers. The double burden put most of the cattle ranchers out of business, and they looked around for something else to do.

Enter wheat farming, the second stage of agricultural development in the state. The missionaries had introduced wheat growing to California when they first came and had shown that the grain would flourish. The now-arid valley plains made excellent wheat fields, well manured by decades of cattle running. Engineers were also opening up the San Joaquin Valley, draining the marshes and shallow lakes. The ranch owners very quickly got the hang of growing wheat and soon were winning competitions in world centers. There would be another twenty years of prosperity based on wheat before world markets changed—including competition from Canadian, Argentinian, and Ukrainian wheat in the mid-1880s—making it unprofitable to send the grain halfway round the globe.

The economic shift from wheat growing coincided with physical and biological changes in the land. Wheat was exhausting the soil, and very few ranchers replaced the nutrients after the initial manuring by the old cattle runs. Yields were falling, and wheat was no longer profitable. As in the 1860s, ranchers looked around for something else they could grow to make money.

Water was the key to the transition in agriculture. Usually there was not enough, but occasionally there was too much. Extremes were the norm. The aftermath of the hydraulic mining era, which ended in the late 1870s, was one source of irrigation canals that could be adapted for use in farming. (One of the best sources of understanding the importance of water for modern California agriculture and its politics is Marc Reisner's book *Cadillac Desert*.[1])

With the new and relatively reliable source of water, mixed agriculture with an emphasis on horticulture became the third stage of agricultural development in California. This stage endures today—though, of course, cattle and wheat also continue to be raised in the state. Olives, though present earlier, grew into an industry during this third stage.

These so-called stages are purely schematic, for ease of discussion. Inevitably there was overlap, as briefly mentioned above. An example of this overlap, and the thinking that presages a significant movement can be seen in a paper given by General N. P. Chipman of Red Bluff before the California State Board of Horticulture in 1892. He listed the reasons to make a change from growing wheat to growing fruit.[2] He quoted the U.S. Department of Agriculture statistician J. R. Dodge's findings that many states had more appropriate climates for wheat and could get better yields. California's yields were too low to compete with other states' production, and the cost of transporting the wheat from California was higher than elsewhere, except from Washington and Oregon.

Chipman suggested that ranchers switch to growing fruit. Orchards were beginning to be popular, although they required a lot of capital to get started and the return was delayed until the trees matured. On the other hand, the unit return for fruit was much higher than for a bulk commodity like wheat. He also understood something about good farming practices. The low yield of wheat was partially due to a lack of fertilizing. He had noticed that orchardists bought manure frequently and thought other farmers should do so too.

Chipman specifically recommended growing olive trees, among other fruit trees, as a good investment. By this time, 1892, large-scale olive growing, as well as that of other deciduous fruits, had already been in existence for about twenty years.

The scene for this change had been set even earlier. The missions had laid the initial groundwork for mixed horticulture, including orchards. This activity continued through the period when California was a part of Mexico (1822–48), as well as when it eventually became a part of the United States in 1848. Oddly enough, the missionaries had shown the potential value of growing fruit, but the original Spanish settlers who emigrated with them hardly copied their example at all. Ulysses P. Hedrick, a horticultural historian, reports contemporary comments that the missionaries actively discouraged other people from growing oranges or lemons by withholding the seeds.[3] I am not sure how to evaluate these remarks. It would not have been not very difficult to eat a few oranges and plant the seeds oneself. Inertia seems to be a much more likely explanation for the lack of imitation.

Yet, from the time the missions closed in the early 1830s, ranchers in the associated "pueblos"— mainly Los Angeles—had been slowly developing horticulture. (Pueblos were separate small towns started by the Spanish government at almost the same time as the missions.) Once wheat growing ceased to be profitable, the possibilities of orchards and other horticulture became a reality. The existing small "Anglo" populace—English-speaking American citizens from the eastern or midwestern states as well as a few other northern Europeans— understood apples and pears, peaches and plums, and learned about grapes and oranges.

Using cuttings and seed from the mission orchards and other sources, these settlers planted orchards to grow fruit for sale. For example, William Wolfskill, a former fur trapper from the Midwest known as "Don Guillermo" once he became a naturalized Mexican citizen during California's Mexican era, had a large orchard with apples, pears, grapes, and a number of orange trees in the tiny town of Los Angeles in the 1840s. He also grew olive trees. The source of many of his trees was the mission orchard at San Gabriel, a place he loved. Wolfskill is considered to be the first Californian to grow oranges commercially.

The gold rush, which began after James Marshall's discovery of gold in 1848, increased the pressure to provide food for the newcomers. Anglo immigrants expanded fruit growing from a localized phenomenon in the missions to a modest commercial level. Carefully packed pears and grapes were sent by sea from Los Angeles to the markets at San Francisco.

Commercial fruit growing was not a totally new experience for some ranchers. Vineyards, orchards, and the fruit business were well established in the European countries as well as the midwestern, southern, and eastern states from whence they came. If the grower did not have enough personal experience, many books could be consulted, including the antique Spanish treatises brought by the Franciscans.

One contemporary commentator on this era was Harris Newmark, who wrote about life in early Los Angeles in *Sixty Years in Southern California: 1853 to 1913*.[4] Among the many topics he covered, the growth of agriculture and horticulture was important. The local population did not expand quickly, but a market existed because there were always ships visiting southern California ports that needed to be supplied. What the fruit growers could not yet do effectively was to send perishable goods back to the eastern United States in a short enough time to avoid spoilage. That era was still a little way off.

Merchants also traded extensively with the Sandwich Islands (Hawaii), Mexico proper, and other countries in Central and South America. William Wolfskill, who had had the inspiration of taking the seeds from a cargo of rotting Hawaiian oranges to grow thousands of new trees, now had merchandise to send back to Hawaii if he chose. There were also new cities and towns springing up in the rest of the state to be supplied.

All the Anglo growers in the pueblos were alert to the possibilities of improving their businesses. If something came along that would sell, they would consider adopting it. That was the Yankee way. They were not content merely to follow tradition and do things in the same way they had always been done. This was a major difference between them and the "Californios." (The Californios were veterans of the war fought against Spain for Mexican independence in 1822. Many became cattle ranchers and took over the mission lands under grants from the Mexican government.) The latter adhered more closely to tradition in every respect.

The Anglo population was responsible for much of the development of horticulture during this period. The Californios had never put much effort into growing fruit or green vegetables, in spite of the excellent example set by the missionaries. Beans and corn were the only vegetables they required. Among other things, they lacked the experience of mixed farming. They also felt that manual labor was demeaning to military gentlemen. Travelers commented on the barren and bleak areas around the houses. Only occasionally did they see flowers growing near the houses, an activity traditionally associated with women.

🌿 GENERAL MARIANO GUADALUPE VALLEJO, SIGNIFICANT PATRIOT, VINEYARDIST, AND MAKER OF OLIVE OIL IN ALTA CALIFORNIA BEFORE AND AFTER THE UNITED STATES TOOK POSSESSION OF THE PROVINCE.

One exception was the home of General Mariano Vallejo. He grew fruit and vegetables and had flowers all around his house. As early as 1830, he planted orchards that contained olive trees and a vineyard at his ranch in Sonoma. After the defeat of the Spanish in the war for Mexican independence, Vallejo had presided over the confiscation of Mission Sonoma and had used its gardens and vineyards to great effect. His vineyard was actually the mission garden expanded and replanted. Agoston Haraszthy, so-called "father of the California wine industry" (a designation that has begun to be questioned) moved to Sonoma because Vallejo had made such an excellent start. He wanted to be near him.

Two of Vallejo's daughters, Natalia and Jovita, married Arpad and Atilla Haraszthy, Agoston's sons, at a double wedding on June 1, 1863. Wine making was now a dynastic affair. Another of Vallejo's daughters married the German immigrant Julius Dresel and lived on part of her father's ranch. They made wine too. Ruins of Dresel's stone cellar remain, and some of Vallejo's original olive trees are still on the property.

The early vineyardists almost all grew olive trees as well. They needed their shade, just as the missionaries had. In many ways the wine industry and the olive oil industry ran in parallel. Olive trees and grapevines both grew well in similar climates, often in the same place. This had been known since ancient times. The same community and individuals understood both crops.

Thirty years before Agoston Haraszthy returned to Europe in 1861 to study vineyards and to write *Grape Culture, Wines and Wine-Making*, the book about wine making that became so influential, Jean Louis Vignes grew excellent grapes in Los Angeles and was truly one of the founders of the California wine industry. He handed his vineyard on to his nephews, the Sansevains. They continued to make good wine that was widely shipped to other parts of the United States.

At first the Sansevains only used Mission grapes. Later they switched to grape varieties imported from France and Spain. This was a pattern to be followed by the olive growers. The latter also widened their choices of trees at a later date. Nurserymen, particularly those from France, played an important role in this development and would subsequently be just as essential for the olive industry as they were for the wine industry in supplying new varieties.

After the missions were taken over by the secular authorities in the mid-1830s, very little olive oil was made for commercial purposes. Residents in the pueblos picked whatever olives they wanted in the deserted orchards and used the fruit for their families. Those who knew how to use the presses could make olive oil if they chose. There are some surviving accounts of life in California during that period which talk about growing olives and being able to buy them in the larger towns. For example, in some correspondence between Lt. E. O. C. Ord and his brothers James and Pacifico out in the gold fields, the lieutenant tells them that he has sent their sister in the city to buy various supplies, including a half-bushel of olives. That was May 21, 1849.[5] It indicates that people enjoyed eating olives and that someone was making them available.

Another source is the story of Eliza Farnham. Farnham, a valiant woman from upstate New York, intended to follow her husband, Jeffrey, who had already gone out to California. He died in 1848, before she could get there. She went anyway, with her children and two other women, and wrote about her life as a California farmer. Jeffrey Farnham had been a lawyer for men in the gold mines and had bequeathed his property in Santa Cruz to her.

Mrs. Farnham arrived in Santa Cruz on February 22, 1850, on the heels of the gold rush. One of her many problems was finding reliable men to work on her farm. All able-bodied men had left for the gold fields. She was tough, very unconventional, and did most of the hard work around her property herself. In her memoir, *California In Doors and Out* (published in 1856, shortly after the gold rush), she describes a visit to a neighbor's ranch to get cuttings of various trees, including olives.[6] She names two neighbors, a Captain Graham and a Mr. Anderson. It is not clear which one had the orchard.

Originally she had ordered fruit trees from New York, but they took so long on the journey around the Horn and were so completely neglected that they were all dead before they arrived. She did not go to a mission to try and get fruit trees, but presumably the neighbor had obtained his trees from that source. When she and her companion, Georgianna, went to the neighbor to get cuttings, she wrote, "[We] soon separated and bound up as many young pears and olives as we thought we could carry." She did not say what she was going to do with the olives. Unfortunately she eventually had to sell the farm and return East, where she died in 1864.

A broader view of the spread of commercial orchards emerges from the records of the State Agricultural Society, chartered in 1854 to encourage the development of agriculture by means of fairs, competitions, and prizes. A committee was appointed and charged with traveling around California in 1857 to recognize the work of superior farmers as a way of rewarding and encouraging them. The society's *Transactions of 1858* record that journey, which in some ways resembles the royal "progresses" of Queen Elizabeth I. They visited numerous small towns and ranches, and included a thorough account of the mission properties in their reports.[7] A valuable outcome of the visits was a statute passed in 1859 by the state legislature "to provide for the encouragement of the culture of the Vine and the Olive." It was an early recognition of the pioneering work already being done.

One of the properties the committee evaluated was Jerome Davis's stock farm where he raised cattle. The town now known as Davis had originally been called Davisville, but both names commemorate the same man. Jerome Davis had become an important property owner after small beginnings working as a ferry operator over the Sacramento River with his father-in-law. Davis's land encompassed a large part of the new town, brought into being by the railroad. When the University of California added the campus at Davis in 1906, part of the property they bought had been Jerome Davis's farm. In an older corner of the campus, there are two gigantic olive trees still bearing very heavily, said to have been planted by Davis in 1852.

The State Agricultural Society's representatives applauded Davis's twelve-thousand-acre farm. They were primarily concerned with the way he cared for his cattle, but they noted the fact that he had an orchard with three thousand trees of different fruits, an extensive vineyard, and large nursery facilities. It is possible that there were more olive trees on the property and that they were cut down or otherwise lost when the university took it over in 1906.

The keys to the change from early, purely Hispanic involvement in olive oil to the next stage in which Anglos took the initiative was a combination of opportunity during a complicated period as well as ready access to a source of the olive trees at the former missions. One of the people who took advantage of these circumstances was General John Bidwell, who would become one of the most prominent citizens of California after it became a new state in 1850.

Bidwell was born and bred in Ohio. One would not have expected him to show much interest in olives in different circumstances. His involvement shows how much the atmosphere in California opened people to innovation.

Like so many of the other great pioneers, such as William Wolfskill, Bidwell had started life in a modest way and had not given any indications of what he would become. He had been a schoolteacher. It is possible that if he had remained in the more structured society of the East, his special qualities might never have emerged. As a pioneer emigrant, Bidwell had crossed over the Rockies and Sierras in 1841. The Bidwell party was the first to complete the

daunting journey with no loss of life. His first position after getting to California was to be John Sutter's bookkeeper, a fairly lowly occupation, but he was quickly promoted to general manager. Sutter, generous and uncritical, recognized his abilities. "Captain" John Sutter had carved out an estate at the site of present-day Sacramento at the end of the 1830s. Gold was discovered at his lumber mill by James Marshall, sparking the gold rush.

A short time later, Bidwell decided to go out on his own. Even his search for gold had a satisfactory ending. He almost immediately found a rich lode, Bidwell's Bar, and he kept the proceeds when so many others lost theirs. He had the advantage of a much better education than Wolfskill and had also displayed remarkable powers of leadership on the original pioneer trek to California. This characteristic continued all the rest of his life, but it was in the seizing of new and hitherto unthought-of opportunities that both Bidwell's and Wolfskill's greatness lay.

Bidwell began to acquire valuable land in 1844 and gradually added to it until he owned a very extensive estate, which he named Rancho Chico. Rancho Chico was the core of the present-day town of Chico. He subdivided it into many smaller farms and ranches, each with its own signature crop. He grew wheat very successfully. Rancho Chico wheat won the gold medal at the Paris International Exposition in 1878.

In 1847, Bidwell wanted to start orchards. He rode hundreds of miles to San Diego where there was said to be a nursery. He recalled this journey many years later but omitted the details. According to the horticultural historians, nurseries as we know them were not actually to begin on a commercial basis until 1851, as a result of the money obtained from the gold rush. Despite this, Bidwell brought back many types of fruit trees, presumably including olives. We do not know how many actual trees he had or if he brought back cuttings. It is not clear how he carried everything back on the long ride to Rancho Chico. Regardless of these details, he accomplished what he set out to do. The end result was a set of flourishing orchards. By the end of the century, Rancho Chico began to sell preserved olives and olive oil. A few original olive oil bottles with the Rancho Chico label (and Bidwell's name on them) still exist. His participation gave weight and credibility to the new direction California agriculture was taking.

When visitors came for dinner at Rancho Chico, everything they ate had been grown there. In addition to the orchards that were attached to his residence, Bidwell also had several large commercially successful ones in various parts of the estate—at Williams Place, Sulam Place, and Drake Ranch. To manage this estate, he had hired the nephew of the noted Harvard botanist Asa Gray.

Originally, Bidwell began his nursery as a necessity for propagating his own plants and trees, but he quickly saw commercial potential in it. He advertised olive trees for sale in his nursery catalogs by the late 1880s, although he never put much effort into the newer foreign varieties. The olive trees could be used for shade, or the fruit could be pickled or made into oil.

During the anti-Chinese agitation in the 1880s, Bidwell continued to employ the hated outsiders in the face of a hysterical movement to remove them completely from California. He pitted his moral authority and prestige against the rest of the community and survived a rather vicious attempt to boycott his products. If the boycott had succeeded, it could have been exceedingly damaging to his business.

Bidwell was an exceptional man, not afraid to follow his own instincts and, if necessary, take a less popular path. He did not take this attitude to the growing of crops. In that regard, he was a follower, changing from one type of crop to another as the times dictated. The changing population of the state helped to determine the market for olive oil. Bidwell lived to the end of the century, dying in 1900. The career of this one man illustrates the nature and degree of the change in the state's agriculture and attitudes.

California's population had begun a slow and steady growth in the first few years of the 1840s, and John Bidwell had personally and constructively contributed to this growth. Others were opportunists, like Lansford Hastings who painted the new country in glowing colors and minimized the difficulties of the journey to California. His book, *The Emigrants' Guide to Oregon and California*, was widely read by the members of church groups and in other places where responsible men congregated.[8] Part of the responsibility for the tragedy of the Donner party can be laid at his door. The leaders of the group were determined to save time by taking his "nigher" route, a supposed shortcut, not knowing that he had never done it himself.

California and Oregon were perhaps the last frontier for a people constantly seeking to move on. Bidwell had shown it could be done safely. Immigrants began to arrive overland in modest numbers, bringing whole families with all their worldly goods in wagons. They tended to be substantial people, not the somewhat questionable type of man who came by himself looking for opportunity. It required a large sum of money to buy the wagon, stock it for a six-month trek, and still have a little capital

☙ OLIVE OIL BOTTLE FROM RANCHO CHICO; NOTE JOHN BIDWELL'S NAME. THE BOTTLE RESEMBLES WHISKEY BOTTLES OF THE PERIOD.

left to get started in the new land. These immigrants settled in quickly. Their families grew with the birth of children. Relatives and old friends from their hometowns were excited by the descriptions in the letters they received, and many decided to go too.

Then came the decade between 1849 and 1859, the crucible of the gold rush. California's population rose astronomically. Men came from all the countries in the world, men of every sort—highly educated in some cases, pathetically ignorant in others. By 1851, San Francisco had grown from its former sleepy torpor as a town of about eight hundred people to one of about twenty thousand. Many more thousands of men found their way to the front lines of the mines, up in the foothills of the Sierras to the remote reaches of Amador County, Calaveras County, Placer County, El Dorado County, and other parts of the state. These very names commemorate the gold mining era. Few found the amount of gold for which they had hoped. More lasting fortunes came from purveying the food, clothing, and shovels needed by miners who continued to search.

The massive influx of miners brought many Italians to California. They were fleeing grinding poverty and political repression. The truly elemental pressure on emigration was the starvation that devastated not just Ireland but a large part of Europe in the mid-1840s. The potato crop that failed in Ireland in 1845 also failed in Germany, Belgium, and France in 1846. Peasants in those countries depended on the potato almost as much as in Ireland. The fungus that caused the blight, *Phytophthera infestans,* was ubiquitous during those cold, wet summers, but the other countries handled the crises in a more humane and reasonably satisfactory way than the English government.

This was also the period of "red" revolutions all over Europe, most of them unsuccessful. The citizens of Paris took to the streets in February 1848 to protest the policies of Louis Napoleon. By June, their protests had been brutally quelled. In Italy, the independent provinces were under the control of the Austro-Hungarian Empire. Until Cavour and Garibaldi arose, the citizens had no hope of ever being free of this hated domination. America offered an escape valve. Men from many other countries were glad to have somewhere to go, to escape possible political retribution.

The arrival of large numbers of Italian immigrants had much to do with the growth of the olive industry. Old census figures show that of all the Italians in the United States from 1860 to 1880, about 80 percent were in California, and the majority of those were in Calaveras County. They came in steady numbers but not in great "waves." Only the German immigrants outnumbered them.

Many of the men had useful skills and knowledge. Their arrival in California played a role in developing a more generalized market in olive oil. Italian immigrants to San Francisco in the 1850s chiefly came from four provinces. One of these was Lucca, a region celebrated for its olive oil. The largest number of immigrants came from this region.

Once they came to their senses and recovered from the mining madness, the Italian immigrants settled down and began to do the things they understood much better. With this critical mass of Italians and other Mediterranean peoples, the new market was born. Here were large numbers of people who knew and wanted olives and olive oil.

These pioneers grew vegetables, planted orchards and vines, made wine, and pressed olive oil. They did this inland, away from the coastal areas. Gradually they produced enough of these commodities to start supplying their fellow immigrants in the larger cities such as San Francisco. The Italian immigrants' produce remained local. It could not compete with the already sophisticated distribution networks of the brokers and grocery stores.

The Italian and French immigrants joining the gold rush often brought fruit seeds or cuttings from home with them. Some of them brought olive seeds too. Their orchards succeeded but were initially on a small scale, for family needs only. At a time when California horticulture was in its transitional phase, the conjunction of a new business opportunity coincided with a recognition that the old trees had already survived a hundred years. It became possible to develop a market in olive oil.

This group of Italian immigrants was very resourceful and versatile. During later downturns in the business cycles, other segments of this new society could not survive the recessions and left for the cities. The Italian farmers survived by diversifying their crops and taking other work in rural areas until things got better. By relying on a barter economy, they could manage with very little actual cash. Several scholars such as Hans C. Palmer and Dino Cinel have examined these events closely.[9]

Apart from the small number of olive trees imported by the Italians, survival of the mission orchards was pivotal for the olive industry and indeed for the rest of California horticulture. All the changes in the composition of the population that led up to the development of a market and industry might not have been sufficient to stimulate California olive growing on a large scale if a ready source of trees had not been available. Possibly something of the sort could have eventually taken place, but it undoubtedly would have been at a much later date. Being able to take cuttings from established trees hastened the process considerably.

In a striking synthesis of business shifts and readiness for agricultural change, two Anglo men, Ellwood Cooper and Frank Kimball (who grew olives along with his brother Warren), came up with the same idea almost simultaneously: start olive orchards by taking thousands of cuttings from the old trees and plant them on many acres. One was to do it in Santa Barbara, the other in San Diego. Neither had any experience of olive growing before doing this, and it is amazing that they succeeded on such a gigantic scale. Today starting large tracts of olive cuttings is extremely complex, involving a source of constant humidity and other elaborate conditions. Cooper and Kimball simply prepared the cuttings and set them out in open fields. They worked from their own common sense.

The goal of all this effort was to make olive oil. Cooper and Kimball were not sophisticated in their tastes and knew little of different varieties of olive tree at that time. The mission olives had been good enough for the padres and were good enough for them. At a State

Olive Oil: **A Cure for What Ails You—and Society Too!**

To the English and other early nineteenth-century northern Europeans, apples, pears, grapes, and peaches were one thing, olives another. They had no desire to eat olive oil or reason to pay much attention to it. It was part of the outlandish, greasy customs of the Greeks or Egyptians, associated with bowel disturbances when the aristocracy traveled to the Levant. They contemptuously called this syndrome "Gyppy tummy" (a contraction of "Egyptian"). They could not know it was the microbial contamination of the food and water that caused their distress, not the oil.

Manufacturers of woolen cloth in the north of England imported olive oil as a lubricant for their machines. The only other way in which English-speaking citizens were grudgingly prepared to accept olive oil was in the context of medicinal purposes. (Even until very recently, up to the 1960s and 70s, the only place to buy olive oil in England was at the "chemist's," that is, at a pharmacy.) At a time when the etiology of very few diseases was known, physicians seized upon odd and disparate substances to reduce symptoms whose origin remained obscure. Compared with previous candidates for this function, olive oil was at least quite benign.

Medical treatises from the seventeenth and eighteenth centuries contained references to the supposed therapeutic value of olive oil. This notion persisted into the nineteenth century and would be used to good effect as a testimonial by the promoters of California oil at the end of the century. (A hundred years later, the health benefits of olive oil are once again being touted, but this time, the claims are backed by a greater insight into the mechanisms of disease.)

A pioneer in commercial olive growing provided just such a testimonial. Frank Kimball was one of the first wave of Anglos who revived olive growing in California. He lived in San Francisco but suffered from chronic bronchitis, exacerbated by the cool, damp climate. His physician suggested he move to a warmer region. Kimball chose San Diego and bought Rancho Nacional near San Diego in 1867. He renamed it National City and by planting orchards with olive trees became part of the history of the state.

Long after he had settled there, Kimball told a story at one of the olive growers' meetings about a neighbor who felt ill. The neighbor took several glasses of the oil by mouth and also used some as an enema. Later he was gratified to find that he had passed a lot of stones, type unspecified. Mr. Kimball stated that if a small amount was good, more must be better—a classic fallacy among the medically unsophisticated.

Other examples of the supposedly curative powers of olive oil abound. For example, Dr. A. E. Osborne, Superintendent of the then-called Home for Care and Training of Feeble-Minded Children at Glen Ellen, now a state institution, found olive oil was useful in building up debilitated patients after serious infections. Luigi Barzellotti, a physician in Santa Clara, recommended olive oil for colic in infants, irritated skin, erythema (reddening of the skin), erysipelas (a bacterial infection of the skin now seldom seen), tumors and other diseases of the glands in the throat, swellings about the ears, "frictions in rheumatic diseases," drunkenness, and veterinary practice—no mean list.

Dr. P. C. Remondino, vice-president of the California State Medical Society, president of the San Diego Board of Health, and a member both of the American Medical Association and the American Public Health Association, was even more enthusiastic. He spoke at the Olive Growers' meeting held in 1891 under the auspices of the State Board of Horticulture. His remarks were published in the report of that meeting presented to Governor Gage.

Dr. Remondino expounded eloquently: "What the ancients knew by taste or by instinct, the moderns have in a great measure lost, and neither the discovery of the telephone, telegraph, celluloid collars, parlor match, peptonoids, nor the delightful torpedo, can in any way or by any odds replace what man has lost by neglect of the use of olive oil. The modern American, with all his patent contrivances, from patent corkscrew and keyring, electric lights and dynamite guns, will never know a slick and unruffled skin and a healthy, optimistic, full-fledged primitive and natural digestion, with its full tide of health, until he returns to the proper admixture of olive oil in his diet. Until he again recognizes the value and uses of olive oil, he will continue to drag his consumptive-thinned, liver-shriveled, mummified-skinned, and constipated and pessimistic anatomy about in vestibule carts in a vain search for lost health." Phew, that's telling 'em! Remondino shared some of the attitudes popularized by D. H. Lawrence about the degeneracy of modern man and expressed himself with some of the same trenchancy.

When Remondino turned to the actual medical properties of olive oil, he once again expressed himself forcefully and idiosyncratically. His topics included olive oil as a fortifier, as a "moral agent," as an appetite "provocator," as a remedy in intestinal irritation, as a vermifuge (removing parasitic worms from the gut), as a remedy for kidney and bladder afflictions as well as gallstones (shades of Mr. Kimball's neighbor). Its moral properties would be "efficacious in driving the devil out of the San Francisco hoodlum" and the "establishment of public baths and the purchase of a few gallons of olive oil would lessen the pressure on Folsom and San Quentin Prisons. . . ."[10]

Board of Horticulture meeting in 1893, Ellwood Cooper reminisced about his sticking with the Mission olive. As he looked back over his more than twenty years of experience, he said, "I commenced with the Mission olive and got five thousand cuttings from the San Diego Mission, from the San Fernando Mission, from the San Buenaventura Mission, the Santa Barbara Mission orchard and also from the Tajiguas orchard. There is a very great difference in the Mission olive as seen in these different orchards and in these different localities, but on my place they are side by side and there is no difference, so that I have made up my mind that a good many of these differences are due to the different climates and different locations. The Mission olive is large, and at Camulos, on the other side of the mountain, the olive is larger than it is with me. It is more orange shaped; it is nearly round. The San Diego olive is oblong; the San Buenaventura olive is very much smaller, . . . but they are all the same olives on my place; I can detect no difference. I have other varieties, but I am too old to experiment. These other young men can begin these experiments, as Mr. Howland has done; it is very creditable in them." John Howland had a very large olive nursery at Pomona. He, working with his brother, also made and sold olive oil.

Ellwood Cooper, one of the pioneers of commercial olive tree planting in California.

Both Cooper and Kimball wrote about their successes and failures in official reports to the State Board of Horticulture and in pamphlets and bulletins put out by the University of California Agricultural Extension program. They were anxious to encourage many others to follow them and to develop olive growing on a very large scale. Their papers convey the mood of boundless optimism and show anyone who is interested how to grow olives and process them. Cooper was the president of the State Board of Horticulture for many years and introduced other plants of varying value into the state. The most notable one with which his name is associated is the blue gum, or eucalyptus, from Australia.

At the same time, olive oil was still being imported into the United States from Spain, Italy, and France. There was a lot of dizzy speculation about how much oil came into the country each year. Most of that oil was for the large eastern cities, but some of it came into California either around the Horn or through Central America, and later by railroad.

Contemporary statistics indicate that Italy exported more oil than any other country. During the 1870s and early 1880s, Italy was supposed to produce an average of fifty-four million gallons of oil per year and a very large percentage of that went for export. These were very impressive numbers. Spain very quickly overtook Italy and still remains the larger exporter. These numbers came from government reports based on the consular and foreign agricultural services' surveillance, as well as aggregate values derived from Customs and other sources. Prospective growers in California rationalized their concern about these numbers by dividing them into the population of European countries and showing that the Europeans could easily consume all of the available olive oil by themselves. The California growers interpreted the results of their calculations to mean that California could supply all the residual olive oil needed in the United States even after accounting for the European exports.

At a time when agriculture, and particularly fruit growing, was being encouraged as an alternative to gold mining, Cooper and Kimball's examples were very impressive. The climate in California resembled that of the Mediterranean countries closely, olive trees had been shown to survive at the old missions and do amazingly well in spite of neglect, and businessmen knew there was a market already because of the amount of oil imported. They hoped to increase that market. Everything seemed to mesh together.

Their joy was short-lived. The wind was taken out of the California olive growers' sails when all the Mediterranean countries began increasing their exports toward the end of the 1890s. They too had heard about the increase in California's population. It was only too easy for them to increase production and exports. The considerably lower prices charged for imported oil were made possible by adulteration with cheap substitutes. It is a commentary on just how cheap cottonseed oil was that it paid olive oil merchants to export it from the United States and to have it sent back again masquerading as olive oil. Liquid tallow was also used very frequently in the United States to adulterate the more expensive olive oil.

In fact, looking back with the clarity of hindsight, one wonders just on what Cooper and the others based their optimism. The astronomical quantities of olive oil exports from Spain and Italy seem to have been their only "feasibility study," and the numbers were probably flawed.

One of the rocks on which they foundered was the development of the cottonseed oil. Ways had been found to produce an edible cottonseed oil domestically in the United States. There really was a Dr. Wesson behind Wesson Oil. In many parts of the country, housewives grew accustomed to an almost tasteless "salad" oil and seemed to prefer it. A speaker at one of the State Board of Horticulture's conferences told the story of trying to send olive oil to Mississippi through a representative and finding out that it was a waste of time. The brokers would not even take it as a gift. The cottonseed oil had become a norm, and the public either never knew about olive oil or had lost the taste for it.

The cottonseed "salad oil" was heavily promoted by very large concerns. It was considerably cheaper than olive oil, and that was important too. It cost about one-fifth, or even less, of olive oil. California olive oil producers had relied on the purity and wholesomeness of their oil as a selling point, forgetting that most women with a limited budget shop by price.

Crude cottonseed oil is very unpleasant. It needs a lot of refining to remove its taste and render it palatable. The incentive to undertake processing of such magnitude must have been a large, seemingly open market. There was no shortage of the raw material. Cotton was grown on a giant scale throughout the South. The oil was produced in such volume and at such a low price that it paid Italy and other oil-producing countries to import it in bulk and use it as an adulterant of their own olive oil. By 1886, more than a quarter of the cottonseed oil was exported to Europe.

Initially, the cottonseed oil processors completely discounted the possibility that domestic Californian olive oil offered much competition. That tolerant attitude would change. They became greedy and wanted to close the market to any oil that threatened their sales.

The British Consul at Leghorn described how the flasks of supposed olive oil were filled in London with cottonseed oil. Another trick dishonest Italian olive oil makers used was to pour the cottonseed oil over the olives in the presses to mix the two types of oil as thoroughly as possible and make it seem that this hybrid oil was actually the real thing.

Many observers alleged that more than 50 percent of the imported oil was adulterated. This was only a guess. Methods to isolate the specific chemicals that give olive oil its unique flavor and taste were being described by that time, but it was still early. Later, they would get help from the chemists at the University of California at Berkeley.

The University of California led the way in applying chemical tests to identify adulterants and was helped by reciprocal studies at French agricultural colleges. For example, Arthur P. Hayne, a graduate student from Berkeley, went to Provence to study at the College of Agriculture there. His father, Colonel W. A. Hayne, was a very large landowner in the Santa Barbara area and grew olives on a number of his properties. Arthur Hayne learned about the newer chemical tests for purity of olive oil.

An assistant chemist at the University of California's Viticultural Laboratory, Louis Paparelli, described six tests to find adulterants in olive oil: iodine absorption, Brulle's reaction (Brulle was a chemist at the French agricultural college in Provence), Bechi's reaction, Fleydenreich's reaction, Baudouin's reaction, and Schneider's reaction. Each one of these tests exploited a different property of the oils, such as their sulfur content, from other sources beside the olive.

The demand for olive oil in California grew. Even though the increased demand was on the West Coast, the foreign oil still came through New York. Food brokers there recognized that business in California was changing. Grocers in San Francisco and Los Angeles were being asked for olive oil and sent East to get it, rather than obtain the local, more expensive kind. There may also have been an element of snobbery and class prejudice involved. For high-class purveyors of expensive foods, an imported article has greater cachet.

Recent archeological studies under the streets of San Francisco confirm the presence of foreign olive oil imports. The excavators unearthed many such bottles, some still full of oil and with the label intact. Connoisseurs preferred the sharply flavored Tuscan olive oil from Italy. They found the local oil, from the Mission olive trees, somewhat insipid. The local manufacturers and promoters had been living in a bubble and probably seriously overestimated the market capabilities. They found that they could not compete successfully with well-entrenched Spanish and Italian exporters nor overcome the effects of cynical adulteration.

Starting in 1880, Congress passed strong legislation to protect the purity of food and drugs on a number of occasions. The Food and Drug Administration was the logical outcome of the accumulated legislation and development of standards. The stimulus came from several sources. "Muckraking" journalists (Theodore Roosevelt's contemptuous term for them) exposed scandalous practices in the meat, dairy, and other industries. Roosevelt may have objected to the journalists' methods, but he signed the groundbreaking Food and Drug Act of 1906. Adulterated oil, whether domestic or imported, was among the stimuli to act, although, in the greater scheme of things, it was far less significant than contaminated milk or filthy slaughterhouses.

ARTHUR P. HAYNE, CHEMIST AT THE COLLEGE OF AGRICULTURE, UNIVERSITY OF CALIFORNIA AT BERKELEY.

The Department of Agriculture enacted regulations, and California's olive oil producers heaved a collective sigh of relief. It meant that there were standards to be met and that adulterated oil could no longer be sold with impunity. In spite of all this, foreign oil remained cheaper and a continuing threat to the California product.

In 1897, only five years after promotion of fruit growing was emphasized officially by men such as General Chipman, but already quite a lot longer from the time fruit growing had begun, a representative of the State Board of Horticulture was writing that the general depression in the market for fruit was particularly tough on the olive growers. This was a segmental depression that mirrored the more serious national depression of the time. There were too many olive trees and not enough control over the quality of the oil and preserved table olives. The oil being produced varied in its flavor and freshness, and there were problems with preserving the table olives successfully. This is a sad commentary on the high ideals with which Cooper and Kimball had started.

While the market remained depressed, growers in one particular locality, Riverside County, imposed a voluntary moratorium on planting new orchards. By 1900, the newspapers were saying that the olive industry in California was dead. This was an overstatement but had an element of truth.

In the late 1880s, as the market for pure olive oil declined, table olives had begun to move to the fore. The bifurcation of the olive industry seen today began at that time. Although olive oil was the reason the missionaries planted olive trees, cured olives were always an important part of the Spanish diet. The fruit has useful nutritional properties and can supply a reasonable number of daily calories from its vegetable protein and fat. Various ways to cure it and rid it of the unpleasant bitterness have grown up simultaneously in different cultures. The Spaniards brought their own methods with them when they came to California and taught the local people how to use them.

For many years the only place to find cured olives was close to where they had been prepared. Either they were made at home or bought loose from barrels at a store. The idea of mass production with prepackaging in smaller, more convenient quantities and transcontinental sales came later, toward the end of the nineteenth century and early in the twentieth century. The necessary conditions for these changes were the same for table olives as for other California products: safe, consistent methods of preparation and preservation, transportation, refrigeration when required, and an adequate distribution network. Many of these improvements were fostered or at least guided by the faculty of the newly established College of Agriculture at the University of California at Berkeley.

Once these prerequisites were in place, the scene was set. Using the newer methods of processing, canners produced an olive that was a milder, less obviously "ethnic" food. No longer was it the sharply flavored Spanish type. Olives had in fact become American. Such changes were to occur in many foods, to accommodate the American palate.

The dominance of canned olives arose from the fact that they had broad appeal. They had a mild taste, lasted a long time in their cans, and could be enjoyed by people who were otherwise very unadventurous in their gastronomic choices. Once safely in the cans, transporting them was not difficult. The market for this food rapidly outgrew that for California olive oil. This is the irony of events. The impetus to expand olive growing and import better varieties of trees came from the vision of oil makers, but they were then left behind. Whatever small market there was for olive oil in the United States a century ago could easily be met by imports from Europe, as the early producers learned very painfully.

Americans of all ethnic derivations across the United States started to buy the neutral tasting delicacy, California ripe olives, although sales were always strongest in California itself. That remains true today. In order to counter the extremes of glut or shortage in the new market for canned olives, and maintain a sound price structure, a group of leading olive canners founded the California Olive Association in 1915.

High-powered marketing was the reason that canned olives became an accepted part of the diet in the first years of the twentieth century. Green olives were the signature of the martini. Black ripe olives became part of a "relish tray." None of these practices had been in existence twenty years before. They would coincide with the Jazz Age, when mixed drinks supplanted the older, standard aperitifs. This wider population did not cook with olive oil and seldom even wanted it for salad dressing. Using a simple marketing strategy, the California Olive Association pushed very hard to make olives indispensable in middle-class homes. The strategy depended on newspaper articles and advertisements, careful

❧ Women labeling glass jars of preserved olives at the
rate of 350 quarts per person per week, circa 1900.

attention to the readers of the women's magazines, recipe booklets, and live demonstrations at promotional events.

Booth Tarkington, a novelist who noticed wonderful details about life in his hometown of Indianapolis, captured this phase in *The Magnificent Ambersons*, published in 1918. One of the characters, an old-timer in the town, is complaining about the habits of the newly rich Amberson family: "My wife says Ambersons don't make lettuce salad the way other people do; they don't chop it up with sugar and vinegar at all. They pour olive oil on it with their vinegar and they have it separate—not along with the rest of the meal. And they eat these olives, too: green things they are, something like a hard plum, but a friend of mine told me they tasted a good deal like a bad hickory-nut. My wife says she is going to buy some; you got to eat nine and then you get to like 'em, she says. Well, I wouldn't eat nine bad hickory-nuts to get to like them, and I'm going to let these olives alone. Kind of a woman's dish, anyway, I suspect, but most everybody will be makin' a stagger to worm through nine of 'em, now Ambersons brought 'em to town. Yes, sir, the rest'll eat 'em, whether they get sick or not!"[11]

From the beginning, the two constituencies in the nascent olive industry, oil makers and canners, followed separate courses. Each group had its own serious difficulties and issues not relevant to the other. The California Olive Association specifically represented the interests of the canners and paid only minimal attention to the oil makers.

The canners had to keep the olives free of bacterial or fungal infestation while holding them for days or weeks, and then get them safely into cans and sterilized. They were concerned with "off flavors" derived from several sources, particularly microbial action and agricultural sprays.

The oil makers who wanted to make premium oil needed to press the fruit as soon as it came into the yard and to make sure there were no contaminants to affect the flavor. They faced different problems than the canners did. All the fruit somehow had to be crushed at once, requiring long hours and expensive labor. They did not have the luxury of holding the olives for a later date. Olive oil can be pressed from preserved olives, but it is not of the best quality.

Such crucial differences in technique were only part of the reasons there was practically no communication between the two groups. Other reasons were ethnic and social. The olive canners were mainly Easterners who had been in California for a long time. With some exceptions, oil making had passed from the original producers to the more recent immigrants from Italy, because it was no longer a mainstream business. Cooper, Kimball, and Bidwell were no longer active in oil making.

Both groups depended completely on the growers, but once the latter realized how much better they were paid for table olives, they responded very quickly. They would grow the type of olive needed for canning and not bother with selling their fruit to make oil. In many cases, that meant changing their trees to different varieties. Mission olives can suffice for table purposes, but trees producing more suitable fruit for canning were now in the state. Originally, these new varieties were imported to make better olive oil, but a few turned out to provide superior table olives.

By the beginning of the twentieth century, domestic olive oil was still being produced, but in much smaller quantities. It was not reduced to the levels of the mid-1840s and 1850s, but it was in a very unsettled phase. Growers who had a lot of capital sunk into orchards and oil-processing plants felt concern, and some businesses did not survive.

It is remarkable that in spite of the uncertainty during this upheaval, smaller, family-run businesses were still being started, making modest amounts of oil for a very local market. For example, Serafino Martinelli, a former shoemaker, built an oil press in his olive orchard in Madera and started to make oil in 1902. Serafino's old Mission trees still stand, but his daughter-in-law, Della Martinelli, a charming eighty-two-year-old widow when I met her in 1996, had them grafted over to Manzanillos, the most popular variety now grown. Della Martinelli died in 1998.

Even while the early olive growers concentrated on olive oil, there was always a small demand for pickled olives. They had tried various ways of meeting it by using recipes and methods taken from Spain, France, and Italy. Ellwood Cooper soaked his olives in water to remove the bitter taste and then put them up in dilute brine. Treatment with lye was another time-honored method used to remove the bitterness. The Kimballs soaked their olives in a weak solution of lye, removed that by washing them in many changes of water, and finally packed them in brine. C. M. Gifford of San Diego, an early olive pioneer, brined his olives and sold them with his olive oil from a wagon.

Although these were old, established methods, the results on a large scale were hit or miss. A lot depended on the stage at which the olives had been picked, whether completely unripe or in different degrees of ripeness. The fruit changed color, from green to dark red or brown, even black, depending on several factors. Controlling the temperature was important. Varying the amount of air in the vats was also a key factor. If no air was permitted, the olives remained green but were cured. California olives were later to be sold as "black ripe" and "green ripe," rather confusing terms. Sometimes the olives tasted unpleasant or looked bad. They spoiled quite easily. It was not easy to sell such a mixed bag on a consistent basis.

It would take till the 1890s before some of the problems of curing olives were solved. This occurred when two scientists at Berkeley's College of Agriculture, George Colby and Frederic Bioletti, worked on these problems and came up with the solutions. Colby was a chemist, second assistant in the Viticultural Laboratory. Professor Bioletti was foreman of the Agricultural Experiment Station. Bioletti was an expert in wine making, but his basic training in chemistry qualified him to elucidate the problems in the olive industry.

The two men could not have been more different from each other. George Colby was heavyset, slightly overweight, and a jovial sort who enjoyed good food and wine in large amounts. In spite of his Italian surname, Bioletti was English. He was small in stature, a formal man very particular about his appearance, sporting a large handlebar moustache.

Together Bioletti and Colby had clarified the canning processes by 1899 and made the techniques reproducible and safe. Using high pressures and temperatures plus evacuation of air from the containers to preserve and sterilize the olives, they improved the way olives could be preserved in metal cans, adapting a method that had already been in use for other fruits for about thirty years. (In 1856, Daniel Provost had been the first person to preserve California fruit as jams and jellies in glass jars. In 1862, Francis Cutting began to preserve California fruit in tin cans, the sheet metal for which had come at first from Baltimore.)

The new technique of sealing olives in metal cans rather than in barrels or glass jars allowed the olive industry to enter the "canned olive" age. Mrs. Freda Ehmann, a widow fallen on hard times, is credited with establishing a true commercial preserved olive industry, something C. M. Gifford had already been doing in a very small way in San Diego. There is no question that Mrs. Ehmann was a most remarkable woman and would have been so in any era. Her work established the modern California ripe olive industry in the shape it still has today. Her accomplishments reflected the culmination of all the forces that worked together and resulted in the market being ready for canned olives.

Mrs. Ehmann was born in Germany in 1839 as Freda Lorber. Her father, Pastor Lorber, came from a long line of Lutheran ministers. Her mother was of Huguenot extraction. When Freda was thirteen, her father died. She and her mother moved to the United States. They went to live with an aunt in Rochester, New York. At the age of eighteen, Freda married Dr. Ernst Cornelius Ehmann in St. Louis. He too had been born in Germany. They settled in Quincy, Illinois. Dr. Ehmann practiced medicine and dispensed pharmaceuticals. At first they lived over the drugstore, but as things improved, they were able to buy the house next door.

The Ehmanns had three children. Tragically, their eldest daughter died of typhoid. Their only son, Edwin, moved to California and became a traveling salesman, or "drummer" as they were known at that time, for the firm of Nathan-Dorhman, china manufacturers. Dr. Ehmann died in 1892. Mrs. Ehmann and her younger daughter, Emma, decided to go to California to be near her son.

From being a sedate physician's wife in a very predictable small town, Mrs. Ehmann underwent extraordinary changes in her life over the next few years. Edwin Ehmann had gone into partnership in an olive orchard with one of his customers. Olive planting was at its peak in the early 1890s. Edwin Ehmann and Herman Juch, a jeweler who was also enthusiastic about the prospects of olive growing, had bought part of a ranch called Olive Hill Grove near Marysville. Edwin had invested his mother's money from the sale of her house in Quincy in this project, together with his own. The widow and her daughter moved to the farm in 1894 but were overtaken by some of the worst flooding for many years.

The timing could not have been worse. The 1890s saw a severe business depression in general and a great drop in the value of olive property and the olive industry in particular. Mr. Juch went bankrupt and Edwin lost all his own and his mother's capital. All that was left was a twenty-acre olive orchard that Mr. Juch deeded to Freda Ehmann in restitution for the harm she had suffered. Most women in their late fifties would have been crushed by all these misfortunes. She had no money, no home, no way to earn a living, and was far from anyone who knew her, but Freda Ehmann was a very strong woman.

Lacking any training, she might have been reduced to menial work or charity, but her daughter did not let that happen. At that time, Emma married a building contractor in Oakland, Charles W. Bolles. The young couple asked her to live with them. Freda Ehmann was not the rocking-chair sort of mother-in-law. She wanted Edwin to pay the debts from his investment and wanted to help him do so. The only asset they possessed between them was the olive orchard. She decided to get busy and exploit this sole asset.

In 1895, there was no crop as the trees were still too young. By 1897, the trees had plenty of fruit, but she had no idea of what to do with the olives. The caretaker at the orchard suggested curing them for sale. Oakland was not too far from Berkeley, and Mrs. Ehmann approached the College of Agriculture at the University of California for advice. Dean Eugene Hilgard obliged with a recipe for curing olives.

Dean Hilgard's recipe was not complex, consisting mainly of frequent changes of water to leach out the bitterness, but because the family could not afford to pipe water to the back porch where she set up her vats, Freda Ehmann carried all the buckets of water from the tap at the other end of the house to the porch by herself. Charles Bolles had made her ten vats from sawn-off wine barrels. Not only did the curing process necessitate several changes of water each day, but sometimes Freda Ehmann also got up in the night to make sure everything was under control.

The whole thing was a punishing process, but in the end, she made excellent pickled olives. The only part that disappointed her was that the olives did not look attractive. Rather than taking a sample to Dean Hilgard herself, she sent her daughter, Emma. The dean told Emma they were some of the best he had ever tasted. Now Mrs. Ehmann could set about selling them.

She began by approaching a grocer in Oakland. He liked the flavor of the Ehmann olives and took her entire stock. As she experimented further, she overcame the problem of mottling and uninteresting color by trial and error. Mrs. Ehmann set very high standards for the future industry, insisting that the pickled fruit keep a high percentage of its oil and flavor as well as having a dark color and good keeping qualities.

The enthusiastic response of local retailers made her think that she might be able to expand the market. Her son helped a lot because his sales route included many grocery stores. They bought china and were obvious targets for his mother's olives. Her debut was in 1897, the year of the Klondike strike. The next year, when the gold rush to Alaska was

at its peak, Mrs. Ehmann started out for the East Coast, first by taking a ship to Vancouver. Neatly dressed and clearly a respectable, superior matron, she was an odd passenger among all the riffraff who were headed for the gold country.

Brokers and grocers in New York were most unkind. They had had previous consignments of California olives that were rotten and stinking from failure to sterilize them in any way. Every one of them had had to be thrown out. It did not matter that Freda Ehmann's samples were delicious. The businessmen were soured by the bad experience.

She next tried to sell the olives in Philadelphia and had much more success. The brokers there ended up by giving her orders for 10,000 gallons. Depending on how she looked at this, it was both good and bad. The good was obvious, but the problem was that her own orchard could only yield 1,000 gallons at most. Mrs. Ehmann immediately began to seek a source of additional fruit.

Edwin once again made a useful contact for her because of his travels. The disaster to their capital had not caused any lack of affection for his mother, and he worked as hard as he could to help her become successful. Her son-in-law, Charles Bolles, also revered her and ultimately became one of her trusted managers in the new business she created.

Edwin had seen the Fogg orchards in Oroville and introduced Freda to Edward W. Fogg. He sold her his entire crop and also leased her the small pickling plant on his grounds where she could prepare the olives. In order to supervise every phase of the process, Mrs. Ehmann moved to Oroville and roomed with the Danforth family. Edward Fogg's plant was just on the other side of the Feather River from the Danforth home.

Each morning she could be seen marching firmly to work over the covered bridge. At that time, menial labor in Oroville was still provided by the Chinese. Mrs. Ehmann employed two Chinese men as laborers but worked equally as hard herself. The season ended with her fulfilling all the contracts and getting new orders for the coming year.

It was clear that this was no longer a "cottage" industry. Mrs. Ehmann had become a commercial manufacturer and needed a formal structure for the business. At the end of 1898, she formed the Ehmann Olive Company, making Edwin the director of sales, and Charles Bolles the supervisor of all plant installation and orchard operation. She herself remained the chief "pickler." There was also no question that she was the supreme arbiter of everything that went on. No one could change anything or let anything out of the plant without her approval.

The siting of new orchards was extremely important. Mrs. Ehmann had learned something about the growth and culture of olive trees and was always concerned that the

❧ FREDA EHMANN TESTING OLIVES
FROM A LARGE VAT AT HER FACTORY
IN OROVILLE, CIRCA 1905.

orchards be in suitable places. One of the few times her son and son-in-law overrode her objections was when they bought 110 acres of unimproved land in Shasta County to plant an orchard, and she thought they should have bought land in Butte County.

Within two years, in 1900, the Ehmann Olive Company had a large processing factory in Oroville, financed by a loan from Edwin's employer, Mr. Dohrman. There were ninety processing vats, an unprecedented number for that time. The men at the lumberyard where the lumber for the vats was purchased thought everyone had lost their minds. However, not only were these vats rapidly utilized, but by 1904, the plant had to be expanded to keep up with the demand. At the same time, the Ehmann Olive Company built an olive oil mill to take advantage of that market too.

At first, they employed Japanese men to sort the olives by hand, but quite soon, the same xenophobia that had led to the anti-Chinese demonstrations in Oroville extended to the Japanese laborers too. Reluctantly, Freda Ehmann had to discharge her men. She had been quite an enlightened employer for the time, housing them adequately, feeding them, and paying them the same wages as American workers doing the same job.

By 1915, Mrs. Ehmann had bought E.W. Fogg's orchard and in 1920 rebuilt her plant in Oroville yet again. She always looked out for her female employees, or "girls," as she thought of them, and included a women-only lunchroom in this building. Each day she sat with the young women who had brought lunch from home and drank tea made in the huge teapots she supplied. No men were ever allowed to enter this precinct. Doubtless their mothers and husbands were pleased about this rule, but one wonders what the young ladies thought of it themselves. We can make gentle fun of this quaint matriarchal attitude, but at a time when there were no safeguards against sexual harassment for women in factories, it made sense.

During the First World War, Freda Ehmann was concerned about the anti-German hysteria that was prevalent in the United States. She had long been an American citizen but took pains to make it known publicly that she held no brief for Germany. It was at that time that she made sure the pronunciation of the name Ehmann changed from the Teutonic "AY-mann" to the American "EE-mann." Many now refer to her as Mrs. "Emmon," another variant.

Initially Mrs. Ehmann sold her olives in barrels, kegs, and then glass jars. Fairly soon after Professor Bioletti perfected the canning of olives in metal, Ehmann Olive Company changed to cans in 1905. Once they did that, the firm joined the California Olive Association. Other firms had embraced the cans sooner. For twenty years, canned olives were sold widely across the country, from the end of the 1890s to 1919.

The Ehmann saga ends sadly. The first outbreak of botulism in 1919 from some of their olives was the cause of their descent from being the leading olive canner to relative failure. It set the company back enormously. Edwin Ehmann retired from the firm after twenty-eight years in 1925. The Ehmann Olive Company merged with the Mount Ida Packing

Company, even though each firm kept its own identity as a sales organization. Years later, the factory would become Olive Products and be folded into a large conglomerate. It has since closed completely.

Freda Ehmann died in 1932 at the age of ninety-three, having worked until very late in her life. In all those years, she had followed two rules absolutely: no alcohol ever came into her house and she never made any green olives. All Ehmann olives were the black "California ripe" type.

In the course of half a century, from the 1880s to the 1930s, California had become known for the "California ripe olive," a unique tasting food, quite unlike anything made previously. Many more trees were planted during this period to take advantage of the increased opportunities, and by 1910, the shape of the modern olive industry in California was established. There were twenty-six thousand acres devoted to this crop. Most of this acreage was now in the Central Valley rather than in the coastal areas where it had all begun.

The division into two separate industries is a modern phenomenon. The great expansion in olive growing toward the end of the nineteenth century was intended to make olive oil on a hitherto unprecedented scale. As that phase peaked, circumstances changed. Olive oil was no longer the principal reason to grow the fruit and the table olive overtook it, but that was not the end of the story, as we have yet to see.

The early pioneers had made their contributions to olive growing, and a new generation expanded the industry. The inflated optimism that had encouraged the initial start of olive growing had, however, now mellowed into a more mature, matter-of-fact approach. It became routine. Olive growing and processing were entering the modern era.

3

Transition to the Modern Era

One of the changes signifying the start of the modern era was where the olives were grown. With the advent of safe, mass canning, heralded by Mrs. Ehmann's business, a much larger and more reliable source of fruit was needed. Modernization in the olive industry also coincided with the growth of agricultural mechanization and improved transportation. Tractors could work harder and more quickly than a team of horses or mules even under adverse conditions.

In the 1870s and 1880s, olive trees were planted along the coast of California. The rise in "factory orchards," complained about by Dean E. J. Wickson, signaled the onset of the modern phase.[1] Edward J. Wickson was the third dean of agriculture at the young University of California. The first orchards laid out by Cooper and Kimball in 1868 and 1869 had been quite extensive, but when the demand for olive oil rose rapidly in the last quarter of the nineteenth century, much larger orchards were planted. They were often financed by outside business syndicates.

California olive growing occupied an aggregate of twenty to twenty-five thousand acres for about forty years, peaking in the 1920s. It then receded with the reduced demand in that decade.[2]

Since the 1930s, commercial olive growing in California has been concentrated inland, in two main clusters of counties in the Central Valley. Very large orchards

❧ WOMEN STEMMING, SORTING, AND
   CLEANING OLIVES.

are quite common now. The techniques to manage them effectively are available and larger orchards can be much more profitable. The modern era may be said to start with this fundamental change in the nature and distribution of the orchards, accompanied by further developments at the processors. Total acreage is now in the range of thirty-five to forty thousand acres.

Time and experience were needed to find out which regions were best for olive growing and to effect this change. In the early years after the destruction of the missions, some modest activity in a number of other parts of the state continued and occasional reports surfaced about this exotic crop. For example, a note appeared in the San Francisco daily newspaper *Alta California* on January 29, 1854, announcing that a merchant in southern California had thirty barrels of olives for sale.[3] Another very brief article in *Alta California* on December 4, 1860, described Major Pierson B. Reading's successful cultivation of olives on his Buenaventura Ranch, near Shasta.[4] The local town was called "Reading" after the major. (Later it

E. J. WICKSON, DEAN OF THE COLLEGE OF AGRICULTURE AT THE UNIVERSITY OF CALIFORNIA AT BERKELEY FROM 1907 TO 1912, CIRCA 1900. WICKSON'S FORTE WAS SCIENTIFIC JOURNALISM.

would change its name homophonically to "Redding," in honor of Mr. B. B. Redding, a senior railroad executive and state official.) The major considered it to be the most northerly point in California where olives would flourish. The reporter added some pleasant background information about olive trees in Greece, their beauty, and longevity.

The tone of this type of report was just a charming footnote, much as we marvel nowadays that someone grows excellent bananas in Santa Barbara. It is not the common practice. Hardheaded businesspeople do not start banana plantations in the temperate zone. Sensible farmers did not plant a tree producing an outlandish crop for which they could see no market.

Soon after this period, as population pressures increased, things changed. With the increased population, many more people used olive oil. There began to be a larger market in table olives.

The notion that olives only flourished within a hundred miles of the coast took a long time to be refuted. It began because the Greeks and Romans had only farmed along the coastal regions in their day and were unsuccessful inland. The Spanish missionaries accepted this as gospel. Eventually ranchers realized that the climate of inland California was actually better for the olive trees, because it was less humid than the coast. A cooler winter was also important. The olive needs some winter chilling and does not produce nearly so well when this is lacking. Other important reasons for the change to the inland valleys were cheaper land prices, proper soil conditions, and the ease of obtaining water.

At one time in the earlier phase, very large olive orchards were common in the southern part of California, because that is where Cooper, the Kimballs, and Gifford began. Once growers realized the disadvantages of this region and that better yields came from more northerly areas, olive growing in southern California shrank rapidly. The only large company still active in Riverside County is Graber's. In 1992, the southern counties only contributed 0.3 percent of the state's olive crop.[5]

At the north-central and northern end of the Central Valley, known as the Sacramento Valley, olives are predominantly grown in Tehama, Glenn, and Butte counties. Growers in Tehama and Glenn counties mainly raise Sevillano olives. Growers in Butte County still stick to Mission olives, because the original plantings in that county were primarily for oil.

In the central and southern parts of the Central Valley, known as the San Joaquin Valley, Tulare County leads in acreage, but there are also large orchards in Madera, Kings, Kern, and Fresno counties. The predominant olive in these more southerly counties is the Manzanillo. Smaller quantities of other cultivars are scattered throughout the olive growing area. Other adjacent counties all produce some olives, but the quantities are much smaller.

The olive will survive as an ornamental or shade tree all over the state except for regions where it gets too cold. It will not give a commercially useful crop in such regions. Enthusiastic individuals are trying to revive orchards and oil making in some of the more marginal sections, such as Calaveras County, where oil and table olives had been produced at the end of the nineteenth century and in the early part of the twentieth. At least one such orchard in "the foothills," as Calaveras is often called, never ceased producing crops and a thriving cannery persisted in that area until very recently.

It has become customary to refer to the San Joaquin Valley and the Sacramento Valley jointly as the "Central Valley." This title obliterates the considerable differences the two valleys once had and the traces of individuality that remain.

The agricultural potential of the San Joaquin Valley was not immediately apparent when the first explorers crossed it. A major obstacle was the marshy terrain, caused by cyclical flooding. The valley's fecundity was not in doubt, but the engineering techniques needed to control it for organized farming had yet to be devised. Early travelers paddled across the valley in canoes during the wet season.

The many native tribes that survived there successfully for centuries were accustomed to its rhythms and lived by gathering the foods that appeared during each of its seasons. The marshes supported thousands upon thousands of fish and birds, and the land produced wild fruits of all types. Numerous deer, rodents, and other small animals rounded out their diet. At one time there were many free-ranging Tule elk, but they have disappeared.

Settlement in the valley began slowly, because the native peoples were still hostile and likely to attack any unprotected farmhouse. Gradually Spanish colonists gave way to American farmers, and by the end of the nineteenth century, the villages and towns we see today had begun to form.

Dr. Samuel Gregg George, a dentist and one-time gold miner who lived and worked in Visalia, planted the first olive tree in Tulare County in 1858. He gave an offshoot of his tree to a man named Wiley Watson and in his turn, Mr. Watson gave away many cuttings to friends and acquaintances. The original George-Watson tree survived for many years. Wilko Mentz, another early citizen, gathered the olives from some of these trees and pickled them to sell in his general store.[6]

The arrival of John J. Cairns, a gigantic and genial Scotsman, defines the start of commercial olive farming in Tulare County. There had been an olive orchard at Bonnie Brae Ranch in Exeter, but Cairns would do things on a large scale. He had begun by growing wheat but almost went bankrupt. He wanted to change to growing fruit, but the persistent drought discouraged many farmers.

Cairns had an idea about how to deal with the drought. He had spent a number of years sheep farming in Australia and astonished the Tulare community when he dug a successful artesian well in Lindsay.

In 1892, Cairns set out orange trees together with grapevines, and added olive trees as a border at about the same time. The olive trees were to be a windbreak, but he also planted them for their beauty, according to an interview Lindsay historian Harold Schutt had with Mr. Cairns's daughters thirty years ago. The hedges of now enormously tall trees still stand at Cairns' Corner in Lindsay. They are about sixty feet high, even after pruning.

Cairns's investment in fruit trees was profitable. The price of olives was rising. In 1911, he received up to $100 per ton for oil olives. This is worth far more in today's dollars, as much as $1,000.

Such prices led to the inevitable cycle of boom and bust. A veritable frenzy in olive planting occurred in the mid-1890s. Within a short time, so much fruit was harvested that the price dropped precipitously. By then Cairns was getting old enough to retire. He was not too distressed about the fall in prices but remained an active member of the California Olive Association during its early years.

Cairns's neighbor and friend, Senator Stockton Berry, also planted an olive orchard and profited during the boom. Other early settlers in Lindsay contributed to the town's growth and development as an olive area. A prominent early family was the Hutchinson family from Scotland. Colonel Arthur Hutchinson bought three ranches shortly after Cairns came to town and grew citrus and olives very successfully. The Southern Pacific Railroad offered land as an inducement for people to settle near their lines and so build freight and passenger traffic. Hutchinson had hoped to obtain certain lands, but the railroad reneged. He very shrewdly overcame the disadvantage of this broken promise by buying other properties.

These early olive-growing efforts led a large part of the olive industry to establish itself in the southern part of Tulare County, chiefly around Lindsay, Porterville, Visalia, Terra Bella, and Exeter. This coincided with the switch to canning olives, and Tulare rapidly became dominant. Firms such as Lindsay Ripe Olive Company and California Associated

Olive Growers, Inc. built plants in Tulare County to be near the source of fruit. The railroads provided convenient transportation to distribute the finished product.

An important factor in the development of the olive industry in California was that no special horticultural knowledge was required to root Mission cuttings and get an orchard started. It was the idea of doing so that took imagination. As orchards and oil making prospered, growers and oil processors began to consider the possibilities of finding other, more productive trees, or olives that would yield more oil when crushed.

Growers sought trees on which the fruit would ripen earlier or that would tolerate slightly cooler weather, so that orchards could be planted in more parts of the state. This work began quite early in the 1870s and persisted for more than twenty years. With different trees, there could be oils with a richer or more complex taste. At this point, the emphasis on an improved table olive was only just beginning. The steps growers took to accomplish their goals were very effective.

In some places, the spread of the trees outran the capacity to process the fruit. Trees were frequently not planted wisely because of failure to understand their requirements and too much haste to cash in on the perceived bonanza. That has actually happened twice on a large scale, once early in the twentieth century and once more recently.

At the end of the nineteenth century, there was a notion that olive trees throve on neglect and that the worse the soil, the greater the yield. This myth is derived from the fact that olive trees can manage to survive without care. Based on this idea, trees were planted too high in the lower reaches of the Sierras, and nowhere near a source of water. The maximum altitude for successful growth of olive trees is 2,600 feet. Predictably, they did not do well and no crops were gathered. They can be seen as one drives through the foothills in the mining country, groups of shaggy, neglected stumps and gnarled old trees bent from the weather. They were rapidly abandoned.

In Tulare County, one such olive orchard was planted as an adjunct to successful citrus crops in 1911. The citrus trees in the flat section of the valley were part of the Merryman Fruit, Land, and Timber Company's holdings. Reuben Merryman came to the Exeter area from Michigan in the 1890s. He joined forces with George Frost of the Bonnie Brae Ranch, a man who had started to grow citrus in Tulare County very early. Once the orange trees in the valley were producing well, they decided to expand the groves up the hillsides.

The growers had to pump water uphill to irrigate them, but the soil was not good enough and after two or three years, they took the trees out. Instead, they turned to olive trees. A veteran nurseryman, Smith Dungan, whose descendants still run a large nursery in Exeter, lived until 1961 and told Harold Schutt that he had helped to plant the replacement trees.

Reuben Merryman took the olive planting seriously. He was an active member of the California Olive Association. Continuing to irrigate the olive trees was too expensive, and so for the next few decades these trees survived completely on their own. They still bear some fruit but nothing on a commercial scale.

To Irrigate or Not to Irrigate?

Olive growers disagree on the issue of irrigation. While the value of irrigation per se has been shown, there is still disagreement about the value of frequent irrigation, because it may reduce the flavor of the olive oil. Irrigation appears to be most effective and necessary in the late spring and early summer months while the fruit is setting. The tree uses the extra water to allow the fruit to swell from the blossom.

Part of the disagreement concerning irrigation arises from the fact that, to some extent, water seems to be relative as far as olive trees are concerned. In 1911, a USDA scientist, Dr. Silas Mason, found some neglected olive orchards in Arizona that still bore good fruit in spite of minimal rainfall, less than fourteen inches per annum. Working in the early years of this century, Mason also saw old trees near Palm Desert in California that had survived with the same minimal rainfall. These old trees stood near others that had died. He noticed that the survivors were planted much further apart than the dead ones. His explanation was that trees planted far enough apart could obtain sufficient water from a distant source, because of reduced competition. This was not the case for trees planted more closely. It seems to be a sound argument. The trees in Tunisia, for example, are planted at very wide intervals and are said to thrive.

A different failure occurred in the 1970s. The great California water project had been completed. Vast amounts of water became available, but it was not inexpensive. The land in the western part of the San Joaquin Valley, in Kern and Kings counties, was rapidly bought up by several holding companies and large corporations in other lines of business. They were looking for ways to modify their tax obligations.

Prudential Insurance and Gulf Oil were among these investors. They hired agronomists and horticultural advisers to find out what should be grown to get a quick profit or what could be manipulated for tax advantages. Any crop had to have a good financial return to compensate for the cost of the water. Olive orchards were one of the prescriptions.

Accordingly, they planted vast acreage with Manzanillo olive trees, assuming that within a very short time, they would have a saleable commodity. Other growers, and processors who already had large inventories on hand, were deeply concerned about the possible impact of this huge increase in production on their own businesses. Sliced olives for pizza had not yet become commonplace, and the market was still fairly circumscribed. The outside businesspeople, experts in petroleum or life insurance, for example, relied on agricultural advisers and did not know that this was a very risky experiment. These advisers were not specifically knowledgeable about olive growing. Experts such as Karl Opitz, the Tulare

County farm adviser from the University of California's Agricultural Extension Service, were acutely aware of the pitfalls awaiting these corporations.

Opitz wrote about the problem in the 1970 *Olive Industry News* and on other occasions.[7] He and others knew that the land in question had been used for long periods to grow cotton. Because of that, it was chronically infested with pathogenic fungi, particularly verticillium wilt. A very disquieting development had been the insidious appearance of the fungus in adjacent territory.

There is no known cure for verticillium wilt once it gets into a plant. Some vegetables have been bred for resistance. A few varieties of tomatoes, and some other annual vegetables such as cucumbers, are resistant. It will usually kill a perennial plant like a tree. The fungicides that can be used safely in other crops like strawberries are not acceptable in olive trees. The concentration required kills the tree's roots.

Olive knot is another disease afflicting olive trees. Both of these problems diminished the likelihood of successful, permanent olive growing. Opitz wrote several articles about this in other journals, but it was too late to stop the executives of the large corporations. They were already committed to the project.

By 1980, his predictions had come true. There was no need to worry about absorbing the additional fruit into the processing plants, because the new trees had all been affected and produced almost no crop at all. The new breed of business "farmers" spent very little time grieving. New tax legislation changed their tax needs. They rooted out the olive trees and planted something else.

After this brief review of the development of the olive industry in the San Joaquin Valley, it is interesting to follow its development in the Sacramento Valley. The Sacramento River defined the Sacramento Valley. Its floods have always been awesome. The river rises from the southern slopes of the Klamath Mountains and provides the central channel to which all the other rivers flow. The flooding was inconvenient, to say the least, but over the millennia, it had been the source of the deep, fertile soil accumulated around the Sacramento River's banks and for some miles on each side of it. It is not unlike the Nile Valley in that respect. The coarse sediment deposited on the higher lands eventually turned out to be ideal for orchards.

Butte County is watered by the Feather River, a tributary of the Sacramento, and its streams. Tehama County and the neighboring Glenn County hug the main channel of the Sacramento River. The valley floor widens as the river flows south. Once the floods of 1861 and 1862 put an end to cattle ranching, and wheat farming was no longer profitable in the valley, fruit farming on a large scale took over. The region was beholden to the gold rush in more ways than one, not only because of creating demand for fruit but also for providing the basis for irrigation.

Wealthy mining companies had constructed huge irrigation "ditches" for hydraulic mining. These ditches became the nucleus of irrigation systems. This useful resource, with the associated title to large amounts of land and access to sources of capital, led the mining companies to take the lead in fruit farming.

The cities of Oroville and Chico became centers of agriculture. More and more people followed John Bidwell's example and planted orchards. Oroville did not call itself an "olive capital," but it could easily have done so. In the late 1880s, Judge John Carleton Gray laid out his orchard, Mount Ida Ranch, in Wyandotte. Edward W. Fogg planted his orchard across the river at about the same time. They wanted to make oil. Both these ventures and that of the Kusel brothers, prominent local citizens, did well, becoming some of the largest such businesses in the state. Mrs. Ehmann had moved her center of operations to Oroville because she would be closer to the source of the fruit. In 1917, the California Associated Olive Growers built one of its plants in Oroville for the same reason.

Other growers began to plant orchards in Wyandotte. They formed the Wyandotte Growers Association in 1915 to market their fruit. Additional communities in Butte County rapidly turned to growing olives: Chico, Biggs, Palermo, Thermalito, and other towns where the irrigation projects had made it feasible. In general, the olive trees and citrus were planted in the same areas.

At the time of the First World War, twenty-eight young professors at UC Berkeley, along with some colleagues from the University of Nevada (all graduates of Berkeley), decided that they should invest in olive orchards to provide an income for their retirement. The university did not offer such a benefit at the time. The men represented various disciplines, but no one was in agriculture. The group designated Professor Herbert W. Hill, a teacher of English, to do the research and report back to them.

Hill thought that Butte County offered the best prospects. The convenient location of the Ehmann processing company in Oroville was an important factor in his decision. It was not long before the group bought land in Coal Canyon, just north of Oroville. Two of the engineers supervised the blasting of holes in the rock to plant the trees. They also experimented with the layout of the orchards, using hexagonal plantings to get the most out of their space.

The professors planted the trees and sat back to await results. During the summers, they camped in the olive orchards. Later, some of them built small retirement cottages on their property. The olives prospered, and so did the professors. By 1922, they were in full swing. It was a good investment. The olive trees continue to bear fruit, and some of their families are still involved in the olive trade.

About ten years after they started their orchards, the Berkeley group joined with the Wyandotte Growers Association in taking over another plant, the Suni-cal Packing Corporation, successor to the California Ripe Olive Company. The combined organization continued to make oil and pack olives until the 1960s.

Another company in the area, the Mount Ida Packing Corporation, was enlarged and recapitalized in 1916. It was renamed Olive Products Company. This group built a very

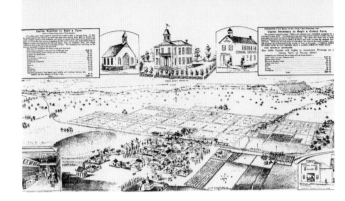

big plant, said to be the largest of its kind in the world. Olive Products bought the Wyan-dotte cannery in 1976. (Everyone liked to brag about their own endeavors. Sylmar Packing Company in the San Fernando Valley was also supposed to be the largest in the world.)

In the Butte County area, a major frost destroyed many trees in Thermalito in 1932. Despite its name, Thermalito was not an especially warm section of the valley. Winter was particularly severe in the northern part of California that year. Icy conditions also ruined orchards near Auburn. The trees in Thermalito were never replanted and the orchards ceased operations. Despite this, olive growing in Butte County occupies about three thousand acres at present.

In Tehama County, the story of Maywood Colony is both charming and interesting. It also reveals another aspect of how the olive industry developed in the Sacramento Valley. It sprang from the mind of Warren Woodson, an inspired real estate developer. Woodson saw the potential in Corning, in spite of the paucity of resources in that town, and decided to develop it. The town eventually would become a community of respectable citizens rather than the unfortunate assemblage of gamblers and drinkers that predominated at the time.

Woodson wanted to build a community of godly people, but he also wanted to make money. Offering many modestly sized lots was a more certain way to attract enough people to his community than trying to sell a few large ones. The idea came to him because of the letters he had received in Red Bluff when he had served as postmaster there. People wrote simply to the "Postmaster" asking for information about farming in the upper Sacramento Valley. He decided to sell ten- and twenty-acre lots as part of a self-sufficient "colony."

Woodson had had very little formal schooling, but he read a lot on his own and loved the Bible. He knew that the climate of California resembled that of the Holy Land. Godliness and the connection with the Bible were symbolized by growing the same kind of fruit, including figs, olives, and grapes. This, Woodson thought, could in turn be fused with his business of selling ten-acre lots to newcomers from the rest of the United States.

Woodson's inspiration was to prepare the lots to be little self-supporting orchards. The fruit trees were to be a lure to get Easterners to move out to California. Railroads made it possible to reach California in a week or less. An additional inducement was paying the railroad fare from Chicago to Corning.

Instead of the newcomer having to scratch for a living, Woodson promised that they could buy a nice little property already producing some income from bearing fruit trees. Even if they were planning to retire, the fruit would supply an additional income. His wording was so glowing in tone that many reputable magazines, fearful of being involved in a swindle, refused to carry his advertisements, assuming they were grossly exaggerated and fraudulent. Though this put a crimp in his advertising, it did not end it, because numerous small church magazines trusted Woodson and carried his notices. He sincerely meant there to be fruit trees bearing and had taken steps to assure this, but unfortunately by the time the first settlers came, almost all the fruit trees had died.

Woodson had gone to a nursery in Oroville in 1895 and bought odd lots of fruit trees, without much concern for the specific character of each one. He had them planted on the lots for sale, but the climate and infestations of vermin quickly destroyed almost everything. Olive trees were jumbled in together with numerous other fruit trees. Only the olive trees survived, and even they acted strangely by not producing any fruit for several years.

Woodson did not know the odd lot of trees he had bought included the relatively new Sevillano, or "queen," olive. When fruit did finally appear, it was unusually large and ultimately became very popular. Warren Woodson had almost unwittingly started a completely new industry, though a problem had to be solved before this new industry could thrive.

It was initially very difficult to cure the Sevillano olive by standard techniques. These techniques resulted in blistered, split, and unattractive-looking fruit. Research at the College of Agriculture in Berkeley and the efforts of local experts such as Fred Beresford corrected this, and the problems were overcome. By 1913, many more Sevillano trees were planted in Corning.

A few growers had planted Mission or Manzanillo trees. They soon grafted them over to Sevillanos. In 1906, Woodson and some other investors started the Maywood Packing Company. Its purpose was to can fruit, but it quickly added olives to its inventory once the canning process became widespread. Corning still calls itself the "Olive Capital" because of Woodson's skill in promotion, but in fact it is not so large a producer as Tulare County. The 1992 agricultural census shows that the San Joaquin Valley produces 65 percent of the olives in California and the Sacramento Valley 35 percent.

This shift in the relative size of the crops led to other changes throughout the state. Because of the great expansion in olive growing in the San Joaquin Valley, the growers in Lindsay and the neighboring towns got together in 1916 to form the Lindsay Ripe Olive Company, a cooperative with a canning plant that lasted until 1992. At one time, it was the largest such facility in the world. Unlike some of the others, this claim could be substantiated.

The momentum, which had been generated in the preceding decade by large-scale nurseries making olive trees readily available, was now carried forward by this giant olive-canning plant. California's agriculture would astonish the world with its scale. We are fortunate that the superintendent of the Lindsay plant during the 1950s and '60s was Harold Schutt, a thoughtful man who cared a good deal about history, because his efforts provide much information about the olive industry's history. Schutt was born in Buffalo, New York, but his family moved to Lindsay in 1908. He studied political science at the University of California at Berkeley. After several changes in career, he returned to Lindsay and entered the Lindsay Ripe Olive Company, where he rapidly rose to a senior position.

Almost from the beginning of his tenure there, Schutt began to look into the history of the olive industry in California. Both George Powell and Ralph Fusano, the men who have more recently saved documents about olive history, were his colleagues at Lindsay. It is likely he had an influence on them. He wrote a number of short articles about his findings but never completed a book. Schutt's interest in history led him to become president of the Tulare County Historical Society for several years. The chapter in this book on the olive processing companies covers the history of the Lindsay Ripe Olive Company in more depth and owes a great deal to Schutt's work.

In the same year that the Lindsay Ripe Olive Company was established, another joint business venture, the California Associated Olive Growers Incorporated (CAOGI) also started. Unlike the Lindsay firm, CAOGI was not intended to be a cooperative but a standard business corporation. The organizers signed up many growers all over the Central Valley and built plants in Oroville and Lindsay. With these major developments, things seemed to be going along very well.

Once again, smooth growth in the California olive industry was interrupted. This time it was a true catastrophe. In 1919, an outbreak of botulism was traced to eating canned olives. This disease is caused by the toxin of *Clostridium botulinus,* a bacterium whose spores are ubiquitous in soil and agricultural produce. Botulism is hard to diagnose quickly without an obvious lead from the patient's history. It is difficult to treat successfully even today, but in 1919 it was almost uniformly fatal.

In that first outbreak, fourteen people fell ill, and seven of them died. Public health officials tracked the outbreak to a shipment of contaminated California canned ripe olives. Once this became known, there was an immediate, severe decline in sales. Everyone across the country was scared. The fearfulness lasted almost ten years and had some effect on the sale of other canned fruits and vegetables as well. Members of the California Olive Association called in numerous experts, taxed themselves to pay for research both by public and private scientists, and worked with the National Canners' Association to make sure this never happened again.[8]

The end of the olive industry's recession due to the botulism coincided with the onset of the Great Depression, which began in 1929. Millions of people lost their jobs and had to subsist as best they could. Almost no one had extra disposable income to enjoy the relative luxury of olives in their diet. It was still hard to sell olives even in the mid-1930s, and several firms closed down. Once confidence in the safety of the product and the stability of the economy were restored, canned ripe olives regained most of their popularity, and business continued to build up to present-day levels. Doing this required relentless attention to marketing.

As we look at the olive industry in California, it may be helpful also to see it briefly in relation to the worldwide olive industry. The modern California olive industry is very small by world standards. To understand its modest size, consider these statistics. Spain has about five million acres of olive trees, or more acres than there are individual *trees* in the whole of the California olive belt. California only has about four million trees at best.

Vast areas are also devoted to olive orchards in Italy, Morocco, Tunisia, Algeria, Turkey, and Greece. There is a successful olive industry in Israel, although it is not as extensive as in the other Mediterranean countries. There are large orchards in France, but many of them were decimated by a disastrous freeze in the 1970s. The French olive industry is now much smaller than it used to be.

Enormous quantities of this Mediterranean fruit go to be pressed into oil. The costs of growing them and picking them are far lower than in the United States, so the oil is less expensive to produce. In some of these countries, there are also governmental subsidies for olive oil exports.

Olives are also widely grown in Mexico, Argentina, Chile, and Peru, as well as in Australia and South Africa. The olive industry in Australia began earlier than in the United States, even though the first olive trees did not arrive in the Southern Hemisphere until 1800. At times in the nineteenth century, a few California growers turned to Australian experts for guidance.

In the United States, California is essentially the only area where olives flourish commercially. Only a minute amount of the total annual U.S. output comes from Arizona. Since the principal end product of the California olive harvest is canned olives, one can see that the amount of acreage devoted to producing oil is extremely small. There is no way oil prices based on the correspondingly high unit cost in California can compete with the relatively inexpensive oil that comes in such vast quantities from the Mediterranean countries. The philosophy of modern California oil makers is to offer a product that is in a special class and thus circumvents competition.

The American public assumes all the imported oil it consumes comes from Italy, Spain, or France and does not know it could originate from much further afield. Current international codes allow the label to list the country where the oil was packaged as the place it originated. Much of the oil produced in many of the other countries is excellent, but not all of it. In a business where the surface presentation accounts for a lot of the appeal, this ignorance can result in the public paying premium prices for less than premium goods.

While oil continued to be produced in California during the early years of the twentieth century, for the faithful few who depended on it for their everyday cooking, it was relegated to a backwater. It was not distributed in Eastern cities through the normal channels, unless the makers took the oil there themselves. The oil did not carry botulism. If anything, it is acid, discouraging the growth of the bacteria, but the outbreak of botulism in 1919 did nothing to improve the sales of oil.

Given these circumstances, it must have seemed like utter madness when the Sciabica family undertook to make and sell olive oil in 1936, but that is what they did. (It was in the depths of the depression, and no one knew the opportunities that would soon be presented by the Spanish Civil War.) The Sciabicas were not alone in their endeavors. Two other Californian families of Italian descent, the Obertis and the Padulas, did the same thing at about the same time. All three families persevered with enormous ingenuity and struggle, and managed to make a living when others could not. During this whole phase, imported oil continued to reach the United States and remained powerful competition.

The rise of fascism in Italy, and its trial run in Spain during the late 1930s, finally gave the California olive oil industry the opportunity it needed to expand. The Civil War in Spain led the way because it diminished the export of table olives and olive oil. Later, when the Second World War began, merchant vessels could not safely cross the Atlantic and all imports of oil from Spain and Italy ceased. Even if it had been possible to transport the oil, there was not a lot of Italian oil to send. Most Italian men were away fighting or in labor camps, and the women, with the help of elderly men too old to fight, could only do so much on their own.

Spain by this time was technically neutral and much less affected by the new war, having partially recovered from its previous one, but the absence of available merchant shipping effectively prevented any oil being exported to the United States. Spanish farmers might concentrate once again on such peacetime activities as making oil, but the American merchant marine was taken over by the war effort.

Between 1938 and 1950, the pendulum swung back and forth, with olive oil and canned olives changing places as the principal activity of the California olive industry. There was much more emphasis on oil for a time, but it quickly came to an end as Italy and Spain recovered from the war.

Everett S. Krackov, an olive grower in Woodlake, Tulare County, was born in Brooklyn. He told me that he went to Italy with his father in the mid-1930s on a buying trip for the family food-importing business. Everett A. Krackov, his father, imported olives, olive oil, and other Mediterranean foods. The political instability of Italy made a deep impression on Everett A., and he was concerned that the family would no longer be able to continue its business. Together with many other thoughtful people, he saw the coming of another world war.

To protect his livelihood, Everett A. bought olive orchards, an olive oil mill, and an olive processing plant in northern California in 1937. Several immediate family members moved to Tulare County to manage these businesses. The Krackovs would manufacture their own delicacies. This was a bold, but somewhat unusual move at the time. It turned out to be prescient. The son, Everett S. Krackov, moved to Woodlake in 1949 to manage an additional olive business for the firm and has remained there ever since.

The families who were already in the olive oil business in California took advantage of the new circumstances very quickly. Those who had not been in the trade before hastened to join in. Dozens of new firms started up the length and breadth of the Central Valley. With this improvement in their fortunes, the California olive oil makers of Italian descent are said to have attracted the attention of the Mafia, always on the lookout for a profitable business. When one firm changed hands in 1947, the new owners were clearing out some closets and supposedly came across a stash of machine guns.

Growers had switched from producing olives for oil to growing them for canning earlier in the twentieth century because the processing companies paid much better for large, table-sized fruit than for olives that were to be crushed. Attractive fruit in perfect condition commands a lot more money from the processors for curing and pickling as table olives than it would if sent to be crushed to make oil. Because of successful marketing, the consumer would pay more for these larger olives. Now the oil makers began to pay the growers more for their fruit than the canners. There was immense competition between the oil-making firms to get fruit. Often, second-level olives, such as culls, had to be used to press oil.

Quite soon after the Second World War ended, these newly prosperous oil-making firms once again slipped back to their former levels of activity. Italy very rapidly resumed making olive oil and exporting it at lower prices. Ships became available once more to carry Spanish imports across the Atlantic. Many small California olive oil firms went out of business.

Only a few tougher ones survived, such as the Sciabicas, the Padulas, and the Obertis, the original oil-making families. West Coast Products in Orland continued to make oil. Marino Garbis, manager and part owner of this firm, obtained his olives from the Krackov ranch in Woodlake.

When the war was over, most of the action in the olive industry again revolved not around oil but around table olives—in cans. The growers had become accustomed to the high prices for oil olives and had a large crop to sell in 1946. Unfortunately for them, the canners were not yet back in full swing. They could not absorb this crop. Residual wartime regulations about the use of metal meant they could not produce enough cans for the fruit.

The growers tried to do something about their plight. They organized and, for several years in the late 1940s, received governmental help. According to Ralph Fusano, they ended up with a further loss of the market to the foreign oil. Matters were made worse when the Commodity Credit Corporation, a wartime agency, decided to reduce its inventory and released stockpiled domestic olive oil at half price. The CCC had lent money to oil firms against stocks of olive oil as collateral.

The canning industry underwent further change during this period and in the years that followed. There were twenty-eight olive processing firms and canners in 1950. By 1975, it was down to eleven. Some of them were divisions of large canning companies such as Libby, McNeil, and Libby. Others were small and independent. The reasons for this shrinkage are explored in chapter 7.

The changes were all exemplified by the town of Corning. At one time, there were eight canning plants there. Family-owned firms were affected during these decades. The heirs of the Stanley Rousch Company did not want to run the business. It was sold to the Maywood Packing Company. Even the strong Glick family eventually sold out. The Glick family worked as a unit, father and several sons. Maywood absorbed most of the smaller firms and then in turn was taken over by Bell-Carter Foods.

Stronger competition both within the United States and from abroad began to force down prices, coupled with the uncontrollable swings in the size of the crops. Jack McFarland told me about his family's experience. (Jack was already eighty years old when I met him, and had been growing olives all his adult life.) His father began to grow olives in Corn-

❧ HARVESTING OLIVES IN THE EARLY YEARS OF THE TWENTIETH CENTURY.

ing in the 1940s. He struggled against many odds without success, never making any money from his crops: too many olives one year, not enough the next. Jack's father died in 1947, without living to see olives finally fetching $600 a ton a year or two later.

Because of the cyclical nature of the crops, huge numbers of cases of processed olives would be left over from a previous year and were difficult to sell. This occurred at fairly predictable intervals. The mounting problems with marketing, and to a lesser extent quality, that resulted were the catalyst in creating a state marketing order in 1955. The marketing order permitted orderly interaction between processors, allowing the group to set price floors and manipulate their output.[9]

The growers and canners had many differences but needed each other to survive and grow. Following the marketing order, further adjustments were made in the size categories, and most important, a combined marketing program helped improve sales. About ten years later, in 1965, a federal marketing order became necessary and is still in existence today. This marketing order has essentially the same provisions as the previous one. It sets standards, regulating the industry and the market.

Things seemed to be on a more even keel in the 1960s, but pressure from environmental legislation and regulations started to have a serious impact in the next decades. This was a combined assault on the viability of some canners and more succumbed. (See appendix C.)

Foreign competition also continued to be a threat. An example of foreign competition is the story of stuffed olives. Costs in the California companies were too high. Preparing one jar of stuffed olives in California was almost as expensive as preparing a dozen jars in Spain. Rather than compete and lose, certain branches of the trade were "given" to Spain because their costs were so much lower than those in the United States. Cocktail olives, the big green "queen" olives stuffed with almonds and pimento, are now almost solely supplied by Spain.

Back in the United States, internal competition affected shelf allocation in supermarkets. If customers cannot see the can, they will not be able to buy it. Large food-processing conglomerates with many diverse products could influence the distribution of olives as pawns in the cause of their other products, and sell the olives more cheaply for a while to gain an advantage. Items that the supermarket wants to sell most urgently are placed at eye level. Others are relegated to the bottom or top shelves, far out of eyeshot. In the elegant grocery shops of Marin County, the expensive foreign olives are at eye level, the humdrum standard ones at the bottom of the case. This is not unique to olives. It is the standard way supermarkets operate.

The effects of the tougher competition were felt much more acutely by smaller companies. A division of a large conglomerate can tolerate fluctuating prices because it cushions the effects with its other lines of business. Independent companies whose assets lie in a single product cannot weather such instability in price. The age of consolidation accelerated. By the early 1990s, there were only four processing companies left in California. Two were independent, Bell-Carter, based in Corning, and Musco Olive Products, based in Tracy. The third one belonged to a large conglomerate, Early California in Visalia, and the fourth to a cooperative, Tri Valley Growers in Madera. The four remaining canners became two when Musco bought Early California in 1998, followed by Tri Valley ceasing independent processing operations in 1999.

There was an improvement in the market when pitted olives became the norm in the 1970s. Increasing the convenience increased the demand. Very few people have the time or inclination to stand around taking the stones out of olives, no matter how exciting the recipe. Almost all California black ripe olives, the standard ones for table use, are now sold pitted. The rise of pizza garnished with sliced olives again led to an increased demand. A very considerable quantity of the canners' output goes to restaurant chains, institutional caterers, and other wholesale users. As a derivative of this, it is also quite commonplace now to find sliced and chopped olives in cans for retail sale. This increase in the market balanced the extra cost of the machinery needed to take out the pits and slice the fruit.

A recent problem has been that the pizza industry needs so many olives that even the newly consolidated olive industry in California cannot reliably supply large enough quantities each year. The number of trees and their biology influence the size of the crop.

Olive trees are cyclical bearers. One year there will be a huge crop, the next a great deal less. In spite of unremitting research, no one has found a reliable way to smooth out this biennial bearing cycle beyond a certain point. Planting more trees will not help in the short run because it takes a minimum of five years for a tree to reach full maturation. By the time that happens, the taste for pizza with sliced olives may have been succeeded by something else.

One company tries to bridge the gap caused by cyclical bearing by bringing in olives from Mexico and processing them in the Central Valley. This is a very sore point with the smaller growers in that district. The firm is the only player left in town and the growers have to accept the prices offered, or else transport their fruit much longer distances to another processing firm. They see the purchase of foreign fruit as a betrayal, since the shortage has not increased the price they receive. By contrast, the processor is concerned about keeping his share of the market. If he cannot meet the demand, next time that contract will go to someone who can, perhaps a foreign firm abroad. In spite of the processors trying to patch things together with the Mexican olives, the pizza chains have turned to Spain to fill the contracts. They are using the canned Hoja blanca olives, which are not as tender or pleasant as the California ripe olive. This is cause for concern. How much else, like the stuffed cocktail olives all coming from abroad, may have to be "given" away?

Another ironic twist in the story is the current shift away from the handsome large "queen" olives that were so sought after and profitable until only just recently. Marketing research has revealed that families want to have more olives in a can, so that they can open just one at a time and give everyone a few olives rather than have to open an extra can. This is seen as an economy. The processors need to furnish consumers with what they want.

The result is that beautiful large Sevillano (queen) olives, grown mainly in the Corning region, are no longer so valuable. Their price has dropped as the processors seek more modest-sized fruit, usually the Manzanillo variety. Growers have been told they should change their variety by grafting the Sevillano trees with Manzanillo scions. It is hard work and fairly costly to do that, and of course, would take four or five years of growth before they could harvest enough to sell.

The olive growers in the northern Sacramento Valley are in a very tough spot. If they do nothing, the market for their fruit will continue to shrink. They could not even get much for them from the oil makers, as they are not such a rich source of oil. At best, the price for oil olives is about 10 percent of the price for table olives. If they go ahead and graft the trees, there are no guarantees. Many of the trees were grafted at least once before—from the Mission variety (originally brought to California and disseminated widely) to the Sevillano (later considered more profitable). Grafting requires a lot of attention to detail and the success of the graft is a matter of technique. Assuming the grafts take and the trees bear Manzanillo fruit, what is the grower going to do without that income for several years?

CLOSE-UP VIEW OF A SUCCESSFUL GRAFT.

American consumers are not simply concerned with the size of olives (or the number in any given can). They are also concerned about taste. Increased prosperity has, directly and indirectly, played an important role in developing more sophisticated tastes. This has been very beneficial to the industry. Prosperity allowed more Americans to travel abroad after the end of the Second World War. For the first time, many Americans tasted foods they had never eaten before—and they liked them. They wanted to continue to eat them once they returned home. The nation's palate was to be broadened by these experiences. It is commonplace now, but pizza was very new and daring when it was first introduced in the early 1950s as a derivative of foods eaten in Italy.

Foods with much more pronounced flavors became popular in the 1960s and '70s. A taste for such pungent delicacies as Greek and Italian olives now spread more widely among the general population. Their consumption was no longer confined to small ethnic minorities. Those olives could be imported, but they could also be made in California by using old recipes. Many small California manufacturers now prepare and sell "Sicilian" olives, "Greek" olives, and "Niçoise" olives, all very much like the imported kinds.

All these developments would lay the foundations of an increased demand for olive oil in the 1970s and '80s. Once that was accomplished, the public slowly recognized that olive oil could be differentiated into various grades and have different flavors. Not all oils were the same. At first the new demand stimulated imports from Italy and Spain, but in recent years, the California olive oil industry has capitalized on this trend. A number of people have been encouraged to plant olive orchards or restore old ones in an attempt to make premium oil.

With a few exceptions, the modern grower of olives is a practical businessperson trying to make a living. The recent "amateur" growers with financial security from other sources are the only ones who can afford to ignore the economic viability of their crops. In that way, the amateurs resemble the nineteenth-century ranchers. Olives at that time were not, in many cases, a principal crop. They were, for example, useful in filling odd corners that would not support orange, lemon, or other fruit trees effectively.

For full-time growers, the price of the fruit is very important. This is also true of the grower who has a small orchard in addition to another job, such as working in an office or plying a different trade. Such people have factored in the additional income from the orchard as a way to improve their finances. Since olives sold for oil only bring in about one-tenth of the price for table olives, it is essential that this fruit meet the canners' standards.

An example of a family that has depended on growing olives for two generations is the Aguiars. There are three brothers—Lawrence, James, and Louis. They were literally born into the olive business. I was fortunate enough to meet all of them.

Their father came from the Azores in the 1920s and bought several pieces of land in Orland. (Orland is a very small town in the northern end of the Sacramento Valley, ten miles south of Corning.) He gradually planted olive orchards on all his lots. Olives had not been his business before he came to the United States, but he learned very quickly. His sons remember him using dynamite to create the holes for the seedlings.

Today Mr. Aguiar's sons all continue to work in the olive industry. Lawrence and James run the family olive orchards. Louis, a comfortable, low-key sort of man, has worked for a number of years as the "field man" for the Bell-Carter packing company in Corning. The years of experience Louis gained from his family business are invaluable for the work he does today. The job of field man is not at all simple and requires a lot of character. The field man has to assess the quality of the fruit brought in by the growers, and is the gatekeeper for all the processing that follows. If fruit does not meet the firm's standards, it has to be rejected, no matter how old a friend the grower may be. The work of a field man is also time consuming. All the time I chatted with Louis, the phone rang frequently. He had many tasks to complete. In spite of that, he found time to suggest people I should interview and get me their phone numbers.

Talking to the Aguiar brothers gave me some of the perspective on the economics of growing olives in California in the 1990s noted here. Other growers, whom I met through the Aguiars, and another expert, Dennis Burreson, confirmed what the Aguiars had told me.

Orchards may look passive and serene, but there are substantial fixed costs in their main-tenance. It is necessary to purchase land and plant the saplings. Time must pass before a crop can be harvested. The trees have to be irrigated at proper intervals, contrary to popu-lar notions about their rugged indifference to water. Even in an organic orchard, there is a need to counteract pests, and in conventional culture the owner has to spray and cultivate.

Pruning is another important activity. Knowing how to prune takes skill and skilled labor is expensive labor, but by far the largest expense is for picking and harvesting. No mat-ter how the grower decides to do it, more than half the year's expenses are accounted for by this crucial phase. Clearly the grower needs to get the best price possible after investing so much money and effort in the orchard.

In the larger Mediterranean olive industries, the economic factors are not the same. The same requirement to earn money exists, but the trees are so widespread and cover so much land that much more is left up to nature alone. In this way costs are controlled. It is not feasible to do things that work well on smaller properties. Irrigation is less common. Only the more enlightened Spanish growers cultivate their orchards and prune effectively.

Another variation in the expenses between the Mediterranean countries and the United States is the cost of picking. Until fairly recently, pickers were paid a fraction of what even a migrant worker in California gets. That is no longer generally true in European Union countries, although it is probably still the case in Turkey and North Africa. Another major difference is attitude of the governments. Olives in those Mediterranean countries are said to be subsidized heavily, which makes it difficult for U.S. producers of oil or of table olives to compete on price.

Olive growers face very real economic challenges, both at home and abroad. In spite of this, each time California olive oil production and sales seem to have reached a low point, someone finds a new positive attribute to the oil and the cycle turns up again. We are cur-rently seeing one of those upturns. It has been caused in part by the new medical findings that olive oil is a so-called "good" fat, monounsaturated rather than saturated or even polyunsaturated. Articles pour forth almost daily about its effect on reducing the low-density lipoproteins or LDLs (source of arteriosclerotic disease) in the blood and boosting the high-density lipoproteins or HDLs, which remove the unwanted fat molecules from the blood.

Arterial disease, especially in the coronary or heart arteries, is found more frequently in persons with an excess of cholesterol in the blood and more particularly, a disproportion-ately low ratio of HDLs in relation to the LDLs. Changing the ratio of LDLs and HDLs by increasing the HDLs can reduce this risk. Olive oil is not the sole unsaturated fat that can do this. Other mono- and polyunsaturated fats achieve the same end, but olive oil does it effectively and deliciously.

Another reason for olive oil's resurgence of popularity is the need to return to foods that still have an authentic taste. So much food in modern life lacks savor. In many cases, it is harvested too early, processed to make it homogeneous, and packaged in plastic for a long shelf life. It is the antithesis of what food should be. Responding to this mood, small companies are making "varietal" oil to match the excellent varietal California wines. They are also making new, more creative blends. The idea is to create an oil that tastes more like the ones from Tuscany. One of the ways this is being done is by importing new varieties of trees, expanding the choice beyond Mission and Manzanillo. These new growers argue that better quality oil with the authentic Italian flavor must come from a different type of tree. They were anticipated in this by growers in the last century.

History, of course, is a living thing, and how the current revival of interest in olive oil fits into the larger picture will only become evident in the days ahead. As we have seen in this chapter, unexpected factors can enhance, damage, or, as in the case of the 1919 botulism outbreak, nearly destroy the olive industry.

Oil was originally the *raison d'être* for the olive industry in California, but it rapidly shrank into a small niche. Once reliable methods of preserving the olives in cans were developed, the growers found they made more money from canning olives and changed almost all their trees to varieties more amenable to table use. California's canned ripe olives are unique in the world of olive fare, with a special taste found nowhere else. Consolidation has reduced competition and streamlined production, but it still cannot stem the inroads of foreign processors. Pizza lovers enjoy the taste of the California Manzanillo olive and complain that the Spanish Hoja blancas are tough and tasteless, but until some magic way is found to boost production significantly without the attendant risks, they will have to make do with the substitute. The consolidation of the canneries is now so tight that it cannot be expected to go much further. Because of this, I think the future of the California olive industry is rather uncertain.

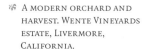 A MODERN ORCHARD AND HARVEST. WENTE VINEYARDS ESTATE, LIVERMORE, CALIFORNIA.

4

Why Olive Growers Changed
to New Kinds of Trees

In the late 1860s, when Ellwood Cooper went to the old mission orchards and took enough cuttings for his new ranch, he and his friends were convinced that olive oil was an important marketable commodity and could be made in California just as well as in Europe. There was plenty of space in the huge, almost vacant tracts and ranches in the fertile sections of the state to plant orchards. Once it was clear that the public would buy the oil, all that ranchers needed were vision and application.

In that early stage, the expansion of olive growing had the feeling of a religious movement, not just a business. Certain men had a sort of epiphany. The proponents talked about it as a way to make money, but it had a special aura that other, more mundane businesses lacked. One feels that the money-making potential was touted to give them cover and justify their enthusiasm. They had to seem hardheaded and practical.

It would not do to appear naive and romantic, yet it was somehow a very gentlemanly activity, perhaps even slightly glamorous, not just a crude manufacturing enterprise like making soap or tanning leather. This probably reflected the old classical and biblical associations of the olive tree. Warren Woodson in Corning, who

❧ HARVESTING OLIVES IN TULARE COUNTY
IN THE 1920s.

79

clothed his real estate development schemes in the righteous robes of biblical allusions, is a perfect example. Ministers of religion like the Reverend Mr. Loop of Pomona were also very comfortable with their orchards. Growing olives was almost a godly thing to do.

Many sincere imitators took up olive growing. They had been encouraged by the rhetoric. A very notable example is Edward E. Goodrich. He was inspired by the work of Ellwood Cooper. Goodrich bought the El Quito Ranch in Santa Clara expressly for the purpose of planting olive trees and making oil. He employed Arthur T. Marvin, author of one of the first treatises on the olive in California, as his manager, but always considered Cooper to be his mentor and frequently consulted him for advice. Another of Goodrich's associates at El Quito was one of Governor Arguello's sons. He assisted in planting the olive trees.

The Del Valle family at Camulos in Ventura County had the very first commercial olive oil mill outside a mission. In 1871, they pressed and sold the first olive oil not made at a mission. Goodrich and Cooper were among the earliest to follow them. All these growers used the same tree, the Mission. No one was yet thinking about trying to find a different tree. The one they had did everything they needed.

At first blush it is hard to see why olive growers would want to change a successful formula. The Mission trees grew vigorously and the oil was excellent. The product was only moderately perishable. If properly stored, oil lasts up to a year. Many householders bought it in bulk. If the previous lots had been satisfactory, the buyer repeated the purchase the following year.

Olive growers did not have the problems of the deciduous fruit fraternity, where single varieties of trees resulted in fruit ripening all at once, thus creating a glut in the market. Despite this, olive growers suddenly wanted to expand their choices. It is tempting to blame that peculiarly American trait of constantly wanting to improve a good thing, of not leaving well enough alone. Even when something appears to be working extremely well and does not seem to have any room for improvement, someone with imagination comes up with a better way of doing it. In this instance, the American penchant for improvement does not appear to have been the only reason growers sought out new types of trees.

Two other factors seem to have come into play. One was California's geography; the other was international geography. As olive growing moved to more distant parts of the state where the soils and climates were different, the growers began to wonder about finding a tree that might perform even better. Early growers had been very lucky with the success of the Mission olive tree, largely due to chance, but it was reasonable to question whether another tree might do as well if not better in other locations.

By the end of the nineteenth century, the Central Valley was beginning to be drained and becoming arable land. Land at slightly higher elevations began to be cultivated. Each of these areas had its own climatic range of temperature and rainfall. The Mission tree is very cold hardy, and this contributed to its success as far north as Tehama County. Other kinds of trees might not have been so cold hardy but could offer variations in climatic adaptability, as well as the size of the fruit, its taste, the overall productiveness of the tree, the date of maturation, and hence the quality of the oil. Susceptibility to pests was also an important variable.

One enthusiastic amateur, Benjamin B. Redding, state official and executive with the railroads, was eager to try out new trees. Redding worked as chief land agent for the Southern Pacific Railroad under Collis P. Huntington. Huntington was very interested in promoting agriculture in California and expected his staff to take up the task too. Redding studied soil types and temperature belts all over the state. There were many other similar, painstaking studies of the same sort at the time.

In some of his most useful experiments, Redding showed that citrus could be made to flourish in the northern section of the Sacramento Valley. It is unfortunate that he ultimately turned out to be wrong when some unexpectedly cold winters caused excessive damage to the trees. He had not allowed a long enough time for a complete weather cycle to run its course. In a study with more favorable results, Redding experimented with olive trees in San Diego, Tulare, and Sacramento, and proved that they would do well in the inland valleys.

The other stimulus to changing cultivars was the increasing prosperity that led to more travel in the 1880s. California ranchers could go to Europe and North Africa. They tasted better olive oil in France, Italy, or Spain and wanted to duplicate it. Redding traveled in France and was impressed by several different varieties. Knowledgeable people immigrated into the state and brought new ideas with them. Some of them brought olive oil itself or even cuttings of the trees their families had grown for generations.

There was also the example of the vineyardists constantly improving their stock with foreign imports from many of the same places where olives grew so well. The State Department's Consular Service and the Department of Commerce's foreign agricultural division encouraged such improvements by sending a steady stream of informational and educational bulletins to California.

American farmers were not bound by the social and economic stasis that afflicted olive growers in the ancient lands whence they sought the trees. They were free men in a democratic society and eager to question all authority, including horticultural. It is a curious paradox that restless and energetic Americans imported specimens of trees that had been grown in one place for centuries and whose originators would not have dreamed of exchanging for another. Tradition and habit are powerful ingredients of inertia. Only relatively recently have the experts in Spain and Italy even decided to try new cultivars in the ancient orchards and compare their productivity with the resident trees.

In 1874, a few years after Cooper and Kimball started the olive industry movement, two Spanish olive varieties were imported into California. This step had extraordinary consequences for the industry. These Manzanillo and Sevillano trees would eventually overtake the Mission trees and become the dominant varieties—Manzanillos in the San

Joaquin Valley and Sevillanos in the Sacramento Valley. That first step in 1874 led to a veritable avalanche of new imports. It signaled a new approach for olive growers, a step that the deciduous fruit growers and vineyardists had taken twenty years before.

In 1882, Redding arranged to have a quantity of French Picholine trees sent to him in California. He thought he was bringing a classic French olive tree, the Picholine from Provence, but in fact it is now known that what arrived in California was another tree entirely. Different trees can be known by the same name in various parts of France, Spain, or Italy, and the same tree can have six different names in six different villages just a few miles away from each other. There are a few articles and at least one monograph in which some of this has been elucidated, but actually clarifying each individual tree and its correct name remains too large an undertaking.[1] (Unfortunately, Redding died before he could see the results of his work. The "true" Picholine has very large olives and is used for pickling. Redding's tree did not work well either for oil or table olives—the fruit is very small and not rich in oil—but it has a place as a rootstock.)

To make things even more confusing, many of the nurserymen who sold these trees after their introduction called it the "Italian" tree, or Picolene. In this they were unwittingly correct. The genuine Picholine had originally come from Italy, brought by a leading horticulturist of the late eighteenth century, M. Picholine.

The explanation for this apparent error on Redding's part only emerged many years later. Byron M. Lelong, secretary to the State Board of Horticulture, revealed it in 1900. Redding was acting in very good faith, but events outside his control took over. The tree he ordered was grafted onto a small, "wild" type of tree. The grafts did not survive the voyage, only the rootstock.

When the trees were planted and began to grow, the resulting tree was actually the rootstock. No one realized that until considerably later. Meanwhile this tree was propagated and sent all over the state as Redding's Picholine. Redding's name continues to be attached to this tree more or less out of sentiment.

By the mid-1880s, these three varieties, Manzanillo, Picholine, and Sevillano, had become standard. This can be seen by the frequency with which they were offered for sale by the leading nurseries. Once the growers recognized the benefit of growing olives for the table olive market, only a very few nurseries persisted in offering the rare and offbeat trees.

The search for greater oil content, more flexible ripening, climatic tolerance, and improved flavor continued throughout the rest of the nineteenth century and into the twentieth. Although over two hundred varieties were brought in, only a very few took hold commercially in the same way as the Manzanillos and Sevillanos. The shift from oil olives to table olives made it uneconomic to propagate most of them.

During the formative stage of the olive industry, all the early growers believed that they had to adhere to the very highest standards and make oil that was pure and wholesome. Like so many new activities, the birth of the commercial olive oil business in nineteenth-

century California was sustained by an optimistic glow. In fact, this period only lasted about twenty years at best. Olive growing resembled the gold rush in some ways. The rewards were never as wonderful as imagined, but in chasing this dream, many marvelous things were found, such as improved horticultural techniques and better ways to preserve and market agricultural products.

Scrupulous attention to detail is required to make a good olive oil, let alone a really fine oil. If the workers are careless, use poor quality fruit, and fail to keep the mill clean, the oil soon reflects these failings. The zeal to convert more and more farmers to olive growing carried the risk that standards would slip. Highmindedness was splendid, but as other crasser individuals took up the trade, highmindedness gave way to the more usual cutthroat business attitudes. Exploiting the new market in California for olive oil attracted some of the wrong people. In some cases, consortia of businessmen from the Midwest or the eastern United States were excited about the possibilities of making money and started orchards knowing very little about what should be done. In others, unscrupulous Californians were as much to blame.

Some of this change can be detected in the reports of the State Board of Horticulture. In the early 1880s, men like Cooper and Kimball, with others of the same mind, wrote glowing accounts of this new crop.[2] They prepared small monographs and pamphlets for wider distribution, including clear instructions for the culture and propagation of the trees and, very often, for making the oil. Like others who have seen the light, they wanted to share the good news with as many people as possible. Olive growing was the next bonanza.

Ten to fifteen years later, the tone of the board's reports began to change. Now they mourned the decline in standards and the shrinking of their market due to very unfair competition from both domestic and foreign sources. The board's secretary laid out some of the growers' shortcomings in an article in 1900. Trees were planted without regard for their cultural needs. This period coincided with the great increase in new cultivars. Many varieties were sent out into the field too hastily before their bearing capacity had been evaluated. He was saying that nature does not reward shortcuts. Even the firm guiding hand of the University of California was not enough to prevent these mistakes from being made.

Olive growing and citrus farming developed at much the same time. Demand for citrus was much less elastic than that for olive oil, except during extreme downturns in the economy. There was not a great deal of substantial foreign competition. The result was that citrus growers did not feel the same need for experimentation. The varieties of orange trees that had started the industry continued to be propagated, no matter where the groves were sited. The standard "Washington" navel and Valencia trees were improved in various ways but formed the backbone of the industry for many more years. Expectations and reality were more closely in touch than in the olive industry. Sturdy Valencia and navel oranges never went out of style, but the olive growers chased the dream of a perfect tree: highly productive, with abundant rich oil, and resistant to swings in temperature and pests of all kinds.

As more new olive cultivars entered the state, growers became curious about the one they already had, the old Mission tree. It had more than fulfilled its promise. Spanish colonial officials back in the sixteenth century had chosen their specimens very wisely without knowing much about the place to which they were sending these trees, nor that the trees would end up a thousand miles further north than the original destination.

Perhaps the officials of the Casa de Contratacion sent that particular tree simply because it was widely grown, useful for both oil and pickles, rather than for any other more complicated reason. Whatever it was, the California growers were curious about its origin and wanted to know more about it.

Soon after Cooper and the others began to grow olives, a man they considered to be an expert, Federico Pohndorff, sent samples of the Mission tree to a noted Spanish authority of the day, Don José de Hidalgo Tablada, for identification. Tablada considered it to be a variety of Cornicabra Cornezuelo, although much modified by the passage of time and its isolation in California.[3] Since then, other attempts to identify the tree have been made. A complete answer might be provided by DNA studies, comparing the Mission pattern with known ones in Spain. Professor Luis Rallo, a Spanish expert on growing olives, had intended to carry out this work but was not able to do so.

Tablada's classification reflects his known attitude of simplifying nomenclature and ignoring minimal deviations that might seem important to another scholar who preferred complexity. If in fact Mission trees belong in the Cornicabra group, Tablada's identification fits well with the notion that the Spanish colonial office sent the obvious standard tree. After the Picual, the present-day Cornicabra is the second most widely grown olive tree in modern Spain. Its oil is excellent.

The Franciscans were thought to have brought only one variety of tree to Alta California from Baja California, still known solely as the "Mission" olive. That interpretation is open to question. An unsigned supplemental report to the California State Board of Horticulture in 1885 puts forward the notion that the padres actually imported two varieties of olive tree, both known now as "Mission." W. G. Klee, foreman of the University of California agricultural stations and inspector of pests at that same period, made a similar point.

Joseph Connell, the current University of California farm adviser for Butte County, thinks that there might have been actually considerably more variation in the early Mission olive trees. It is his opinion that the missionaries originally "brought both seedlings and rooted cuttings." He bases this observation on the variation in size and shape of olive pits found in old adobe bricks at the mission sites, and work done by Professor George Hendry, historian at the University of California, and his associates.

Connell believes that what is now called the Mission olive is the result of the selection of wood or buds from the better trees found growing at the missions for vegetative propagation during the latter years of the nineteenth century. His theory might help to explain why Wickson noticed seven very different types of fruiting olive trees at Mission San Jose. Arthur P. Hayne, a graduate of the University of California College of Agriculture at Berkeley, noted at least three principal varieties of Mission olives in an 1893 article. He used the terms "common or broad leaved," "narrow leaved," and "early Mission" to define them. The USDA lists four separate types of Mission tree in its inventory.

Whatever its origin, this widespread mission tree has been a workhorse, its fruit useful both for oil and table olives. Its advantage was its adaptation to the high temperatures of the Central Valley. The author of the anonymous article in 1885 commented that the putative other type of Mission olive tree was not so adaptable. (He did not specify the name of the other olive variety, if indeed there ever had been one.) In a not dissimilar way, vineyards based on the almost indestructible "Mission" grape spread widely over the state.

Pohndorff, who earlier had sent samples of the Mission tree to Spain for identification, arranged to import two varieties of another widely grown Spanish olive tree, the Manzanillo, in 1874. The original imports were simply called no. 1 and no. 2.

Manzanillo olives flourished near Seville. One of Pohndorff's reasons for choosing these trees was that the fruit ripened earlier than the Mission type. This was particularly true of Manzanillo no. 1. Another was that the fruit is large and easier to handle. The Spanish name, which means "little apple," reflects the round shape of the drupe. Manzanillo grows very rapidly and is a prolific bearer. It is considered a table olive in the United States, although a reasonably good oil can be made from it.

Who Was **Federico Pohndorff?**

Federico Pohndorff, the man who first imported two varieties of the Manzanillo olive to California, remains something of an enigma. In 1880 and 1881, Pohndorff gave his address as "Brunswick House," at Sixth and Howard Streets in San Francisco, but his name does not appear in the census records of that ward. Entries in the San Francisco directories for 1880 and 1882 list a "Frederick Pohndorff" who was the cellar master for a large firm of wine and spirit merchants, Dreyfus and Company. (Dreyfus, a Bavarian Jew, represented the Anaheim group, acting as their salesman in San Francisco. He also made wine himself and is credited with making the first kosher wine for Passover in California.)

William Heintz, a historian of the wine industry in the Napa Valley, found an 1881 letter from Pohndorff in the *St. Helena Star* recommending grape varieties to Charles Krug. It was written from San Jose. Mr. Heintz adds that Pohndorff was highly regarded in the wine industry, based on records from various meetings that Pohndorff attended. Pohndorff was the man called upon to represent the California wine industry at an international conference on the problems of adulteration in wine, and he was sent to Washington, D.C., on related missions.

On a few of the occasions Pohndorff's name cropped up in the old olive literature, the authors called him "professor," but he was not on the faculty of the University of California. He was also not on the faculty of any other California college of the period. Most probably he was not an American. "Professor" seems to have been a purely courtesy title.

Despite these tantalizing uncertainties, it is known that Pohndorff worked closely with the University of California College of Agriculture. Presumably Eugene Hilgard, dean of the College of Agriculture, knew Pohndorff in a viticultural capacity and called upon him to be a consultant. The Bancroft Library has thirty-three letters, dated from 1882 through 1888, from Pohndorff to Hilgard. The letters are written in English, Spanish, and German. (Hilgard had spent two years in southern Spain as a young man, for the benefit of his health. A few years later he returned to marry Doña Jesusa, the daughter of a Spanish army officer. Hilgard seems to have been completely at home in Spanish as well as German—his mother tongue—and English.) Some of the letters contain all three languages, though Pohndorff's English was almost perfectly idiomatic.

Whenever Pohndorff traveled on business for the wine industry, he wrote most deferentially to Hilgard, either requesting his consent, and promising to do his very best, or thanking him for the recommendation and opportunity. Other correspondence in the Bancroft Library files indicate that Pohndorff and his son, Federico Jr., were working on Hilgard's own property in San Jose, planting various crops, including grapevines and olive trees.

In his own writings, Pohndorff disclaimed any practical expertise in growing the olive tree but indicated he was an outsider who happened to know something about the field. This may have been purely modesty, because a number of people engaged him on issues involving olives. For instance, during the course of his curating the California exhibit at the New Orleans Exposition in 1885, he notes he visited Ambrose Maginnis's estate at Ocean Springs, Mississippi. In his words, Maginnis was a "large cottonseed oil man, [who] has succeeded [in raising] some 150 olive trees five years from cuttings brought by a ship's captain from Italy, and [there is] fruit on the young trees. He plants 1500 olive cuttings this season. . . ."[4]

Pohndorff also had connections to vineyards in San Jose and St. Helena. Over the six-year period covered by the correspondence in the Bancroft Library, he changed positions a number of times. From Dreyfus and Company he moved to Charles Meinecke, and then to "To-Kalon," a vineyard belonging to H. W. Crabb in Oakville. By 1888, he was working for the Gallegos Wine Company at the former Mission San Jose.

The previous discussion shows that the wine and olive industries have much in common. Federico Pohndorff seems to have exemplified those characteristics, for his expertise crossed the boundaries between them.

Pohndorff could not have foreseen that the tree he brought to California in 1874 would become the most widely grown and commercially suitable cultivar in the state and would remain so for over a hundred years. He presumably brought the Manzanillo because it had been so successful in its native region. He had no way of knowing just how well it would adapt to the new conditions.

Wickson notes that the University of California sent out samples of the new olive cultivars—Manzanillo no. 1 and no. 2—to many locations for trial. In the first edition of *The California Fruits and How to Grow Them* (1889), Wickson says that the Manzanillo was already widely distributed by that time. He named several growers who were participating in the trials: George Ladd of Atwater, Dr. J. M. Stewart of Santa Cruz, Señor Juan Gallegos of Mission San Jose, as well as ranchers in Santa Barbara and Niles. The trees were also tried out at the university's own experimental stations. Everyone applauded the vigor of the trees and the early ripening.

There is still a question as to which cultivar of Manzanillo is the standard one today. The differences between the two lie principally in the shape, or "habit," of the tree and the time of ripening. The fruit itself is almost identical. Gallegos, a major propagator of the cultivar, probably made an error in nomenclature when he began to distribute the stock, confusing the two cultivars.

Because of careful pruning, it is hard to see the habit of a modern tree. The pattern of growth is not the best basis on which to make a determination, but today's Manzanillo is considered to be a late ripener. Therefore, it is likely that cultivar no. 2 was distributed. This is truly an academic question and of no practical significance at present, but it could become important if there were ever a catastrophe and new germplasm is needed to restart the crops. The USDA National Clonal Germplasm Repository at Winters has more than one type of Manzanillo in its inventory.

From its inception, the State of California has had a strong interest in promoting successful crops. This has already been noted in the chartering of a State Agricultural Society, and somewhat later, a State Board of Horticulture. The new College of California, later the University of California, was expected to pay very serious attention to agriculture, and the College of Agriculture was integral to the school as a whole.

Looking for valuable crops and their by-products was a major responsibility of the College of Agriculture. In the case of olives, the initial search for an economically successful crop had been done by private individuals. The college consolidated the finds, extended the terrain where olive trees would grow successfully, and improved techniques of cultivation by examining the basic requirements of the trees. The departments of chemistry, physiology, and pomology proved to be extremely valuable to the olive industry.

The early growers were prominent Californians who had access to politicians in Sacramento. The latter were able to get the attention of federal officials in Washington concerning agricultural matters. An introduction to the consul at Palermo or Marseilles would smooth the way of a California farmer traveling through Sicily or France. The consul in turn could arrange for the visitor to be pleasantly received by well-placed citizens, making the sojourn not only more comfortable but also more useful. Although most of the consular duties revolved around the needs of American shipping and seamen, particularly in the earlier days, the Consular Service and the Foreign Agricultural Service were heavily engaged in seeking all sorts of useful plants throughout the world. Another agency that operated in this sphere was the Department of Commerce.

The Consular Service regularly sent back reports about the principal crops of the areas where they served. In Italy, Spain, and France, this included olives, together with citrus and other agricultural products. Consuls were responsible for a town or small region, and so there are annual records (going back to the 1860s) of crop futures and actual yields from the major olive-producing regions.

One of the reports to the State Board of Horticulture contains reprints of three such documents from consuls—Vincent Lamantia, consul for Catania (Sicily), W. Harrison Bradley, consul for Marseilles (France), and Charles Trail, another consul for Marseilles. Lamantia sent a lengthy and detailed report in 1890.[5] He took a quite scholarly approach, quoting from then fairly recent work by Italian experts. Three hundred varieties of olives were grown in Italy, broken down by district. He arranged his article by topic: climate, propagation, sites, soil, fertilization, and so forth. Finally, he spent several pages in a careful discussion of the olive pests of Italy. A prospective grower could learn a great deal from a piece of work like this.

The other paper by W. Harrison Bradley used a similar method of organization, though in a little less detailed manner.[6] He noted that in France growers did not press their own oil but took the fruit to mills, whose owners had no orchards of their own. That system worked very well in his view. Not surprisingly the pests he noted were very similar to the ones in Italy. The dacus fly was, and remains, the worst, ruining the center of the fruit as it approaches ripeness.

All this was part of the very focused way that California growers were encouraged to try new varieties and experiment. In that same annual report to the State Board of Horticulture, a very interesting paper by the Reverend Charles Loop of Pomona was reprinted. Rev. Loop actually went to France and Italy to bring back olive trees for his orchard. He took a letter from the American ambassador in Paris with him to smooth the way. He, too, was a scholar, carefully beginning his paper with the usual quotations from ancient history.

Loop then moved on to what he saw during a journey through the two chief olive-growing areas. As far as he could tell in 1889, there were fifty varieties of olive trees grown in France. When he got to Italy, he heard there were three hundred kinds of Italian olives. He felt that probably represented one hundred actual cultivars at best. Tuscan oil was considered to be the very best. The varieties needed to produce it were Razzo, Leccino, Morinello, Belmonte, Rosselina, and Grossajo, according to Signor Rafello Pecori of Florence, the "foremost horticulturist in Italy." Razzo was at one time considered another name for Frantoio or Frantoiano, but current Tuscan authorities do not accept this. All these varieties of trees are growing at the National Clonal Germplasm Repository at Winters.

In Sicily, Loop saw the Saracena olive, an ancient variety perhaps so named because of Arab settlers on that island centuries ago. It grows to a great height and is a heavy bearer, with tiny black fruit. The Birdsall orchards in Colfax restored by Amigo Cantisano contain this type of olive. Loop also consulted with M. Audibert, a director of the National Experiment Station of France at Hyères, from whom he obtained the "true" Picholine, or St. Chamas, variety.

Rev. Loop eventually imported a number of varieties into California. Through the goodwill of M. Audibert, he obtained Rubra, Atro-violacea, Uvaria, Oblonga, Regalis, and Hispania, in addition to the Picholine, in 1888. In 1889, he imported Razzo, Grossajo, Rosselina, Belmonte, Olivastro, Leccino, Piangente, Morinello, Correggiolo, and Infrantojo for oil and Santa Caterina, San Agostino, and Ascolano for pickles, from Signor Pecori at Florence. The year after that, 1890, he planned to import six new kinds for oil and four more for table use.

One of Loop's goals was to propagate these new trees in his greenhouses. He thought he could produce as many as fifty thousand such young trees, and make saplings available to all who would want them. Beyond that, his next journey would be to Mytiline in Greece and to Syria, where he would be on the trail of three different kinds of olive said not to be as bitter as the others.

It is intriguing to wonder whether Rev. Loop ever did this. We do know that the USDA National Clonal Germplasm Repository at Winters has a cultivar from Mytiline and at least two from Syria, though they are listed as having been imported in the 1940s. Loop is a wonderful example of the dedicated amateur, a species very well known in horticulture. One of the largest nurseries selling olive trees—John Calkins—started in Pomona, perhaps partly due to his influence.

Apart from the direct activities of such men as Loop, information from Washington was distributed across the country, reaching the growers in California. It complemented that of the private individuals who had visited these countries. New varieties were imported by both groups.

On the state level, the University of California had five experimental field stations, Paso Robles, Jackson, Berkeley, Tulare, and Kearney. In Chico (Butte County), the U.S. Department of Agriculture opened an experimental field station to receive new plant materials of all sorts, including olives, and to learn how they would grow in California.

The combination of public and private activities in the United States resulted in numerous plant introductions for more than half a century. Olives were a part of this. Later, just after the end of the Second World War, more olive varieties began to be imported, largely due to the efforts of Professor Hudson T. Hartmann at the University of California Department of Pomology at Davis. Even now, there are still very useful importations, such as the Tuscan olive trees growing in Marin and Sonoma orchards, although many of them had come in a century ago, only to be forgotten.

Climatic adaptability was one of the key factors in seeking new trees. The climatic temperature zones of California mimicked those of Spain quite closely. There are the warm coastal sections, the hot interior valleys, and the cooler uplands. Cooper and the Kimballs began operations in coastal southern California, close to the missions. The putative descendant of the Spanish Cornicabra tree, the Mission olive, flourished in this climate. The newly imported Manzanillo came from the great olive-growing region near Seville. This is a very warm area, much like the Central Valley of California. Further south in Spain, the heat is even more torrid in the summer. In spite of these broiling summer temperatures, all the Spanish regions had a long enough period of winter chilling for the olive tree to produce flowers and, later, fruit. Without a minimum number of cold nights, olive trees continue to look very nice but produce no fruit. That is why there is no olive industry in equatorial Africa or the equivalent regions of South America. Even in the warm Central Valley of California, winter meets this minimum threshold of chilling. The olive trees produce abundant crops, and the Manzanillo does best of all.

Temperature cannot be considered without the concomitant humidity—or lack thereof. The Spanish climate is very arid. Mission trees did not flourish very well in San Francisco or its immediate vicinity. The weather on the west side of San Francisco Bay was damp and foggy, rather different from the ancestral sites in Spain. Across the bay in Contra Costa and Alameda counties, the air was dryer and warmer, and the trees grew perfectly well.

Susceptibility to pests was connected to climatic tolerance. In the very warmest areas of Spain, the dacus fly lays its eggs near the pit of the developing berry. As the fruit ripens, the growing fly feeds on the olive and erodes the integrity of the fruit, allowing fungi and other pathogens to colonize it. Spanish growers combat the dacus fly in various ways, but it has always been a redoubtable foe. It was fortunate that the young Manzanillo trees imported into California in 1874 did not carry the dacus fly's eggs with them.

The Mission tree did develop fungal and entomological diseases in California's coastal regions, in part because of the slightly more humid atmosphere. Peacock spot and black scale are the most common. Raising trees in the southern and central sections of the Central Valley and further north in Tehama and Butte counties reduced this risk. While growers did not use resistance to disease as a key factor in choosing a new kind of tree, it was something to consider.

The size of the fruit was also important in selecting new trees. Very small olives are often the best for oil, but the disadvantage is the cost of picking them. Pickling, or table, olives can be any size depending on the process and market, but even though the early olive growers were only involved in making oil, a larger olive offered some benefits.

Taste and flavor are closely connected. Degrees of bitterness affect the final product. Soaking alters this in the pickling process, but olives to be made into oil are not subject to the same treatment. If the fruit is too bitter, some of that strong taste will remain.

The overall productiveness counts a great deal in the value of a tree. It is elementary economics. The input—use of land, labor, fertilizer, water, and so forth—are the same whatever the size of the yield. A greater yield brings a better return on investment.

The date of maturation at which the fruit could be harvested was very significant. To make a smooth, sweet oil, the fruit must be mature. Unripe fruit makes a tart, green oil that has become voguish lately, but the oil level of unripe fruit is lower than that in mature fruit and the resulting reduction in yield has to be offset in some other way. The olive growers of

A BRANCH OF MANZANILLO OLIVES MOST LIKELY IN CORNING.

the 1880s did not consider green oil to be desirable. They wanted to make a pure golden-yellow oil.

Olives ripen late into the fall and early winter. This is the rainy season in that narrow belt of climates coming under the rubric of "Mediterranean." If an olive could be found that ripened early enough to escape the worst of the rain, it would have an immense advantage. The grower was probably only minimally concerned about the risks and discomfort of the pickers on wet slippery ladders in a sodden orchard, but he was very concerned about the risks of fungal infestation in fifty-pound lugs of soaking wet fruit. Water can ruin the fruit very quickly. Ellwood Cooper insisted that all the olives be carefully dried for a time before sending them through the press. If the air was not warm enough, he had a system of gently heating the sheds where they were held.

All of these factors had to be measured against the final quality of the oil. The growers were interested in trying new varieties in order to make better oil. If such an oil was ready earlier in the season (to gain an advantage in the market) and could be had in larger quantities (as long as it did not dilute the flavor), that was an added virtue for a new tree.

This set the stage for an extraordinarily creative epoch in the history of olives in California. From 1875 to 1895, new varieties positively poured into California, and then as suddenly stopped because the market emphasis shifted to table olives. As growers sought new varieties of trees, nurseries played a crucial role. They also responded to the shift that moved growers away from the new varieties. In the next chapter, we will look at this critical aspect of the California olive industry: the propagation and dissemination of olive trees, both private and commercial. To set the stage for this, we will consider the more general area of fruit growing and the appearance of the first nurseries in California. Then, after examining the more specific role that nurseries played in the olive industry, we will round out our exploration with a visit to some olive orchards where old varieties are still being cultivated today.

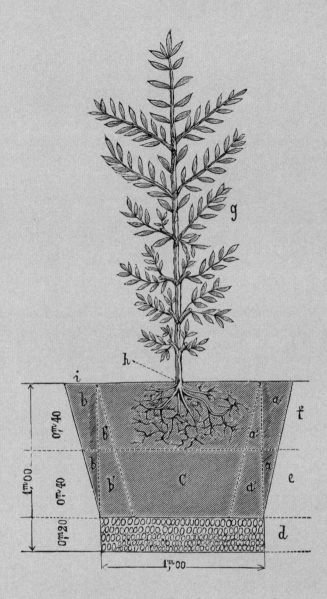

PLANTING OF THE YOUNG TREE. ONE METRE IN DEPTH.

d. Layer of stones and sticks.

e. Strata of earth upon which the roots rest.

f. Strata surrounding the root system.

c. Central part underlying the root, which should consist of well worked earth.

g. The plant itself interred as it stood in the nursery.

5

Nurseries and the Dissemination of Olive Trees

Olive growing in California did not exist in a vacuum. It developed together with agriculture in general and fruit growing in particular. Orchards with deciduous fruit took hold in California quite early, mainly in Los Angeles, after the missionaries were expelled in the 1830s. The abandoned orchards at San Gabriel were plundered for cuttings. All the mission property now belonged to the government of Mexico, which began to sell off the mission lands and orchards to private owners.

Although professional nurseries did not start until 1850, there is some evidence that commercial nursery activity was taking place at the former missions. General Vallejo's brother, Juan Jesus, took over Mission San Jose with its fields and orchards in 1834, right at the time of secularization. Guadalupe, one of Juan Jesus Vallejo's daughters, grew up at the mission. Many years later, she wrote about her early life and listed what was in the orchards and gardens of the time.

E. L. Beard, an American shopkeeper in the town, began supervising the mission orchard for Juan Jesus Vallejo in 1852, but he also planted an orchard on his own land. He ordered peach seeds from the East in preference to using the local variety. By 1857, Beard, an early president of the State Agricultural Society, was selling peaches, cherries, and pears. Because the missions were the only local source for fruit

🌺 DIAGRAM OF OLIVE SEEDLING
   PLANTING, 1888.

95

trees, most of the varieties grown were the same as the ones grown there. The trees were well adapted to the climate and soil conditions by now. Less vigorous types had perished early. If anyone wanted something else, it had to be ordered from a long distance, as Beard had done. Although settlers from other parts of the United States knew about many more kinds of fruit, for the time being, most Californians were quite satisfied with the narrow selection.

Beard's orchard was later acquired by Señor Juan Gallegos, a wealthy Spaniard from Costa Rica. Señor Gallegos had a sentimental attachment to the old mission fruit and enjoyed keeping the old varieties alive. He called his orchard a "fruticetum," a variation on "arboretum." In the 1870s, Gallegos would participate in evaluating newer types of olive trees from abroad. Other settlers were also entering the field of orchard cultivation. The State Agricultural Society's journeys of inspection revealed this. In a simple, informal way, orchards spread quietly across the state at a steady pace. Most of the fruit was for the use of the families themselves who grew it, but a small commercial industry did exist.

These commercial activities were reported for the first time by the California State Agriculture Commission in 1851.[1] Another report on fruit production was prepared for the U.S. Patent Office Record in the same year, using data from a ranch in Alameda County.[2] In the following year, a more detailed report was issued. It listed the market value of fruit from different counties. Santa Barbara recorded the sale of 1,370 barrels of olives worth about $27,500. This was a small fraction of the $366,900 aggregate for all fruit grown in Santa Barbara that year.[3]

The outside world was beginning to hear about other early achievements in California horticulture. An article about fruit growing in California appeared in 1857 in *The Horticulturist*. It mentioned a large orchard in Marysville laid out by E. L. Beach and a man called Shepherd, former storekeepers, with thousands of trees, and introduced several new nurserymen, such as A. P. Smith, G. G. Briggs, and a "Mr. Llewellyn." Perhaps the author meant Seth Lewelling, who, with his brother Henderson, opened a nursery in Alameda County in 1854. The Sansevain Vineyards were also noted.

The drive to obtain more varieties and increase the productivity of their vines and trees, including the olive, was set in motion by nurserymen coming from other parts of the United States and wealthy citizens who traveled abroad. They had the knowledge and horticultural sophistication required to facilitate this.

Then came the crucible of the gold rush, another factor that precipitated the growth of nurseries. It had an immense impact on fruit farming and the preservation of fresh foods, as it did on all the rest of agriculture. Suddenly there were thousands more men to feed, and in an even more interesting shift, many more men with a great deal of money to spend. The thousandfold (or more) increase in food production that the gold rush demanded was not accomplished easily. At first, food had to be imported quickly. Without competition, food prices rose astronomically. Diaries and letters from the miners constantly record unbelievable prices for everyday staples. Then, in some of the diggings, a few enterprising women started small dining rooms with reasonable prices. Some of the women ended up with huge catering establishments. Such catering activities and the spread of population promoted the sale of fruit where previously it might not otherwise have been considered. The menus in these informal diners were fairly limited, but apple pie was a favorite dish. Men who would not think of eating a piece of fresh fruit would always want pie. Apples for the pies came from orchards a long distance away.

At first nutritious food for the body was the most important need, but it would not be long before display and ostentation would emerge as almost equally important incentives to the astute entrepreneur. These factors coincided. Agricultural output, including the cattle trade and other staples, expanded to supply the new market. Horticulture also blossomed. It encompassed truck gardening and the related commercial fruit industry, but ornamentals were not far behind. The unprecedented need for food in enormous quantities meant that there had to be an efficient way to propagate food plants quickly. This increased the impetus for commercial nurseries. It was further strengthened by the need to feed social aspirations by means of ornamental plants. Given the double stimulus, nurseries multiplied fast.

City nurseries tended to stock primarily ornamentals, but many of them also offered fruit trees and vegetable seeds. Rural nurseries concentrated on seeds and plants for food. The effect of the need for ornamentals can be seen from the entries in the San Francisco city directories over the next few decades. The first directories listed no more than five nurseries. By 1871, fifteen San Francisco nurseries advertised in *The American Nurseryman*. In 1883, there were 67 nurseries in San Francisco alone, and 160 in the whole state.

When food production stabilized, horticulture could move into the next phase. Wealthy miners who stayed in California wanted to show off their wealth—as did the merchants who had made huge fortunes by supplying essentials to the mining camps. In many cases, the merchants' fortunes were far larger; the names of Leland Stanford and Collis Huntington come to mind. A very good way to display wealth was to build a large house and adorn it with a fancy, luxurious garden and possibly a conservatory for hothouse plants. Huge mansions were constructed on the hills of San Francisco. The architecture was often garish and the gardens gaudy, but their existence led to a demand for plants that had to be met by the growth of commercial nurseries.

A corollary of this development was the appearance of opulent florist shops. In some cases, the same establishment combined the functions both of nursery and florist. A florist is definitely a sign of civilization and the maturation of a city. Flowers are important at weddings, funerals, and in many civil and religious celebrations. In the 1850s, flowers were also a social currency—a means of paying attention to and perhaps gaining the affection of the many women—"nice" and less nice—who had flocked to San Francisco during the gold rush. (An interesting aside: a middle-class woman could own a florist shop and still be respectable. In the surviving city directories from that period, this is one of the very few times that women's names appear.)

Because the growth of San Francisco was so overwhelming, one tends to forget how explosively Sacramento developed at the same time. (It became the state capital because of its proximity to the gold fields.) As in San Francisco, nurseries also developed here. The first was started by Colonel Joseph L. L. Warren, a successful Massachusetts nurseryman, who first visited California briefly in 1845. He returned in 1849 to join the gold rush, but he soon returned to his previous work. In 1850, he opened the New England Seed Store, a commercial nursery, at 15 J Street in Sacramento, and sold the first camellias ever seen in California, "Wilder" and "Miss Abby Wilder." Warren's commercial venture is considered to be the start of the professional nursery industry in California, if one ignores the tentative beginning made in the mission orchards. For the first recorded time, a skilled nursery operator opened a place of business in the new state. San Francisco did not have any nurseries at that early date.

Warren issued his first California catalog in 1853, the first of its kind in the state, although it had been printed in Boston. The plant stock originated in Massachusetts. He listed fifty-three varieties of pears, sixteen cherries, thirty-seven apples, and twenty peaches. Even though he went to the trouble of packing up everything from his nursery in Boston and sending it out to California, he decided not to continue as a nurseryman. In 1854, he sold the business with all the fixtures and moved to San Francisco.

What he did next was perhaps more influential even than starting the nursery. He began a weekly magazine called the *California Farmer,* doing almost all the necessary tasks from sweeping the floor to setting type by himself for many years. The magazine was a powerful force in educating several generations of horticulturists, ranchers, and farmers. In addition to publishing the *California Farmer,* Warren privately sponsored shows of flowers, agricultural produce, and artists' works, which became the nucleus of the state fair. They generated excitement and interest in horticulture, and this led to rapid improvements in the nursery trade. Warren also lobbied and agitated in Sacramento to get the State Agricultural Society formed, and was very gratified when Governor John Bigler signed a bill authorizing the society on May 13, 1854. The idea behind starting a state agricultural society was to capitalize on the power of competition. The desire to win prominence and renown would lead farmers, ranchers, and horticulturists to develop new ideas and work very hard.

Warren's Sacramento nursery was not the only one for long. In 1851, A. P. Smith laid out a nursery on the banks of the American River a few miles from Sacramento. Anthony Preston Smith, of Rome, New York, was drawn to California by gold. He made a great deal of money trading skillfully on the sea voyage to Sacramento. With those gains, he bought land for his nursery from John Sutter at $100 per acre. The nursery covered sixty acres originally and was a most ambitious project. Later Smith added another forty acres.

The citizens of Sacramento used to go there on summer evenings to enjoy the soft air and beautiful surroundings.

Originally Smith sold only deciduous fruit trees, reflecting the need for increased food production caused by the gold rush. He soon also offered ornamentals. Roses were always extremely popular, but he had many other delightful plants too. Part of his expansion came when he bought much of Colonel Warren's nursery stock as the latter dissolved his business. At one point, Smith had fifteen thousand rosebushes and two thousand camellias on display. All these plants were first described in an 1856 catalog of which two copies have survived.

Another early nursery was the work of Henderson and Seth Lewelling. In 1854, the Lewelling brothers came into California from Oregon. Henderson had taken grafted fruit trees to Oregon from the eastern United States for the first time in 1847. Seth took a box of grafted apples, pears, plums, peaches, and cherries to Sacramento in 1851. Three years later, the Lewellings opened their nursery in Alameda County. Another brother came in 1859 and planted many successful orchards. For the first time, the new types of fruit trees being grown in California had been developed and propagated in the West. It became less and less necessary to send to Prince Nurseries in Long Island, or Elwanger and Barry in Rochester, New York, which for years had been two of the best known suppliers of fruit trees to California.

G. G. Briggs settled in Marysville and planted very successful orchards in 1853. He won a medal at the state agricultural fair for a "first class orchard" in 1858. Briggs's peaches were still winning prizes twenty years later. The state's policy of promoting excellence by means of competition at these fairs was effective. It is uncertain whether Briggs actually had his own nursery or simply obtained young trees for local people from somewhere else.

About this same time in Nevada City, a French immigrant named Felix Gillet started out in a humble occupation as a barber. He had come to the United States in 1852 at the age of seventeen to work with Julia Ward Howe in her antislavery campaign. After two years in Boston, during which he learned the barber's trade, he left for California. No one knows why he did that or why he settled in Nevada City, but he stayed there until he died fifty years later, having contributed enormously to the development of horticulture in his adopted land. Gillet had only attended school in France for seven years but was a consummate autodidact.

Gillet carefully saved his money from the barbershop he opened in Nevada City. With it, he bought a piece of barren land on the outskirts of the town, presumably the only one he could afford. Gillet obtained $3,000 worth of nursery stock from France and rapidly built up a renowned business. The nursery he started was called Barren Hill. It is a paradoxical name because the place grew into a thriving orchard and garden. Gillet imported numerous cultivars of almonds, plums, prunes, filberts, walnuts, chestnuts, grapes, and strawberries. He did everything enthusiastically and methodically and kept voluminous records of every planting, together with the weather conditions each season.

Many of Gillet's imports and cultivars are still standard commercial crops. The thriving California walnut industry is an outgrowth of his efforts. He also wrote a number of brief, useful monographs on fruit and nut growing, encouraging their spread across the state. Barren Hill Nursery remained in business well into the twentieth century, even after Gillet died. It is a pity that he is almost totally forgotten today, but one can still see the remnants of his property in Nevada City.

William Walker's Golden Gate Nursery was another pioneer business. Walker, a lawyer, came to seek gold in California but decided to sell plants instead. He was one of the first men to bring eucalyptus from Australia, which he did very early, about 1849. The California Historical Society has Walker's handwritten catalog and mailing list for 1858 and 1859.

In response to this rapidly growing market for seeds and plants, professional nurserymen came from other states and quickly brought in a rich and diverse stock. Most of them were experts in the growing and propagating of deciduous fruits, and skilled in many of the grafting techniques. They knew how to extend the seasons by growing a selection of varieties that ripened at different times. A tree whose fruit ripened very early in the season or very late had an advantage over one that produced its fruit at the same time as all the others. In some instances, all the mission peaches or pears might ripen at once. This would be too much for the market to absorb. The result was a temporary glut and lower prices. Then there were no more peaches or pears until the following year. One way to overcome this problem was by pitting the fruit and drying it in the hot California sun, but dried fruit was not so enticing as fresh. Knowing about numerous cultivars and skillful plantings permitted the grower to avoid or at least reduce the cycle of glut and shortage.

The huge influx of plant material affected the native flora of the state, totally changing its nature forever. Not only were there large numbers of the newly introduced cultivated fruit trees and vegetables as well as the many ornamental plants used in making gardens, but the very weeds themselves changed permanently and ineradicably. The entire landscape was completely transformed after 1850, and by 1875, almost all the plants we take for granted today had been imported.

Although the very early efforts of men like A. P. Smith and J. L. L. Warren have been documented, little tangible remains. The properties have long since been used for other purposes. Two fragile catalogs remain from Smith's many endeavors. An 1856 catalog from a contemporary of Smith's, advertising fruit trees and ornamental shrubs from the Shellmound Nursery in Brooklyn, Alameda County, is in the Bancroft Library. It is one single sheet. The owner simply offered apples, pears, and other plants and trees without specifying any particular variety. He also had a few "foreign" cultivars. The future rich and complex choices had not yet materialized.

Fortunately, considerable written material does persist in the form of catalogs from other nurseries which were established later. Rather amazing numbers of catalogs have survived. Captain Charles Weber, cousin of Eugene Hilgard, dean of the UC College of Agriculture, not only founded the city later known as Stockton but was also a noted horticulturist. He collected the nursery catalogs as they appeared. After his death, his daughter kept them safe and later bequeathed them to her niece, Mrs. Gerald Kennedy. Mrs. Kennedy donated them to a museum in Stockton. Other people also saved enough of them to allow modern scholars to follow the initial nursery businesses in California. This has also enabled me to track the dissemination of olive trees throughout the state.

Olive growing in California followed the course set by the spread and propagation of deciduous fruits. It began with the simple expedient of using cuttings from the mission stock to lay out orchards, which may be considered the first, primitive stage in the development of nurseries in California. Then, as more orchards became established, an intermediate stage evolved. The previously developed orchards did duty as nurseries. Almost all the pioneer growers sold slips, cuttings, or saplings. General Bidwell's nursery business and the Reverend Loop's greenhouses provided additional income for these men. Thus they began nurseries partly out of a desire to make money but also from a desire to proselytize and share a good thing with others.

Later, commercial nurseries emerged as the third stage in this development process. Once large commercial olive orchards had developed, the old informal method of going out to a mission or a larger grower and getting cuttings would no longer suffice. It did not matter that the farmer only wanted the mission tree. He had to be sure he could get as many saplings as he needed, in the correct size, and take delivery when he wanted them. Commercial nurseries could meet this demand. Also, after many new varieties of olives were imported, the most efficient way they could reach growers was by being centralized in professional nurseries and sold from there. The concentration of stock, skill and knowledge, and the reliability these connoted, all combined to make nurseries pivotal in getting any new horticultural trend established. (For a list of commercial nurseries from the late nineteenth and the early twentieth centuries, see appendix F.)

There seemed to be several kinds of nurserymen, much as there are now. One type is the scholarly horticulturist who uses his or her knowledge to earn a living, but whose real interest is in the plants themselves. There are many of these small, highly specialized nurseries whose owners have an almost encyclopedic knowledge of horticulture.

The opposite extreme is a more conventional businessperson who happens to purvey plants but might just as well sell something else. Because a successful nursery depends on knowing plants, these businesses employ horticulturists as managers and supervisors. Somewhere in between is the well-trained nurseryman or -woman who wants to make money but not at the expense of good quality. This latter type played the largest role in spreading the cultivation of new, possibly better olive trees.

Some nursery owners actively pursued new olive cultivars because they genuinely cared about getting the very best trees they could find. If this gave them a competitive advantage, that was an additional benefit. They took action in various ways. Some of them sought fresh varieties from foreign colleagues. Some were chosen by the University of California to carry out trials, either because they volunteered for this task, or because their reputation made them the obvious choice.

Time was a very significant factor for nursery owners to get a return on their capital investment in fruit trees. Keeping the time from starting the growth to reaching a point at which a tree could be sold as short as possible was an advantage. The cost of the stock was negligible. The cuttings themselves were not costly, and often came in for nothing.

The investment lay in other quarters. Fruit crops take several years to reach maturity. At that period, the end of the nineteenth century, olive experts thought trees needed five to eight years to mature and to yield a useful crop. In the end, they learned that this was too pessimistic, and that adequate bearing began within three to five years. Even during that shorter amount of time, the nursery had to devote space, staff, and other resources to trees that could turn out to be useless. Careful observations from the start helped them to find out sooner if a tree were no good and move on to different varieties.

It is clear that such risks could only be borne by a large, efficient, and well-organized nursery. It was too hazardous for a small- or medium-sized operation. Small nurseries rode on the coattails of the larger ones, because they could not afford a costly mistake. The brochures and catalogs of these nurseries tell this story. For example, A. F. Boardman, owner of a small nursery in Auburn, commented in 1889 that some new kinds of olive trees had recently been introduced. Although he said he had a few of them, he added "... [we] have not seen them fruiten [sic] enough to judge of their merits." Even as late as 1893, W. R. Strong, owner of Capital Nurseries in Sacramento, was still suspicious of the new varieties.

The introductory acclimatization of olive specimens to California most often took place in the nurseries. The University of California had its own experiment stations at Kearney, Paso Robles, Jackson, Berkeley, and Tulare, but it also frequently sent samples out to cooperative nurseries under an informal contract to make sure the specimens could survive and perform well. Two of the most prominent and cooperative sites were John Rock's California Nursery at Niles in Alameda County and George F. Roeding's Fancher Creek Nurseries in Fresno, but John Calkins of Pomona and others also participated.

The connection between the ability to grow numerous cultivars and commercial nurseries is very close. The missions themselves functioned as the original nurseries for their own type of tree. The first wave of orchardists who took cuttings from the missions also performed a nursery function as a next step. They continually propagated young trees from the truncheons and suckers that were removed by pruning. In many cases, they gave these young trees away free, or charged a nominal ten cents each. Only when there were choices in varieties to be made did the professional nursery become indispensable.

It is useful to understand what the choices of trees were and which varieties were imported. This is more than a dry academic exercise. One of the functions of this book is to try and record in one place all the cultivars of olive that were imported and grown, however briefly, in California. There is a point to doing this.

Many people are now interested in bringing more new cultivars into the state, and most are unlikely to know about these previous efforts. Detailed accounts are still in existence but quite widely scattered. The information assembled here should save prospective growers considerable trouble by being easily accessible. If they choose a cultivar that was tried in an earlier era, even if it was known by one of its

ADVERTISEMENT FOR OLIVE TREES BY THE CALIFORNIA NURSERY COMPANY OWNED BY JOHN ROCK. NOTE THE EMPHASIS ON THREE COUNTRIES OF ORIGIN: FRANCE, ITALY, AND SPAIN.

many synonyms, they will get some idea of whether it can be expected to do well. If it has succeeded at the USDA National Clonal Germplasm Repository in Winters, or, in a few cases, another orchard, then it may reasonably be considered acclimatized to California. Even if no details about its cultivation remain, the mere fact of its being listed is valuable. It means someone else tried it at one time.

A complete list of trees imported between 1870 and 1960 can be found in appendix D. Appendix E provides an accompanying table with the many of the synonyms for the trees imported. This chapter includes a partial list of the imported varieties. The list contains comments on some of the characteristics of the more frequently grown European olive cultivars of the nineteenth century, since quite a few of them are being grown in California again today.

To prepare the account that follows, records of a total of 234 varieties were gleaned from a handful of sources, both nineteenth and twentieth century. The work of four early experts forms the basis of these remarks: Arthur T. Marvin, author of the monograph *The Olive* and general manager of El Quito Olive Farm in Los Gatos; Byron M. Lelong, secretary to the State Board of Horticulture in the 1880s and 1890s; Arthur P. Hayne, graduate student at UC Berkeley College of Agriculture who spent a sabbatical year in Provence and very methodically translated work from the French National Agricultural School at Montpellier; and Waldemar Gotriek Klee, foreman of the University of California's agricultural experiment stations. In addition to these four, George Colby, although a chemist by training, also submitted careful reports about the response of the different cultivars to varying climatic conditions, listing their yield of oil and growth characteristics.

In the twentieth century, scholars are indebted to the late Hudson T. Hartmann, professor of pomology at the University of California at Davis, for extending and cataloging the inventory at the university's grounds. John Whisler, technical assistant to Professor Hartmann, and now a vigorous octogenarian, was very instrumental in keeping it up. He can still recall all the details about each specimen, why it was included, and where it came from.

The USDA started its plant introduction center at Chico, but it was later moved to Winters, using cuttings from each tree to reestablish the orchard there. When Hartmann assumed responsibility for the collection, he once again took cuttings and started another new orchard. The USDA National Clonal Germplasm Repository at Winters has since absorbed this second collection. The U.S. Forest Service now occupies the land at Chico.

The entries in the lists forming the basis of appendix D pertain only to cultivars that were imported into California. In a few cases, Arthur T. Marvin included varieties from the Montpellier catalog for which there is no correlate in the USDA inventory. The USDA inventory is the most comprehensive list, but it is by no means exhaustive. It covers the trees brought in the 1920s, 1930s, and beyond, after the first wave of enthusiasm, but it does not mention all the types that Lelong and Klee stated were being grown in California previously. I note the source of each comment when it is in question.

The USDA list alone has 137 entries, but it does not go into the many and confusing synonyms. Lelong, Marvin, and Hayne did do so. Marvin thought that at least seven varieties were actually the Mission olive, although no one else came up with this idea. He was probably not correct, since the names he gives are mostly French and Italian imports. (Note the word "imports" and not "trees" is used here, because the origins of a particular type of tree are not always able to be determined.) One thing at least is very clear, the Mission olive tree came from Spain. From there, it may have then traveled to other countries at some unspecified time, just as it eventually traveled to the New World.

A number of the French trees have names, such as Pendulina and Rubra, that sound Italian or Spanish, and not like modern French. This is the persistence of the old Latin terms. The culture of the olive in the Mediterranean rim is so ancient, it predates the division into modern nations. The Romans took olive trees to North Africa and Spain as they expanded their empire. Just as the names of rivers and places in Europe commemorate earlier occupants and ethnic groups, so too do the ancient names of trees, which were already old when Europe started to differentiate itself into nations, continue to be used.

A remnant of the next epoch is the hint of Arabic in a few types of Italian trees, distinct from the clearly Arabic names of the trees from Syria or North Africa. One of the trees, included in the list in this chapter, is called Mouarou. The sound suggests that it was a Moorish tree from old Spain. A very similar tree is named Morinello, an Italian version of "Moorish."

The majority of olive tree imports came from France. Italy was next, then Spain, Greece, North Africa, Turkey, and a few other countries. The present-day crops reflect how significant the Spanish varieties have been, in spite of the small number of types that were imported. Manzanillo, Mission, and Sevillano are the primary olives grown in California. This could not have been foretold a century ago.

One of the reasons for the success of the Spanish trees is that they came to California at least ten years before most of the others. The larger nurseries had plenty of time to propagate them in the increasingly enormous orchards they developed. There was also time to see how reliable and productive these trees were. Federico Pohndorff's insights had been prescient. So much acreage was devoted to these dependable cultivars within a short time that few growers wanted to take a chance on trying the succeeding kinds, even though a number of them were considered to be excellent for pickling as table olives.

An example of this attitude can be seen in an anecdote from that time. In 1879, William West, owner of the Stockton Nursery in Stockton, traveled through Spain, Italy, and France studying the olive trees. He wrote an article about his trip in the *San Francisco Weekly Bulletin.* Among his other observations, he noted that when there are only one or two varieties of olive trees, there is little need for commercial nurseries. There were few such nurseries in Spain, because the olive growers propagated their own stock.

In West's opinion the olive orchards in Granada and Andalusia were far larger and finer than any others he had seen. He planned to import some of the trees he saw there. In addition, he also intended to try out some of the ones he had seen in France and Italy. In his 1880 catalog, the only one of his to survive, West offered Mission and Picholine trees. Perhaps in later years he was able to sell more varieties.

Another reason for this adherence to the Spanish trees is probably the fact that although some of the French and Italian imports were widely touted to be productive and reliable, they fizzled quietly after being cultivated for a few years. The soil and climate did not suit them as well as the trees from Spain. It is also likely that these olives were not economically practicable. Otherwise it is hard to understand why more of the French and Italian table varieties are not found today. An example is the Ascolano. This is a fine Italian table olive that persists in a few orchards, but the fruit is easily bruised when picked and this increases the cost of harvesting. Wastage is expensive and so is the resulting need to pick the fruit more slowly to avoid it. Because of this, growers quickly grafted the trees to more remunerative varieties.

In order to see how the olive trees were distributed throughout California, I found tracing them by means of nursery catalogs very helpful. Thomas Brown's *A List of California Nurseries and Their Catalogues: 1850 to 1900* has an alphabetical list of the nurseries by community, with valuable comments on each one, and tells the present location of the catalogs that still exist.

Brown specializes in reconstructing historic landscaping. In order to restore a town square or historic site to its pristine state, he had to find out not just what plants were in the garden but also which cultivars had been used. If he were using anachronistic varieties, he would not achieve the authentic appearance. Having worked with Harry M. Butterfield, an agriculturist with the University of California's Agricultural Extension Service and a student of the history of California horticulture, Brown knew that a good place to find what he needed was in the old nursery catalogs.

An additional source of information about past nurseries is Butterfield's own work. Over a period of more than twenty years, he wrote many articles about early horticulture in California. He also kept all his original notes and sources. These were bequeathed to the Special Collections department at the University of California at Davis after he died. Unfortunately the catalogs he collected seem to have been scattered and were not saved with the papers.

U. P. Hedrick's *A History of Horticulture in America to 1860* also contains a number of references to pioneering nurseries in California. Some of the nurseries mentioned by Butterfield and Hedrick are not included in Brown's list. Very few of these nurseries' catalogs survived and the information concerning them is sketchy at best, but there are indications that these nurseries grew olive trees.

In the usual, haphazard way of such things, many of the series of catalogs became split up over the years. Unlike weightier works, they are technically known as "ephemera," transient and disposable. They did not appear to be academically relevant. There was no pressure at first to seek them or keep them carefully. They only became important with the passage of time. It was a while before scholars recognized their role as transmitters of social and technical history. The same is true for other industrial catalogs and brochures. Now they are treasured, and librarians display them proudly.

Even though the catalogs in question are all from California, they have been spread, for many reasons, widely across the country. The largest repository is the National Agricultural Library in College Park, Maryland. The University of California at Davis holds an impressive number of them. The stimulus for this collection came from Harry Butterfield, whose papers, as mentioned above, form part of the Special Collections there.

Cornell University is a rich resource of nursery catalogs because of Professor L. H. Bailey, who was the dean of American horticulture for thirty years. (The Bailey Hortorium at Cornell is named for him.) The Massachusetts Horticultural Society has a small number as does the California Historical Society and the Bancroft Library at the University of California at Berkeley. Other libraries, societies, and a few individuals own small numbers of them. In a couple of instances, the rarest documents are in these latter private hands.

Visits to Cornell's Arthur Mann library in Ithaca and the National Agricultural Library in College Park, as well as the Shields Library at UC Davis, the Bancroft Library, and the California Historical Society's library in San Francisco, gave me a sense of the continuity of each nursery's wares and showed me when a cultivar was no longer fashionable or saleable.

In addition, seeing the entire pamphlets with the covers and reading the (usually) charming comments was really delightful. The occasional strong differences of opinion about the care and culture of the olive trees lent an additional spice to the reviews. One nurseryman insisted that grafting the cultivars onto Picholine stock was the only way to go, while another swore it was the worst possible thing to do.

Fancher Creek Nurseries and the California Nursery Company at Niles are of most interest because they specialized in olive trees. Both nurseries were owned and operated by very remarkable men of German extraction. Rock, who owned the California Nursery Company, came as an adult to California and literally translated his original name of Johann Fels to John Rock. George Roeding was born in Fresno, the son of Frederick Roeding, a very successful German immigrant who started Fancher Creek Nursery.

George Roeding would play a dominant role in propagating figs commercially in California. He feuded with James Shinn of Niles over which of them first brought the fig wasp from Turkey. Without this wasp, the fig cannot be effectively pollinated and no fruit will form. The process is called "caprification." He devoted twenty years to working on the fig. During that time, he also paid a great deal of attention to the olive.

In the reports on olive growing to the State Board of Horticulture, there are numerous references to the cooperation of Rock's and Roeding's nurseries with the university's extension services. These nurseries had the space and organization to do the detailed, careful work needed to grow the new trees and identify useful varieties. Reading nursery catalogs from participating firms serially over the years clearly outlines the way in which many olive varieties were introduced, had a brief vogue, and then were discarded because they no longer met the needs of growers.

Roeding and his manager, Gustav Eisen, in particular wrote in great detail about the different varieties of olive, just as they did about the fig and indeed all his stock. Roeding's catalogs are miniature horticultural texts. If no other catalog were to survive, Roeding's catalogs alone supply enough information to form a very complete picture of late nineteenth-century fruit cultivation. Fancher Creek catalogs were quite different from those that simply listed a plant and its price, and left it at that.

The different styles of pamphlet presumably lie in the expense involved to print them. Firms like those of Rock and Roeding could afford the cost of printing a veritable small book each season, whereas the owner of a more modest enterprise had to think very carefully before spending money on that scale. Rock and Roeding put delightful colored covers on their pamphlets, and the pictures still glow brightly. Of course, many large, ornamental nurseries also used luscious, romantic paintings of flowers such as lilacs, lilies, orchids, marigolds, and roses on their covers to promote sales, but for a small firm selling mainly vegetable seeds and fruit trees, the cost of such catalogs could be prohibitive.

Enough catalogs survive to see how they ran the gamut of size, layout, complexity, and choice of nursery stock. They reflected the structure and practice of the business. The pamphlets range from the most modest price sheet of small companies in farming towns to the extravaganzas of fashionable San Francisco nurseries.

Then there are the "anti-catalogs" of Luther Burbank, which are a parody of other catalogs. They testily claim that Burbank is too busy to do anything as mundane as selling his wares and ask people please not to bother him! In spite of this pose, Burbank carefully followed the usual layout. Each page had all the relevant information about the plant variety in question. What distinguished his pamphlets were the constant reminders of how clever he was, puffing his own skill and acumen in identifying the variant and bringing it to maturity. All this is framed at the beginning and the end by very pointed instructions on how to contact him without causing him to take any trouble.

Burbank paid very little attention to olives, offering a single, unnamed variety some of the time. I imagine he was not too interested in them because he could not do very much with them. After he sold part of his concern to others, the nursery took on more conventional tones, and there was a brief flurry of activity with the modish new imported olive seedlings offered for sale. In 1900, the new manager, a realist, saw that there was no money to be made with olive trees. The Santa Rosa Nursery had a giant sale, drastically reducing the price of the olives by 40 percent to get rid of them, together with other unsatisfactory wares. Nothing could have been more businesslike.

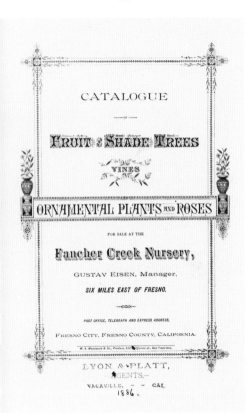

COVER OF THE FANCHER CREEK NURSERY CATALOG FOR 1886.

Nurseries grew up across the state but were mainly concentrated in the Central Valley's farming towns and the large cities at the coast. They were found in fifty-nine towns over all. If one narrows one's focus to the availability of olive trees, the distribution was fairly even. San Francisco had six nurseries where a grower could buy olive trees, probably reflecting the status of the city as it grew into a business capital, even though the trees did not do well in the city or its environs. Santa Barbara had four. Fresno and San Diego had three each, while there were two in Los Angeles, Niles, Oakland, and Sacramento. The rest were fairly evenly distributed with approximately one nursery per town. Aggregating them by county does not really change this pattern of distribution.

The earliest date at which there is evidence of a nursery with a surviving catalog offering olive trees was 1872. Six more offered them by 1879. In the 1880s, there were eleven more nurseries selling olive trees. After 1890, fifteen more companies took them up, at least as far as the documentary evidence goes. In most cases, they ceased to sell the complex new varieties by about 1900, although Fancher Creek and the California Nursery Company at Niles went on much longer.

In those early days, olive growers were widely scattered throughout the state. Gradually they began to collect in the areas in which they are now found. It did not matter where the nursery was. Shipping the trees they had ordered was not difficult once the railroads were

ADVERTISEMENT FOR OLIVE TREES,
AMONG OTHERS, BY SANTA ROSA
NURSERIES, ORIGINALLY OWNED BY
LUTHER BURBANK.

completed. Growers today still buy their trees wherever they choose. Proximity is not important. Growers go to a nursery where they believe they can get the best quality and price.

It is a pity that none of the older nurseries survived the state's transition to modern industry and urban spread. A few remained in business until the mid-twentieth century, but their land was so valuable, and tax incentives often so perverse, that it made economic sense in most cases to sell the property for development. Large wholesale nurseries today are found quite deep in the countryside, not occupying prime acreage downtown.

Nursery stock varied from a single kind of olive tree to a vast array of cultivars during the final decade of the nineteenth century and the first few years of the twentieth century. The widest selections, not surprisingly, were to be had at the three nurseries that acted as auxiliary experiment stations for the University of California: California Nursery Company (John Rock), Fancher Creek (George Roeding), and John Calkins. Other, less ambitious nurseries carried intermediate numbers of varieties. It is entirely possible that they obtained their supplies from Rock, Roeding, or Calkins, unless they explicitly stated that they had imported the trees themselves. The extraordinary expansion of cultivars began in about 1885, with Rock and Roeding releasing the results of their trials.

The expansion of imported cultivars persisted until about 1900. When the commercial canning of table olives became technically feasible at that time, the market for oil olives swiftly diminished. This was soon after the economic depression of the 1890s, when there was a glut of fruit trees of all sorts in California, a situation which must also have had an effect on the nursery business.

Even after the interest in foreign curiosities cooled, giant "factory" types of olive nurseries continued to develop to feed the insatiable appetite for more and more trees of the now standard Manzanillo, Mission, and Sevillano types. There are photographs of thousands of rows of pathetic little specimens—"toothpicks" in Wickson's contemptuous term—that were a source of pride to the owners, who bragged about offering more than half a million trees for sale at any one time. Wickson was being a bit harsh because every tree starts off as a tiny plant and needs time to grow. The purchaser could see how large the tree was and gauge whether the price was fair. What irritated Wickson was the application of mechanized, big business methods to the previously very slow-paced traditional field of agriculture. Similar endeavors involved the economically more significant fruit trees, such as apples, peaches, apricots, and prunes. California was starting to do what it would do so well in the coming years: develop, mechanize, and standardize its horticulture.

The current renewed vigor of the olive oil business in California has led to a revival of orchards that otherwise would have continued to be neglected and lie dormant. They are in such vogue that it will soon be difficult to find any left to reclaim. In a few exceptional cases, the French and Italian trees, which were considered to be such an improvement in the 1880s, have been kept going. Most of the rest of the orchards have the more mundane Mission or Manzanillo trees.

One such historic orchard is in Marysville. Its existence brings to life the dry records of cultivars dredged up from the depths of dusty archives and libraries. About an hour and a half north and east of Sacramento, one starts the gentle climb up into the foothills of the Sierras. Peggy and Michael Henwood live on an old ranch near Smartville in Yuba County, next door to Michael's parents, Mariana and Carroll Henwood. The ranch is set fairly high in the hills, at about four hundred feet, surrounded by cattle farms and sheep runs. The gravel driveway winds for over a mile through the green pastures. There is a true feeling of peace and quiet. Life flows at a different pace there.

The ranch was originally the property of the Excelsior Water Company, which belonged to Frederick Ayer. He had come from Ayer, Massachusetts, a small town near Groton. The company brought water to the mining district, digging the gigantic ditches needed to help generate enough water pressure for hydraulic mining, a process in which water was used to wash down the sides of the hills containing ore. The mining business petered out by the early 1870s, and Mr. Ayer decided it was time to go into the fruit business. Fruit cultivation was being heavily promoted throughout the state during that period. Mr. Ayer was responding to the trend.

In 1875, Mr. Ayer bought 250 acres in what is now part of Marysville in Yuba County and called the estate the Excelsior Ranch. His son was in charge of the day-to-day activity. They planted many fruit trees in different sections of the property. It is clear the Ayers were very observant and prudent, using all the natural shelter the land offered to protect their trees from strong prevailing winds.

The Henwoods now possess a hand-drawn map of the Ayers property from 1895, showing the disposition of the various fruit trees. There were two main olive orchards plus a small olive nursery next to the house. In addition, a large, uneven-shaped field contained several olive trees that were not the same as those in the neatly laid-out orchards. This appears to have been the Ayers's experimental area or "lab." Other fruit included Joppa oranges, grapefruit, pears, figs, persimmons, almonds, walnuts, and nectarines. Eventually

JOHN S. CALKINS' NURSERIES

— AT —

POMONA, LOS ANGELES CO., CALIFORNIA.

OLIVE TREES A SPECIALTY.   FRENCH, ITALIAN AND SPANISH VARIETIES.

ADVERTISEMENT FOR OLIVE TREES BY JOHN CALKINS' NURSERIES IN POMONA, CALIFORNIA. NOTE THE CHOICE OF FRENCH, ITALIAN, AND SPANISH VARIETIES.

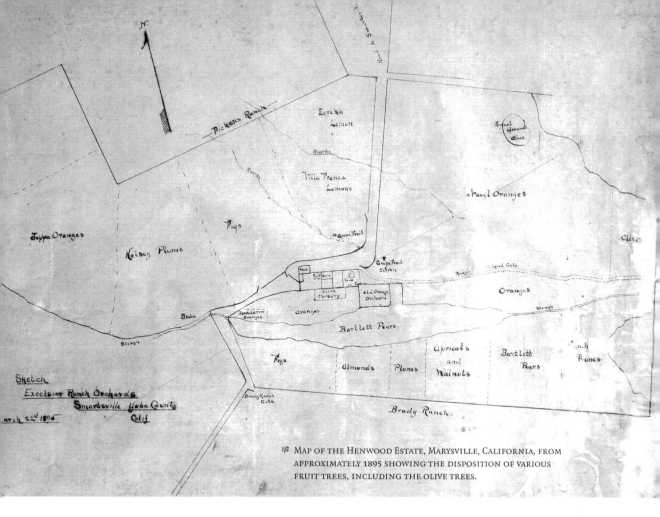

Map labels (as visible on the sketch):

N.

Pickens Ranch

Eureka Lemon

Villa Franca Lemons

Ravine

Ravine

Toppa Oranges

Kelsey Plums

Figs

10 Grape Fruit

Grape Fruit Citron

Navel Oranges

Olives

Highest Ground Olives

Road

Island Gate

Oranges

Slough

Olive Nursery

old Orange Orchard

Barn

Shed

Mandarin Oranges

Oranges

Bartlett Pears

Figs

Almonds

Plums

Apricots and Walnuts

Bartlett Pears

Prunes

Cabin

Slough

Brady Ranch Gate

Brady Ranch.

Sketch
Excelsior Ranch Orchards
Smartsville Yuba County
Calif
arch 22d 1895

🌿 MAP OF THE HENWOOD ESTATE, MARYSVILLE, CALIFORNIA, FROM
APPROXIMATELY 1895 SHOWING THE DISPOSITION OF VARIOUS
FRUIT TREES, INCLUDING THE OLIVE TREES.

the Ayers learned that it was too cool for grapefruit and oranges up in the hills, but the persimmons did well for many years. The fruit was sold under the name "Bonanza."

The Ayers owned the ranch for fifty years, but then it was sold intact to a Mr. Wolf in about 1920. He in turn sold it to a Mr. Bell. Under Mr. Bell, the property became a cattle ranch. It was then sold to a Mr. Johnson before the Henwoods took it over in 1974. During these changeovers, the estate shrank until only the olive orchards were left. The small number of owners in a hundred years is quite remarkable in itself, but the other wonderful characteristic of this estate is the fact that the olive trees are all vigorous specimens of trees brought here experimentally in the 1870s and 1880s to make an improved oil.

The Henwoods have an orchard of Columella and Uvaria trees that still bear heavily, and one or two Rubras that are also quite productive. The Columellas produce very superior oil. After I learned which varieties had become available at particular periods from the nursery catalogs, it was extremely exciting to see the living trees themselves.

Michael Henwood trained as a cabinetmaker and sells furniture he has made from walnut. He has a great feeling for trees and wood. For many years, he went past the olive trees in the fields, making observations about them without even realizing that he was doing so, but only recently did he think about using the fruit as a resource. This happened partly because Peggy became interested in making soap with olive oil, and they realized that they had the capacity to make their own oil. In a very short time, he learned how to cultivate and prune the trees, and then he built an oil press in his barn. The press meets all the specifications of the California Department of Health. There is now a fine Henwood Estate extra virgin olive oil on the market.

Michael told me that when the property changed hands for the first time, Mr. Wolf grafted all the Columella trees over to Mission. It is unclear why he should have done that, since the Manzanillo was already becoming far more fashionable at the time. It was already a little late for the oil industry. Some of these grafts have not done very well, and one of Michael's first priorities is to cut out all the Mission growth and let the Columella reassert themselves. There are plain Uvaria trees and also other types grafted onto Uvaria as a rootstock. In Michael's experience, Uvaria is a fine rootstock, much better than the now standard Redding Picholine so widely used. The Uvaria does not create the vast thicket of suckers that the Redding Picholine produces every year.

The orchard was laid out in rows of four, alternating Columella, Mission grafts, and Uvaria. Michael introduced a gravity-fed flood method of irrigating the trees, but he does not fertilize them at all. The Butte County farm adviser, Joseph Connell, visited the orchard and suggested that Michael continue to be very conservative in his culture. The trees have flourished under the benign neglect of years, and it makes sense to leave things alone. There is a lot of water under the surface and that must have had a lot to do with this vigorous survival. Most of the trees are balanced at a very good height, not too tall and "leggy." In spite of the fact that the soil is red clay over rock, it has good natural drainage. The area is too high to be flooded by the Yuba River.

One of the fascinating methods used by the Ayers to encourage growth was to plant some of their trees in the center of a small outcrop of rock, actually displacing some of the rock. At the top of a ridge, there is a separate small grove of olive trees dispersed among rocks, looking like a scene from an ancient Greek drama. Evidently they had the idea that there was a source of water under the rocks, and they seem to have been correct. This may be what happens in Greece and Turkey, where ancient olive trees sit in beds of rock.

Identifying the trees provided a challenge for the Henwoods. It should not be imagined that the trees were neatly labeled with their names, nor were the varieties listed on the map. Michael had to identify them himself, using the old reports to the California State Board of Horticulture as a guide. The Columella (named for Lucius Columella, a Roman agriculturist in the first century B.C.E.) is a very distinctive tree. It was first imported into California from France by John Rock of Niles. Arthur P. Hayne, a graduate of the UC

College of Agriculture in Berkeley and whose father and brothers were olive growers and vineyardists, described the Columella, among many different olive varieties, in an 1892 report to the board.

Hayne said that "Columbella" was the more frequently used name. The tree branches in a distinctive way, each twig coming off at a very sharp angle. The fruit changes from yellow to red, a unique feature, and then turns deep blue to black when ripe. Michael has also noticed tiny yellow pits on the surface of the olive itself, even when fully ripe. Possibly these are encapsulated oil droplets. It ripens a bit later than the Mission. The seed is small and straight, with a sharp point. The flesh is far less bitter than Mission, so the oil is extremely sweet.

Byron M. Lelong, secretary to the State Board of Horticulture, had also commented on Columella in 1888. He listed three synonyms for this variety: Pasala, Loaime, and Columbella. It is also known as Figaniere. The fruit is so heavy, he said, it almost weighs the branches down to the ground, requiring props. He added that it was cold sensitive and ripened unevenly. I saw that at the Henwood Estate. Branches loaded down with ripe fruit were side by side with branches just coming into flower.

In his 1889 first edition of *The California Fruits and How to Grow Them,* E. J. Wickson leaned heavily on Lelong's descriptions of the olive varieties, quoting him almost verbatim. He gave Lelong credit for the information. Wickson noted that Columella flourished in Livermore, Niles, San Jose, and Saratoga, just as Lelong had said.

Lelong and Wickson may not have known about the orchard up in Yuba County at Marysville. It was probably not planted yet. Their reports deal with observations on trial plots in leading nurseries. John Rock and George Roeding would not sell Columella until 1885. They needed that time both to prove its hardiness and bearing qualities as well as to propagate enough plants for commercial purposes. The world of the olive growers was small and clubby. They usually knew what the others were doing, but perhaps Marysville eluded them.

Lelong and Wickson also described Uvaria, the other principal variety in the Ayer-Henwood orchards. Lelong thought it was a very valuable olive, both for oil and pickles. (John Rock had imported this tree.) It is a rapid grower and very prolific bearer. The unique feature is the clustering of the grapelike fruits at the end of each bearing branch. (That is the source of its name, *uva* being Latin for grape.) Lelong noted fifteen drupes at the end of one very heavily laden branch. The fruit ripens in November, and the Uvaria was successful in San Jose, Niles, and Saratoga. Wickson echoed Lelong's remarks. Hayne simply mentioned it in a list, without any other comment.

Michael Henwood disagrees about Uvaria's value as an oil olive. It does not seem to be nearly so rich in oil as the Columella or the Mission, and it has a less attractive flavor. In fact, he has not decided whether to keep all the Uvaria trees in production or to use them solely as rootstock. This is an interesting question, though not a new one.

In an 1898 report to the State Board of Horticulture, George Colby, assistant chemist at the UC College of Agriculture, presented an analysis of the oil content of different varieties of olive grown in different regions of the state, for 1895 and 1896. He listed the place of growth and the actual date of harvesting.

The average oil content of Uvaria, sampled from twenty-three sites, was 18.48 percent. The percentage of oil content ranged from 11 to 29. Columella yielded an average of 19.64 percent, sampled from nineteen sites, with a range of 13 to 30. In other words, there was hardly any difference. What was different was the amount of usable flesh, or the "flesh-pit ratio." In Uvaria, the pit took up over 25 percent of the weight, whereas in Columella, it was only 17 percent. This is a reasonably large difference.

It is interesting to compare these values with those of the Mission olive. There were many more samples of Mission, as it had been so much more widely disseminated. Its oil content hovered around the 18 percent mark. The pit averaged out at 17 percent. At a generic level, purely comparing the oil content of the fruit, there is little to distinguish one from the other. Missions were said to be better for oil than for pickles, though it was adequate for both.

Nevadillo blanco, an olive imported specifically for the quality of its oil, had almost the same oil content as the Mission, but it had a very high pit average, 29 percent. The Manzanillo olive is seldom used for oil. It has an average oil yield of 17 percent, and its pit occupies 15 percent. One would think it should be excellent for oil, and yet it is not often used. The reason is probably that it brings so much more money as a table olive that very few growers will sell it for oil. (The Sciabica family presses Manzanillo occasionally and sells its oil as a varietal. It tastes very good.)

These analytical data, though old, are almost certainly reliable and confirm the fact that oil quality depends on many other factors than the mere raw content in the fruit. It is interesting to consult these old reports, especially in light of Michael Henwood's experience with these old trees.

Michael also has the orchard of "unknowns" planted among the rocks. These trees are exceptionally prolific and produce wonderful oil. One tree of medium height and broad growth yielded 226 pounds of fruit in 1996 and looks as if it will continue to do the same in subsequent years. This belies the biennial cycle usually associated with bearing olive trees. These trees seem to have Columella ancestry in the shape of their branches and the sweetness of their oil. It may be that the Ayers were trying to hybridize their trees. There are no written records that Michael can find, but it is a very likely assumption. There are also several trees with a strong "weeping" habit. They could be specimens of the French Pleurer or Pendoulier, both of whose names connote the drooping quality. They might also be hybrids from those varieties.

The earliest date at which Columella trees were available commercially was 1885, at Roeding's Fancher Creek Nursery in Fresno and John Rock's California Nursery Company at Niles. They continued to sell them until 1893. Columella could be bought from Leonard

Coates at the Napa Valley Nursery in 1893. Other nurseries selling Columella trees early include the Central Avenue Nursery in Los Angeles (1891) and the Silver Gate Nursery in San Diego (1889). Four more nurseries also offered them: Luther Burbank's Santa Rosa Nursery (1890—the year Burbank wanted to get rid of them at fire-sale prices), Morris in San Bernardino (1895), Trumbull and Beebe in San Francisco (1895), and the Orange County Nurseries in Fullerton (1900). G. G. Briggs was active in Marysville at the time, but no catalog has survived. Uvaria was sold in tandem with Columella. In general, these two were slightly more common than some of the other types.

The Henwoods do not know whether the Ayers bought their trees or propagated them in their nursery from cuttings or perhaps seed. Possibly they ordered their other fruit trees from Briggs. He might have accommodated them by getting olive trees, even if he were not in the habit of selling them as a rule. Because the Henwood's map from 1895 shows olive orchards in existence, one assumes that they were planted before that date.

Henwood Estate has a unique oil in the Columella as well as in the "unknown" varieties. Paul Vossen, farm adviser for Sonoma County and a certified oil maker himself, encouraged the Henwoods in their venture, supplying a lot of technical advice and skill. Darrell Corti, the oil expert in Sacramento, told Michael that his Columella is in the finest class of oils. As far as is known, no one else has a working Columella orchard or oil available. The new oils made in Marin, Napa, and Sonoma counties are from other varieties that have recently been imported—Leccino, Frantoio, Maurino, Pendulina, and maybe a couple of others—plus the standard Mission type.

Another historic orchard has also been restored in the foothills of the Sierras. It is in Auburn. This property, at 1,200 feet, is about halfway to the limit for olive cultivation. At much higher elevations than that, the temperature may drop too low and frost is a serious hazard. The orchard is principally planted with an old Italian olive known as Saracena, but there are also about twenty other varieties. The Saracenas are really tiny fruit, very black when ripe, and a source of excellent pickles and oil. They strongly resemble the minute olives from Provence. A historian of Placer County, May Perry, who wrote many essays describing the county's early industries, called the trees Picholine.

The present owner, "Amigo" Cantisano, is a master organic farmer, known across the state for his skill in coaxing people to grow all their crops organically. He provides skilled assistance and psychological support, acting as a consultant to several agricultural industries. Amigo presses a fine, golden-yellow oil from his olives and has sold it under the original name of the orchard, Aeolia Olive Oil Company. His land is in the Aeolian Heights district of Auburn. He also marinates olives in several ethnic styles. Cantisano's company is now called "Aeolia Organics."

This orchard and oil business were started in 1887 by Frederick Birdsall, an engineer. His daughter recalled that he went to Italy and brought many types of olive trees back to grow on his land. Although he was an engineer, he used a simple, old-fashioned hand method to press the oil. His manager later built a hydraulic press in a separate building. This structure has now become independent of the olive ranch and was recently sold as a residence. The hydraulic press has been restored to working order by the current owner of the house, also an engineer. The original glass bottles with the Aeolia impress are still in existence. They are avidly sought after by bottle collectors.

The Wente Brothers property in Livermore, Alameda County, incorporates several old vineyards, olive orchards, and ranches in its present complex. One olive orchard was at Mel's Ranch, where Louis Mel originally planted imported trees. These trees still produce fruit, and the fruit is pressed into oil by the Sciabica family.

Another segment of the Wente holdings is the former Olivina Vineyards, so named for the olive trees that were planted there. Olivina was an early independent winery. Both wine and olives were produced at the vineyard. The Lucques variety of olive trees was planted between the rows of vines, and the fruit harvested for pickling. Another old winery, Cresta Blanca, is now the Wente Brothers visitors' center.

In the Napa Valley, another old orchard continues to be in production. An illegitimate son of Mariano Vallejo, Tiburcio Parrot, had perhaps the largest olive orchard in the county, with between five and six thousand trees. He sold olive oil under the name Miravalle. Parrot had two stones to crush the fruit and two oil presses to extract the oil. This property is now owned by Safra and has become the Spring Valley Winery. Olive oil and wine are currently both sold under the name Spring Mountain.

A century ago, there was a successful olive oil operation in Santa Rosa, owned by Captain Guy Emmanuel Grosse. His orchards are said to be still functioning under new ownership. The older vineyards and estates had numerous olive trees, dating from the end of the nineteenth century when olive oil was a growth industry. The climate was very suitable for growing olive trees, suffering from less fog and cold winds than the coastal region.

In Calaveras County, there is more ferment. Former city dweller and businessman Ed Rich took over an old orchard and olive oil business in Copperopolis. He grows a number of different varieties of olives experimentally, including the Greek variety, Kalamata. Mr. Rich presses oil from some of these old varieties.

François Vitrac, a young French master oil maker, is working with several enthusiastic citizens of Calaveras County to get the olive oil business restarted in that region. His father is also an expert part of the group. Because they are from Provence, they have decided to import French olive trees for this project. That is a complete departure from the past. Louis Sammis, former owner of the Rocca Bella Olive Company in Calaveras County, grew Sevillanos and Ascolanos together with Manzanillos for canning. He was not an oil maker. (The Rocca Bella orchard is now owned by the Sciabica family.)

François took his associates on a journey to Provence in 1996 where they saw the type of tree they wanted. It remains to be seen if it will flourish in their orchards. There are certainly many other historic fruit trees in that area. Judith Marvin, historian of the county, showed me pear and fig trees in her garden at Murphys dating back to 1860, and still bearing fruit every season. Maybe the new French olive trees will fare better than the ones that came here in the 1880s, all traces of which have essentially vanished.

With the restoration and renewed cultivation of old orchards and the establishment of new ones using new and different varieties of olives, we can more clearly understand the excitement and fervor that accompanied the introduction and dissemination of new olive cultivars beginning in the 1880s. In these old orchards, we see the living history of the olive in California—moving from the simple distribution of original mission stock to the more sophisticated and extensive distribution of imported varieties made possible by commercial nurseries. On an even more concrete level, we see the skill, patience, and dedication of olive growers as they care for the trees and explore new possibilities and contemporary uses of the olive—an exploration that touches all who love olives.

Varieties of Imported Trees

Please note: I have used the spelling of the period in which the variety was imported, not necessarily the spelling employed at present.

Amellau: This variety, from southern France, was originally imported by A. C. Wetmore of Livermore. It was not very prolific in France, but it did better in Biggs (Butte County). The berry itself is very large, thus making it good for pickles.

Atro-rubens: This is an excellent oil variety from southern France, but the tree is susceptible to cold. As a result, it was not found in the oldest orchards, because a series of cold seasons had destroyed it in many places. It is moderately productive and produces some sort of crop every year. John T. Doyle brought the seed to California in 1880. Mr. Doyle was a lawyer in San Mateo and a friend of the writer Gertrude Atherton.

Columella: John Rock brought this tree from France. It is a source of very good oil, though the fruit is not as rich in raw oil as some of the other cultivars. One of its identifying characteristics is the bright yellow color of the fruit before it ripens to a rich purple-black.

Empeltre: Small and vigorous, this tree resists the cold well and the fruit ripens early, but it needs a lot of water and fertilizer. The oil is said to be good, but very few specimens of the trees were imported from Spain. It is used for grafting. The name means "grafted" in Spanish.

Frantoiano (Correggiolo, Frantoio, Frantojo): This cultivar creates oil with a true Tuscan flavor. It is not a very vigorous grower and has to be pruned very carefully. It does not do well in the fogs and cold winds of the lowlands but should be set out on a protected hillside. High winds or excessive heat cause it to drop its fruit. Hayne said that it did not produce as much oil in California as expected, whereas in Italy, its very name, Frantoiano, denotes an oil press. Hayne's assessment was disputed by Lelong, who thought it was quite prolific. Judge J. R. Logan was the first to import it from Italy and grew it successfully in Santa Cruz. There is disagreement as to whether this variety is synonymous with Razzo. Some French and American

Line drawing of the Grossajo or Frantojo cultivar from 1888.

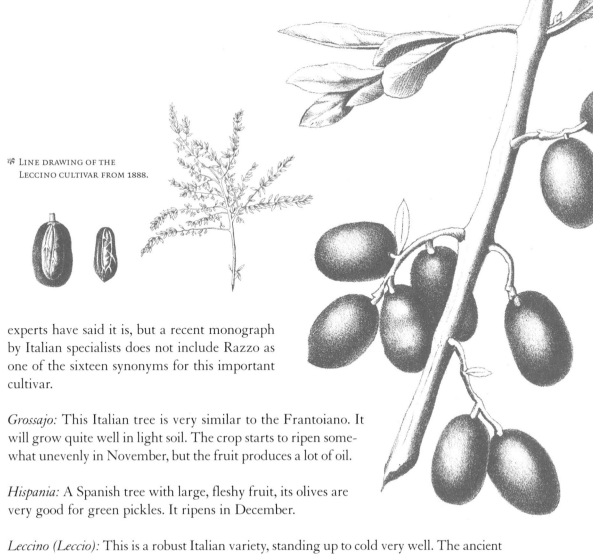

✧ LINE DRAWING OF THE
LECCINO CULTIVAR FROM 1888.

experts have said it is, but a recent monograph by Italian specialists does not include Razzo as one of the sixteen synonyms for this important cultivar.

Grossajo: This Italian tree is very similar to the Frantoiano. It will grow quite well in light soil. The crop starts to ripen somewhat unevenly in November, but the fruit produces a lot of oil.

Hispania: A Spanish tree with large, fleshy fruit, its olives are very good for green pickles. It ripens in December.

Leccino (Leccio): This is a robust Italian variety, standing up to cold very well. The ancient Romans grew it and described it accurately. Despite these favorable qualities, Hayne did not think it was very useful in California. The oil clouded easily and did not have such a fine flavor as the others. The tree looks a little like the shrub oak, *Quercus ilex,* and, in fact, that is the source of its name, though the word "ilex" has been somewhat corrupted.

Lucques: This tree does best on a protected hillside. It is not exceptionally sensitive to the cold but needs very long hot summers to complete its ripening. It also has to have deep, rich soil. The experts all agreed that it requires vigorous pruning to get it to bear annually. In late nineteenth-century France, it sold for a very high price because of the size and quality of the pickles. There is an orchard of Lucques olive trees at the Wente Brothers property in Livermore. They were originally planted by Louis Mel at Mel's Ranch. This ranch was later incorporated into the Wente lands.

Macrocarpa: This dwarf tree produces poor crops, but the fruit is very large. It does not produce much oil. John Rock brought it from France.

Mignolo (Gremignolo): This Italian tree survives well in damp, foggy areas where other, more sensitive trees do poorly. It needs to be aggressively pruned. The fruit is not too rich in oil, but it has a reliable crop each year.

Morinello (Moraiolo): Both Hayne and Lelong agreed that this is a hardy Italian tree, resistant to cold and adapting well to different types of soil. The fruit ripens early and makes good oil.

Mouarou: This tree, also from Italy, strongly resembles the Morinello above.

Nevadillo blanco: This variety seems to have done much better in California than in its native Spain. Unfortunately, it is very sensitive to frost. It bears very heavily, but in France it ripened so early that the growers had to have two separate harvests, something of a disadvantage. An early harvest was a benefit in California, as was its productiveness. The fruit is almost exclusively reserved for oil.

Nigerina: The tree grows to be very large. Lelong called it a "thrifty" grower, an old-fashioned term that, from other contexts, seems to mean abundant. The oil was said to be of high grade. John T. Doyle brought seed from France in 1880.

Oblonga: The oddly shaped fruit accounts for this tree's name. It ripens two weeks earlier than the broad-leafed Mission. It is not bitter and so makes very good pickles. John Rock imported it from France.

Pendoulier: The fruit ripens "medium early." Hayne's and Lelong's original notes indicate that its oil was exceptionally delicate. It requires deep soil in the United States, but in southern France where it originated, it grew reliable crops each year, despite poor soil quality. The name records the fact that the branches droop toward the ground.

Pendulina: This useful French tree was imported by John Rock. It is known for good growth, good crops, early and even ripening, and medium to large fruit that does well both for oil and pickles.

Piangente: Another French tree with a weeping habit, it ripens early and has a great deal of small fruit that makes good oil.

(True) Picholine: Unlike the tree known as Redding Picholine, this variety has very large fruit. It came from the Languedoc in France but is also widely cultivated in Provence. The trees bear crops each year quite reliably. Because of the large size of the fruit, it is primarily used for pickles. Hayne commented that this was known as "Lucques" in the markets. He also noted that some authorities believed it was synonymous with Oblonga, but that was not his opinion. The tree is only fairly hardy but can be pruned quite severely.

Pleurer: The tree has a typical "weeping habit," hence the name Pleurer. It grows very vigorously to a very large size. The oil is esteemed in Provence, its original home.

Polymorpha: A tree with large fruit and an excellent crop, it is most suitable for green pickles. John Rock brought the tree from France.

Praecox: As the name (Latin for "early") indicates, this is an early ripening variety. It has oval, purple-black fruit, which makes good oil and comes from France.

Puntarolo: The fruit is pointed, hence the name. It is not very fleshy and does not contain a great deal of oil. It ripens late. Puntarolo came from Italy.

Racemi (Racinoppe): Of modest size, this tree is very hardy. It requires deep, rich soil but can withstand fog and cold quite well. The fruit forms in clusters, like the Uvaria. It is small and good for oil and came from Italy.

Racimal: This Spanish tree resists the cold quite well but does not give reliable crops each year. The fruit also tends to fall off too easily, thus reducing the amount of the crop. The oil is good.

Razzo: Comments by Lelong and Hartmann indicate they thought this tree was synonymous with the Frantoiano. It is a fine oil tree, very similar to Frantoiano but not the same according to Prevost, Bartolini, and Messeri, experts in olive nomenclature. Razzo is also an Italian tree.

Regalis: This tree grows very large and its fruit ripens late. It is used for pickles. John Rock brought it from France.

Rouget: Hayne said this tree was very hardy, hanging on in very poor soil in its native Languedoc. It also resists cold well. The crops are regular, and its oil is of quite good quality. The name comes from the red color of the fruit as it goes through the ripening stages.

Rubra: This is a French tree that really does do better in poor soil than rich bottomland. It is possibly a source of the persistent myth that olive trees prefer poor soils. Its chief problem is its oil content, which can vary as much as 20 percent in different years.

Salonica: Although this sounds like a Greek name, the tree actually originated in Salon, a town near Marseilles. The fruit, though large, ripens late in modest quantities, but the oil is good.

San Agostino: This is another Italian tree that has very large fruit good for pickles. It ripens early.

Santa Caterina: This Italian tree has extremely large fruit that makes good pickles.

Sweet Olive: There are two types of sweet olive, one with large fruit and one with small fruit. As the name implies, it is not bitter, and the fruit is used for drying. The sweet olive comes from Italy.

Uvaria: Although this is a hardy and vigorous tree, the fruit gives only mediocre results as either oil or pickles. It is useful as a rootstock. The olives form in clusters, like grapes. John T. Doyle brought the seed from France in 1880.

Verdale (Verdeal): A dwarf variety with small crops, this French tree is sensitive to the cold and the fruit ripens early.

❧ Line drawing of the Razzo cultivar from 1888.

6

The Olive Oil Trade

Olive oil has been made in California, originally at the missions, since about 1800. As olive trees spread, so did the making of oil. At first, it was made for home use, and then during the 1870s, it began to be manufactured commercially. After the missionaries, the earliest commercial olive oil makers lived and worked in southern California. Ellwood Cooper and the Kimballs started their orchards and had fruit to press during the 1870s. The Del Valle family sold the first oil from their press at Camulos in 1871. Since then, over 120 firms, large and small, have made and sold olive oil in California. (See appendix B: Olive Oil Makers in California [1869–1996].)

The story of the making of olive oil cannot be separated from the stories of the people who made it in the past and who continue to make it today. Often these are stories of perseverance, determination, and survival. As we look at the olive oil trade, I want to share some observations with you about both the process and the people, for both are part of the history of the olive in California.

The essential process of making olive oil is not complex. Fresh, undamaged fruit must be crushed to release the oil globules from the cells in which they are contained. The crushed "mash" is then pressed to extract the oil. This releases a mixture of oil, vegetable water, and solid matter. Separating these three components to single out the oil comes next. The final product is usually filtered after being allowed to settle for

❧ OLIVE CRUSHER AT CAMULOS,
VENTURA COUNTY, CIRCA 1872.

some time. The water and solid matter must be disposed of appropriately. No other physical or chemical processes may be used if the oil is intended to be "extra virgin."

Crushing may be done in a traditional stone or granite trough fitted with a stone or granite wheel crusher, which is rotated by some form of external power, or the fruit may be crushed in a hammer mill. A hammer mill is a grinder or crusher in which materials are broken up and homogenized. The extraction of the oil is done in a variety of ways. If the fruit has been processed through a hammer mill, the resulting "slurry" is separated in a centrifuge. The centrifuge may either be a two- or a three-phase machine, depending on whether there are two end products or three. When there are two, the oil is separated from a combination of water and residue. When there are three, the waste matter is also separated, leaving water and solid residue in different containers. In either case, it is important for the separation in a centrifuge to follow the crushing quickly, to avoid emulsification.

To extract the oil from a traditional crushed mash, the material is spread on mats, now made of an impervious polyethylene fabric, which are piled into a press or left for the oil to percolate slowly in a "sinolea." The sinolea is a system allowing the oil to accumulate passively. "Cold pressing" refers to room temperature, usually the same as the ambient outdoor temperature, and the fact that no additional heat is applied to speed the process. Very cold olives yield smaller amounts of oil than warmer ones. This is important because olives are picked in the late fall and early winter months. The fruit may not only be too cold for optimum yield but

☙ OLIVE OIL PRESS ROOM SHOWING FIVE-TON ROLLERS PREPARATORY TO MAKING OLIVE OIL. DATE UNKNOWN.

also very wet. If such fruit is left piled too deeply for too long, it very quickly starts to putrefy. The resulting oil has an unpleasant flavor.

Ellwood Cooper, working in the 1870s, believed that it made sense to prepare the fruit carefully before pressing it into oil. In an earlier chapter, I mentioned Cooper's drying sheds, which were attached to his olive oil factory near Santa Barbara. Cooper maintained these sheds at about 120 degrees, and left the fruit in them for thirty-six to forty-eight hours. The olives were spread in very shallow heaps to avoid fungal growth at the warm center of a pile. Eugene Hilgard, dean of the College of Agriculture at UC Berkeley, wrote about the insidious effect of even one moldy olive on the oil. Cooper felt that removing some of the moisture from the fruit allowed him to make a finer grade of oil. There is still merit in this notion.

There are several varieties of olive presses. In the hydraulic type, presses are bolted to the floor. Pressure is applied to the mats so that they are pushed upward and the oil drips downward. The disadvantage of hydraulic presses is that the process has to be stopped from time to time in order to clean the machinery.

The system known as "sinolea" allows the oil globules to percolate down through the mats under gravity only. This is considered the best way to obtain an oil with as few defects as possible. It releases about 80 percent of the oil. The remaining mash may be treated again with water in a decanting centrifuge, pulling out another 18 percent of edible oil. After that, only a low-quality "pomace oil" can be made from the residue. Sinolea machinery avoids the problems associated with hydraulic presses, and it works in a continuous manner.

In other machines, pressure is exerted by a beam, using Archimedes' principle. The antique method of pressing with a heavily weighted long lever, or beam, is still effective. It is used in the West Bank and Israel by the Palestinians, and by Israelis who choose to work in the time-honored manner. A working replica of an ancient mill has been built at the Eretz Israel Museum in Tel Aviv, and children are taught how it worked.[1] Ellwood Cooper's press in Santa Barbara was of this type.

The missionaries made their oil in this crush-and-press way. The stone crusher, turned by a burro, can still be seen at Mission La Purisima (near Lompoc), and so can the heavy press. The volunteers who serve at the mission nowadays are planning to revive oil making. They have started by training a burro to turn the crusher. The missionaries used woolen bags to hold the mash, so the weaver at La Purisima has been spinning wool from the mission sheep and weaving the bags. The missionaries knew that everything had to be kept extremely clean in order to make edible oil, but the woolen bags posed a problem. It was hard to remove the rancid residue from woolen cloth using the primitive laundry methods of the day.

Today oil makers use an inert polyethylene fiber, which can be thoroughly cleansed after each pressing. Other materials that have been used throughout history include plant fibers woven into porous baskets. These allowed the oil to drip out slowly as the pressure was applied; they were a little easier to keep clean than the previous materials, such as wool bags. Such baskets can still be found in traditional Palestinian oil mills in the West Bank. Jute and esparto grass are the fibers most commonly used.

Once the oil is ready, it is put into bottles. The color of the glass for the bottles is important, because oil becomes rancid when exposed to the light for a long time. Heat is equally as bad as light. Olive oil will last much longer if it is kept in the dark. One way to do that is to use dark-tinted glass for the bottles. Unfortunately, this obscures the color of the oil, a key selling point. The shape of the bottle, of course, has nothing to do with conserving the

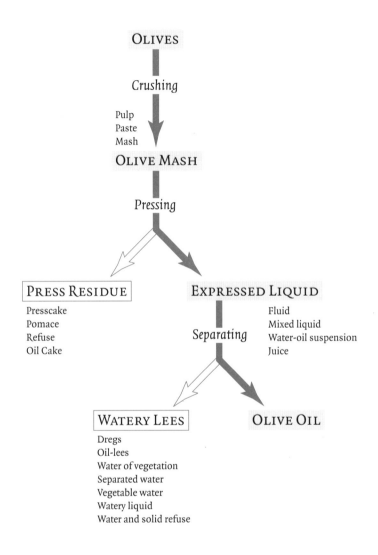

OLIVES

Crushing

Pulp
Paste
Mash

OLIVE MASH

Pressing

PRESS RESIDUE   EXPRESSED LIQUID

Presscake   Fluid
Pomace   Mixed liquid
Refuse   Separating   Water-oil suspension
Oil Cake   Juice

WATERY LEES   OLIVE OIL

Dregs
Oil-lees
Water of vegetation
Separated water
Vegetable water
Watery liquid
Water and solid refuse

❧ FLOW CHART SHOWING THE EXTRACTION OF OLIVE OIL
FROM THE RAW FRUIT.

oil, neither does its design. The cost and practical requirements of the bottles have to be balanced against gaining attention through aesthetics. An elegant, elongated bottle seems to justify the higher price paid by a consumer. Its disadvantage is that most pantry shelves will not hold it, and the oil is exposed to the light.

For a long time, much of California's olive oil has been made from undersized culls, together with the olives that fell to the ground during harvesting or as a result of storms, and other rejects that are not sufficiently attractive for the table olive processors. Culls are olives that are too small to be suitable for canning. Rejects are olives that may have been frozen or left on the orchard floor too long. Any oil made from them is only suitable for rectification, a chemical treatment that strips all the signature flavors from the olive oil, leaving it completely neutral. Olives that are too small or blemished in some way can be used to make an adequate grade of oil. Consignments of olives from scattered properties with only a few trees are also used quite often. The large processing companies will not accept delivery below certain minimal quantities. Oil can also be expressed from olives that have been in brine for some time or that have been frozen when the temperature falls below zero. These types of fruit do not make superior oil or exceptional oil.

COVER OF A PAMPHLET ON OLIVE OIL PUBLISHED BY H. J. HEINZ IN THE EARLY YEARS OF THE TWENTIETH CENTURY.

The life of an olive oil processor is made up of a few quiet times followed by periods of merciless haste. If the processor wants to make perfect oil, he or she has almost no margin for error. The fresh fruit is totally unforgiving. Normally placid people get edgy and irritable at harvest time because of this pressure. Whatever can go wrong will go wrong in the usual way of Murphy's law. The machinery breaks down just when it is required to work at its peak. Workers get sick, whereas the rest of the year they were in excellent health. It rains when no rain is supposed to fall. Oil making is not for the faint of heart.

Veteran manufacturers of olive oil in California have held on through thick and thin, and they now are seeing the market expand very gratifyingly after long dry periods. Listening to some of them tell their stories makes one feel very humble because of the hardships, diligence, dedication, and sheer hard work that was necessary for their families—and their businesses—to survive. Due to the variable business cycles, none of the current producers have been in business uninterruptedly for more than about sixty to sixty-five years. They are nonetheless part of a chain of California olive oil makers that has lasted more than two centuries. Reviving the stories of their predecessors is an act of piety. Many of them had small family businesses, which were the backbone of many small communities. All of them, however modest their accomplishments, contributed something to life in this state and as such should be remembered.

Ellwood Cooper of Santa Barbara gets the credit for restarting the olive oil industry in California after the missionaries ceased their work. Cooper ended up with six separate orchards in the region around Santa Barbara. The main one was at Goleta, the present site of the University of California at Santa Barbara campus.

Cooper was a very practical man. Born in 1829, he had grown up on a combined farm and gristmill in eastern Pennsylvania and had been put in charge of the milling operation very early. His brother ran the farm. Subsequently Cooper went to Philadelphia to learn merchandising in an early "politically correct" grocery store: the owner would sell nothing known to be made by slaves.

From Philadelphia, Cooper went to Haiti for eight years. The political and social atmosphere on that island must have been extraordinarily different from that of Philadelphia. He was a partner of Colonel Oliver Cutts in the latter's import business. By the end of eight years, the political hazards of life in the Caribbean led him to take his family back to the United States, where they lived in New York for two years.

The attraction of the gold rush turned Cooper's mind to California. He and his wife went there for a long visit early in the 1860s. They met the Wolfskills, two brothers from Ohio who had found their way to Los Angeles in the late 1820s, in Los Angeles and saw the orange groves as well as the old mission orchards at San Gabriel. The Coopers thought very seriously about living in California. Ellwood made another trip west on his own. By chance he met Colonel John Hollister—the town of Hollister near the Gavilan Mountains is named for the colonel—at the San Juan Bautista stagecoach station. They became friendly. Using Hollister as his agent, Cooper arranged to buy two thousand acres of farmland in Santa Barbara County. He borrowed the money from Mrs. Oliver Cutts, the wife of his former business partner, a very wealthy woman. The Coopers moved to Santa Barbara in 1870.

Cooper and his wife opened a girls' school in Santa Barbara, because there was no adequate school for their own children. Mrs. Cooper was a former headmistress and well qualified for this work. She was also an authority on ferns, so she and her husband shared strong interests in botany and horticulture. The leadership qualities latent in him were expressed as he transferred his activities to California, not unlike William Wolfskill and John Bidwell.

A fortuitous observation played a role in his ultimately choosing to grow olive trees. He had had difficulty in obtaining good quality olive oil from Europe and recognized that olives would do well in the Santa Barbara area. He moved very fast to plant the new ranch with cuttings from the mission orchards.

Cooper had a lot of energy, which he spent in numerous important projects. For many years, he was the president of the State Board of Horticulture, a most influential body in its time. His activity with the board was in addition to his work with the six orchards he owned and the olive oil factory he built. Ultimately he owned eight thousand olive trees as well as numerous eucalyptus, Japanese persimmons, figs, English walnuts, and other types of fruit trees. His ranch, Rancho Ellwood, extended over two thousand acres. The eight thousand olive trees yielded fifty thousand bottles of olive oil in one year.

In Cooper's opinion, the Ojai Valley, slightly inland from Santa Barbara, was the perfect place to grow olives. Perhaps he felt this way because of the valley's elevation, east-west orientation, and bowl-like shape, which collected the heat from the sun effectively. The current principal crop in the Ojai Valley is Valencia oranges, which respond to the same climatic conditions. Perhaps in part because of Cooper's enthusiasm and guidance, there was a burst of activity in the Ojai Valley during the 1880s. Several hundred acres were planted with olives, and later a cooperative built an olive factory there. The factory burned down in 1910, and the olive industry never recouped.

Cooper was tireless in his promotion of the olive and its products. In the winters, wealthy tourists visited his ranch and admired the olive factory with its drying rooms and beam press, the orchards, and all his property. He created a thirty-foot column of olive oil at the 1893 Chicago World's Fair that was much admired. Although he was happy with the Mission trees he had started from cuttings, he was somewhat interested in the foreign imports and had a few on his property.

Cooper played a crucial role in the establishment of the olive industry in California. In particular, he both helped establish the early commercial viability of the olive oil trade in the state and also motivated many other people to start growing olives.

Frank and Warren Kimball of San Diego share the distinction of reviving the growing of olives with Ellwood Cooper. The Kimballs were true pioneers in the olive industry. They began their work at much the same time as Ellwood Cooper did further to the north.

Frank Kimball was a building contractor who was advised to leave San Francisco because of chronic lung disease. The doctors thought the cool, foggy climate exacerbated it. While on a journey to find a more congenial place to live, he bought the old Rancho de la Nacion near San Diego.

The ranch was originally part of the mission lands, but Pio Pico, the governor of Alta California in the period after secularization, gave large amounts of it away on his own authority. This particular ranch went to his brother-in-law, Don Juan Forster, from whom Kimball bought it in 1868. Kimball founded the town of National City there when he built a wharf and various other essential structures.

Frank Kimball wanted to grow a commercial crop and drew inspiration from the mission orchards nearby. His diaries record the laying out of the early orchards using cuttings from the missions. At first, he brought a few branches back and planted them behind his house. In 1872, he noted in his diary, "Staking out lot south for my little trees," and the next day, he added, "[S]et out my little olive trees." A year later, the diary states that he "got 100 cuttings from my little trees."

Also in 1872, Kimball decided to raise sheep on another part of the land. He later used those fields for another olive orchard. The residual sheep manure formed a rich fertilizer.

Kimball returned to the mission orchards and wrote in his diary, "By leave of Father Farley and Charley Morse, I got 101 three foot cuttings." Father Farley was a Franciscan priest who served at the mission church. Two years later, when visiting the mission with his brother, Warren, they bought one thousand more olive cuttings for $11. Frank and Warren also visited the mission at San Luis Rey in 1868 and counted only seven remaining olive trees.

In later years, Kimball bought 726 cuttings from a Mr. Machado in Tijuana, and 3,500 from Francisco Arguello's orchard in Baja California. He recorded the transaction with Arguello. He would either pay $75 for the lot as a whole or $150 if 50 percent of the cuttings sprouted. In the end, he paid the $75.

Kimball experimented with different methods of planting, not always copying the way the missionaries had done it. For example, he started out planting the cuttings in sand but learned that he needed to add some real soil. Transplanting tended to destroy the long, fragile root that the cuttings formed. The new tree did not have to be transplanted once it was started in the kind of soil it needed. The missionaries' method of burying the truncheons six feet deep did not work for him. It is not clear how he found out what they had done, unless the lore had passed down through the neophytes, native people impressed into the missions by the Franciscans, and thence to Father Farley and Charley Morse.

By 1878, he had determined the best way of doing things. His diary records, "Planting cuttings obliquely in the earth with one and a half feet above ground. In that way the largest and sturdiest sprout of the cutting can be preserved."

Kimball wrote many brief articles about how to make olive oil and how to preserve olives. The olive oil factory he built at National City started to work in 1886. His oil machinery was very traditional, with a granite basin and rotating granite wheel crusher. The crushed fruit was put into bags made of camel hair or vegetable fiber, specially imported by Kimball for this purpose, and pressed in a press with a long "ratchet lever." Unlike Cooper, he never left the olives in a drying room but pressed them quite quickly after picking. Kimball also preserved olives for table use, using the old lye process. One of his diary entries said, "Visitor from San Diego says my olives are better than any others. He should like them. Ate most a quarter of my best olives."

Kimball also sold olive cuttings and young trees. The cuttings cost ten cents each. When a customer complained about the cost, Kimball replied, "In 1880, when I could not get enough cuttings from the San Diego Mission, I sent a four horse team down the Peninsula [probably Baja California] to a good orchard. The men had to repair the road as they went along. I found the cuttings were all from Mission trees. The cuttings cost me five cents apiece even before they were planted. Ten cents is a fair price for sprouted cuttings taken from bearing Mission trees."

The U.S. Department of Agriculture called on Kimball to experiment with new varieties they were importing. He imported some trees from Syria but was very unimpressed with the fruit. The government sent him Redinolla, Nevadillo, Empeltre, Racimal, Gordale, Verdugo, Madrileno, and Orcada. He also tried the "Mansanillo" [sic] and the Cornicabra, but he thought nothing did as well as his Mission trees. As a pioneer orchardist, Kimball served on the State Board of Horticulture for many years and was active in trying to stop the importation of adulterated olive oil from Europe.

The Kimballs also grew citrus and other fruits. The business prospered, and Frank Kimball became very wealthy. He entered into dealings with the railroads, deeding them property for their lines. Unfortunately, he was not a hard-headed businessman, and at the end of his life, he lost all his holdings, having been manipulated out of them. A nephew took pity on him and allowed him to live in a flat over a restaurant he owned. One of Kimball's last diary entries reads, "I spent the best years of my life trying to make those around me happier, and the result is unsatisfactory. I am confronted at every step by ungrateful people, but I look back and thank God I have lived. As far as I know, I have done my best." This quiet dignity is very poignant.

Also working in the San Diego area was C. M. Gifford. Charles Gifford was born in Pennsylvania in 1856. As a young man, he went to sea. When he settled in the San Diego area, he established a ranch called Jamacha north of the city. Initially he grew oranges and grapefruit. Gifford then became very interested in the horticultural pioneering at the missions.

Gifford left a record of the events that precipitated changing his principal crop to olives, a change that occurred in 1896. A neighbor gave him a pickled olive to eat, the first one he had ever tasted. He really liked it and decided to make some for himself. The neighbor, an American citizen who was the honorary consul for the Portuguese Azores, had a ranch near Gifford, and Gifford bought raw olives from this man. Somehow Gifford then pickled them himself and began to sell the results.

From that small beginning, Charles Gifford went into the olive business. He planted olive trees on the ranch at Jamacha. It was the heyday of the California olive movement, and the enthusiasm of Cooper and Kimball was still widespread. The first olive oil factory he built at his ranch was made of adobe and used the same sort of machinery as the missionaries had used.

Then he built the C. M. Gifford Olive Oil Works at the corner of 13th and M Streets in San Diego, where he made both oil and pickled olives by himself. Each week Gifford, a very distinctive character with a large shaggy moustache, went around San Diego with his horse and wagon and sold his

Chas. M. Gifford.

C. M. GIFFORD, PIONEER OLIVE OIL MAKER AND CANNED OLIVE PROCESSOR.

wares in bulk from barrels. The first time his name appeared in the San Diego directory as an olive processor was in 1897. During this period, Frederic Bioletti perfected the technique of preserving olives safely in metal cans. Gifford consulted with Professor Bioletti at the University of California at Berkeley and became the first person in California to can olives commercially, even before Mrs. Ehmann. In 1902, he was the first Californian to win a prize for canned, pickled olives at the Panama-Pacific Exposition.

When the California Olive Association started, Gifford was an early member. He and his son Orville attended the meetings religiously and always spoke up forcefully. Eventually Gifford sold his olive orchards to the Obertis, whose story will be told below. Later, during the 1960s, Orville Gifford corresponded with Harold Schutt, manager of the Lindsay Ripe Olive Company and historian of the California olive par excellence. Two of C. M. Gifford's grandsons continued in the olive processing business even after it was acquired by the Westgate Company in the 1950s.

El Quito Olive Ranch in Los Gatos was another early olive ranch that was very influential. The owner, Edward E. Goodrich, was an unabashed admirer of Ellwood Cooper. Born in Massachusetts in 1845, he went to Yale and Albany College to study law. Following that, he came to California and married the daughter of a California Supreme Court judge.

Goodrich bought the eighty-acre El Quito Ranch in 1882 specifically for the purpose of emulating Cooper and making olive oil. The ranch had been the property of Don José Ramon Arguello, an early settler and descendant of a Californio family. ("Californio" is the term used to describe families that came to Alta California with the Franciscans.) The land was originally named Rancho Tito, after the Indian who took care of the Mission Santa Clara dairy farm, which had been situated there. In 1841, a teacher from the mission, José Zenon Fernandez, obtained the thirteen thousand-acre grant from the provincial governor. He owned it jointly with a man named José Noriega. They later transferred the grant to Manuel Alviso, and in 1859, the latter sold it to Arguello.

Arguello had planted Mission olive trees and grapevines there as early as 1865. The ranch contained an olive oil factory with a crusher and press, a winery with a large barn, and houses for the workmen. When Arguello died in 1872, the land was subdivided for sale. Goodrich bought the land ten years later. One of Arguello's sons worked with Goodrich to plant the olive trees.

In order to do the job of raising olives and making oil thoroughly, Goodrich spent four years in Europe, learning as much as he could about olives. At the ranch, he employed Arthur Tappan Marvin as his manager. Marvin later wrote a useful monograph on olive growing, one of the first of its kind in California.

The olive trees were bearing when Goodrich bought the land, but they were planted only sixteen feet apart. He had learned in Italy that this was too close for complete growth. In 1883, he removed every second tree. This opened up space and allowed the roots of the remaining trees to expand. The discarded trees were turned into truncheons, which were used to develop a whole new generation of trees. In the end, more than fifty thousand new trees were added to Goodrich's ranch, and many more were given to neighbors and friends. This remaking of the orchard took six years, but during that time Goodrich began pressing oil and won prizes for it at various California state fairs. He also won a diploma for his olive oil at the New Orleans Exposition in 1885.

Goodrich interspersed grapevines between the rows of olive trees, an old practice he had seen in Italy and Spain. To improve his oil, he subsequently grafted newer types of Italian trees on some of the old Mission stock. He kept careful records of the results and published them in the reports of the State Board of Horticulture and Olive Growers Convention. Olive growers met annually at a convention under the auspices of the California State Board of Horticulture.

In 1892, Goodrich reported in the proceedings of the State Board of Horticulture on the performance of the Razzo trees he had imported. He wrote, "This variety on my place does not seem to be as great a success as some of the others and I practically count it out. It is a light bearer in Italy and it will evidently be such on my place."[2] He preferred Correggiolo but was also trying Moraiolo and Grossajo. Grossajo was at one time a synonym for Frantoio, a fine oil olive. Goodrich noted that the Italian olives separated out better in the oil-making process than Mission, and also did not spoil (ferment) so quickly. Another variety he began experimenting with was Cucca (also called Cucco), a large olive suited to pickling for table use.

The tone of his comments was cool and measured, unlike the almost missionary zeal of some of the others. Goodrich worked the ranch until 1919, when he sold it to G. Bruces. Goodrich died in 1920. Since then, the ranch has been broken up into subdivisions and no longer exists. Olive trees from the property were dug up and transplanted for landscaping on Treasure Island in 1939.

A few years after Goodrich began his olive venture in Los Gatos, the Oberti family, which would become very well known in the olive business, was starting their own venture in the Central Valley. Giovanni Oberti was born in Alfi, near Genoa. When he first left Italy, he emigrated to Argentina. Later, he came to the United States, where he landed in New York and was processed through Ellis Island. After finding his way to Madera, he bought eighty acres of land from a bankrupt property, which had twenty acres planted with olive trees. He planted his first olives in 1890. The Obertis had five children, four sons and a daughter. One son died young. Like so many others, the family grew grapes and other fruit besides olives. Their sons—Frank, Adolf, and James—grew up helping in the orchards, and all went into the family business after leaving school. Their future was shaped by the depression, as were the lives of so many adults who came of age during that period.

Selling olives in 1935, when money was exceedingly scarce even for necessities, was an almost impossible task. The Oberti trees produced very good crops, and Giovanni's sons had

Collecting Olive Oil Bottles

Olive oil bottles have attracted collectors for many years. The older bottles, made of hand-blown glass and embossed with the name and brand, are considered rarer and more precious than the other bottles. The embossing, which is done directly into the glass, allows a maker to be identified even without a label. The most desirable, and the most valuable, is a bottle with the original label.

❦ ELLWOOD COOPER OLIVE OIL BOTTLE.

Three olive-oil makers mentioned in this chapter registered the designs of their olive oil bottles with the California Secretary of State in 1891. A number of Ellwood Cooper's bottles still exist. Cooper was the first large-scale commercial olive oil maker in California. On April 10, he registered his design. On June 5, Edward E. Goodrich, owner of El Quito Ranch in Los Gatos, registered his design. Some of his olive oil bottles are still in existence. In July, Frank Kimball, who grew olives about the same time as Cooper, also registered the design of his olive oil bottle. These registrations help document the history of particular oil makers. Even without registration, bottles can sometimes help establish the existence of an early oil maker who might otherwise be forgotten.

❦ EL QUITO OLIVE OIL BOTTLE.

Collecting olive oil bottles is a very practical form of history. The collectors learn as much as they can about the company that made the oil, and they foster studies in local history work as a result. There are bottle clubs in many counties that hold meetings several times a year to sell the bottles and exchange news.

One remarkable collection belongs to Dr. Thomas Jacobs, a dentist in San Francisco. It has been an avocation of his from a very early age. A few years ago, he bought all the bottles collected by another enthusiast, Mrs. Annette O'Connell (and her late husband) of Redwood City. They had carefully checked the history of many of the former olive oil companies in California. Based on the O'Connell collection, Dr. Jacobs is proud of owning one bottle (or more) of every manufacturer mentioned in Betty Zumwalt's book *Ketchup, Pickles, Sauces: Nineteenth Century Food in Glass,* a pioneering study of the subject.

the idea of making the fruit into olive oil. That too was a risky and highly competitive business in California, but if they did nothing, all their assets would perish.

Giovanni gave them land, and the brothers pooled their money to buy a small, galvanized iron building to use for making the oil. The cost of new oil presses was far more than they could afford, so they bought three used hydraulic presses from the tire industry. These worked just as well, as did a McCormick-Deering feed grinder they bought instead of a stone olive crusher. They understood what the tasks were and could substitute cheaper machines with the same function. The final steps of separation and filtration were all done by manual methods using gravity and cotton rather than an expensive centrifuge and machinery. After all, their forefathers in Italy had managed to accomplish the same ends with simple and unsophisticated equipment.

The Oberti brothers made very good, virgin olive oil right after they began. Selling this oil was another story. It was essentially impossible. When they could not get brokers or grocery chains to take it, they started to go door to door in California cities and towns with dense Italian populations. Even this only yielded a very small return. On some days, it cost them more to rent trucks than they made in sales. Only when a grocer in Gilroy unexpectedly sampled their oil and liked it, did they break through. In the long run, the door-to-door approach had been effective. The grocer ordered 150 gallons because his customers, who had enjoyed the oil sold to them at home by the Oberti brothers, wanted to be able to buy it in the grocery store. That was a turning point.

The brothers divided up their efforts. James led the marketing efforts. Once when he tried to get a foothold in the Chicago market, he was warned off very sternly. That territory was taken. Frank had the family "nose." Each morning a worker had to bring him an oil sample—the Obertis always blended their oil with several kinds of imported oil—and he would decide whether it met their standards. One of his tests was to fry an egg in it.

As their business expanded, the Oberti brothers needed more fruit. Not only did they produce olive oil, but had begun to can table olives as early as 1937. To meet this need, they started the Madera Corporation as a business vehicle. Adolph Martinelli, another Madera olive grower and oil maker, joined them in this. The additional exposure led to larger demand, and their oil production rose. By 1960, the demand for olive oil fell. The old galvanized iron building in Madera was torn down to build a cannery. They moved the oil section of the business to Oroville, where they bought the former Villa d'Oro plant in 1974 and rehabilitated it. James had purchased Villa d'Oro from the company's former bookkeeper, the owner's brother-in-law, after the owner had been deported to Italy. A Pieralisi machine from Italy, which reduces damage to the raw fruit and extracts the oil more efficiently than older methods, was installed to make the olive oil.

Until 1989, the Oberti family expanded their orchards hand in hand with their canning business. They grew olives in Madera, Merced, Fresno, Kings, and Tulare counties. They added a ripe olive processing unit after merging their operation into Tri Valley Growers, a

🍇 WOMEN FILLING OLIVE OIL BOTTLES
AT A FACTORY IN LOS ANGELES, CIRCA
1920.

cooperative. The firm they founded is now a part of Tri Valley Growers and is no longer independently known as the Oberti Olive Company. The Oberti family made olive oil for many years. Their story is described in more detail in chapter 7 ("Olive Processing Companies"), because they went on to can olives on a very large scale. Eventually processing table olives eclipsed the making of Oberti olive oil. Unfortunately, the Oberti brand of canned olives will no longer be in existence after 1999. Tri Valley Growers ended this activity after the last harvest of that year, but will continue some processing activity under an arrangement with Bell-Carter.

A little known olive oil maker, but a well-known film director, was Frank Capra, who worked in Fallbrook. His story is a significant variation on the theme of oil making—a theme that often emphasizes the importance of family relationships. In his autobiography, *The Name above the Title,* Capra described his early childhood in Bisaquino, Sicily, and his immigration to the United States in 1903 when he was six years old. His family members were farm workers. The eldest son had somehow managed to get himself to Los Angeles, and so the rest of the family packed up and joined him. Frank was too young even to have known the brother who influenced their decision to emigrate.

The Capra family left terrible poverty behind them but found that things were not so different in the Los Angeles of the early 1900s. The only good thing was that there was plenty of work for those who wanted it. Both parents worked ten- to twelve-hour days, six days a week—his father in a glass foundry, his mother in an olive oil factory, where she pasted labels on the cans and bottles as they came off the line. Capra did not say which olive oil factory it was, but Ralph Fusano, a former Lindsay Ripe Olive Company employee and a historian of the olive industry in California, guesses it could have been Matranga's. Capra's father and mother earned $12 and $10 per week respectively.

In memory of his father, Capra planted orchards on two properties he eventually acquired in Brentwood and Fallbrook, which is near San Diego, in the 1940s. He bought 150 fruit trees from the Armstrong Nursery, together with cuttings of grapevines and berry canes. At the peak of the McCarthy era in the 1950s, he took his family and lived quietly at the ranch in Fallbrook, working on the land.

Capra did not mention olive oil in his book, but Ralph Fusano remembers buying oil from the ranch on one or two occasions. Vladimir Sliskovich, a veteran olive oil maker, also remembers the Capra ranch and buying the oil from them. Frank Capra died in 1991 at the age of 94.

Giacinto Maselli, like Frank Capra, emigrated in 1903. Maselli was born in Bari, Italy, and became a very successful enologist there. He also managed his family's estates. In 1887, there were great financial upheavals in the Bari wine trade, and Maselli was unable to continue his work. He had to turn his property over to a receiver and take a paid position. For almost ten years, he tried to get his property back, but in the end he had to give it up.

Eventually Maselli came to the United States. Unlike many immigrants, he was not impoverished. He was well educated and accustomed to a comfortable life, but he had a rather difficult time getting established in California. He first sought a position with Italian Colony, a large winery in Fresno. Italian Colony did not take him on, and neither would Frank Borello, A. Mattei, nor Frank Giannini, other vintners. It is not clear why he could not get work in the wine industry, considering his knowledge and skill. Possibly it was a manifestation of the still continuing prejudice of northern Italians against those from the impoverished south. By 1907, Maselli was virtually forced to go into business for himself. He rented the Horseshoe Bend Ranch in Mariposa County and began to make olive oil. He had learned to do this in his native country.

In a few years, he became very successful at making olive oil, winning the first prize in the Panama-Pacific Exposition and many others in state and county fairs. An entry for Maselli Olive Oil first appeared in the Fresno City Directory in 1926. The address was listed as 2310 South Railroad Avenue, the same address as olive oil maker Vincent Florio's Log Cabin company. Maselli presumably bought Florio's business. (This might explain why there were no more entries for Florio after 1925.) Maselli Olive Oil continued to be listed in the directory for many years, both under the name Maselli and under the brand name Sphinx.

Eventually Maselli formed the G. Maselli and Sons Corporation and established two plants, one in Lindsay and one in Fresno. His four sons worked with him in his business. Renato D. Maselli had an olive oil plant in Orland. Leo and "Rip" (Ribelle) ran plants in Lindsay, the original family business. Another son, "Lat," worked in the Fresno plant. At one point, the Masellis sold oil to the Obertis.

I looked Maselli up in an old directory in the Madera County Library. The community respected him, and he was mentioned in one of the county histories, something that was rare for an Italian immigrant at that time.

Cristo Fusano, who like Giacinto Maselli was from Bari, Italy, came to Los Angeles in 1909 and went to work for the Sylmar Olive Company (previously the Los Angeles Olive Growers Association). This was apt because he had worked in the field before he came to the United States. He then left the Sylmar Olive Company and started his own firm. He began by making olive oil but later shifted to canning olives. In 1938, he installed a new olive processing plant. Cristo Fusano sold his oil strictly by mail order. The brand was initially called Fusano, but after the Second World War, he changed its name to San Fernando Valley Oil.

Fusano had seven children. His three sons are still involved in olive production, though not olive oil. They maintain an olive orchard of 230 acres near Lindsay. In 1977, they sold their father's business to the Lindsay Ripe Olive Company.

I have mentioned Ralph, one of Cristo Fusano's sons before. Ralph held several positions at the Lindsay Ripe Olive Company, and when it closed, he became a consultant to Early California Foods in Visalia. One of his most important activities has been to collect all the old documents he can find about the olive industry, especially the Lindsay Ripe Olive

Company's papers. He also safeguards several sets of documents collected by his former colleague George Powell. Both men shared a concern for the history of the olive industry in California.

My first contact with an olive oil maker, as I mentioned in the preface, was when I met Dan Sciabica of Modesto. While many others shifted from making olive oil to canning table olives, the Sciabicas were one of the families that continued only to make olive oil—often in the face of difficult challenges. In many ways, the Sciabica family exemplifies the capacity to survive and thrive in business, a quality shared by many in the olive industry.

Dan's grandfather, Nicola Sciabica, came from Marsala in Sicily. Marsala is a wine-making region well known for its dessert wine of the same name. Olives were also grown there. After Nicola arrived in the United States in 1911, he found his way to Connecticut. A few years later, in 1920, he went to San Francisco. He did not care for life in San Francisco and moved his family to the farming community of Modesto. The Sciabica family made their living in those early days by growing tomatoes, peaches, and grapes. They used the grape cuttings to fuel their bread oven. For a few years, they also dried some of their fruit. Initially they sold their produce on the streets of San Francisco. In 1936, Nicola, along with his son Joseph, decided to make olive oil, which Nicola had learned to do as a young

man in Marsala. At first, he bought a small ten-acre olive orchard in Carmichael, near Sacramento. Next, on his family farm of 134 acres in Modesto, he took out some of the peaches and grapes and planted another forty-five acres of olive trees. He bought Mission and Manzanillo trees from a nursery. These properties were sold before they could make any olive oil from these trees.

The Sciabicas intended to press oil themselves. Although they bought equipment for pressing in 1936, it was not used until 1941. At first, they took olives to the Oberti factory in Madera to be pressed. The Sciabicas were not the first people to make olive oil in Modesto. The Bambecino family's

🌿 THE SCIABICA FAMILY AT JOSEPH AND GEMMA'S GOLDEN ANNIVERSARY.

Modesto Olive Oil Company produced oil under the brand name of Barletta.

Nicola Sciabica had three sons, Joseph, Peter, and Vincent. The whole family worked in the fledgling business, which was called Nick Sciabica and Sons. Peter died young, but Vincent worked in the family business until the 1950s. Now Joseph runs the firm with his two sons, Nick and Dan. In his mid-eighties, Joseph gives no sign of slowing down and can be found at many olive oil fairs and events, wearing the signature turquoise vest and beret crocheted for him by his wife, Gemma, whom he married in 1943. All those who deal with him solely at a business level attest to his fearsome skill at driving very hard bargains. This is hardly surprising. Anyone who had to make a living from selling olive oil during the last phase of the depression would doubtless have absorbed some very effective lessons.

From the beginning, the Sciabicas made very good quality oil. They used ripe olives to ensure a sweet flavor and rich golden color. It was not an inexpensive product. One way Joseph survived was to take his oil to the Italian communities of New Jersey and Connecticut, and sell it door to door. That was in addition to the direct sales he made within a two hundred-mile radius of Modesto.

On one occasion while working in the East, Joseph tried to sell his olive oil in Philadelphia. He was told to stop immediately, because "This is a Bertolli town." He drove his rented truck back to Swedesboro, New Jersey, and began to deal with a Mr. Retino, the leader of the Italian (Sicilian) community in that town. Joseph was fluent in the dialect they spoke, and this cemented the connection. Former immigrant farmers getting ready to harvest crops of sweet potatoes in rural New Jersey would place orders with Joseph for the coming season's olive oil.

One of the obstacles the Sciabica family faced was foreign competition. Imported Spanish and Italian oil was always cheaper and remained their most difficult competition. As protection against this, Joseph maintained vineyards and, during really difficult times, augmented his income by selling grapes to Italian families.

Joseph's persistence paid off, and business became steadily successful. There was a turning point in 1980, when the health benefits of olive oil began to be publicized. The improvement in their business meant that they could expand a little. The Sciabicas bought the old Rocca Bella orchard, originally owned by Louis Sammis, in Calaveras County. They now grow Manzanillo, Picholine, and Mission olive trees there.

With the improvement in the market, the Sciabicas bought new Italian machinery a few years ago. The machine produces olive oil in a continuous process. This reduces the risk of damage to the fruit, which might possibly spoil the oil. They recently moved into additional much larger premises, still in Modesto, still within a short distance from home as before.

The Sciabicas continue to press oil for other people, but occasionally have difficulty finding enough fruit to press for their own oil, even in good years. The biennial bearing habit of the olive tree gives them a hard time too. The orchard in Calaveras County is a valuable asset in these times. In spite of that, Joseph Sciabica complained about the high cost of harvesting the fruit, something I heard from many others. It is another aspect of the California agrarian dilemma. Successive waves of poor immigrants have graduated from the harsh life of picking fruit on a seasonal basis, and the local populace does not want to do such a tough job. Machines are still not reliable enough and cannot work properly in old-fashioned orchards with the trees planted at inconvenient distances.

The increased number of effective outlets for their premium olive oil has not made the Sciabicas give up the steady methods of selling that kept them going in the bad periods.

They still have a booth at the San Francisco farmers' market every Saturday. Participation in many demonstrations and special events helps to promote their name and wares. Sciabica oil has won prizes and commendations, and this too improves sales. It also gained them entrée into the lucrative restaurant supply business. About 50 percent of their output is sold directly to restaurants.

When I visited the Sciabica family in March 1996, I asked Joseph what he thought about the trend of bringing in different types of olive trees from Italy. That did not bother him, nor does the increased level of competition in a field he and his family have held almost alone for so long. He is all for experimentation and innovation. The only thing he deplores is someone making shoddy, poor quality oil. That spoils the market for all olive oil makers.

The Sciabicas built their house in Modesto in 1925, and the family still lives in it. Nicola Sciabica's vineyards and orchards still surround the house, even though it now sits in the midst of a built-up residential area. Doubtless the developers are gnashing their teeth, but Joseph has no intention of selling his father's land.

I went to visit the Sciabicas soon after their move to the new premises. We had tried to set a time that would not be too inconvenient. Joseph was very preoccupied and not inclined to spend time with me at first, but his son Dan explained what I wanted to do and he very quickly made space for me. All the foregoing information came from our chat that day.

In addition to all the other information I gathered, my visit to the Sciabicas gave me a small taste of the everyday life of a close-knit oil-making family. Dan's wife, Genevieve, works in the business every day. She is an impressive woman and helped to smooth my way. After about an hour of interviews, Joseph had to go to the post office and get his mail. When he returned, he invited me to go home with him for lunch. The house is only about a mile away. Joseph's wife, Gemma, had prepared her usual lunch for a working day—feeding her husband, both her sons, one daughter-in-law, two grandchildren, and strays such as I was. It was a sumptuous repast of Sicilian dishes: pasta with pesto, spinach salad, sautéed peppers, sweet potatoes, Swiss chard with onions and tomatoes, homemade pizza, and several other dishes followed by a delicious ricotta pie whose crust had been made with a specially mild olive oil from the spring harvest. Homemade wine was handed round, but I had to drive home and feared taking any alcohol.

Everyone sat down to enjoy this meal after Dan said a simple grace. We ate gratefully, though Mrs. Sciabica did not really join in. She said she had had a large, late breakfast and was not hungry. The scene was one of enormous warmth and reminiscent of an older period, before the fragmentation of families and all the forces that pull them apart. Nick Sciabica's son John is a college student who works in the business during his vacations. John's mother is a schoolteacher, and was not able join us for lunch.

No obvious changes have been made to this house built in 1925, other than updating the kitchen about thirty years ago. Gemma Sciabica has all kinds of charming knickknacks scattered around the counters and furniture of her kitchen and attached dining room. The unpretentious character of the whole place spoke volumes for the continued adherence to the old standards of religion, work, family, and home that animates the Sciabicas.

When I left, Joseph picked me a big bag full of grapefruit and gave me a bunch of the sweet peas from Gemma's flower garden. I felt privileged to have shared in their family life, if only for a brief time.

Anyone who starts to make olive oil in the northern California area knows that the Sciabicas are wonderfully generous with time and help of a very practical sort. They have pressed the small opening harvests of a number of flourishing companies, before anyone knew if the new enterprise would survive or not. Ridgley Evers, a new oil maker about whom we will learn more later in this chapter, took his first fruits to them. At the suggestion of Darrell Corti, a highly regarded California expert in olive oil and other fundamental foods, Sciabica presses oil for Wente Brothers from their old Lucques trees. As long as the goal is to make the best olive oil, they are on your side. They do not fear competition.

During my visit, Dan Sciabica suggested that I ask his friend Jerry Padula to see if he could help me with my research. He showed me one of the early Padula Golden Eagle olive oil cans that he thought even Jerry did not have. I arranged to meet with Jerry, both to gather more general information about oil making in California and also to learn more about his own family's oil-making history.

Further south in the San Joaquin Valley in Porterville, the Padulas still make a fine oil with the brand name Golden Eagle. Jerry is the current senior partner, and his daughter Tracy is taking over the business from him. Jerry is a soft-spoken, gentle sort of man, extremely cordial and helpful. It was not the oil-pressing season, and the plant in Porterville was quiet. This was in contrast to the bustling Sciabica plant, which I had visited during the oil-pressing season, where Joseph Sciabica could barely make time to talk to me because of the demands of business. Only Jerry and Tracy were there the day I visited.

Jerry's grandfather Joseph worked for the Sylmar Olive Company near Los Angeles, as did Ralph Fusano's father, Cristo. (Cristo Fusano later went into his own business as we learned earlier in this chapter.) During the Second World War, Jerry's father, Louis, tried to stabilize olive oil prices by starting a cooperative for olive oil. Unfortunately, the Office of Price Administration put a very low cap on the prices, and most of the oil ended up on the black market. Jerry also had three other relatives in the olive oil business besides his father.

The Padulas currently use a French machine with a continuous screw press to make their oil. Louis originally had hydraulic presses. Much of their activity is pressing oil for other firms to bottle and sell with their own labels.

The older generations of Sciabicas and Padulas were friends for a long time, and the connection continues to the present. Jerry told me he remembered his father selling Nick Sciabica his first olive press many years ago. He went with Louis to Modesto to watch him install the new machines. It seemed foolish to the men gathered at the new plant to break a perfectly good bottle of wine over the machines to launch them, so they drank it instead.

The Sciabicas and Padulas represent the traditional, standard way olive oil has been made in California until recently. Marino Garbis of West Coast Products in Orland is another one who works in the same way. Careful honest workmanship characterizes their products.

West Coast Products Corporation/Orland Olive Oil Company began making olive oil in Orland in the late 1930s. Marino Garbis, part owner of this firm at present, was born in Greece but grew up in New York. His father imported olives from Greece. When Marino got married, he asked his father to find him work on the West Coast. The senior Mr. Garbis was a friend of the owner of West Coast Products, Everett A. Krackov, who agreed to hire Marino. In 1957, Marino and his wife came to California, where Marino joined the firm as manager.

Garbis made olive oil in Orland using fruit from Krackov's Woodlake Ranch and his own orchard in Shasta County. This orchard once belonged to the Ehmann Olive Company. Recently he decided to sell the orchard, because it no longer paid to grow the Sevillano olives there. The Ehmanns had grafted the old Mission trees over to Sevillanos. He also buys olives from other, smaller growers in Tehama and Glenn Counties.

West Coast Products used hydraulic presses that dated back to the 1930s. The only oil they made was extra virgin quality. Some was bottled for their own label. They sold the rest to other firms to be bottled under different labels. In 1997, they ceased making olive oil. West Coast Products now makes ethnic-style olives, such as Sicilian-style green and dry salt-cured olives.

Marino collects artifacts connected with the olive industry, and his office is chock-full of pictures, books, ornaments, and other treasures. He also has a good deal of olive lore in his head and is very generous about sharing it.

It is hard to say exactly when the recent movement to reproduce a European type of olive oil began in northern California. Several people seemed to come to it simultaneously. In the early 1990s, Lila Jaeger had the idea of starting an organization to share information and promote marketing. The California Olive Oil Council now has about 250 members. It is very eclectic, with enthusiastic amateurs from various professions plus professional olive oil makers, and some vintners.

The council is deeply concerned about the quality of the oil sold by its members. They sponsored a bill in the California state legislature to define a premium, extra-virgin California oil. It must be made from olives grown in California; it cannot be made from imported olives or be an imported oil simply repackaged and sold under a California label. The product will be accompanied by a certificate that attests to the origin and quality of the oil. SB 920 passed in 1997 and became law. Unless they can deliver such a guarantee, California oil makers are at the mercy of merchants who will adulterate the oil and pass it off as a premium California product, benefiting from the very high price the best oil commands.

The California vintners have been attracted to the notion that they could make a premium olive oil under their own estate names, to accompany their wines. The majority of the new olive growers are in Napa and Sonoma counties. This happened because most of the varietal wines originate in these counties and a number of people recognized the trend toward a signature California olive oil early.

Some winemakers make the oil themselves, using the fruit from old olive trees that have not been exploited again until recently. These trees were planted as ornamentals along driveways and as shade trees as well as for their fruit. Very few growers have invested in all the necessary oil-making equipment. In 1997, however, a consortium of growers in Glen Ellen, Sonoma County, created a state-of-the-art olive oil factory there. The factory, which uses the finest Italian machinery, is called The Olive Press. Here the fruit from orchards in Sonoma County can be turned into excellent oil without the delay and expense of a long journey to presses further south in the Central Valley.

Until now, most of the smaller growers arranged to have the fruit harvested and taken to one of the established firms, such as Nick Sciabica and Sons, for pressing and bottling under the vineyard's label. They will probably send it to the Glen Ellen facility in the future. As each new olive oil operation succeeds, the owners plant more olive trees. In a small number of cases, they are even replacing some of their vineyards with olive orchards.

The old trees being used for this oil are almost all Mission and, occasionally, Manzanillos. The Mission fruit makes an excellent California style of oil, though it does not taste like Tuscan oil from Lucca. At this level, things get very subjective. No one can argue usefully about how something tastes to another person, but the Lucchese oil does not have its reputation for nothing. It has become a challenge to the California producers. They want to make oil in the Tuscan style.

The new ambitious standards have been brought about by many separate personal experiences, almost always because of repeated travel to Italy. No one can forget the beauty of the Tuscan landscape. In addition, food in Italy tastes completely different from that in the United States, fresher, closer to the actual essence of the raw materials. No one forgets that either. A few obstinate souls have become obsessed with re-creating both the beauty and the taste of Tuscany in California. In order to do that, some of the olive oil makers are obtaining different varieties of trees from France and Italy. They believe that one must start with Tuscan varieties in order to make a Tuscan style of oil.

Once the trees are planted, the imponderables of soil and climate take over. They are bound to make a difference in the flavor of the oil. The nineteenth-century growers learned this, and the experts recorded their observations. It is a risk the modern growers are willing to run.

There is a lot of discussion about single-source oil (from one type of tree) versus blends. The classical Tuscan oil is a blend. Unlike wine, it is probably not such a good idea to use only one variety of olive. There has never been a period in which a truly varietal olive oil

❧ Labeling and packing olive oil bottles at the Old Mission Olive Oil Company, San Diego, in the early twentieth century.

was a serious contender for the highest honors, although the concept was instrumental in getting many people started. If one is serious about reproducing the true Tuscan oils, a single variety cannot provide depth and complexity of flavor in the same way as a blend.

It is most likely that the distinctive flavor and appearance of Tuscan oil owe more to the stage at which the fruit is picked almost more than any other single characteristic. The pale green color and sharp tang both reflect immaturity. The reason for this state of affairs has little to do with tradition, but everything with necessity. After the Second World War, Italian farmers were faced with making oil from trees that had been neglected. Previously, the ideal Italian oil had been golden yellow and very mellow in taste. (Charles Morgan in his novel *Sparkenbrook* extolled the virtues of golden Lucchese oil in the 1930s.) Now they had to hurry the process and began to pick the olives earlier in the cycle. The resulting oil was marketed as representing the unique signature of Tuscany. Thus are traditions born.

Ridgely Evers is typical of the new wave of California growers. He is a man with prodigious energy and strong feelings about life, a life that lists Lucchese olive oil among its essentials. His primary work is in the computer industry. In 1982, he bought some land in Healdsburg, Sonoma County. He began by remodeling the house on it. At the same time, he knew that he wanted to use the rest of it for agriculture but had not yet formed any clear idea of what he should grow.

He decided not to plant grapevines. It was a period when vineyards were not doing well financially. On one of his trips to Tuscany a few years later, he saw the olive trees there with new eyes. (Tuscany has three major oil growing regions. One is in Chianti with the vineyards, another is around Lucca. The third is in the southern region of Tuscany called the "Maremma," near Grosetto.) Together with the tall narrow cypresses, olive trees are the signature of the landscape. It occurred to him that here was a noble undertaking. He would plant olives and make oil in the Tuscan style.

Ridgely found the farm where the oil he liked best was made. It was in the Lucca area. At the Fattoria Mansi Bernardini in Segromino in Monte, he requested cuttings of the four varieties of olive trees from which this blend of Lucchese oil is prepared: Frantoio, Leccino, Maurino, and Pendulino (or Pendolino). He then returned to Sonoma County to prepare his land for the planting. Meanwhile back in Tuscany, the wheels were turning slowly.

He had bought 2,400 two-year-old trees, to be sent from Milan through Frankfurt to San Francisco. That was what he thought was going to happen, but the dispatchers had other ideas. They considered it unpatriotic to use a German airline when Alitalia flies to California directly. How far could Los Angeles be from San Francisco? Accordingly, the trees were sent to Los Angeles. Very late one night he received a call from the customs official at the Los Angeles International Airport to come and deal with his trees. The official told him ominously that there was still soil attached to the roots of said trees.

One of the USDA's strictest regulations prohibits the importation of soil because of all the pests that lurk in it. One may import plant material under very careful conditions, but it has to be certified free of soil. In some ways this resembles Portia's challenge to Shylock. Getting the trees without any soil is like getting a pound of flesh without any blood. Ridgely was going to have to take care of this matter.

Among his other characteristics, Ridgely is very resourceful. He rousted out some old friends in Los Angeles, and they obligingly went over to the airport in the wee hours to clear up the problem. He told me they rinsed off all the soil, and the trees were allowed to be sent on to San Francisco.

The cuttings arrived before Ridgely had completed the soil preparation, so they were put into pots and left outside for the winter. There was a bad freeze that year, but most of the young olive trees were spared because the pots froze solid and the ice acted as an insulator. Later he planted them in their permanent sites and watched them grow and develop. After the losses, and subtracting the group of trees he gave to some friends, there were twelve hundred trees in the ground.

Even within one property, there are substantial differences in the soil from place to place. The trees Ridgely planted at the same time are markedly different in size, depending on where he put them. All of them are beautiful, with tender gray-green leaves on spindly, young flexible branches. Ridgely is carefully controlling the height of the trees so that the olives can be picked by standing on the ground. Using ladders leads to many difficulties.

Ridgely Evers has harvested five crops so far. Each one was larger than the last, a sign that the trees are maturing. In order to reproduce the Lucchese character in the oil, Ridgely has adopted the same blend as the original Tuscan farm: 50 percent Leccino, 25 percent Frantoio, 15 percent Maurino, and 10 percent Pendulina. If he wished to make an oil more reminiscent of Chianti, the proportions would be reversed. The dominant ingredient would be Frantoio.

Nan McEvoy is another Californian who was enthralled by the possibility of making a Tuscan oil. She too had not started out with the intention of growing olive trees. Mrs. McEvoy wanted a rural retreat where she could gather her family together at times and relax after their busy lives in the city. Once she bought her land in western Marin County, she found that the authorities would only permit her to alter its buildings if she declared an agricultural purpose. Western Marin is zoned strictly for agricultural use.

Mrs. McEvoy had grown up in California, and her father, among his other possessions, had owned a cattle ranch. She did not want to raise cattle. Sheep were not a good idea, because coyotes steal too many of the lambs each season. Her thoughts then turned to orchards, and she happened to go to Italy just as she had to make up her mind. The olive trees suddenly struck her in a new light. She returned from Italy with the idea of growing olives and making oil.

As she began to look into the feasibility of doing this, she turned to local experts. The pomologists at the University of California at Davis thought her land was not suitable because it is very close to the sea, with a great deal of fog and cool wind. They also believed it would cost an enormous amount of money to get the land properly contoured to grow the trees. She decided to ask an Italian expert for his opinion.

Mrs. McEvoy met with Dr. Maurizio Castelli, a recognized expert in the production of olive oil, in Chianti. They conversed through an interpreter, but he clearly understood what she wanted and told her that olive trees would do very well on the land she described. His faith heartened her and she decided to go ahead.

Dr. Castelli chose the varieties of trees and arranged for her to receive the cuttings. Mrs. McEvoy bought Frantoio, Leccino, Pendulina, Maurino, Coratina, and Leccio del Corno varieties. They came from Italy as bare sticks, and she did not have the same problem as Ridgely Evers with USDA rules. The only requirement was that she not allow any tree to leave her property for two years. Under Castelli's guidance from afar, her staff prepared the land and planted the trees. He has since come over to California twice a year to follow her progress and make any modifications that are necessary.

The olive trees have done very well. The wind can be a problem, but the trees are bearing ahead of schedule, and very prolifically. Another difficulty was the unusual heat during the blossom- and fruit-setting periods in 1997. The farm adviser from the University of California at Davis has helped Mrs. McEvoy overcome some of these problems.

All these efforts are dictated because of one crucial fact, the "nakedness" of olive oil. Nothing is done to the fruit besides the pressing, and so the fruit is destiny. If everything is done properly, good fruit should engender good oil. Wonderful fruit by analogy should produce wonderful oil. The oil should taste solely of the olive that was used to make it. Grapes can be manipulated enough to make different wines from the same fruit at the same period. This is not true of olive oil.

A slight variation on this "nakedness" of the oil theme has been offered by Napa Valley Kitchens, which is part of a holding company connected with the popular restaurant Tra Vigne in St. Helena. It also reflects the recent regeneration of interest in oil making. The restaurant's chef, Michael Chiarello, developed some flavored oils sold as "Consorzio." The olive oil is made from the company's own Mission and Manzanillo olives. Napa Valley Kitchens bought the orchard in Butte County that once belonged to Joseph Cooper, and his father before him, in 1995. The oils are pressed, using the hammer mill process, in their factory in Corning, under the careful management of Bob Singletary.

Napa Valley Kitchens is at the forefront of the marketing changes that are promoting California oils. Flavorings such as rosemary and basil are one innovation taking advantage of a new interest in fine cooking and olive oil. On a recent trip to London, I saw their oil prominently displayed at Fortnum and Mason, a fashionable and very expensive shop. This is quite a contrast to the days when oil makers had difficulty selling their wares.

Olive oil making in California has come a long way since the early days of the missions. There have been periods when businesses have thrived and periods when it was difficult just to survive. The recent move toward varietals and the importation of new varieties of trees has added a new and lively dimension to the story of olive oil in California. The oil-making business has evolved greatly from its early beginnings, and one of the factors in its evolution was the growth of table-olive processing. In the next chapter, we will learn about the olive processing companies in California—how they came to be and how they themselves have evolved in face of market changes and environmental challenges.

Olive Oil Classifications

There is a strong movement afoot to standardize olive oil categories internationally. The International Olive Oil Council leads the way in this endeavor. Without a reliable classification, no valid comparisons can be made and fraudulent claims cannot be exposed.

The most recent classification system contains four main grades with a total of seven subcategories. The main grades are "virgin," "refined olive oil," "olive oil," and "pomace oil." Within the designation "virgin olive oil" are the subcategories "extra virgin," "virgin," "virgin corriente" (ordinary virgin), and "lampante" (lamp oil). "Refined olive oil" and "olive oil" have no subcategories. "Pomace oil" contains three subcategories: "crude pomace oil" (industrial), "refined pomace oil," and "pomace oil."

The concentration of oleic acid, a substance that occurs naturally in the olive fruit, is one of the principal determinants for defining each category. The other is the degree of defects permitted. "Extra virgin" olive oil must have 1 percent or less by weight of oleic acid. The concentration of oleic acid in the very best "extra virgin" oils may be as low as 0.1 percent.

❧ "Virgin" olive oil contains 2 percent oleic acid by weight. "Virgin corriente" and "lampante" oils both have 3.3 percent of oleic acid. These three classes of olive oil are not available to the consumer but are used in various industrial processes, such as making soap or for certain textiles.

❧ "Refined olive oil" has been completely "rectified," which means that almost all the chemical markers of its origin from the olive have been erased. The oil becomes, as it were, tabula rasa. It has only 0.5 percent oleic acid. This product is the basis of "extra light" oil. By adding about 2 percent of extra virgin oil to this liquid, the category of "olive oil" is created. "Olive oil" is widely sold in food stores everywhere.

(continued)

❧ "Pomace" is the solid matter that is left after olives are crushed and the oil extracted. Further extraction leads to the formation of "crude pomace oil" (oleic acid content 1.5 percent), "refined pomace oil" (0.5 percent oleic acid), and "pomace oil" (1.5 percent oleic acid content). These latter classes are also industrial.

❧   ❧   ❧

The other standard for true "extra virgin" olive oil is the degree of defect permitted. Defects are unpleasant smells such as mustiness or a rancid taste. Defects are identified by smelling and tasting the oil. In rating olive oil, the taster starts with the hypothesis that it will be perfect, with all its identifying components in perfect balance. These include freshness, spiciness, fruitiness, and a hint of attractive bitterness, which lasts very briefly. Fruitiness is particularly important in the rating process. Desirable fruit flavors are similar to those of green tomatoes, green apples, artichokes, and grass.

Any smell, flavor, or taste that affects this harmony reduces the quality rating. Professional olive oil tasters can detect exceedingly subtle differences. Scoring goes down from ten. For example, the international definition of "extra virgin" oil states that the score must be above 6.5 for it to be designated "extra virgin." The very finest oils seldom score that low, because they have few defects. The goal of the olive oil maker is to produce oil with no defects, and this is attained quite frequently.

The University of California at Davis trains reliable olive oil tasters in California to conform to the International Olive Oil Council's standards, so reproducible results can be achieved. Experts like Paul Vossen, University of California cooperative agricultural extension agent for Sonoma County, and Darrell Corti of Sacramento both participate in this effort. These men have spent a lot of time in Spain and Italy learning about the methods of tasting.

Any elaborate classification system, such as this one, can be manipulated. Consumers seldom carry all these refinements in their heads. Very skillful packaging and pricing that has little relation to true value compounds the complexity. In other words, consumers can easily be seduced into thinking that a very expensive oil in a beautiful bottle is also the very best quality. From that point, it is then sometimes only a short step to outright, intentional deception.

Deception can be accomplished in two ways: by adulterating imported olive oils with other vegetable oils or by using olive oil that does not meet the clearly defined standards for the "virgin" product. When the prime quality product is in short supply, purveyors are tempted to make up the difference with cheaper oil simply to fulfill their contracts. Even when the finer grade of oil is plentiful, this is still a temptation. The price, of course, remains the same, and this is fraud.

A few years ago, a scandal hit the international olive oil market. Due to a prolonged drought (1990–95), Spain was only able to harvest about 20 percent of its usual crop. Even in normal times, much of the oil sold as "Italian" actually comes from Spain. Italy cannot physically produce the volume of oil sold under its labels. During the drought, a cheaper oil from Turkey was imported into Spain, and then sent to Italy. It was palmed off as the premium product. Another case during this period named three importers for adulterating their olive oil with the cheaper canola, soy, corn, and cottonseed oils.

A hundred years ago, the burgeoning California olive oil industry ran into both these problems, the low cost of imported oils and adulteration at home and abroad. The details were different, but the lessons were the same. In some ways, using liquid tallow, a very unhealthy form of fat, to adulterate the olive oil was even worse than the ruses adopted in the current era. Today's growers are moving swiftly to prevent such scandals from tarnishing their image.

7

Olive Processing Companies

By the time of the First World War, California olive oil had declined to a very small industry. The transition to canning table olives, which had started at the end of the nineteenth century, now rapidly overtook the parent industry and left it far behind. Increasingly large proportions of the California olive crop were going to the canneries. At present, 99 percent of the crop is devoted to processing table olives. For this reason it is essential to follow the course of the fruit as it undergoes its transformation. Even though olive growing started in order to make olive oil, one cannot ignore the fact that the industry has been completely transformed.

Olive processing companies have three very basic things in common: olives, a method of processing them, and people who do the processing. In this chapter, we will look at the process and some of the people who have played, and continue to play, an important part in olive processing in California.

An initial question that must be answered before the process of curing begins is exactly when and how to pick the fruit. Although the growers are responsible for picking, the processors have a vested interest in seeing that the fruit is picked to suit them. Large canning firms have a "field man," who is very knowledgeable about each

❀ CONVEYOR BELT MOVING FRUIT
   THROUGH A FACTORY, EARLY
   TWENTIETH CENTURY.

orchard's methods and practices. He is the intermediary between grower and processor, and to a large extent, his skill determines the success or failure of the operation. He sees the fruit as it is brought to the canner's yard and decides whether it meets his needs. During the summer and early fall, the growers bring him bulletins about the prospective crop, and he knows more or less what he will receive from each grower.

Once the olives have been picked, the curing is done in a series of steps, each one extremely critical. The degree of ripeness is a key factor, because it determines taste and texture. Although the name is "California ripe olive," this is actually a misnomer. The olives cannot be successfully canned if in fact they are completely ripe. Fully ripe olives are used to press olive oil, but even in that case, the sharper taste of unripe, green olives is becoming more fashionable. It is different for the ethnic or salt- and oil-curing methods. Mature, ripe olives must be used for the Greek style.

For the canner, if the raw olives are too green, the taste is not fully developed, but the texture holds up well. At the next level of ripeness, there is more flavor, but the fruit is softer and it deteriorates with processing. The majority of processors prefer the less ripe fruit, but one company, Graber, has persisted in using fruit at a more advanced stage since the firm was begun by Clifford Graber in 1894. Graber olives are distinctive in appearance, mottled light brown and not shiny black, which is how the standard method cures them. They are also very mild in flavor. People in New York and other East Coast communities enjoy this brand.

After picking and before processing begins, of course, olives must be transported to the processing plants. In earlier days, processing plants were located in close proximity to olive orchards. Today olives are transported all over the Central Valley. Companies in the middle part of the valley obtain olives from Corning and Orland, in addition to the crops they buy locally, while firms at either end of the valley get some of their fruit from the other end of the valley. For example, Musco Olive Products' principal plant is in Tracy, San Joaquin County. Staff at their Orland center receive the olives from the northern part of the valley, hold them, and arrange to have them transported to Tracy in good condition. The next steps in curing the fruit are all done in Tracy. It does not matter where the olives start out or where they go, the process is the same.

After the fruit is received at the canner's yard, it should ideally start to go through the curing process immediately, but when there is a large inventory, the olives have to be held for a while. Until recently, enormous tanks filled with a saline solution were used for storing the olives until they could be cured. The amount of salt and level of salinity were very important variables. Too much or too little affected the olives badly. The tanks were left open to the air. The records of the California Olive Association's technical conferences show how much work went into this decision. When the plants were first in operation the tanks were open, but then state inspectors were concerned about dirt and insects getting into them and recommended they be covered. Many types of cover were tried, but whatever was done ended up by damaging the olives. The change in temperature and evaporation affected their chemistry, and many olives were lost to fungal infection. Finally the recommendation to go back to keeping the tanks open was accepted and the problem abated.

In more recent times, methods to store the olives without using salt have been perfected. By making a dilute solution of lactic and acetic acids, olives can be stored without losing weight or texture and in this case can be safely covered. The olives do not ferment but simply remain static until they can go to the next stage. This all improves the environmental compliance of the processing plants.

Before anything can be done with the fruit, whether fresh or held over in liquid, it must be inspected by the joint Federal-State Inspection Service. This inspection, which is paid for by the processor, is one of the tasks authorized by the federal marketing order.

Following the inspection, the raw fruit is sized and graded. Sizing machines are quite simple; they divide the large, medium, and small olives from each other by means of a series of graduated holes as water carries them along in flumes. The need to achieve a uniform and consistent grade is a good reason to take fruit from a grower with a long track record and in large quantities. Picking over a small lot of fruit from an uncertain source is time consuming and may lead to variation in quality.

The field man has to answer to state inspectors about compliance with environmental regulations based on the grower's records. Toxins and pesticides are the principal cause for concern. If this history is unknown, the olives must be rejected. After the olives have been graded and weighed—this weight is the basis of payment for the grower—the inspector certifies them and processing can begin.

Oleopurein is an amygdaloid, the chemical that makes olives so bitter, rendering the olive inedible until it is cured. Removing it is a key part of the curing process, requiring considerable skill and expertise. When lye is used, its concentration is titrated (adjusted) very carefully, usually between 1 and 2 percent. The longer the olives have been held, the weaker the solution of lye required. The lye must go through the flesh of the fruit slowly, but stop just before it reaches the pit, or center. This process is assisted by pricking the skin of the olives with very fine needles to make tiny holes.

The pits are removed after this is done. It was found that removing the pits before the lye treatment would spoil the cure. As the lye process continues, the olive begins to turn darker. Light and air make the olive black. At this stage the olives are intermittently covered to control the amount of light and air, and thus the degree of color. The same change in color occurs when water is the sole agent for leaching out the bitterness.

After all traces of the lye are washed out with plain water, the olives are put into brine where the pickling takes place. For the black ripe type, this stage lasts up to seven days. Small quantities of lactic acid occur spontaneously during this stage from the transformation of the sugar in the fruit. To turn the olives into "green ripe," curing has to continue in the dark to prevent the change in color.

🌿 A modern processing plant: olives awaiting processing at the Musco Olive Products plant in Tracy, California.

All these stages sound simple in the telling, but in reality many choices and decisions need to be made continually, and their results affect the quality of the olives very materially. The canners have an olive specialist in charge of the process—someone who has the skill and experience to handle all eventualities—just as there is a wine maker in a vineyard.

Once these steps have been completed, the olives are sorted again. The pits are removed and the olives are sliced or chopped if required. Then they are ready for the cans. The range of can sizes was ultimately decided upon by the California Olive Association after considerable discussion over several years. Initially, there was no standardization of cans, but the retailers wanted it. All the other fruit and vegetables, regardless of the brand, came in standard-sized cans. Things that seem self-evident to us today were not always so. Besides the size, the composition of the metals and the thickness of the can, as well as its contents, are all very important for safety and purity.

The last crucial step is the "retorting," in which the sealed cans are heated to 240 degrees Fahrenheit for forty minutes. Some minor changes have been allowed by the health department, using higher temperatures for shorter periods in some plants, but the essentials will never really change.

After this is done, the cans are labeled and packed in cases. Large processors such as Bell-Carter pack olives for numerous other smaller companies, as well as the house brands for supermarkets. They also put out olives using the brands of their predecessors, such as Lindsay Ripe Olive, which they bought in 1990, to stimulate sales.

All processors today face the same difficulties: they have to comply with environmental regulations, keep the olives sound until they can be processed, and minimize the use of salt wherever they can. These difficulties are in addition to the ongoing need to acquire fruit in both the quantity and quality needed, find and retain adequate and skilled labor, and deal with all the other realities of running a business. In the stories that follow, we will see how four olive processing companies—Bell-Carter, Oberti Olive Company, Lindsay Ripe Olive Company, and Musco Olive Products—came into being and how they have dealt with their common problems.

Arthur Bell and his brother Henry bought an olive orchard in Reedley, near Fresno, in 1912. Although they started out solely as growers, by 1930 they recognized that they would have to do more if they were to stay in business. They would have to cure the olives, pack them, and distribute them. The Bells chose to be independent rather than go in with one of the large cooperatives.

Arthur Bell began the Bell Packing Company in a disused cleaner's store in Berkeley. It was not an auspicious time for new endeavors. He did all the work himself at first. The old cleaning vats were useful for washing the olives. He packed the cured fruit too.

In spite of the depression, he was able to secure a number of good accounts. Soon he could afford to pay a woman to do secretarial work but also to double as the olive chopper at times. Arthur Bell developed the chopped olive. Selling olives already chopped was a useful innovation for that period, since chopped olive sandwiches and salad dressing with chopped olives in it were very popular items. The "islands" in Thousand Island dressing were chopped olives. A busy chef was glad to buy them in such a convenient form. It saved him from paying someone to do that job in a rushed and crazy kitchen.

Arthur Bell also invented, or assisted in the invention of, an early prototype pitting machine, which made it simpler to pit the olives before processing them. The company grew and changed from glass jars to metal cans. In the late 1930s, Bell produced seven thousand cans a year. Daniel Carter, his stepson, joined the firm in 1938 to supervise the Berkeley operation. That allowed Mr. Bell to go on long marketing trips across the United States.

The advent of the Second World War meant that they had to retrench. Daniel Carter went into the Navy, leaving a void in the Berkeley plant. Metal was in such short supply that they had to revert to using glass jars. In spite of these difficulties, Bell-Carter remained active and kept its share of the market.

Once the war was over, Daniel Carter returned to work, and the company went back to its pattern of growth and expansion. Carter's two sons, Tim and Jud, entered the business in 1964, and continued to develop and build it even more. After buying the Maywood Packing Company's plant in Corning in 1978, they moved everything up to Corning where it remains today. The Carter family also moved, from the Bay Area to the Sacramento Valley.

During the past decades, Bell-Carter has expanded and grown by acquiring Olives Incorporated, other firms in Corning, and the Lindsay Ripe Olive Company in the San Joaquin Valley. In Corning, the self-designated "Olive Capital" in the northern part of the Sacramento Valley, the only canning company left is Bell-Carter. There were eight canners in the town's heyday. As they ceased working either because of financial losses or because there were no successors to take them over, Bell-Carter absorbed them one by one.

Bell-Carter's main receiving station is on Fig Lane, a quiet, narrow street on the edge of the town, across the railroad tracks from the main part of town. The only other large, industrial building on that street is the Napa Valley Kitchens' plant, where the herb-flavored Consorzio olive oils are made. Otherwise, it is a street of very modest houses, and it quickly peters off into open countryside. The two olive plants are just a few yards from each other.

In the canned olive world, Corning is a one-company town now. About 250 growers supply Bell-Carter with fruit. Bell-Carter has never returned to growing its own olives. The drive to shift from the large Sevillano olives, originally planted by Warren Woodson, to the now more desirable Manzanillo olives comes from the marketing needs of Bell-Carter.

Like Arthur and Henry Bell, the Oberti family also began business in the San Joaquin Valley, but its activities are still there. Madera is the town in which Oberti is a well-known name. Giovanni Oberti and his wife, Maria, started growing olives in the Madera area after immigrating to California from Italy early in the century. Some of their history is also included in the chapter on olive oil. (See chapter 6.)

The Oberti family added a plant to can table olives on their property in Madera quite early on, in 1937. They also bought the Villa d'Oro plant in Oroville. The market for canned ripe California olives had begun to improve late in the 1930s after the double assault of the botulism crisis and the Great Depression, although it was still a bit shaky. For about twenty years, Oberti continued to make both olive oil and canned ripe olives. In addition to the standard California ripe olive, they also processed "Spanish" style olives.

In about 1960, the Oberti company ceased making olive oil, and closed that operation. From then on the Madera plant only put out canned ripe olives. Gary Oberti, grandson of Giovanni, and son of James Oberti, one of the principals in the business, decided to return to pressing olive oil independently early in the 1970s and did that until recently in Madera.

After a fairly short time solely in the canned olive business, the Oberti family sold the processing plant to Tri Valley Growers, a cooperative which has owned it ever since. Oberti did not give up their olive orchards, but sold the fruit to the new owners. Tri Valley Growers continued to use the brand name "Oberti" as it was already so very well-known. This company ceased its olive canning operations at the end of the 1999 season. No more olives will be sold under the Oberti label. Growers will sell their fruit to Bell-Carter. Another Central Valley landmark is going by the way.

The Oberti Olive Company employed a chemist, Marvin Martin, for many years who carried a great deal of responsibility for the end result. He was the plant manager, the man who could handle any problem that arose and ensure that the olives were properly cured and of consistent quality every time.

Marvin Martin has been president of the California Olive Association twice, an acknowledgment of his skill and understanding of olive processing in all its aspects. It was Martin who came up with an innovative way to recycle the salt in the brine used in olive processing and thus reduce the environmental exposure so damaging to all the olive processing businesses. The process involves bacteriological degrading of the excess salt. Once soil becomes permeated with high concentrations of sodium chloride, it can no longer support the growth of crops.

James Oberti's son Gary represents the third generation in the olive business, though he is no longer employed directly by Tri Valley Growers. He grows olives in his family orchard and vineyard, and is active in the olive trade organizations.

A bit further south of Madera and the Obertis, olive growing expanded in southern Tulare County. Here the town of Lindsay became the center of the olive-growing district. The early editions of the *Lindsay Gazette* contain steadily increasing references to growing olives from the first issues in 1901 over the next fifteen years. Curiously, although J. J. Cairns and Senator Berry were known to be the first to plant olive trees in the area, they carefully avoided any publicity on this subject. Harold Schutt, the general manager of the Lindsay Ripe Olive Company and a keen local historian, commented that they were very shrewd and cautious. They did not want to be ridiculed if the olive trees were unsuccessful.

The other growers were not as reticent about publicity as Cairns and Berry were. According to the *Lindsay Gazette,* at least six men planted orchards in 1908: W. B. Kiggens (five acres), F. S. Wormer (five acres), G. W. Fletcher (ten acres), Burr Brothers (twenty acres), J. W. Irwin (seven acres), and J. F. Sophy (fifteen acres). All these new plantings were fairly far out, because orange groves occupied the land closer to town. One year later, Fletcher planted another ten acres and sold the entire twenty acres to C. P. Grogan of Los Angeles for $3,000. At that point, olives were fetching $160 a ton. Over this changing period, the price varied between $75 and $300 a ton.

The big companies like Libby and Heinz were thinking about building canneries in the early years of the twentieth century, but held off because fruit remained in short supply. One report indicated that 1,500 acres were planted with olives, perhaps to act as an inducement to the large companies to build facilities in the community, but that does not fit with the numbers available.

In 1916, a small group of growers in southern Tulare County wanted to start their own canning operation. The growers were reacting to the fluctuation in prices paid by other canners. In good years, the price was low; when fruit became scarce, the price rose. More serious than price fluctuation was the appearance of favoritism. Three men complained at a meeting in 1914 that they had each sold olives to the same canner through the same buyer and of probably the same quality. One received $139 per ton, another received $83 per ton, and the third received a price somewhere in between. They believed they could do it better themselves.

The growers decided to start an organization called Lindsay Ripe Olive Association, intending it to be a cooperative. The town of Lindsay was an obvious place to start such an enterprise. Committees looked into the feasibility of doing this and obtained letters of support from one or two large canners, offering to buy their output once they started. The original incorporators were A. M. Drew, L. H. Emery (who had been in charge of pickling olives at STOMA, the Southern Tulare Olive Marketing Association), R. D. Adams, George McLees, and R. C. Winther. The group built a plant near a source of water and close to the Southern Pacific Railroad.

Their activities were fairly modest at the beginning. A newspaper article in November 1916 noted that two dozen people were employed there, twelve men and twelve women. It sputtered along for several years, with changes in management and an occasional leasing of the premises to tomato and other vegetable packers. The company competed with the cannery of California Associated Olive Growers Incorporated.

Some of the brokers who handled Lindsay's olives introduced the directors to a W. O. Johnson, and in 1920, Mr. Johnson assumed control of the plant. He had considerable experience from his work in Los Angeles, particularly in sales. The name was changed to Lindsay Ripe Olive Company in 1921, and a new shareholders' agreement was developed. The number of shares was tied to olive acreage, and an exclusive contract for four years was enforced. The grower could not sell any fruit to any other canner during that period. A schedule of prices accompanied these changes. At times, when they needed extra fruit, they brought it in from Corning and Oroville by rail.

Also in 1921, the plant was rebuilt to accommodate the increased amount of fruit. Johnson developed wonderful sales over the next few years, managing to reach the populations of Mediterranean descent in big cities all over the country. The plant's capacity had to be tripled because more growers joined. By 1923, the floor space had been enlarged again, so that the claim of being the largest olive packer in the state was true.

Johnson continued to do very well, but sometime during the next ten years, he fell out with the board over his compensation. In 1933, they reluctantly let him go. The board reorganized again, this time into a standard cooperative. They appointed one of the directors, Earle Houghton, to be manager temporarily. The initial intention was to find a new chief executive, but Houghton remained on the job until 1955.

Earle Houghton was a remarkable man. A former colleague, Bob Webster, spoke about him at an olive meeting. Houghton had grown up on a farm in Iowa in a prosperous family. During the First World War, he joined the Army Air Corps and learned to fly in France. One of his passengers during his last mission was a war photographer. Many years later that photographer published a story about Houghton's heroism in 1917. He brought his plane and his passenger safely back to the airstrip in spite of being severely wounded and bleeding profusely.

This streak of self-confidence made him a formidable manager. He was able to manipulate the prices paid for olives by taking on a line of credit to back his deals with the growers. The other olive companies were startled to see how much he paid for fresh olives, and the ruse worked so well he never had to draw on the money from the bank. The maneuver pushed the price of processed olives much higher, the goal he sought in the first place.

A large and strong man, Houghton made himself felt. Staff members had to justify their recommendations and present solutions to any problems they noted. In spite of this tough surface, and a seeming indifference to the niceties of formal religion, those who knew him were aware that he gave frequently but unobtrusively to many charities, including to any of the workers at the plant who got into difficulties. It was also notable that he remained on good terms with all his constituencies, especially the board.

Houghton not only maintained the current volume of sales; he also wanted to get into "secondary" markets to increase sales further. When the salespeople were reviewing their program, his sole contribution was to point out that they had only sold one case of olives in

Alabama that season. He planned to improve on that. Much of his time went into marketing trips all over the country. They were very successful.

One of Houghton's concerns was to improve the quality of their product. Two of the men who worked with him on this, Richard Ball and Edward van Dellen, later left to start their own business, the Pacific Olive Company.

Another task Houghton set for himself was to develop a mechanical olive-pitting machine. Selling the olive already pitted was a sure way to increase sales, but pitting olives by hand was prohibitively expensive. He was adamant that any such machine should have a minimum of moving parts. Bob Webster, a senior employee of the Lindsay Ripe Olive Company, mentioned that Houghton had a strongly mechanical turn of mind and had studied engineering at college. This knowledge had been supplemented by his experience with airplanes in the war.

One of the mechanics at the plant, Herbert Kagley, invented a pilot machine and later, two engineers, Edward Drake and Fred Alberti, improved it. This machine pitted 1,000 olives per minute. It went into immediate use and sales definitely picked up.

Almost simultaneously, George Ashlok, an industrial engineer working with other stone fruits, adapted his cherry-pitting machine for olives. Nowadays olive companies use either type. (Harold Schutt noted that he did not think schools would have bought unpitted olives for their lunch programs. He could just see the mayhem in the lunchrooms with flying olive pits.)

Following Houghton, Thomas Read became manager, and after him, Richard Henderson, who took over in 1960. Even with good managers, the board always retained full authority for the direction of the cooperative, and members served for long periods of time. There were only four presidents from its inception until 1960: A. M. Drew, C. E. Goodale, Thomas Pogue, and Roy R. McLain.

It was after 1960 that the full force of environmental requirements came into effect. The proper disposal of waste effluent was the one that affected the food canning industry the most. The leadership had trouble in dealing with both this and increased competition from foreign imports. The Achilles heel of such an organization is its dependence on a single product. There was no way to redistribute costs or cushion losses. The Lindsay Ripe Olive Company struggled for some time to meet the new requirements, but was always burdened by them. In the end, they were not able to continue in business. Bell-Carter took over the company and maintains the Lindsay name as one of its lines.

Another olive processor, Musco Olive Products, Inc., began many years after the Lindsay Ripe Olive Company. Just as the Oberti company was, Musco Olive Products is a family business. Nicolo Musco was born in Italy and came to the United States when he was

⁂ EARLY VERSION OF AN OLIVE-PITTING MACHINE FROM THE BEGINNING OF THE TWENTIETH CENTURY.

twenty-two years old. At the time, he was the only one in his family who decided to emigrate. Today the California branch of Muscos still keeps in touch with their Italian relatives.

Nicolo imported cheeses from Sicily before going into the olive business. From 1942 until 1967, he made olive oil in Orland. The company shifted into the olive canning business in 1969 after twenty-five years of making olive oil.

Two of Nicolo's sons, Nicholas (Nick) and Damian (Danny), took over the business in the 1968, after the death of their father. After Damian died in 1978, Nick took sole charge of the now-expanded company. In 1987, Nick's son, Felix, joined the business and is thus carrying on the family tradition. (It is through Felix that I had the pleasure of meeting Freda Ehmann's descendants.)

The firm has been enlarged considerably under Nick's management. The original plant in Orland is not only a receiving center but also processes and packs standard California ripe olives in institutional sizes. Olives are sorted, weighed, and put into brine there. Once a year, the olives are turned into "Sicilians," a sharp, tangy green olive. Fruit that is not needed for the Orland processing cycle then goes to the main plant in Tracy. The firm also has a receiving center in Lindsay and another combined receiving, storage, and processing plant in Visalia, the result of Musco's purchase of Early California Foods in 1998. Musco does not grow its own olives but deals with about three hundred suppliers.

Matt Koball, a grower in Corning who sells olives to Musco, took me to meet Musco's director of field operations, Dennis Burreson, manager of the Orland operation. Dennis is a former basketball player of Norwegian descent: hardly a typical olive person. After his basketball career ended, he went into food processing and learned all about managing food processing plants in Wisconsin. These skills are readily transferable. Nick Musco recruited him in 1979. He has been happy with the move to Orland and its olives. He told me much about the olive scene in Orland and Corning.

One of the people Dennis introduced me to was Gail Terry, a whirlwind of energy. Gail not only manages her olive orchard and does all the hard physical work by herself, but she also owns a set of laundromats and an apartment house in Orland. Over a cup of coffee in her kitchen, she told me a sad tale about the effects of machine harvesting on her almond trees. The majority of machines used to harvest fruit have depended on transmitting vibration to the trunk and major branches of the tree. The ripe fruit then falls off the branches. The trees had been weakened by severe winter storms and the vibration of the machines did a great deal more damage to them. Gail is not an enthusiast for machine picking.

After initially being somewhat skeptical about me, Dennis became very helpful. Through him, I met two of the Aguiar brothers who grow olives in Orland. (See chapter 3.) Dennis also took me to see an olive orchard that he had given to his son. The three of us bumped along the narrow irrigation levees in his small truck and I thought I might not live to finish this book, but he is made of stern stuff and the truck stayed in its appointed place.

✿ AERIAL VIEW OF MUSCO OLIVE
PRODUCTS IN TRACY, CALIFORNIA.
NOTE THE LARGE SALT PONDS IN
THE REAR.

I also spent some time at the Musco factory in Tracy, which is very modern. The family built it on the hills outside the town itself. There are no other buildings anywhere near it, only the characteristic California scenery. In honor of Nick's father, the lane by which one approaches the plant is called "Via Nicolo." The architecture is so spare and the surrounding country so uncompromising in the hot dry summer one almost has the feeling of being in North Africa.

Nick Musco, a dapper and charming man, showed me all over the huge plant himself. I admired the smooth system he had designed and the sheer size of everything. The day's processing was over so the machines were silent, but I could see how the fruit was separated and sized, and the way in which pitting is done. Some of the workers were still putting the finishing touches on labeling or stacking the cans for retorting, the essential immersion in boiling water to sterilize the contents. Giant holding tanks spread out over many acres.

Before we went out into the summer sun to tour the processing plant, we sat over a cool drink in Nick's office and he told me about his father and the company. He is very proud of his son, Felix, and the continuity he represents. Felix will be a worthy successor. My idea of collecting all the scattered bits of information about the olive in California appealed to Nick. He spent quite a long time telling me who else to contact in the industry, taking the trouble to find addresses and phone numbers.

Musco's is one of the two major olive canners left in California, along with Bell-Carter, and they are both family-owned. Massive changes have occurred since the early part of the twentieth century when the market for table olives was quickly growing, and numerous canneries were being built in an attempt to ride this wave of growth. Market changes and environmental regulations have drastically altered the face of olive processing in California over the past few decades. As I commented elsewhere, there is not much more room for further consolidation in this industry. Yet it is interesting, and encouraging, that in the midst of all these changes, two of the remaining processors are family owned. They exemplify the hard work of the many dedicated families through the years, and they give hope for the future of the industry.

8

Botulism

Botulism entered the American consciousness in a terrible outbreak due to canned California ripe black olives just after the First World War. It was, and remains, a lethal disease. Treatment in 1919 was rudimentary. It is far more sophisticated today, but people still die.

The 1919 epidemic was not the first time canned fruit and vegetables from California had caused botulism, but it was the first in a modern era of transcontinental markets. The extensive promotion required to sell the canned olives also worked in reverse. No one could be left in ignorance of what had happened. For ten years, canned California ripe black olives were shunned and the industry constricted in on itself. The course of events can be partially reconstructed in skeletal form by looking through the minutes of the California Olive Association.

When an epidemic of botulism occurred in 1919 and was traced to the consumption of canned California ripe olives, the very heart of their industry was at risk. In Ohio, fourteen people became ill, and seven of them died, from eating canned California ripe olives. Here was a veritable disaster. The deaths had occurred a few months before, but public health officials did not complete the connection with canned ripe black olives until the autumn. Worse yet, several more epidemics

☙ REMOVING CANNED OLIVES FROM THE RETORTS, WHICH HEAT THE OLIVES AT 240 DEGREES FAHRENHEIT FOR FORTY MINUTES TO DESTROY ANY PATHOGENIC ORGANISMS. BELL-CARTER FOODS, CORNING, CALIFORNIA.

occurred in other parts of the country and were once again traced to the canned California ripe olive. In a very short time, the livelihood of California olive growers and processors stood at the brink of complete dissolution.

Botulism had been recognized since 1735 in Europe, but the causative agent, *Clostridium botulinus* (originally known as *Bacillus botulinus*), was not isolated until Louis Pasteur and Robert Koch established the science of bacteriology at the end of the nineteenth century. A paper published in 1920 presented this history briefly.[1] The original French and German cases in the early nineteenth century were traced to imperfectly preserved meats and fish, long before canning was invented. The name "botulinus" means a little sausage. Cases of what were known as "ptomaine" poisoning from preserved fish may well have been botulism. The authors of the 1920 paper noted that the majority of cases in the early twentieth century had been in California.

Fruit canning began in the late nineteenth century in California with peaches and apricots, and was soon followed by pineapple in Hawaii. Canning of vegetables came later. Public health authorities noticed that episodes of botulism had become more frequent and traced them to the canned fruit and vegetables. Canned pears, string beans, peas, spinach, asparagus, corn, apricots, and peaches were all implicated. It was only a matter of time before the olive industry would be struck, because no one yet realized that canned olives could also be a source of botulism.

There are two essential requirements for botulinus toxin to develop in canned foods. The first is a neutral or alkaline environment. Foods that are neutral—that is, neither acid nor alkaline, such as spinach or asparagus—pose a greater risk of incorporating the botulinus bacilli in the can than acidic foods; but foods that are alkaline are the most dangerous of all.

Pineapple and most of the deciduous fruits have considerable natural acid. It was fortuitous that these foods were the first to be canned in metal, but even acidic foods need care and attention in the canning and sterilizing process. Microorganisms that can cause food poisoning, including botulism, may well escape detection and lead to disease.

Acidic bulk foods, such as properly pickled cucumbers in barrels, were safe as long as the concentration of vinegar was high enough. The development of lactic acid in Mediterranean methods of pickling olives and the use of vinegar to season the ethnic types of olive also protected the consumer during those earlier epochs. In their need to keep food over the winter, farmers and housewives learned it was essential to use a lot of vinegar. By this means, they were also unwittingly protecting the food from unwanted fungi and bacteria. Foods we regard as condiments, to stimulate the appetite, were necessities for our ancestors, part of a very scanty diet through the lean seasons. It always amazes me how people had found such effective methods of preservation. Vinegar is an ancient substance.

The second essential factor in the development of botulinus toxin is the reduction or complete removal of oxygen. *Clostridium* belongs to the class of bacteria called "anaerobes," that is, they thrive when the oxygen level in their environment is below a certain concentration. In such an environment, the spores mature and produce the lethal toxin. Conversely, the presence of oxygen slows down clostridial growth, preventing the formation of toxin. As long as the olives were sold in bulk from large barrels, with either no lids or very loose ones, and not hermetically sealed in metal cans with all the oxygen evacuated, the risk of acquiring botulism from early preserved olives remained low, particularly when they were in an acid liquid.

The spores of *Clostridium botulinus* are found in all soils, and thus are ubiquitous in natural produce. They are destroyed in a sufficiently acid environment, but flourish in an alkaline one. Foods that are preserved in an alkaline medium, such as canned ripe black California olives, have to be specially treated to ensure that all the spores which are inevitably present are killed. After all the investigations into the epidemics, it was learned that forty minutes heating at 240 degrees Fahrenheit effectively killed the spores.

Botulinus toxin causes disease by paralyzing the neuromuscular junction. When this happens, the muscles supplied by the nerves in question can no longer respond to the signals and are unable to function. Most typically, the disease starts with muscles of the head and neck, such as the eyes or throat, and very quickly respiration is affected. Many other muscles in the body can be affected, but the involvement of the head, neck, and respiratory muscles is the most common and the most serious.

Modern neurologists take advantage of this characteristic for therapeutic purposes. They use minute amounts of the toxin under carefully controlled conditions to alleviate symptoms produced by the muscles of the head and neck being in constant spasm. It cures people whose eyes are held tightly shut by squeezing of the eyelid muscles, or whose necks are constantly distorted by abnormal muscle contraction. It has been tried for people who cannot write clearly because their hand and arm muscles are cramped in chronic spasm, but this is a less well-accepted use. Dermatologists who specialize in cosmetic procedures use it to remove frown lines. What a paradox! The most feared bacterial poison on earth has been trivialized into "Botox," the trade name of purified botulinus toxin used for injection.

Foods preserved at home are the more likely source of outbreaks. Often women from immigrant communities are the ones most likely to preserve foods at home. They are uneducated in proper sterilization processes, and yet want to maintain their ethnic customs and also hope to save money by starting with inexpensive raw materials. They are not aware of the risks that this entails. Preservation in the home usually involves glass or ceramic containers that are tightly sealed in a variety of ways. Outbreaks of botulism throughout the twentieth century have often been traced to such practices, and they have not only come from fruit or vegetables.

One of the problems of botulism in canned products is that there may be little exterior sign of anything going wrong. The can does not always change its appearance, and the food may not taste noticeably different. Olives, like many other products, are susceptible to several unpleasant conditions, such as "soapy center" and other sorts of microbiological decay and deterioration. These are detected immediately when the can is opened by the smell and appearance of the food.

The insidious nature of botulism, together with numerous other significant facts, was firmly established as a result of the very thorough examination the California Olive Association and the National Canners' Association carried out after the epidemic directly affected them. (In one case report, published in 1920, the authors commented that it was only by the merest chance the pathologists and microbiologists even thought of looking for botulinus.[2]) The National Canners' Association was an organization formed for scientific purposes by the much larger fruit and vegetable companies such as Libby, McNeil, and Libby, and Del Monte. It is now known as the National Association of Food Processors. Through the years, it has promoted applied scientific research of a very high order. The safety and wholesomeness of preserved food in this country is one of its legacies.

The two associations participated in the investigations, contributing large sums of money raised by a tax on each ton of olives processed and sold. The relationship was not altogether amicable at times, because the National Canners' Association wanted to make sure the public did not connect them and their products with botulism. They allowed some slightly derogatory articles about olive canners to be published in the press. The California Olive Association made strenuous efforts to get these refuted. In the end, the two groups would jointly raise more than $100,000 for research into the cause of botulism, which was in addition to the money spent by the public health authorities. They worked with the best scientists they could find. Chemists and microbiologists from private foundations as well as city, state, and federal agencies were all involved.

The *Public Health Reports* for December 19, 1919, contain an exemplary review of the first outbreak and its elucidation.[3] It was written by Dr. Charles Armstrong, assistant surgeon in the United States Public Health Service, and Professor Ernest Scott, the pathologist at Ohio State University College of Medicine.

The first outbreak due to the California canned olives occurred at a banquet on August 23, 1919, at a country club near Canton, Ohio. Out of two hundred diners, the only people who became ill were all seated at the same table, as the guests of a Mrs. I. W. G. (Her full name is deliberately withheld in the original paper for confidentiality.) The article shows a plan of the table and its seating arrangements. In her desire to be extremely hospitable and exceed the standard menu, Mrs. G. had served special hors d'oeuvres at that table, and had included canned ripe olives among the delicacies. The other tables had the standard celery, pickles, and green olives supplied by the management. This table did not take those items. The rest of the menu was the same for all: turkey, potatoes, corn, stuffing, tomatoes dressed with mayonnaise, crackers, rolls, and ice cream.

A careful epidemiological survey of the entire menu, item by item, indicated that the only people who became ill were the ones who had eaten the canned ripe olives. The patients who eventually died had eaten more olives than the ones who recovered. The investigators found that the severity of the illness was proportional to the amount of toxin ingested. The reason will emerge below.

The investigators learned that the affected olives were received in a sealed glass jar, but once it had been opened, they could not find out if the seal had been in any way defective. The waiter in charge had spread the olives over three small dishes. He had washed the olives before putting them into the first two dishes but not the ones he put into the third. It is unusual to wash food taken from a jar, and one wonders if he smelled something out of the ordinary. The washing accounted for the difference in taste noted and the degree of disease.

Among the victims who could speak, several commented that the olives had not tasted quite as they had expected and yet they ate them. Some of the guests who did not become ill had tasted them but rejected them because of the unpleasant taste. Two waiters at that table also ate some of the olives. They fell ill and one later died.

One of the waiters was suspicious of the olives because he did not like their taste. He took them into the kitchen at the end of the banquet and asked the chef to taste them. The chef ate two of the unwashed olives and subsequently died of botulism. The waiter developed a mild case of the disease and did not die. This reinforced the fact that the spoiled food was not completely inedible and that the washing had partially removed some of the toxin.

There was also a hint that the amount of whiskey drunk before and during the cocktail hour had a protective effect. A waiter who recovered told the doctors he had had considerable quantities of whiskey that night. A guest who ate one olive had drunk whiskey both before and after dinner. He had very mild symptoms.

Once these essential clinical data were established, the investigators performed laboratory tests on all the foods from the banquet. The animals that were given samples of the olives themselves, or just the saline in which they had been preserved, all died of botulism. Culture media revealed a heavy growth of the *Clostridium*. They even tested the possible protective effect of alcohol, and indeed animals given toxin mixed with varying amounts of alcohol did not get nearly so ill as those given the plain toxin without alcohol.

The evidence that the disease came from the canned ripe olives was meticulously assembled and could not be faulted. A minute quantity of the toxin, half a milliliter, was sufficient to kill two hundred guinea pigs. A short time after they completed these studies, they tested a protective antitoxin prepared in another department of the USDA. It was very efficacious.

The scientists then traced the source of the contaminated olives. They had been prepared by the Ehmann Olive Company. Mrs. Ehmann had changed to individual glass containers after she established the market with her work on bulk olives. Glass jars can be sealed very effectively, almost as well as cans, and botulism will still occur if they are not sterilized appropriately after closure. It was a tragedy for Mrs. Ehmann, a woman of extreme rectitude and the utmost probity. Mrs. Ehmann's granddaughter told me she could never come

● Ill ✛ Died

✛ Mrs. I.W.G.

C.C.W. ✛

Mrs. F.M.

W.E.D.

OLIVES

Mrs. L.H.B. ●

C.B. ●

OLIVES

Mrs. J.C.S. ✛

FLOWERS

L.H.B. ●

Mrs. W.H.M.

OLIVES

W. H. M.

● Mrs. C.C.W.

W.F.S.

● Mrs. C.B.

F.M.

✛ Mrs. W.F.S.

✛ J.C.S.

Mrs. W.E.O.

● I.W.G.

❦ Seating plan of Mrs. I.W.G.'s table at the Ohio country club dinner where the first major outbreak of botulism caused by imperfectly canned olives occurred. Four guests, along with Mrs. I.W.G herself, a chef, and a waiter died.

to terms with the fact that something for which she was responsible had done so much harm. She continued to work for many years, into extreme old age, but business had somehow changed for her.

In 1920, another study was done by the Bureau of Chemistry at the USDA. A total of 480 containers, both glass and metal, all from the Ehmann Olive Company, was examined for contamination by botulinus and any other organisms. Some of the cans looked normal. Others were obviously deformed and the contents spoiled. All the containers were opened under sterile conditions.[4]

CHART SHOWING WHICH GUESTS ATE THE TAINTED OLIVES AT MRS. I.W.G.'S TABLE, LEADING TO ILLNESS AND DEATH.

Of the cans that looked normal, 8 out of 181 had identifiable pathogenic organisms, including *Clostridium botulinus,* whereas only 3 of the cans out of 157 that appeared abnormal had completely sterile contents. This was hardly surprising but clearly the authors were most concerned about the eight bad results from what seemed to be normal cans. Tests on the glass jars yielded very similar results. The other bacteria that were found also could cause serious disease but not so uniformly fatal as botulism.[5]

There were a few other outbreaks, in Michigan and Pennsylvania, but always from olives prepared in California. The various scientists who worked on the problem showed conclusively that adequate heat treatment of the olives after the cans or jars were sealed would sterilize the contents completely. The water bath had to reach 240 degrees Fahrenheit and be kept at that temperature for forty minutes.[6]

Dr. Dickson of the U.S. Public Health Service, Dr. Ebright, president of the California State Board of Health, scientists at the University of California and at the private foundations that had all done tests concurred in this remedy. All this work was finished by 1921. They had found the right answer, and there should be no more outbreaks. There was nothing very complicated about it, but the California Olive Association and the National Canners' Association feared that it would not be taken seriously enough.

A privately sponsored scientist, Dr. Karl Meyer of the George Williams Hooper Foundation, noted the ubiquity of the spores and advised canners to be vigilant. Dr. Meyer would continue to work with both associations for many years. At the same time, the Food Products Laboratory at UC Berkeley, a new and unique department conceived of and led by Professor William V. Cruess, took up the problem and worked closely with the public health authorities. Professor Cruess was not only a remarkable academic scientist. He was also alert to the possibilities of contamination in home kitchens and wanted to make sure everyone knew about the need for sterilization. He prepared a version of the sterilizing procedure for household use, based on the use of a pressure cooker.

The Food Products Laboratory would later become the Food Technology Department and migrate to the University of California campus at Davis. Dr. Cruess never worked at Davis—that move took place after he retired—but the building in which the department is now housed is named Cruess Hall in his honor. The members of the California Olive Association pressed for a program of inspection by the California State Health Department. The state provided funds and a team of inspectors for several years after this initial epidemic, but when the funds ceased the association raised money itself to continue the program. The inspectors traveled from plant to plant, reviewing the temperature records from the retorts in which the cans were heated. Cannery employees had to record the temperature of the water and length of time each lot of cans was immersed and keep the results to show the inspectors. Nowadays, these tasks are done automatically, with markers to show that sterilization is complete.

In spite of the continued bad publicity and need to reestablish consumer confidence, a few canners seemed to remain slack and careless. This can only be assumed from the fact that botulism broke out twice more in the 1920s after all the facts were known and disseminated. In 1921, a woman died from eating contaminated olives in Greensburg, Pennsylvania. On March 1, 1924, nine people fell ill while at a dinner of the Growlers' Club in Coalinga, California, a Central Valley town southwest of Fresno. Two of them died. Botulism from canned ripe olives was the cause again. The contaminated olives were traced to a jobber in San Francisco who had sold them under a private label. Dr. Meyer delivered a scathing address to the California Olive Association board, with very good reason. Everyone knew exactly what had to be done, and it was really very simple to do. There was no excuse for such a catastrophe.

The state put all olive canning factories under a quarantine and stepped up inspection of the temperature charts. The state inspectors found that many cases of canned olives had to be resterilized because of "deplorable laxity." On March 9, 1924, the president of the State Board of Health, Dr. Ebright, addressed the group of olive processors. The large processors had been right to be concerned. The first outbreaks could be put down to ignorance and lack of skill. This one was totally avoidable and inexcusable. Even though it seems self-evident now that Dr. Meyer was correct to be so angry, one of the processors present would not accept the collective, symbolically shared blame. This processor, Mr. E. Bentley, claimed that there was a lack of adequate inspection and said that the industry should not have to police itself. He spoke only for himself. No one agreed with him.

The matter was so serious that Governor Richardson met with the olive canners on March 19, 1924. He wanted to be sure that this time there would be no recurrence. In order to raise sufficient money to pay for the inspections, the association levied one penny per case of canned olives on all processors, not just on their own membership. Later that year, the association sponsored tests of a continuous strip thermometer, to improve recording of the temperatures.

One last possible case of botulism occurred in December 1924. A woman died of uncertain causes in Vallejo, California, and some newspapers, which could be just as irresponsible then as they can be now, inflamed public concern by attributing her death to eating canned ripe olives. By now the California Olive Association had more confidence, and it challenged this report. They paid a toxicologist to examine the contents of her stomach at the postmortem. The toxicologist's report was not in the board's minutes, and we will never know what the cause of death was. Fortunately, no more cases of botulism caused by olives were reported. The measures the processing companies adopted were ultimately very successful.

CALIFORNIA OLIVE ASSOCIATION

9

The California Olive Association

In 1915, a group of owners and managers of olive processing companies decided to start an industry trade organization. Competition between the olive canning companies was exceedingly severe. Prices varied wildly. The market was fickle, and the processors felt it needed to be expanded and stabilized. Some degree of cooperation was now essential if order were to come out of this chaos. They had the example of other food industries, such as the peach canners, doing this successfully, and the National Canners' Association already existed.

The group duly started the California Olive Association in May 1915. The minutes of the association provide an interesting series of vignettes of what happened over the years from the narrow point of view of a group of men involved in a particular set of activities. The parochial emphasis is sometimes very odd, especially when it came to major world events. One would never know what was happening in the world at large from the entries in the California Olive Association minutes. Such myopia would not be surprising in the diaries of a private individual, but it does raise a question when a major industry is involved. Their priorities clearly had to be those connected with the olive business, but external events often had a big impact on their trade. The narrative that follows is based on their records, showing events through this prism.

꽃 THE CALIFORNIA OLIVE ASSOCIATION
   LETTERHEAD LOGO.

Many people were invited to be part of the initial organizing meeting. Invitations were sent to the owners and operators of the following companies: American Olive Company, C. M. Gifford and Son, Akerman and Tuffley, A. Adams, Jr., California Ripe Olive Company, Loma Ranch Company, J. C. Kubias, Charles P. Grogan, Curtis Olive Company, McNally's, Roeding Olive Company, Fair Oaks Olive Company, Ehmann Olive Company, Maywood Packing Company, and Phoenix Brothers. In addition, two growers' associations were invited to join: Los Angeles Olive Growers' Association and Tulare County Growers' Association.

On May 19, 1915, despite the numerous invitations, only six men met in Los Angeles to lay out the structure of the new association. The initial members were the Los Angeles Olive Growers' Association (represented by Frank Simonds), American Olive Company (M. M. Bryant), Curtis Olive Company (E. S. Moorhead), Gifford and Son (C. M. Gifford himself), Fair Oaks Olive Company (W. W. Hinsey), and a Dr. Charles Pratt, representing Pratt Olive Company, which was not listed in the initial roster of prospective members. Mr. Simonds was elected president and eventually served for fifteen years in that capacity. During that period, his company, the Los Angeles Growers' Association, became the Sylmar Packing Corporation.

Though not present at the initial meeting, Flavel Shurtleff was drafted to be the secretary pro tem. At the succeeding meeting, Mr. Shurtleff was requested to continue as the corresponding secretary. After the Lindsay Ripe Olive Company was formed, Flavel Shurtleff joined that company as an executive.

The new association elected a board and adopted bylaws. Dues were set at $5 per quarter. The annual meeting would be on the third Monday in April. Within six months, the association had taken an office in the Wilcox Building in Los Angeles and was looking for a permanent employee to run it. They chose a man named P. R. Lance and paid him $100 per month.

The first article of incorporation stated that the "object and purpose for which this Association is formed is the promoting of the Ripe Olive in all its branches." This rather broad statement did not technically restrict the agenda to table olives. In order to become a member of the association, it was only necessary to be "actively engaged in the Olive Industry."

Olive oil is made from ripe olives, and so it seems that oil makers should have been included in the association. In fact, there was relatively little communication with the olive oil makers, except on rare occasions, because it seemed the two groups had practically nothing in common. Occasionally an issue would come up that crossed this boundary. The association did receive a letter in November 1915 from the American Olive Company questioning some remarks of former State Senator Del Valle (of the Camulos family) about olive oil. The initiating letter was not preserved. On another occasion, the association helped to defeat an unfair bill put forward by the cottonseed oil makers. (This will be treated in more detail below.) There were a few other sporadic joint efforts.

The association seldom included the processors of ethnic varieties of table olive (the "Greeks" and "Sicilians") in its deliberations either, despite the fact that all these processors used ripe olives. The association referred to these commodities as "by-products," a somewhat pejorative term.

In reality, the words "ripe olive" had a code meaning. A "California ripe olive" was not an olive at the peak of its ripeness but an artifact of processing. The California Olive Association was composed of a group of companies that processed raw fruit into table olives and sealed them in metal cans, a very important point. The others either sold their wares in bulk or put them up in glass. The association's affinities were with other canners, such as the National Canners' Association and other users of metal cans.

As the executive committee considered what the processors were doing, it was concerned about the integrity of claiming that the member companies sold ripe olives when the fruit had been pulled from the tree long before it ripened. The committee grappled with an adequate definition of a "ripe olive" on several occasions, and on March 18, 1916, it presented a statement with its conclusions for the record. The olive was not to be accepted for processing unless it had begun to turn color, at least to a reddish hue. They did not want the constituent companies using completely green and immature fruit.

These men were not scientists. They did not have the skill needed to come up with the concept of "horticultural" maturity versus "physiological" maturity. Horticultural maturity is a compromise between unripeness and true ripeness, based on a statistical index of the number of sufficiently ripe fruit on a given tree. Once that was accomplished at a future date, their difficulties with this matter were over.

In addition to defining the "ripe olive," the association also needed to define the difference between table (or pickling) olives and oil olives. This was, in fact, one of the first definitions to be adopted. Maybe because of the calibration of their grading machines, or perhaps because of a dedicated Manzanillo grower, the members selected eleven-sixteenths of an inch to be the threshold. Olives that were larger than that were for pickling. Smaller olives were to be used for oil. Very soon after they made this decision, they came up with a description of what a ripe olive should be, at the time of picking. The association wanted to make sure that when they sold an olive as "ripe" it was indeed ripe, although this was to change as techniques changed.

Whatever money they raised in these early days of the association was used for advertising. The cost of a full, double-page advertisement in the *Los Angeles Times,* with an editorial writeup, was $1,200 in 1915. We think that advertising is expensive today, but considering the change in the value of money, that was certainly a very steep price.

That first year a foundation was laid that would serve the association for the next eighty-two years. Members were concerned with standardizing the sizes of the olives, marketing them in cans, and establishing the essential definitions of ripeness, the canning process, and good quality. A crucial question each year was how many of the aggregate number of cases of canned ripe olives would be sold ("the pack") and how many would be left to carry over into the following year. Handling that excess inventory tested all the ingenuity their marketing advisers could summon.

Through the years, association members were to meet at regular intervals to taste the olives each had canned to ensure uniform flavor and quality. These events were called "cutting bees."

Wholesomeness and safety were important, but after the botulism outbreak of 1919, they would take on the characteristics of a crusade. The crisis due to the botulism epidemic forced the association to adopt scientific methods to handle the daily problems of their plants and rely less on the empirical approach. Holding annual technical conferences to share the results of the research became an important aspect of the association's work. In this, the association established a tradition that continues to this day.

Labor issues were to be discussed many times, as was advertising, but perhaps the most common item on the agenda was the size structure of the canned olives themselves, or "unit quantities." It seemed to be the most contentious issue, equaled only by the continued problem of what to call the different sizes. These two matters come up again and again in the minutes of various committees, board meetings, and annual meetings.

On October 18, 1915, the following nomenclature was adopted: "jumbo" (60 olives per pound), "extra fancy" (72 per pound), "fancy" (90 per pound), and "select" (105 per pound). All these values were approximate. This terminology would change time and again to accommodate various types of olives and the numbers per can. Part of the problem came from the fact that olives grow in a range of sizes according to the variety of tree. Just what is large or medium is hard to clarify when there are so many gradations in nature. C. M. Gifford, who dealt in two varieties of very large olives, the Ascolano and Sevillano, initially wished to dissociate his firm from these standards. He later suggested a separate set of grades for the Ascolano and Sevillano, and this was adopted unanimously. Ascolanos were to be "special" and Sevillanos "mammoth," if there were sixty to the pound. Gifford also proposed another category for the larger Mission and Manzanillo olives: "special extra fancy" (fifty to sixty per pound).

Less than a year later, in March 1916, a new set of definitions was adopted. Instead of four categories, there were six—ranging from "standard" (the smallest) to "mammoth" (the largest). This was not the end of it. After all this work, the system was scrapped when they switched to seven grades. "Mammoth" gave way to "colossal" and "giant" as the largest sizes.

1963 OLIVE TECHNICAL CONFERENCE

SPONSORED BY THE CALIFORNIA OLIVE ASSOCIATION

SANTA BARBARA BILTMORE SANTA BARBARA, CALIF.

JUNE 20-22

✽ COVER SHEET FROM THE 1963 ANNUAL TECHNICAL CONFERENCE PUT ON BY THE CALIFORNIA OLIVE ASSOCIATION.

✺ AUTOMATIC GRADING MACHINE CAPABLE OF SIZING FROM 200 TO 240 BOXES OF OLIVES PER DAY.

In June 1916, P. R. Lance, who had been hired to run the association's office, resigned. No reason was recorded, although he might have been fatigued by all the traveling required to sign up new members. The members looked back with satisfaction as the association passed the end of its first year. Although many of their colleagues had not joined them, the group had held together and had succeeded in accomplishing much of what they intended. The names and sizes of the olives were now standardized, and no one was supposed to be processing the completely immature olive. Members hoped the other companies would want to come into the association.

From the beginning the association had sent copies of its bulletin at intervals to all the packers, not just members, as a way of demonstrating how useful the organization could be to everyone. The next significant task was to adopt a uniform contract with the growers.

At the same time, there were minor annoyances. The state marketing director, Colonel Harris Weinstock, seemed to be arrogating too many powers to himself for their taste. He was an energetic and enthusiastic man, anxious to promote California produce and get the markets organized, but they thought he insinuated himself into too many of their affairs.

The First World War was in full swing during these years, but its existence did not enter the written record of the association. That may be because the United States did not get involved in the war until 1917. Strongly isolationist views in Congress and among many members of the public prevented the President from taking action. It was not until the intentional sinking of the *Lusitania* by the German navy that the resulting outrage generated enough political momentum to change course. Isolationism did not protect American citizens on the high seas.

The reduction in transatlantic shipping capacity during hostilities was not a problem for the California olive processors. They did not need imports, and their customers were in the United States. The mobilization of internal transport systems for military purposes also must not have affected them.

They continued to be concerned with freight costs, as in civilian days, but mentioned no difficulty in getting the goods moved. The war had no visible effect on their business, nor on their use of metals and other resources. Promoting membership, contracts with the growers, internal and external tariffs, and particularly advertising remained their principal concerns. Nothing changed when the war ended. They continued to do all the same things.

During this early formative period, a situation arose in which the association could assist the makers of olive oil. Although the purpose of the association was clearly to promote the canned olive industry, there were still some members who made oil. The Giffords did, and so did Akerman and Tuffley. The California Olive Association was the sole organization at that time that could represent the interests of all parties involved in the olive business. Today the makers of olive oil have an organization of their own but not back then.

Early in 1919, the association got wind of a bill (AB 1075) in the state legislature sponsored by the cottonseed oil manufacturers, attempting to get olive oil off the shelves. Californian olive oil already suffered from much unfair competition. Here was one more attack on their livelihood. Not only were the olive oil makers unable to compete against the very low prices of foreign oil, but now there was an American attempt to put them out of business.

The manufacturers and refiners of cottonseed oil, a set of very wily characters, wanted to grab the salad oil market for themselves by making it seem that olive oil was impure. They used the concentration of oleic acid in olive oil as the basis for their contention. They tried to deceive the legislature into believing that olive oil was unfit for human consumption because it had 1 or 2 percent of oleic acid in it. The manufacturers of the bland and tasteless cottonseed oil, with less than 0.025 percent free fatty acids in it, argued that it should be the standard for edible oils. Any oil with more than this entirely arbitrary value of fatty acids should be labeled adulterated.

In fact, the 1 or 2 percent of oleic acid in olive oil is not the slightest bit harmful to human beings. The cottonseed oil makers were making an invalid comparison, and, of course, they knew it. Olive oil has been safely consumed by human beings for millennia. It was just a ruse. Unfortunately, the legislators were not sophisticated in food science. The argument sounded very plausible.

Without knowing the harmless nature of oleic acid, the bill seemed to be an innocent enough way to protect the public with little or no political cost. The board of the California Olive Association took action, educating the members of the legislature, and the bill was dropped. This was an occasion on which the canners helped the oil makers very materially.

After the war years, during which the association had no full-time manager, the board hired J. J. Hoey to manage and run their office. Hoey was the editor of the *Fig Journal,* and he suggested he could work part-time on olives, gathering similar statistics for the association. Initially, he was only taken on part-time, but it was soon apparent that he was a very competent man. He received $250 per month, and the use of a rented car whenever he had to travel any distance outside Los Angeles. He was an excellent choice and worked for the association diligently for many years. Because he now covered both spheres, the name of the *Fig Journal* was changed into the *Fig and Olive Journal.*

The year 1919 would turn out to be much more fateful than they had ever expected. The association weathered the cottonseed oil threat quite easily. Olive oil was not at the core of their business, and the possibility of losing that battle, while a nuisance, did not alarm them too profoundly. This was not the case with the next crisis, the outbreak of botulism.

Up until that time, the association had been run on a rather cozy and informal basis. This could not continue. The executive committee recognized that a serious new situation existed and that it had to take appropriate action. The simple, friendly, almost clublike attitude had to be replaced by something more formal. They feared the enormous liability both for themselves as officers of the association and for their member companies. The possible legal ramifications of the epidemic led the organization to reincorporate itself in 1920 as a formal entity, hoping to limit exposure to liability suits.

For more than ten years, the effects of the botulism outbreak colored all the actions of the association. The members of the association responded to the outbreak and its fallout by encouraging a great deal of scientific research that ultimately would be beneficial on a much wider front than just the olive industry.

Beside the essential scientific studies, the association needed a very effective advertising campaign to try and overcome the public fear of canned foods in general and canned olives in particular. Their market had collapsed almost immediately, and it would not fully recover for a decade.

A very important component of the campaign to restore confidence in canned ripe olives was the need for reassuring and positive statements from sources that were unimpeachable, such as state boards of health, city health departments, and the railroad commissary department. None of these would be seen to have an ax to grind. The association itself prepared a clear statement detailing its actions for publication in the Hearst press. It prevailed on the National Canners' Association to withdraw its derogatory remarks about olive canners and processors, which had appeared early on. To pay for this advertising, the members were assessed one dollar per ton of processed olives.

During all the turmoil, canning companies came and went in the California Olive Association. The Lindsay Ripe Olive Company joined soon after all this happened. The Giffords had resigned in 1917 but later joined again. They were finally able to reconcile their special needs with the association's philosophy and C. M. Gifford was a staunch member of the association's inner councils for many years to come. Initially, the Ehmann Olive Company had not joined as it stuck to glass containers for a long time and would not be bound by the association's requirements. Later in the 1920s, the Ehmann Olive Company changed its mind and joined. The botulism outbreak had had a very sobering effect and the management realized they needed to be part of the group.

It was hard for the association to collect all the money it levied because of this movement in and out. Companies that seceded refused to honor commitments made earlier. For example, the Old Mission Olive Oil Company went bankrupt in 1925 and simply could not pay its dues. New members felt they should be prorated, and everyone moaned about the fall in prices due to the weak market. Also in 1925, the association forgave Lindsay Ripe Olive Company its assessment for $1,800. It was allowed to continue as a member. Maywood Packing Company wanted to be exempt from the assessments because it dealt only in Sevillano olives. This request was denied as it might set an unfortunate precedent.

The various advertising campaigns were not satisfactory, and the association kept changing advertising firms until finally coming across the Lord and Thomas Agency. After the first few years, the agency deputed L. B. Williams to concentrate on the association's account. He was a very dynamic man and led the association's advertising with many innovative techniques until his death in 1959. At a previous time in his career, he had once had a part in a movie playing a deacon and was known affectionately as "Deke" for the rest of his life. Williams had also been a journalist and still knew many people who worked in newspapers and magazines. He had something of the charismatic style associated with preachers, which stood him in good stead.

The market continued to be very bad for canned ripe California olives, and more attention was paid to olive oil during the next few years. The National Canners' Association (NCA) stood by the olive processors, and in November 1924, the then-president of NCA, Royal Clark, addressed the board. He noted that other canners had similar or related problems. He proposed federal inspection as a way to recover public confidence. This was important because canners in other states were not subject to the jurisdiction of the California State Board of Health. The federal umbrella would extend across all states. He suggested that as an economy the olive industry could be covered under appropriations for the salmon industry.

Flavel Shurtleff, now an employee of the Lindsay Ripe Olive Company and a member of the association, was given the task of traveling to the cities in which botulism had occurred. He would work with merchants and others in those cities to try and demonstrate that things were now different. The association spent several thousand dollars on this critical work and was very pleased with the results.

Marketing remained the association's most serious challenge once it had overcome the scientific aspects of the botulism epidemics. The members were always concerned about the threat of foreign competition, and they watched the tariff schedules in Washington very closely. The last thing the industry needed at this critical juncture was a flood of pickled olives from Spain or some other prolific olive-producing country. They approached one of the California senators, Hiram W. Johnson, to take up their cause in Congress. Through Johnson's efforts, they were able to ward off this danger for the time being.

Over the next few years the association refined and consolidated many of its basic positions. The Canners' League, a California industry association, had a good contract with growers that the association modified and adopted. It rearranged the size grades of the fruit and began to try and make the actual cans conform to standardized ranges. In order to establish a basis for prices, they introduced the idea of cost accounting and had various member firms experiment with it. They relentlessly raised money from the members to pay for more and more advertising campaigns.

We have now reached 1929, that fateful year. The market for olives was still chaotic and rather weak. Membership in the association had now grown to about twenty of the twenty-eight firms packing olives. As an example of participation, the special membership meeting of the association held on September 7, 1929, listed representatives of seventeen firms in attendance.

At that meeting, some of the representatives suggested pooling leftover stock and sending it to brokers and jobbers in secondary markets, where there had previously been very little history of success. They hoped this would help boost sales. Another topic at the meeting was a complaint from the fruit canning companies that the olive packers were not paying their full share of the cost of state inspection. The secretary recommended that the California Olive Association increase its contribution from 10 percent of the state's overhead to 15 percent. The suggestion was adopted.

Lest anyone imagine that the great naming pastime was over, the minutes also record suggestions to expand the medium grade for Mission to three categories, and to add "giant," "jumbo," and "colossal" to the Sevillano and Ascolano grades.

Later in that same September of 1929, the officers of the California Olive Association (COA) created another organization, California Ripe Olive Distributors, Ltd. As an offshoot of COA, it was developed to strengthen their grip on markets. The officers of the organization worked with B. H. Critchfield of the Federal-State Marketing Service to draw up the plans for this new corporation.

In October, the stock market crashed. The California olive growers seemed to be sublimely oblivious to this signal event. One can only assume that the estimable Mr. Hoey did not think it was his business to include anything so extraneous in his minutes. It is hard to imagine that the members did not discuss the crash as they waited to go into the meetings or while they ate dinner afterward, but Hoey was paid to record the deliberations of an olive organization, not national disasters.

In August 1930, a federal canners' bill was proposed, which would establish federal standards for ripe olives. Olive oil also appeared in the Federal Register that year. The USDA proposed to lay down standards for labeling virgin olive oil, and the association reached out to the olive oil manufacturers to assist them.

A year later, the association continued to help the olive oil makers. It paid for a representative to go to Washington and lobby to get the tariff increased on imported olive oil. The association also invited G. Maselli of Fresno, A. Benatti and L. M. Drew of Lindsay, Charles Livoti of Roseville, and H. P. Burt of the California Packing Company in Palermo, all olive oil makers, to attend a strategy meeting on this problem. These steps paid off and the tariff commission sent examiners to California to review costs.

By July 1931, the association was considering taking on a full-time chemist to study the canners' problems scientifically and come up with solutions. In other words, things seemed to be going well. Nowhere in this recital is there any mention that the bottom had dropped out of American business in October 1929, that millions of people had lost their jobs, and no one had any money. It would be July 1932 before any hint of this appears in the minutes. It was necessary to pay for the Board of Health's inspection costs, but they noted "in light of the extremely depressed condition prevailing among all packers, . . . only a limited amount of money could be raised this year. . . ."

Now shortage of funds became a recurring theme. The association was able to make economies in the inspection process and saved $3,500. Its own operating costs had to be reduced by 35 percent. In spite of the gloom, there were discussions about participating in the Chicago World's Fair the following year. Members wondered if olives could be part of the school lunch program, though children are notoriously hard to please. At the same time, there was no way they could afford to hire a full-time chemist. That proposal was shelved.

Late in 1932, the minutes recorded the death of Freda Ehmann, the woman who had made it all possible. She was ninety-three years old and had lived to see enormous changes. One important change she missed would be the adoption of a federal marketing order and code of fair practices in August 1933. A marketing order permits the processing companies to plan how much inventory is sent to the market each season and to compel members to abide by this agreement. It is a form of fixed or ordered market. The purpose is to even out the gluts and shortages that are such a nuisance for commodity dealers. One of the decisive factors that led the ripe olive processors to adopt this almost revolutionary measure was the constant difficulty with the residual pack every year.

There was a sort of symmetry to the two events—Mrs. Ehmann's death and the adoption of the federal marketing order and code of fair practices—occurring so closely together. The woman who began a business in more primitive times departed just as the realities of the twentieth century engulfed the industry. If the cliché can be forgiven, it was truly the "end of an era."

The rabidly independent leaders of the ripe olive industry had resented the much gentler and almost tentative activities of the California state marketing director back in 1916. Now they were inviting not just the state but the federal government into their business, a really surprising move. It bespeaks a sort of desperation that was not voiced in the official documents of the association but must have underlain the decision.

Many executives of the large processing companies may well not have voted for Franklin Roosevelt in 1932, but the philosophy of an activist government had intruded into their consciousness almost willy-nilly. Perhaps they did not quite realize what a momentous step this was. Maybe they were worn down by the struggle to keep going through the depression and its aftermath. No sign of this mood enters the businesslike minutes, but their business lives would no longer be their own once they had to conform to the all-encompassing federal regulations. One cannot pick and choose which regulations to obey. They all have to be obeyed. A new bureaucracy would take up residence in their midst and dictate much of what they could and could not do.

Marketing orders were not new to California agriculture, but this was the first time one had been applied to the olive industry. It was so important that the association opened its annual meeting on August 11, 1933, to all persons involved in the olive industry—growers, canners, and oil producers, and not just members—in order to have the widest possible discussion of such a fundamental change.

The marketing order went into effect at midnight on August 15, 1933. Because of its importance, another meeting was held a week later. Now the association would be able to manipulate the amount of the commodity going into the market and try to even out the huge swings in sales. An economist at the University of California at Berkeley, Dr. H. R. Wellman, told them how this change would affect their expectations, comparing it to the results in the peach industry.

The federal and subsequent state marketing orders led to complex and elaborate arrangements to handle every minute aspect of their industry. One very important change was that the association's articles of incorporation had to be rewritten to allow price setting.

Many of the other fruit and vegetable industries in California were also subject to marketing orders. After almost fifty years, in 1981, two government economists, Edward V. Jesse and Aaron C. Johnson, decided to see what had been accomplished by these orders. They published the results of their thorough investigation into those industries and concluded that the impact had been considerably less than anyone thought. Commodity prices were still very fluid, and markets were not as stable as had seemed. Jesse and Johnson did not study the olive industry, but their conclusions appeared to be relevant and transposable. In spite of recognizing that fact, most of the executives interviewed by Jesse and Johnson still wanted to keep the orders. Perhaps they all believed that things would have been a good deal worse without them.

J. J. Hoey resigned as manager of the association office in August 1934. They gave him a pension at half pay. The association still needed a full-time manager, and they looked to the peach industry for a man who could guide them through the new era. They chose Oscar Hoffman. A Miss Lindrose was taken on to be the secretary. She was energetic and helped boost the membership. By mid-1935, Hoffman resigned and Miss Lindrose took on his position as well.

Things began to go more smoothly by 1936. Sales were up, their publicist, Mr. Williams, was getting the message out very well, and once again there was talk of taking on a full-time chemist. In the meantime, the association benefited from a close relationship with Professor William V. Cruess of the Food Products Laboratory at UC Berkeley. He and his department worked on many of the problems facing the association and its members. In one of the association's records, there is very pleasant report of the professor acknowledging how much each of his graduate students had contributed to all the projects. The association made contributions to the food technology department each year in gratitude for Professor Cruess's work.

Once again, in 1936, a major world development indirectly affected the association's activities but was not overtly mentioned in the minutes. The Spanish Civil war broke out, and all available Spanish men were away at the front fighting. Harvesting and processing olives for commercial use virtually ceased in Spain. The COA minutes only note that there was a shortage of Spanish green olives, and this gave rise to new opportunities for the California producers—not only for table olives but for oil too.

The State of California came up with its own marketing order for olives in May 1937. By now the concept was accepted, and this change did not occasion much discussion. Another milestone occurred when *Good Housekeeping* gave canned California ripe olives its seal of approval.

For the first time in 1937, the minutes note the presence of Miss Erline Hevel as assistant secretary to Miss Lindrose. Miss Hevel was to be the moving force at the association for the rest of its existence, after Miss Lindrose retired. There would be one more manager, Everett W. Hogle, but after he left, Miss Hevel ran everything. Many of the industry executives of today, whose fathers or other relatives were active during the 1930s and 1940s and who themselves joined the association in the 1950s or 1960s, remember her very fondly.

Whatever had to be done, Miss Hevel did it. She was a "one-woman band." She was not a scientist, but she understood the importance of the scientific inquiries. In addition to numerous other duties, she made all the arrangements for the annual technical conferences, took the minutes, duplicated the reports, sent them out, and did all the follow-up required by the findings of the conference. Once in a while, she permitted herself to take on some temporary secretarial assistance. In one set of minutes, where the temporary person had signed them in Miss Hevel's absence, that woman's name is firmly crossed out and "E. Hevel" entered. She was jealous of her prerogatives. The association responded to her skill and loyalty by voting her raises, a special retirement program, and other marks of esteem.

Surprisingly, in 1937, there was once again concern about poor sales and a weak market. Mr. Williams, the active advertising executive, suggested other avenues. The federal government was approached about buying table olives for military personnel. The association had to scrap the idea of getting olives into school lunches. Predictably the children did not want them. The report notes dryly that children do not like a variety of small objects in their food, unless they are chocolate chips!

In 1938, seven packing companies wanted to resign because they could no longer pay the dues. The canners still had to observe all the health and safety precautions when they packed the fruit, because doing anything else was business suicide. The association's advertising agent was concerned because the association no longer represented even half of the packing companies. To prevent the seven packing companies from resigning, the association cut its budget in half, from about $10,000 per annum to about $5,000. They cut out all temporary stenographic help, reduced wages, and ceased paying the directors' expenses. The growers were doing badly too. When they sold olives for the federal programs, they only received payment at the level of oil olives.

As mentioned above, the association had taken on Everett W. Hogle to be the manager after Miss Lindrose left. He was paid better than his predecessors and traveled very extensively up and down the Central Valley to see firsthand what was happening at the canneries. With the continuation of hard times, many members resigned. Although the association participated in the New York World's Fair of 1939 and sent Mr. Hogle to supervise their display, they reluctantly had to fire him right about that time. His response was a reserved and dignified letter that nevertheless conveyed true emotion. His last task was to prepare a lengthy and detailed report of their position at the World's Fair, and what had been accomplished. I hope he found another position, with his rather specialized talents and skills.

With the money they saved, the association was able to increase their honorarium to Professor Cruess, and yet they continued to economize in every other way they could. For many years, the COA had been contributing to the California Chamber of Commerce, in its efforts to prevent "left-wing forces" from overcoming local agriculture. In 1940, the association ceased to pay the dues. Additional research could be done by federal agencies supported by tax money and not by the association. The USDA, for example, had a fine laboratory in its western region.

The Second World War had broken out in Europe on September 3, 1939. Once again, an event of cosmic magnitude was ignored in the minutes. The explanation is probably similar to the lack of notice of the First World War. The United States did not get involved at the beginning, and for much the same reasons. Like the sinking of the *Lusitania,* the attack on Pearl Harbor in December 1941 was the defining event for the new generation of Americans. By April 1942, the minutes still say nothing of the war, but they do note difficulties in obtaining tin for cans.

The war now began to have an impact on their business. There were some additional orders from the military purchasing units, to feed the troops, but it became very hard to complete the canning process because of the lack of raw materials. The processors even began to look into using glass again. The new market for olives in the armed forces was a positive feature, but it was also very difficult to deal with the Quartermaster Corps. The officers drove very hard bargains and laid down tough specifications, something for which they continue to be known. Their attitude was "If you don't like it, there are lots of other people out there who would love to have these contracts." The quartermasters defined olives as a luxury, not an essential food, and ordered modest amounts of them.

Another obvious effect of the war was the manpower situation. Men were drafted, and it was hard to keep the plants going. When women were taken on, they were paid at a lower rate than the men.

It was still possible to hold a technical conference in 1943 but not in 1944. There were too many restrictions on nonessential travel and hotel accommodations. By 1944, the members of the association began to look forward to the postwar period and started planning. In the meantime, the army, navy, and marines continued to take reasonably large consignments of canned ripe California olives, but not the air force.

The war ended on May 8, 1945. That date did not coincide with any of the usual meetings of the COA and is not recorded. The next meeting took place on August 24, but concerned itself solely with the association's own issues, such as sending a wedding gift for an employee of their advertising agency and refusing to send copies of the news bulletin to A. Guirlani, founder of the Star importing company.

In spite of the war being over, association members were still restricted in the use of metals for cans. Plating on the cans could not be above a certain thickness.

There were, however, some new undertakings. The association began to publish *Olive Industry News,* a trade bulletin. A note in the board's minutes states, "A man at the Pomology Department at the College of Agriculture at Davis has been assigned full time to carry on agricultural research on olives." He was not named at the time, but I believe this was the first introduction of Dr. Hudson T. Hartmann to the association.

Dr. Hartmann devoted a large portion of his professional life to olives and was a truly important figure in that sphere. His articles on olive culture in peer-reviewed scientific journals started to appear in the late 1940s. The College of Agriculture evidently underwrote his research for the industry, rather than canners having to pay for it themselves. In 1947, Dr. Hartmann and his associate, Dr. Papaioannu from Greece, were invited to address the annual technical conference. At a more pragmatic level, the board permitted Miss Hevel to buy a new typewriter in 1948.

In keeping with most other American industries, the olive processors had never given much thought to the unpleasant residue of their trade. The steel industry was notorious for the grime and black dust that covered whole cities. Paper mills caused dreadful smells and left ruined rivers in their wake.

Business was too important to waste any time mourning the loss of beauty in their towns. The owners and senior executives were only one generation removed from the men who had resisted the forty-hour week and minimum age limit for child workers. A few do-gooders pounded away on the health problems of dirty air and dirty water, but no one listened to them. Besides, even if anyone believed change were needed, who was going to pay to do anything about it? Overhead was high enough already. Business leaders could not afford to raise it further and still make a profit.

After the war, several factors acted in concert to make people open their eyes to environmental issues and hazards. The specific issue in California was water. Water had always been a contentious topic, and now more than ever, its shortage caused concern. The supply was limited and pouring contaminated water away wasted more than could be replaced. Canners began to worry whether they might be made to do something about this. In August 1947, the president of the Canners' League appointed a waste disposal committee to look into methods of reducing this loss.

The Canners' League (now the California League of Food Processors) was an organization jointly supported by the members of the California canning industry. Its mandate includes the study of scientific problems in canning fruit and vegetables. Its then president asked the COA to participate in these preliminary meetings. Two very senior members, Henry Titus and Lee Newkirk, accepted this responsibility.

For the first time, the COA board had to take note of questions about pollution. Such questions had never been voiced before. There was no announcement that the age of environmentalism had arrived. The science of ecology was still an obscure little branch of biology, known only to a few specialists studying hedgerow communities of plants and animals. The canners' inquiry about polluted water was based on enlightened self-interest.

Once the notion arose that processing companies should begin to clean up, the more knowledgeable men in the industry thought about salt. Salt caused considerable concern. Few other fruits and vegetables required as much salt as the canning of ripe olives, with the possible exception of pickling cucumbers. The California Olive Association's members actually had one of the worst possible problems among the food technology industries: using exceptional amounts of salt in their processing.

As part of the strategy to defend the industry, the canners had come together and formed the Western Fruit and Vegetable Canners' Association (WFVCA). Canning companies that did not belong to the Canners' League could join the WFVCA. The new association would act as a lobbying organization. It subsumed the work of the Canners' League's committee on waste disposal. The motive behind the WFVCA's activity was not philanthropic. It was to try and circumvent or preempt legislation from forcing them to deal with the problem.

Henry Titus and Lee Newkirk, who had been invited to the preliminary meetings sponsored by the Canners' League, reported back to the California Olive Association's board at a meeting on April 30, 1948. By then, the Western Fruit and Vegetable Canners' Association had begun to measure the nature and extent of water pollution resulting from their processing methods, and to start to consider how it could be reduced.

Titus and Newkirk's presentation was a truly seminal event, although no one realized it at the time. It signaled the beginning of the end of the world as they knew it. The cost of cleaning up polluted water and earth around their plants would eventually lead to the demise of almost all of the companies, including the very unfortunate bankruptcy of the Lindsay Ripe Olive Company in 1992. There were twenty-eight olive processing companies in business in 1950, reduced to eleven by 1977. There are only two now.

The canners' worst nightmares came true. They could not prevent the legislation they had predicted, no matter what they did. The state and federal governments enacted statutes and regulations that could not be flouted. The water and land would be cleaned up regardless of any individual's wishes.

The failure of Lindsay Ripe Olive Company is a truly cogent example of the domino effect the legislation caused. There were many difficulties within the company, but the cost of pollution control was probably one of the principal causes of its financial problems. The company set up all sorts of systems to get rid of the enormous amounts of salt in the wastewater. They also had to think of ways to get rid of the mountains of pits that accumulated year after year.

Finding solutions to the problems was very expensive, partly because of Lindsay's enormous size. It got more and more costly as the years went by. As an outsider, I cannot make any really informed comment on the affairs of Lindsay, but it seems that the company had many years of notice in which to get things done before everything spun out of control. In the end, the Lindsay Ripe Olive Company had to cease operating, overwhelmed by the overhead.

The empty Lindsay plant was sold in 1998 to a new consortium led by a former executive of Early California Foods, Gerald Murphy. He had been president of the COA for one year in 1968. The premises will now be used to pack a variety of vegetables but not olives. The cost of finally cleaning it all up after years of pollution has run into millions of dollars. The final sum was arrived at by negotiating with the city, the county, the state, and the federal governments. If the authorities had not yielded slightly in their demands, the sale still would not have gone through. This vast expense had precluded sale and revival of the moribund plant for a very long time. The closure of the Lindsay packing plant had led to the loss of 150 jobs in a small agricultural community, a blow that was hard to absorb.

The town of Lindsay is still somewhat depressed economically. The land around the former Lindsay Ripe Olive Company plant may never really be free of saline contamination. Salt in the soil prevents anything from growing. This land will be useless for any other purpose except industrial use. One hopes that Lindsay's citizens will find new jobs at this plant. The plan to pack many sorts of vegetables will permit them to work all year, unlike the highly seasonal nature of olives.

This discussion of environmental issues, which first were raised in the late 1940s, has led us into the 1990s. Let's return now to the late 1940s to fill in a bit more of California Olive Association's story.

Recovering from the difficulties of the war took longer than expected. Although the Second World War ended in 1945, there was still a shortage of metallic tin in 1950. Even in 1951, this was a problem, perhaps accentuated by the onset of the Korean War and its need for armaments. At the same time, the Korean War meant that the quartermasters continued to have large numbers of troops to feed. Military requirements would continue through the 1950s and beyond, absorbing useful amounts of their products. This was helpful.

The usual variation of the crop from one year to the next was a perennial concern. Regardless of the marketing and stabilization orders, if the crop were too variable, nothing could even out the quantities for sale. Selling a pack that was too large, with a big carry-over to the next season, still haunted the processors.

Finally, though, some prosperity returned. The association collected more of its dues. One of the first uses for the money was to renew their subscription to the California Chamber of Commerce. The increased funds also allowed them once again to focus hard on advertising.

"Deke" Williams, who was responsible for their advertising, racked his brain to come up with better ways to promote their product. Cooking demonstrations, showing how to incorporate ripe California olives into salads and main dishes, and the invention of recipes always helped considerably. He made sure that a new recipe book came out from time to time. In 1952, the association joined with Pet Milk Company to promote "Olive 'n' Tuna Super Supper" as a Lenten meal. In other words, the association's activities resembled the way things had been between the wars. Nothing much would change from one year to the next.

There was still a threat from the cheaper Spanish stuffed olives. It emerged again and again, but on each occasion their Washington lobbyist, Mr. Ehrlich, managed to make it go away. The records show that he worked with the Commerce Department and the USDA. He kept in touch with the Spanish commercial attaché. The Commerce Department exacted promises from the Spanish authorities to keep the volume of imports low. These promises were sincere but could never really be made to stick. The Spanish product was just too cheap and enticing to American wholesalers.

In 1960, Mr. Ehrlich took the line with the USDA that there would be excessive pesticide residues on the Spanish olives, and therefore the United States should not import them. He was always resourceful. Finally, the Spanish prices were too low to fight and the association realized it could not compete. It ceased to pay to have the olives pitted and stuffed in California by 1970, and henceforth these olives were imported from Spain.

The state had enacted an olive marketing order in May 1937. It took over from the federal one, which had been in effect since August 15, 1933. The Olive Advisory Board was set up to supervise this order. On October 2, 1965, another federal marketing order for olives was enacted, superseding the state order. The Olive Advisory Board ceased to exist on that date. This federal order was approved by the growers and is still in effect. It is administered by the California Olive Committee. The committee is composed of eight growers, each from a different section of the state, and eight representatives of canning firms.

On all matters pertaining to the grading, sizing, and inspection of olives, the California Olive Committee can develop standards and regulations. As long as the USDA approves of the proposed rules, these recommendations have the force of federal law. The committee supports and encourages basic and applied research at the University of California, raising the funds from the olive industry directly. In some ways, it has taken over the mantle of the prior California Olive Association (which ceased to exist in its original form in 1972). The California Olive Committee is deeply concerned with the promotion of olives in general, following much the same strategy as the association, with cooking demonstrations, recipe booklets, and advertising in relevant magazines. In addition, the committee maintains industry statistics.

The California Olive Committee owes a great deal to the work of Al Burling, an olive grower in Corning and a member of the committee. He died in 1993 but is still missed by many who knew him. He too was an unlikely candidate for olive farming, coming from

London in 1937. His first venture in California agriculture was raising poultry, but he switched to olive growing soon afterward. In the Second World War, he served in the British Navy, but after his discharge, he returned to Corning and married his wife, Sarah. They had no children, but Al was a scoutmaster for many years and helped to influence many of Corning's citizens in their formative years.

Burling had had very little formal education but used all his native capacity to its utmost. He understood more quickly than most just how important research was to the success of the olive industry, and he would always support whatever program was proposed. Strength of mind and breadth of vision characterized Al Burling.

Because of the need to regulate the market for the finished product, canners had to adjust the amount they paid for raw fruit. The tension between growers and processors had simmered gently over the years. Such tension is inevitable. They have opposite interests. Growers want as much money as they can get for their fruit, while the processors want to get the fruit as cheaply as they can.

The entire idea of controlling the market by means of marketing orders has come under fire recently. Small producers and growers in other fruit businesses feel that they are paying for benefits they do not receive. There have been some lawsuits over this matter.

Complying with environmental requirements has continued to be a serious matter. Reducing the residues of pesticides on fruit and vegetables in the United States to as low a level as possible was a serious regulatory hurdle. Growers learned that the health department had strict rules about which pesticide to use and how to apply it. The processors found that some of the unpleasant tastes, so-called "off flavors," resulted from excessive pesticides.

In the manifold scientific tasks before the California Olive Association, pesticide control was an important topic. Much work was accomplished. It was all reported at the annual technical conferences that began in the 1920s to disseminate the information to the members. They still continue to the present. Many of them have dealt with the pesticide question.

Pesticides were a burden to the growers. Even if they themselves were scrupulous, the behavior of neighboring farmers and ranchers could not always be foreseen or controlled. The effect of the winds was random. Pesticides could be blown across boundaries if the wind changed direction. As each new type of pesticide was introduced and considered to be tasteless or harmless, longer exposure to its effects showed them that these claims were not true. Rachel Carson had eloquently revealed the tragedy wrought by DDT in *Silent Spring*. The chemists then came up with lindane, malathion, and parathion in quick succession, only to find that all of them had serious drawbacks.

Processors also faced scientific problems. Difficulties that are not an issue for the home cook emerge as significant when hundreds or thousands of tons of fruit must be handled. The actual steps are not complicated. There are five basic ways to cure and preserve olives. They can be treated with lye, then rinsed; steeped in water alone; steeped in brine and rinsed; dry cured with salt; or cured in olive oil and then salted. It is the finite time needed to move millions of small individual fruit through the line that is part of the problem. Very large tanks are required as are methods for keeping the olives from either spoiling or getting excessively cured along the way.

The association dealt with all these steps, and explored the best ways to handle them with the assistance of the University of California. Members who paid very little attention to the association's administrative affairs attended the technical conferences and benefited from what they learned there.

As mentioned earlier, the California Olive Committee had begun to take over some of the association's key functions in 1965. With the numbers of processing companies shrinking, it made sense to reduce the size of the California Olive Association. In 1972, it ceased to exist as an independent entity. Miss Hevel was no longer involved. There were no particular reasons to keep it going. The board of directors made an arrangement with the Canners' League (now the California League of Food Processors) to move into their premises in Sacramento. They are still there today. William Grigg has been the full-time manager of the present California Olive Association, a section of the California League of Food Processors, for a number of years, and serves as their legislative advocate when necessary.

The California League of Food Processors is very useful in that it can provide access to health benefit plans for the employees of its constituent associations. Other tasks such as generic advertising for olives as a class of foods now fall under the purview of the California Olive Committee and are not Grigg's responsibility. Once or twice a year, the association puts on a special olive day or holds some other event to promote olives and bring all the people together.

In 1997, the California Olive Association celebrated what it says is its seventy-fifth anniversary. From my research, I think it was actually their eighty-second anniversary. What confuses the issue is that in 1922, the association reincorporated under new articles. It is as if the first seven years no longer counted.

The members of the California Olive Association from its inception to its demise have become like old friends to me as I delve through the history of the industry. The names are quite familiar, because the same people participated year after year. In a few cases the principals are still active, such as G. K. "Pat" Patterson.

There have been a few father-son presidencies of the California Olive Association. J. V. E. Titus of Albers Olive Company, a much respected member for over thirty years, was president in 1930. His son, Henry Titus, held that position in 1953. (The name of Titus goes back into early California agricultural and horticultural history. In the 1850s, L. H. Titus was a prominent vineyardist in Southern California.)

Dan Carter, stepson of Arthur Bell who founded the business now called Bell-Carter, was president in 1957 and again in 1960. His son, Jud Carter, was president twice, in 1977 and in 1989. The Oberti family is another family with two generations represented in the presidency of the California Olive Association. Frank Oberti presided in 1961, his brother James in 1973, and James's son Gary in 1981. The firm they founded is now part of Tri Valley Growers and no longer independently known as the Oberti Olive Company. Nicholas Musco, owner of the Musco Olive Products, was president in 1993. His son Felix has joined him in the family business.

Besides the men who became president, there are many others whose names appear time and again, doing hard work on the committees every year. They too have descendants in the business today, and I have enjoyed meeting many of them since I began the research for this book.

Although the California Olive Association no longer exists in the form in which it was originally founded, olive processors and growers still work together in the current organization and in the California Olive Committee to promote their products, lobby for appropriate legislation, and deal with challenges facing the industry. The metamorphosis of the association into later forms is another sign of the determination of people working in the olive industry to preserve their livelihood, offer the fruit of their labor to consumers, and continue the long and rich heritage of olives in California.

California Olive Association and Committee

Presidents and Vice Presidents 1915–2000

1915	Frank Simonds, Los Angeles Olive Growers and Sylmar Packing Company—President
1930	J. V. E. Titus, Albers Packing Co.—President
1935	C. E. Hazen, Maywood Packing Corp.—President
1936	S. J. Tupper, Olive Products Co.—President
1942	O. D. Gifford, C. M. Gifford & Sons—President
1946	J. M. Glick, B. E. Glick & Sons—President
1949	L. B. Sammis, Rocca Bella—President
1953	Henry S. Titus, Mawer-Gulden-Annis—President
1954	G. K. Patterson, Sunland Olive Co.—President
1957	Dan S. Carter, Bell Packing Co.—President
1958	T. H. Read, Lindsay Ripe Olive Corp.—President
1960	Dan S. Carter, Bell Packing Co.—President
1961	Frank J. Oberti, Oberti Olive Company—President
1964	Elton J. Leggett, Wyandotte Olive Growers—President
1966	Lee Newkirk, Maywood Packing Co.—President
1968	Gerald Murphy, Early California Foods—President
1969	Bruno A. Filice, California Canners and Growers—President
1969–1970	Gerald D. Murphy, Early California Foods—President
	Bruno A. Filice, California Canners and Growers—Vice President
1971–1972	Bruno A. Filice, California Canners and Growers—President
	Dan S. Carter, Bell-Carter Olive Company—Vice President
1973–1974	James Oberti, Oberti Olive Company, TVG—President
	G. K. "Pat" Patterson, Early California Foods—Vice President
1975–1976	Earl S. Fox, Lindsay Olive Growers—President
	G. K. "Pat" Patterson, Oberti Olive Company, TVG—Vice President
1977–1978	H. Jud Carter, Bell-Carter Olive Company—President
	Gary Oberti, Oberti Olive Company, TVG—Vice President

1979–1980 B. J. McFarland, Early California Foods, Inc.—President
Gary Oberti, Oberti Olive Company, TVG—Vice President

1981–1982 Gary Oberti, Oberti Olive Company, TVG—President
Robert D. Rossio, Lindsay Olive Growers—Vice President

1983–1984 Robert D. Rossio, Lindsay Olive Growers—President
(No Vice President according to Mr. Rossio)

1985–1986 Marvin Martin, Oberti Olive Company, TVG—President
Nicholas Musco, Musco Olive Products—Vice President

1987–1988 Marvin Martin, Oberti Olive Company, TVG—President
Nicholas Musco, Musco Olive Products—Vice President

1989–1990 H. Jud Carter, Bell-Carter Foods, Inc.—President
Pat Coghlan, Aunt Nellies Farm Kitchen, Inc.—Vice President

1991–1992 Gary Oberti, Oberti Olive Company, TVG—President
Horace Wells, Vlasic Foods—Vice President

1993–1994 Nicholas Musco, Musco Olive Products—President
Tim Carter, Bell-Carter Foods, Inc.—Vice President

1995–1996 Horace Wells, Vlasic Foods—President
Tim Carter, Bell-Carter Foods, Inc.—Vice President

1997–1998 Bob Moore, Oberti Olive Company, TVG—President
Ken Wienholz, Bell-Carter Foods, Inc.—Vice President

1999–2000 Ken Wienholz, Bell-Carter Foods, Inc.—President
Nicholas Musco, Musco Olive Products—Vice President

10

The University of California's Role
in the Development of the Olive Industry

Since the earliest days, when the publicly funded Agricultural, Mining, and Mechanical Arts College of California merged with a small private college in Oakland, the College of California, to create the University of California in 1868, the resulting institution has been deeply involved in all aspects of the California olive industry. One reason was that the College of Agriculture at the new university was the first separate school to be established. Classes began in 1869 at the Oakland site, but the university began to build in Berkeley soon afterwards. For almost forty years, until the agriculture department expanded to Davis in 1906, Berkeley was the sole campus of the university. Other campuses followed over the next decades, developing the now familiar organization spread across much of the state.

At various times, some faculty in the agriculture and science departments at Berkeley virtually devoted themselves full time to studying the olives. The Pomology Department was one, food technology was another. Now that science has been "deconstructed" into component disciplines, such as genetics, molecular biology, and so forth, the divisions are no longer by specific fruit or vegetable. Modern generic techniques enable scientists to study a strawberry, orange, grape, or olive in the most

🐚 EUGENE W. HILGARD, PROFESSOR OF AGRICULTURE, DIRECTOR
OF THE UNIVERSITY AGRICULTURAL EXPERIMENT STATION
FROM 1875 TO 1905, AND DEAN OF THE COLLEGE OF AGRICUL-
TURE, UNIVERSITY OF CALIFORNIA AT BERKELEY.

appropriate way. Only a very few of the largest and most lucrative agricultural sectors, such as viticulture and the citrus industry, still have dedicated faculty.

While the olive was never among the most valuable crops, it did rank among the top fifteen agricultural products of the state in the early 1970s. It was worthwhile to maintain olive specialists in departments such as pomology and food technology. One of those specialists, Professor George C. Martin of the Pomology Department at Davis, retired in 1996. He has no specific successor.

The early days of the University of California, then known as the College of California, coincided with the tide of enthusiasm about olive growing. The College of California began as a private school in Oakland, but then the small institution became a public university under a charter from the State of California in 1868. The College of Agriculture was incorporated in it shortly afterward. All this occurred only twenty years after California became a state and the gold rush had filled it with people. Other colleges of higher education had started sooner, such as the University of Santa Clara at the former Mission Santa Clara in 1851, and Mills College, also founded in 1851, in Oakland, but once the resources of a great state were made available, the new foundation for the university grew rapidly.

Two major forces shaped the approach to higher education in California. One was the desire to continue the tradition of liberal arts for their own sake, the ethos of colleges like Harvard and Yale. The other was the need for a strictly practical training program for farmers and others who had to wrest a living from the soil. The founders of the College of California belonged to the former party.

Support for a school to train farmers stemmed from the passage of the federal Land Grant College (Morrill) Act in 1862. Its provisions deeded 30,000 acres of land to each state for every senator and congressman representing it. Once the land was sold, the proceeds were used to establish land grant colleges for agriculture. The availability of these funds led to the establishment of the Agricultural, Mining, and Mechanical Arts College in 1866. Little was done to get the college actually built. It remained a skeleton plan only. Joining this college together with the College of California to create a public university was the inspiration of Governor Frederick Low in 1867.[1]

The first dean of the new College of Agriculture was Ezra Slocum Carr. While he was in some ways a worthy man, he was ill suited to the post and only stayed for four years. He was replaced by Eugene Woldemar Hilgard, a physical scientist born in Germany but brought up in the American Midwest.

Original chemistry building at the College of Agriculture, University of California at Berkeley.

Hilgard was the consummate professor who would have shone at an old, well-established university. Hilgard's father was a prominent legal scholar who fled Germany about twelve years before the revolution of 1848 because he feared persecution for his liberal views. Eugene, the youngest of ten children, was well educated in the sciences and the humanities and brought strong principles of academic rigor to his task. He believed that even the most basic practical training needed to be anchored in an atmosphere of research and study of the fundamentals. There was nothing provincial about him. Eugene Hilgard was sophisticated both in science and in the politics of universities. He brought supreme credibility to the young, struggling university.

Hilgard was an authority on soils. Fertile soil is a prerequisite for any type of successful growth. He lectured extensively to farmers all over the state on the need to maintain fertile soil. These men had not had the advantages of a university education and were initially rather cool to him. They did not believe that a college professor had anything to tell them about farming. His skill and sincerity were so obvious that this state of affairs did not last long.

Dean Hilgard shaped the College of Agriculture firmly and effectively from the start. He studied soil conditions systematically all over the state, identifying the best places to grow particular crops. One of his jobs before going to California was with the United States Geological Survey, so he knew soil very thoroughly. He recognized the soil depletion caused by intensive wheat farming, he pondered the possibility of growing cotton and other new crops, and he established the scientific basis for growing grapes successfully in California.

Hilgard quickly took on the olive and directed many of his staff in special studies for almost twenty years. He himself gave papers on its culture, the preservation of the fruit, and production of oil. His attention to detail was very important. In 1891, he wrote about the pitfalls of both the pickling process and of making olive oil: "We should make *first class* pickled olives of those which we pickle at all, but this has to be learned. . . . Perhaps a dozen will be very good indeed; then you come to one that isn't good, that has a nasty taste. The cause of that was simply this: the olive was bruised in harvesting. Instead of taking them off carefully, as is done in Europe, it was beaten off, and bruised olives are unfit for pickling. You can use them only for oil. . . . Again, if olives are bruised, provided that they have no mold on them, they are still good to make oil if the oil is made at once; but a few moldy olives will contaminate the oil that is made of them. An injured olive that has become moldy may injure a whole cask of oil."[2]

He was a bit confused about the difference between the European and American methods of harvesting. Beating the trees is an ancient way of getting the olives down, depicted on Attic vases made in 500 B.C.E. (see page 5) and still widespread in the Mediterranean countries.

Hilgard paid a good deal of attention to the pickling process. He established that different types of olives needed to be handled differently. If the same method that was successful with Mission olives were used for Sevillanos, the fruit became blistered and the resulting product was unreliable. Later, two men, Fred Beresford, a grower and processor

in Corning where the Sevillano predominated for historical reasons, and Professor Frederic Bioletti, a wine expert at the university who also studied olive processing, overcame this problem.

When Mrs. Ehmann, "mother of the California ripe olive industry," went to the college for assistance in curing her olive crop, she was referred to Hilgard. He then farmed out the work to specialists such as Professor Bioletti.

Olives and wine were key practical topics requiring attention in the Department of Agriculture. Wine in particular would become a huge source of income for the state's growers and vintners, and hence commanded a good deal of the university's resources. This remains true today. Hilgard criticized almost everything about the wine industry of the 1880s, effectively goading the people involved to raise their standards.

Hilgard was able to get cooperation from members of other departments for his work on the olive. He received many requests for help, such as Mrs. Ehmann's, and he distributed them to the Department of Chemistry, among others. Frederic Bioletti and George Colby, both chemists, found answers to problems of pickling olives and preserving them safely. Hilgard never gave up his involvement in such questions.

Hilgard's tenure lasted from 1875 to 1905, during which time there were many changes and much growth at the university. One change he did not favor was the development of the University of California campus at Davis. He feared that it would put the clock back to

a time when agriculture was only a practical subject based on rote learning and not leavened by academic study. The Davis campus opened in 1906, after he had retired. It was one of the few times he was wrong. Davis has continued the tradition of academic excellence until the present.

For his many years of dedicated work at the University of California, Hilgard is commemorated in the journal series called *Hilgardia,* which contains articles on all the basic sciences of agriculture. A street in Berkeley, just north of the University of California campus, is also named for him, as is Hilgard Hall on the campus itself.

At the end of Hilgard's tenure, William Vere Cruess joined the faculty as an enzymologist. Professor Cruess was born in 1886, on a farm in the small California mission town of San Miguel. He came of staunch Presbyterian stock. Hard work and frugality were instilled into him early. In 1906, he entered the University of California and worked his way through, studying chemistry. Soon after he was graduated, he was offered a position in the enzymology laboratory and rapidly developed his skill and reputation.

Colleagues and graduate assistants were in awe of Cruess's prodigious energy and accomplishments. At the Department of Chemistry, Cruess performed numerous valuable experiments, taught several courses, wrote five books, and eventually published 895 papers in the scientific literature. He applied the same principles of hard work to all aspects of his life. One young scholar remembered being asked to do some farm work, together with another young man, during the busy season on Professor Cruess's property. The two younger men between them never did as much as the professor by himself, and that was just his weekend relaxation.[3]

WILLIAM VERE CRUESS, PROFESSOR OF ENZYMOLOGY AT THE UNIVERSITY OF CALIFORNIA AT BERKELEY AND DIRECTOR OF THE FOOD TECHNOLOGY LABORATORY. PROFESSOR CRUESS NEVER WORKED AT THE DAVIS CAMPUS, BUT THE DEPARTMENT'S BUILDING THERE IS NAMED IN HIS HONOR.

Of particular significance for the olive industry, Cruess created the Food Products Laboratory, which focused on the study of food science (now called "food technology"). It was the first of its kind anywhere. The Food Products Laboratory was created as a response to the rapid changes in the ways food could be preserved on a very large scale. California was the premier fruit-growing state, and it needed this type of service, a scientific basis for safe canning principles, for the food preservation industry.

The origin of the Food Products Laboratory was almost accidental. Two Argentinian students enrolled at the university and requested training in canning methods. Nothing like that existed and in order to accommodate them, Dean Hilgard's successor, E. J. Wickson, suggested that Professor Cruess take them under his wing. Together they explored the canning factories and a course was devised.

Forty-seven of Cruess's scientific papers were devoted to the olive and its chemistry, approximately 5 percent of his output. During the botulism crisis in the 1920s, he devoted himself to solving the bacteriological problems of canned olives, making sure nothing like that ever occurred again. He published a series of papers showing the effectiveness of proper temperature control and other factors in preventing bacterial contamination of canned olives.[4]

Cruess traveled extensively in search of better ways to prepare olives. His reports in the *Bulletins* of the Agricultural Experiment Station of the University of California describe his findings in great detail. It was Professor Cruess who introduced two Egyptian varieties of olive trees into the United States. Although he focused on the California ripe olive and its problems, he was also interested in olive oil. In 1941, he published some suggested standards for premier olive oil, in which he defined qualities such as color, viscosity, acid concentration, and degree of rancidity. His work is the basis of current standards.

The California Olive Association valued Cruess's interest and knowledge, and supported his department generously through the years, including his travel. The association frequently honored him at its technical conferences. Professor Cruess died in 1968 at the age of eighty-two. He had always worked at Berkeley and never moved his office to Davis. The Department of Food Technology is now located on the campus at Davis in the appropriately named Cruess Hall.

In more recent years, some of Cruess's former graduate students, such as Reese Vaughn, have continued to work on the best techniques for preserving olives in metal cans. Avoiding bacterial and fungal infection remains a priority, but maintaining texture, color, and flavor comes very close behind.

"Sandwiched" between the soil (Hilgard) and the metal can (Cruess, Vaughn) was the olive tree. Professor Hudson T. Hartmann was its advocate. A graduate of the University of Missouri, with a doctorate from the University of California at Berkeley, Hartmann joined the Department of Pomology at UC Davis in 1940 and remained there until he retired as full professor in 1980. He died in 1994 at the age of seventy-nine.

Hartmann wrote more than three hundred papers on the physiology and production of the olive. Among his achievements was the revitalization of the olive industry in Egypt, but his discoveries and insights into the behavior of the olive tree in this country were invaluable. He covered all aspects of the olive tree—from the growth and transplanting of seedlings, to the pruning of mature trees and optimal methods of picking the fruit. Much current thinking about the olive tree in California is a gloss on Hartmann.

🌳 HUDSON T. HARTMANN, PROFESSOR OF POMOLOGY AT THE UNIVERSITY OF CALIFORNIA AT DAVIS.

Hartmann edited the *Olive Industry News* and wrote much of it himself. When he began to slow down and reduce his responsibilities, the journal ceased to appear.

Hartmann wrote many *Bulletins* of the Agriculture Extension Service about the best ways to grow olives. He wrote in clear simple prose so all could read and learn. He issued the first UC Davis compendium of olive growing, the *Olive Production Manual,* a text that is still being used and updated by the present faculty.[5] The most recent edition came out in 1994.

Hartmann was also a favorite of the California Olive Association, for very good reason. Soon after his arrival at the University of California at Davis, he was participating in the technical conferences and began directing research for them. Many people who knew him and worked with him recall him as a very decent human being, fair-minded and pleasant to know.

Hartmann's technician, John Whisler (now in his eighties), was glad he could go with Professor Hartmann to scientific meetings. Technicians are not always invited to go to these meetings by their chief. Whisler helped to lay out the experimental orchard of different olive varieties at the Winters campus of the university, and he told me a great deal about each one. He also participated in the physiological work in the laboratory, but principally he did the outdoor orchard work for Hartmann, who was more of a bench scientist.

Professor Hartmann traveled a good deal, to the Mediterranean countries and also to Australia, looking into the olive industries wherever he went. One of his valuable findings in Australia was the Swan Hill variety of olive tree, named for the town where he found it. His hosts on that occasion showed him an olive tree that had been closely observed for thirty years and was never seen to bear fruit. Hartmann immediately recognized its value as a landscape plant and arranged for samples of it to be exported to California. After the tree passed its period of quarantine, it was propagated and is one of the most widely grown specimen trees in California today. It allows people to have their cake and eat it too: it is a handsome olive tree, but it has no oily, black fruit to fall onto lawns and driveways.

George C. Martin is a former professor of pomology at Davis who also focused on the olive during his academic career. He assumed research into the olive tree and its fruit upon the retirement of Hudson Hartmann, and concentrated on studying the olive's physiology. He too is a bench scientist with an interest in the growth patterns and biological functions of this fruit. Martin is one of the editors of the latest edition of the *Olive Production Manual*. The other editors are also affiliated with the University of California at Davis: Louise Ferguson in the Department of Pomology (based at the Kearney Agricultural Center in Parlier near Fresno), and G. Steven Sibbett, farm adviser for the Agricultural Extension Station in Tulare County (based in Visalia). Joseph Connell, farm adviser for the Agricultural Extension Station in Butte County, contributed the chapter on the history of the olive in California.

One of the issues that university researchers studied involved the maturity of an olive: in short, when is an olive ripe? Eventually, they determined a technical distinction between "horticultural" maturity and "physiological" maturity. "Horticultural" maturity denotes a period at which sufficient numbers of the fruit on each tree are large enough to justify picking them, even though all of them have not gone through the full stages of ripening: "physiological" maturity. The former occurs about four months before the latter. Presumably because of its origin in the Mediterranean lands, the olive ripens in the winter, after the period in which the deciduous fruits have been gathered. This allows growers to use crews that have been released from the earlier harvesting of other crops. Picking crops in the late fall in California means that very often the workers have to contend with rain and wind, conditions that can slow them down. If the olives are left on the trees throughout a cold winter, many will shrivel and lose water content.

One of the results of the cooperation between the California Olive Association, the U.S. Department of Agriculture, and the University of California has been to standardize the signs by which a grower can assume the fruit has reached horticultural maturity and therefore can begin harvesting. These are based on color and texture, including the amount of juice exuded when an olive is crushed by hand in the orchard. Because the fruit continues to gain size and weight through the season, there has to be a point of compromise at which the advantages of increased size are outweighed by the disadvantages of wind damage, overripeness, and cold injury. This point is agreed upon in most cases by the growers and the field men from the canners. Speed is essential in harvesting, since the crop continues to ripen and thus deteriorate as time passes during the picking period. The weather too must be factored in. It is best if picking is completed before the end of October.

If one wants unripe olives picked quickly and efficiently by human beings, then some way to hasten their detachment from the branches would be helpful. If one is using a machine to pick them, it is essential. Ripe fruit has chemicals that cause it to separate and fall spontaneously. Unripe fruit has a vested interest in staying on the tree longer and so resists separation prematurely.

Professor Hartmann spent many years working to develop a chemical agent that would allow unripe fruit to be separated more easily from the tree. Out of a number of possible agents, he found that naphthalenacetic acid (NAA) was the best one. Instead of being used at harvest time, NAA works at the very beginning of the season. George Martin also spent much of his time working on loosening agents. Unlike NAA, he studied those that could be used at harvest time.

NAA can also sometimes be used to remove the excess fruit in the bumper years so as to have a better crop in the succeeding thin year. This biennial pattern of bearing is coded into the olive tree, regardless of its variety. The pattern can be slightly modified by good cultural practices, but it does not completely disappear. The theory of reducing the heavy crop is that the tree somehow stores energy for the following year. NAA has to be applied about two weeks after full bloom to reduce the size of the crop.

NAA is by no means perfect, and it can do all sorts of unexpected things if not very carefully handled. Even when it is used properly, the trees may react differently from the way they have reacted before. Gary Oberti, son and nephew of olive growers and processors in Madera, told me that he had wanted to thin a very heavy crop one year, so as to allow the trees to bear more fruit the next one. Although Gary carefully followed the instructions about timing and quantities, the chemical removed his entire crop for that year and he had no fruit left. The following year, the trees bore fruit again. Such experiences can affect one's attitude very quickly, creating considerable skepticism about a particular chemical.

Another issue at harvest, in addition to the need to loosen the fruit from the tree, is the picking itself. Picking the fruit by hand is very costly. In many other commercial crops, picking is now almost completely done by machine. Agronomists have developed special varieties of tomatoes, peas, and beans that lend themselves to this type of harvesting. Grape harvesting is now coming into this phase. One key requirement for mechanical harvesting is that the crop ripens all at the same time. In annual crops like beans, the whole plant is gathered up by the machine. No attempt is made to pick just the beans. The machine separates the beans later.

The concept of the mechanical olive harvester is fairly simple. A vibrating machine shakes the trunk of the olive tree, and the fruit falls into a canvas receptacle fastened round the tree. Early California models of such machines were made by the firm of Louis Gerrans in Colusa. The mechanical harvester is based on the old Mediterranean method of beating the olives off the tree. Mechanical harvesting of olives was studied very carefully throughout the 1960s and 1970s, but in the end, the vibrating machines were not successful on a large enough scale to warrant their capital cost. Although a ton of olives could be harvested for $45, compared to $250 per ton for hand labor, growers could not recoup their investment.

There were several disadvantages to using mechanical harvesters. Among the most significant was the timing of the harvest. As noted previously, olives for canning must be picked before they are fully ripe. Calculating the degree of force needed to remove incompletely ripe fruit from a tree against the damage it inflicted on the branches and trunk proved to be an insuperable problem. Mechanical harvesting resulted in too many broken branches and damaged trees, which reduced subsequent crops. Trees with a single trunk did better than those with several main stems. The cambium layer of the trunk was also very susceptible to damage, compromising the trees' survival. This difficulty could be overcome by training the operator to control the unit better.

Another serious fault with mechanical harvesting was that too much fruit was damaged as it fell into the catching frames; careful padding of the frames could mitigate this a little. Mechanical failure and the loss of time in making repairs also had to be taken into account. The terrain played a role too, as did the layout of orchards. A very steep property was unsuitable for mechanical harvesting. The distance between trees and the trees' relation to others near them were crucial. Very few orchards had been planted with such a machine in mind.

Recent experiments with artificial fingerlike machines, adapted from ones used in vineyards, look as though they may be more practical. If they become widespread, it will require the orchards' configuration to be radically altered. The trees have to be closer together, and much lower in height, rather like the rows of grapes in a hedgelike configuration, so the machines can go down along both the front and back of the trees.

Maurice Penna, an independent grower in Orland, is considering replanting his orchard to conform to this type of mechanical harvesting. He is a man who thinks for himself. In a very competitive field, he has found niches. He sells raw olives to brokers in New York and other cities with large populations of Italians and Greeks who liked to cure their own olives. He now processes his crop with classical recipes for the ethnic markets in the same large cities. Maurice has thought about the problem of harvesting very thoroughly. His colleagues in the olive growing business respect Maurice but secretly think he is a little eccentric. I am not so sure.

One of the disadvantages of machines is that the fruit may be handled more roughly than when picked by hand. It is very important to control the process in the orchard to avoid bruising and blemishes. Here is where the field man of an olive processing company may be crucial. He will reject damaged fruit immediately, so the grower has to supervise personally or make it clear to anyone in charge that care is essential. As the machines are improved, this problem will be reduced. American processors have exceedingly high standards for raw fruit.

Just as the issues and concerns about growing and harvesting olives are complex, so too are the issues and concerns about processing them. Of course, methods of preserving olives were already in existence when the university began its association with the industry. They were based on very old recipes brought from Spain, Italy, Greece, and France. The faculty at the university worked to improve these methods but did not originate them.

The most frequently used method of curing olives for canning in California is with lye. After the olives are picked and transported to the plant, they are steeped in brine or a mixture of weak organic acids. Once out of the acid solution, they are treated with graduated doses of alkali to hasten the removal of the bitter glycoside, washed to get rid of the alkali, pitted, and then placed in metal cans. These steps lead to the "California black ripe olive." Controlled exposure to the air and light helps to turn them dark before canning, but small amounts of ferrous gluconate can be used to enhance that reaction. To create the ethnic varieties such as Greek or Sicilian olives, the methods vary somewhat but not the underlying principle.

In the immediate post–Second World War years, the University of California chemists studied the nature and process of the color. They found that it was due to the development of anthocyanins, dark pigments found in many plant organs. The color change occurs by itself, in a spontaneous chemical reaction, hastened or retarded by the amount of light available. The specific chemicals causing blackness in olives are cyanidin-3-glucoside and cyanidin-3-rutinoside.

Small amounts of ferrous gluconate were sometimes added during the curing process. The function of ferrous gluconate was to fix the color, not to cause it. This was very significant for the Food and Drug Administration labeling laws. The FDA truth-in-labeling standards required that anything used in the processing had to be listed as well as the actual ingredients. The public does not like too many artificial chemical constituents. Ferrous gluconate appears on the labels when it is used, but the FDA accepted the fact that it only played a very subordinate role. In many processing plants, the canners avoid it altogether.

It was fortuitous that Professor Bioletti came across a process that made the olives shiny and black right at the beginning of the modern era of olive processing. This is almost the same as the color of the true ripe olive left on the tree. The process might just as well have created a red or purple olive that would have had the same taste. The public relations benefit of having this artifactual resemblance to a really ripe olive was inestimable. Most people have no idea that the olive they are eating began life quite differently. The processors have re-created the normal color that would have been present had they left the olive on the tree.

Olive processors do not only make "black ripe olives." They also make green ones. To create a "green ripe olive," air and light must be excluded from the vats so that lactic acid is formed and can last long enough to do its work. Lactic acid works anaerobically, meaning that no oxygen must be present. Seasonings and spices are added later to give them the special tastes. Over the past decades, improvements in the process have reduced the time needed to create a well-cured olive. While the process used to take between three and four weeks, it now takes less than one week.

Even in this very brief recital of issues involved in the growing, harvesting, and curing of olives, one can easily see how important the scientific underpinnings are. In the modern world, all food processing on the scale of the California plants is closely backed by scientists, whether publicly supported or private. Too much is at stake to allow anything to go wrong. In spite of this, processors live in fear of episodes of infection and contamination, which can lead to recall of the products and loss of public confidence.

The collaboration of the University of California with the olive industry, which began at the end of the nineteenth century and spanned the twentieth, now continues as we move into the twenty-first century. From Eugene Hilgard's early outings to speak with farmers about maintaining fertile soil to the development of safe and reliable canning methods, from Frederic Bioletti's method for ensuring a shiny, black "ripe" olive to the discovery of NAA's usefulness as a fruit-loosening agent, the University of California and the olive industry have faced many challenges together. Undoubtedly, more problems lie ahead. If the past is any gauge, the hard-earned, practical skill of olive growers and processors combined with the focused scientific methods of University of California faculty will help sustain the olive industry through the twenty-first century and beyond.

Appendix A

CHRONOLOGY OF THE OLIVE IN CALIFORNIA

CALIFORNIA OLIVE EVENTS	WORLD/CALIFORNIA EVENTS

1492	Christopher Columbus lands in the Bahamas and discovers the New World
1497	First record of olive trees being sent to the Caribbean and Mexico; the trees were from Olivares, near Seville, Spain
1503	Father Valencia arrives in Mexico City with the "twelve apostles"; they plant many olive trees at the Franciscan "college" (monastery) there
1524	Start of Augustinian, Franciscan, and Dominican missions in Mexico
1524	Don Antonio Rivera takes a dozen olive trees to Peru; only two survive after being planted on his grounds; considered to be the origin of all the olive trees in Peru and, later, Chile
1560	Jesuit missionaries start to work in Spanish America
1697	Father Salvatierra founds first of Jesuit missions at Loreto in Baja California
1767	King Carlos III of Spain dismisses the Jesuit order and instructs the Franciscan order to assume their duties
1769	Governor Portola and Father Junipero Serra land on the shores of Alta California; they found Mission San Diego de Alcala and in succeeding years lay foundations of future agriculture, including cattle, wheat, fruit, and vegetables
ca. 1775 to 1780 (Exact date unknown)	First olive trees planted in the mission orchards, probably at San Diego, San Jose, Santa Clara, and others
1776	American Revolution succeeds; United States founded
1803	First written record of olive oil being pressed in California; Father Fermín Lasuén mentions it in a report to his superiors
1822	Mexico breaks with Spain and becomes independent

1834	Mexican government secularizes the missions, annexes the land and all its contents to State; missionaries removed from office and no longer in charge of mission lands
ca. 1830 to 1840	Commercial orchards are started in and around Los Angeles; William Wolfskill is first to grow oranges on a large scale; Jean Louis Vignes lays out vineyards and makes wine commercially; both Wolfskill and Vignes used cuttings from the defunct San Gabriel mission's trees and vines
1841	First large-scale wagon train, led by John Bidwell, comes overland to California safely from the Midwest
1848	Gold found in Coloma; California's population rises from a few hundred to over 100,000 in two years
1850 to 1885	Many Italian immigrants come to California, particularly to Calaveras County
1851	First commercial nurseries started in California
1854	California State Agricultural Society is chartered
ca. 1855	Great wealth from mining and other businesses stimulates development of Sacramento and San Francisco; florists and nurseries expand, providing necessary basis for later extensive commercial fruit growing
1862/63	Unprecedented floods in the Central Valley destroy the cattle industry, which is replaced by wheat farming as primary large-scale agricultural activity
1868/69	First commercial olive orchards laid out; Ellwood Cooper uses cuttings from Mission Santa Barbara orchard; Frank Kimball uses cuttings from Mission San Diego
1871	Olive oil produced commercially in California for the first time at the oil mill in Camulos (Ventura County) belonging to the Del Valle family
1874	First Manzanillo and Sevillano olive trees imported from Spain
1880s	Over 150 nurseries now in California; many sell olive trees; movement to change to different types of olive trees for flavor, yield, and other qualities; eventually almost 300 varieties are imported from the Mediterranean countries
1890s	Wheat no longer successful; California's agriculture shifts to horticulture: fruit and vegetables
1899	Ripe olives successfully preserved in sealed metal cans; more olive companies begin canning
ca. 1900	Nurseries no longer carry most of the fancy olive varieties; only standard varieties now; California olive oil can no longer compete with imported oil; industry declines; table olives grow in popularity

1914 to 1918	First World War
1919	First of several epidemics of botulism traced to California canned ripe olives; industry devastated
1924	Last outbreak of botulism due to California canned ripe olives
1924/25	Combined research by federal, state, and private scientists leads to safer methods of canning olives
1929	Great Depression and financial panic begin
1933	First federal marketing order issued for California canned ripe olives
1936	Spanish Civil War begins; olive oil and table olives not prepared or exported; new olive oil businesses start in California, using Mission olives
1939	Second World War starts; traces of the depression remain in the U.S.; exports of olive oil from Italy cease
1939	Opportunities expand to manufacture olive oil in California
1945	Second World War ends
1947	Spain and Italy resume olive trade; California olive oil business settles back into former pattern; many companies engendered by the war close
ca. 1950	First stirrings of environmental concerns; disposition of wastewater now seen as a problem for all food processors; it is a worse problem for olive canners because they use more salt than any other processor
1960s	Completion of California Water Project in the Central Valley
1965	New federal marketing order promulgated; still currently in effect
ca. 1970	Consolidation of olive canning companies begins, partially driven by high cost of complying with environmental laws; number of firms drops from twenty-eight to eleven
ca. 1985	New wave of specialized California olive oil makers begins, using unusual varieties of olive trees, often imported from Italy or France
1999	Consolidation of California's olive processing companies continues; only two companies left

Appendix B

At one time, more than a hundred firms made olive oil in California. Most of them have been out of business for years and are now forgotten. This list re-creates what is known of their activities from archives of various sorts. The efforts of local historians have been the mainstay in recovering at least basic information, supplemented by entries in old city directories and the memory of living persons. Most of the companies that have been described in some detail in the main text do not appear here.

❧   ❧   ❧

Aeolia Olive Oil Company (Auburn)

This olive orchard and olive oil company were started by Frederick Birdsall in 1887. Birdsall came to California from Peekskill, New York, in 1851 at the age of twenty-one. He was attracted by the prospect of gold. Birdsall, an engineer, built a narrow-gauge railroad between Woodbridge and Valley Springs in Calaveras County. After that, he ran a reduction mill for silver at Dayton, Nevada. At one point, he was a shopkeeper in Paradise (Butte County) and sold supplies to the miners in Placer County. One of the most important things he constructed was the water supply system for the city of Auburn, which was still in use in 1924.

Very soon after Ellwood Cooper and Frank Kimball publicized olive growing, Birdsall started his orchards on sixty-five acres in the Aeolia Heights section of Auburn. He brought the trees from Sicily in the late 1870s and early 1880s. Many of those trees are still producing for the current owner, "Amigo" Cantisano. Birdsall died in 1900, and his son took over the business. By 1950, the family could not compete with imported olive oil, and they ceased producing their own oil. Instead they switched to pickling olives. Birdsall's descendants ran the orchard and press until 1970. A number of the original Aeolia olive oil bottles are still in private collections.

Akerman and Tuffley (San Diego)

R. L. Tuffley was listed in a San Diego directory in 1895 as a rancher in the Mission Valley. He also appeared in one entry as a mechanic. In 1901, E. W. Akerman joined with him and they ran an olive oil press and pickle factory in the Old Town section of San Diego. There were two Akermans, E. W. and John T., in the business. Possibly one or other of the partners had worked for the Kimballs and learned about olives from them. Some of their olive oil bottles are still in existence.

Albers Olive Company (Riverside County)

A young man named Albers from St. Louis, Missouri, started an orchard in Elsinore but built his oil mill in Riverside. It was a large operation with a 135-acre orchard and very big factory, making both olive oil and pickles. His neighbors thought he was very rash, and he himself laughingly called his operation "Albers' folly." In spite of the jokes, it prospered and became an important landmark. "Elsinore is known for its olives," according to Brown and Boyd's 1922 *History of San Bernardino and Riverside Counties*. The expansion of olive growing in this region was noticeable by 1887, when a survey listed over one thousand acres under cultivation in the southern counties of California. An 1890 information guidebook for the town of Redlands in Riverside County noted that there were eighteen acres of olives in the town. This was still a fairly small percentage of the three thousand acres planted with citrus trees, but it was a sign of activity.

In 1914, the town of Redlands gave a banquet for fruit growers who had been there since the 1870s. It was only for those whose residence predated 1880. In addition to Albers, the list included three men with olive orchards: James Boyd with ten acres, J. B. Huberty with 112 acres, and J. E. Cutty with six acres. The others all grew citrus.

A senior official of the Albers Company, J. V. E. Titus, was an early and enthusiastic member of the California Olive Association, and his son, Henry, followed in his footsteps. The firm was still active in the 1930s.

American Olive Company (Los Angeles)
This company made olive oil at the turn of the century. It operated at 1701 East Adams Street.

Bambecino Olive Company (Modesto)
Nick Bambecino made olive oil early in this century.

Bayview Olive Oil Company (Napa)
Felix Borreo owned the Bayview Vineyard and made olive oil very early. He came to Napa in 1866. Borreo was born in Italy in 1837 and went to sea at the age of fourteen. In 1852, he arrived in California. He worked in various enterprises, as a fisherman, as a gold miner, in grocery stores, and even in a restaurant. Once he got to Napa, he settled down, opening a general store that sold supplies for humans and animals, and buying the four hundred-acre vineyard. He put in olive trees and pressed the oil to sell in his store. There are some Bayview bottles in private collections.

Bosse Ranch (Placer County)
This ranch later became S. J. Samson's Spring Creek Ranch.

Bolivar Olive Oil (San Diego)
There is not much information about the Bolivar firm apart from the name. Two of its senior officials were active in the California Olive Association during the early period before 1930.

Bowen and Goudge (Pomona)
Bowen and Goudge were in business in the 1890s. They registered the design of their bottles with the California Secretary of State on May 11, 1891.

Bowles Brothers (Los Angeles)
The Bowles brothers were listed as olive oil makers in the 1896 Los Angeles City Directory.

Brown Olive Company (Strathmore)
No other information exists about the Brown firm apart from the name.

Bruno Olive Oil Company (Fresno)
There was a large family of Brunos in Fresno early in the twentieth century. The first one to appear in the Fresno City Directory was Salvatore, who lived at 1909 F Street in 1913. His occupation was laborer. In 1914, there were three Brunos: Joseph and Frank, who were listed as laborers, and Salvatore, who was now noted to be a farmer. Presumably they were brothers. By 1924, the family had grown to five, with Frank now working as a grocer, and another brother, Nicholas, appearing as a fruit shipper. Salvatore was still a farmer. I assume he grew the olive trees and pressed the oil that Frank sold. Nicholas worked in the Bank of America Building erected by Amadeo Peter Giannini, founder of the bank. Bruno olive oil was available through the 1930s, according to John Ugaste, Sr., a veteran maker of olive oil.

Fred Busby (Concord)
Busby was not listed as an olive grower or maker of olive oil in an Oakland directory until 1907, though he was already doing it at an earlier date. The Oakland Board of Trade's brochure for 1887 listed Busby and his brother as olive growers on a very large scale. The article in the brochure noted that Busby was the first man to make olive oil on his own premises "instead of in a dingy cellar in San Francisco." This is rather fanciful since dozens of other people were pressing olive oil in many quite salubrious places at that period. His wife, Mary, and his brother were both active in his olive oil business. The president was R. N. Busby. Some of the Busby bottles have survived.

The Busbys moved twice within the Oakland area, from Grove Street to Adeline Avenue. His formal occupation was given as a glover in the Oakland directory. He manufactured gloves and gauntlets of every description.

California Olive Growers Company (Los Angeles)
This company worked from the Henn Building in 1906.

Luigi Canepa (San Francisco)
Canepa was making olive oil in San Francisco in 1893. Canepa is a very common name, and I have not traced any descendants of this particular Canepa family.

Santo Catania (Fresno)
Santo Catania listed himself in the Fresno City Directory as a manufacturer of olive oil for the first time in 1920. After 1925, there were no more entries for him.

Chaffin, Long Olive Company (Oroville)

The Chaffins were part of the Berkeley Olive Growers Association. George Chaffin still grows olives on the family property, following his father before him.

William Wallace Chapin (Acampo, San Joaquin County)

Chapin, born in Philadelphia in 1874, bought the El Rubio Ranch in Acampo. When he bought the ranch, the trees were already old, having been planted in 1876. Chapin continued to grow the olives and pressed oil. Some of his bottles are still available. In 1907, he sold his orchard to Mrs. Ehmann, and she had the trees dug up and sent to Marysville. Chapin later went into the newspaper business. He died in 1957.

🎕 Bottle from W. W. Chapin's olive oil company.

Leo Chrisafulli (Sylmar)

Leo Chrisafulli leased one of the Sylmar Packing Company plants, Supreme Olive Oil, with Leo Maselli, one of Giacinto Maselli's sons, in the mid-1930s.

Closs Quisiana Ranch (Placer County)

[Perhaps the name was intended to be "Quisisana," which means "health."]

Fedor Charles Closs was a very early olive grower in Placer County, competing with Frederick Birdsall. By 1886, he had five hundred Picholine olive trees. He built his own olive mill. After he died in 1897, two men from San Francisco, F. W. Dohrmann and Dr. Pischel, bought the ranch. They owned it jointly, and it was managed by R. C. Williamson. Their relationship was cemented when one of Dohrmann's daughters married one of Dr. Pischel's sons. The couple had a son who became a prominent San Francisco ophthalmologist, Dr. Dohrmann Pischel.

The Dohrmann family had other connections with the olive oil business. A. C. Dohrmann and Company, crockery merchants, employed Freda Ehmann's son as a salesman. When Mrs. Ehmann wanted to expand her operation and move to Oroville, it was the Dohrmann firm that lent her $3,000 to do so.

Conant Olive Company (Ontario)

The Conant Company was producing oil in 1893.

Coronet Olive Oil (Oroville)

No other information exists about the Coronet firm apart from its name.

J. C. Curtis (Pentz)

J. C. Curtis was making olive oil in 1899. There are olive oil bottles with the name of G. Curtis but none from J. C. Curtis in existence. I do not know if J. C. Curtis was connected with this other firm or not.

Mrs. S. S. Cutler (San Jose)

Very few women worked in the olive oil business. In most cases, a woman would take over a business after her husband's death. Sarah S. Cutler lived on McKee Road, San Jose, during the first years of the twentieth century and appeared in the directories as an olive orchardist. She pressed her own olive oil and the bottles are still in existence. Little else is known about her.

Jerry Del Olio (San Fernando)

Mr. Del Olio made olive oil for a time, but then moved to Tipton after the Second World War and began raising grapes rather than olives. No other information has come to light about this man, whose name is so extremely appropriate.

Del Valle (Camulos)

This was a very historic ranch near San Diego belonging to a family that settled in California right at the beginning of the Spanish occupation. The first Del Valle was a soldier in the colonial Spanish military. He was rewarded for faithful service by a very large grant of land. During all the turmoil over the transfer of California to the United States, the family was able to hold onto the land, a most unusual circumstance for the times. Descendants of the original settler were prominent in California affairs a century later. The lasting fame for this ranch came from Helen Hunt Jackson's book *Ramona*, even though Mrs. Jackson claimed that she never spent enough time there to describe it thoroughly and had a different family in mind.

De Salvo (San Jose)

No other information about the De Salvo firm exists apart from the name.

Dixon Olive Company (Dixon)

No other information about the Dixon firm exists apart from the name.

Drobbish, Smith (Palermo)

No other information about the Drobbish firm exists apart from the name.

❧ SAMPLE OF FREDA EHMANN'S OLIVE OIL BOTTLE.

Ehmann Olive Company (Oroville)

Mrs. Ehmann merited almost a whole chapter to herself. She was born in Germany in 1839 and came to the United States as a girl. After her husband, Dr. Ernst Ehmann, died, she moved to Oakland to live with her daughter. Her only asset at the time was an olive orchard. In order to pay her debts, she learned how to process olives and sell them in the late 1890s. As her business succeeded, she moved to Oroville and gradually expanded the company in a most remarkable way. (See chapter 2.) Although her chief contribution was to make the canning process consistent and open the market for canned olives across the country, the Ehmann firm also made olive oil for a number of years. There are many bottles with the distinctive pale green and gold label in various collections. Each label has a wreath of olive branches circling the print. It was likely that the Ehmann Olive Company made the oil from the culls and rejects that accumulated during the canning process.

Ekman and Stow (Oroville)

🍂 E & S OLIVE OIL
BOTTLE.

Norton and Ekman took over the Crystal Drug Store in 1888 from D. F. Fryer, who began it in 1874. By 1895, Ekman was the sole proprietor, but in 1900, Stow joined him. At some point in this decade, Ekman elected to make olive oil, which was then considered to be a pharmaceutical substance. In 1900, Ekman and Stow won the Grand Medal for olive oil at the Paris Exposition. Ekman and Stow's bottles can still be found today.

Fair Oaks Fruit Association (Fair Oaks, Sacramento County)

Fruit growing began in Auburn in the 1880s. Growers mainly promoted citrus and almonds, but olives were always part of the program. A suburb of Auburn was known as Citrus Heights. In 1901, the Fair Oaks Fruit Association was organized. The owners built a packing house and an olive oil mill. It merged with the Fair Oaks Fruit Company in 1902. The fact that the association made olive oil is attested to by the survival of bottles. They are very rare, especially if they have the original label.

The association quickly became prosperous, according to reminiscences in 1906. It had eight hundred acres planted in oranges and lemons and four hundred acres devoted to other fruit, including olives and almonds. The oil was pressed initially in an old wooden shack, but later they built a proper concrete building. All went well until the early 1930s, when the citrus crops were destroyed by extremely severe frost. The association never recovered, and even though the olive trees might have come back, the company ceased business.

Vincent Florio (Fresno)

The first time Vincent Florio appeared in the Fresno City Directory was 1914. He lived on a rural route outside the city but gave no occupation. In 1922, he had moved to Fresno proper and was listed as a laborer at 2310 South Railroad Avenue. A new olive oil company appeared in 1924, making a Log Cabin brand. It belonged to Vincent Florio at the same address. The firm moved to 22 White's Bridge Avenue in 1928 and continued to be listed there for many years.

Edward Fogg (Oroville)

Edward Fogg was a horticulturist in addition to being a banker. He owned an olive orchard with his wife, Alida, and was a trustee of the city. He had started by working in his father's shoe store and then became a "printer's devil" at a press in town.

His rise in the world began when he went to work for Wells Fargo Bank in 1866. As he rose, he received more and more responsible assignments, such as reviving mines that had been shut down. During these years, he developed his interest in horticulture. He began with oranges, and his citrus groves were very successful.

In 1888, he joined with a Major McLaughlin to plant forty acres of olive trees. Fogg and McLaughlin pressed their own oil in their plant at Thermalito. Mrs. Ehmann bought his entire crop of olives in 1898, because she had contracted to sell ten thousand gallons of olives that season and only produced one thousand gallons herself. The McLaughlin-Fogg operation continued until 1918 and was then sold to Ehmann Olive Company.

Fontana Olive Company (Fontana, Riverside County)
Remnants of the old orchard can still be seen in this town.

Anthony Forestiere [or Foristiere] Olive Oil Company (Fresno)
The name appears under both spellings but most likely Forestiere is correct. Starting in 1929, Anthony Forestiere made olive oil at 3116 Belmont Avenue in Fresno. He continued the business until the late 1930s.

Dr. J. M. Frey (Newcastle)
Dr. Frey's name is all that remains of his company.

Garafalo (unknown)
Nothing else is known about Garafolo, not even his location. Ralph Fusano recalled his name.

Giovanoni Olive Oil Company (Oroville)
This company was making olive oil in 1895.

B. E. Glick and Sons (Corning)
Glick was better known for his canned olives though he started out making olive oil. The family began its business in Corning in 1913 by drying fruit and collecting olives to sell to the Maywood olive oil factory. By 1920, Glick had bought the Maywood olive oil plant and went into oil making himself. He changed to canning the olives in 1928 and became one of the largest employers in the town. By 1964, Glick merged with Early California Foods and his canning works moved to Visalia. Ultimately all the empty plants in Corning were taken over by Bell-Carter Foods.

The Corning town museum has photographs of the Glick plant, original cans and labels, together with advertisements and samples of uniforms worn by the women workers. The oil was most likely made from leftover olives of all sorts.

Goldberg and Bowen (San Francisco)
Goldberg and Bowen were large wholesale grocers, "wine and tea merchants," and distributors of olive oil, which was sold under the brand name of Sierra Madre. In the early years of the twentieth century, they were quite advanced in promoting their wares. One of their advertisements shows a beautiful young woman with the legend: "Sierra Madre olive oil is used by the great Russian dancers." The young woman in the picture is clearly not a Russian ballerina. She has rounded curves and a great mass of hair loosely pinned up, quite unlike the slim and tightly coiffed dancers. The olive oil label is more

conventional, showing a circlet filled with a branch of olives. In the Oakland directory for 1907 Goldberg and Bowen were listed as olive growers, together with Elliott Diehl Company, Inc. and J. V. Ralph and Company. Remnants of an olive orchard can still be seen on Hegenberger Road, on the way to the Oakland Airport. Possibly this was once the property of these growers. Diehl and Ralph were not known to make olive oil. Because of the entry in the directory, Goldberg and Bowen should be included here as primary processors of olive oil. Most likely they also imported a lot of foreign oil in bulk and put it up in bottles. There are many of their bottles in collections.

Golden Eagle Olive Oil Company (Porterville)

I have previously discussed the Padula family, who owned the Golden Eagle brand. (See chapter 6.) The firm was started by Joseph Padula, grandfather of the present owner. He had worked for the Sylmar Packing Corporation near Los Angeles.

🌿 Goldberg and Bowen
olive oil bottle.

Gonella (Merced)

Only the name of the Gonella firm exists.

W. P. Gould (Montecito)

Gould operated near Santa Barbara in the orbit of Ellwood Cooper. Gould came from New York and was an associate of Colonel Hayne in the olive business. He was known to be making oil in 1893.

Edwin Gower (Fowler, near Fresno)

Edwin Gower was the secretary of the Armstrong Fruit Company but also owned a ranch in Fowler known as the Bois de l'Arc Farm. He listed himself as a maker of olive oil in the 1904 Fresno City Directory. He claimed that his oil was "pure and unadulterated." The entries in the directory ceased after a few years.

Judge John Carlton Gray (Wyandotte, Butte County)

Judge Gray sat on the bench of the Butte County Superior Court for twenty-five years. In August 1887, he began to plant the first commercial olive orchard in Butte County at his Mount Ida ranch. He was said to have made olive oil, but none of the bottles have survived.

Wyandotte was named for a tribe of Native Americans from Michigan who went to California in search of gold in the 1850s. A few years later, another immigrant arrived in Wyandotte with Mexican orange seeds and found that citrus would flourish there. One of the original trees, known as the "Mother" orange, is still standing at Bidwell's Bar. This success with a semitropical fruit was the underlying condition that led to the planting of olive trees there twenty years later.

Charles P. Grogan (Los Angeles)

Grogan was listed as an "olive curer" at 1744 Albion Street in 1896, but he also made olive oil. He owned part of Panorama City, north of Roscoe City in the San Fernando Valley. One or two of his bottles are still available.

James Hall and Sons (Los Angeles)

The Halls appeared in the 1906 directory as makers of olive oil. The office was at 750 Keller Street.

Hay Ranch (Mount Vernon, Auburn)

Little is known about this ranch except that it was listed as a place that produced olives.

Colonel W. A. Hayne (Montecito)

Colonel Hayne bought two thousand acres of rough land in Montecito, covered with brush and chaparral. After clearing the land, he planted one thousand acres with orange trees, moving them from Los Angeles. He also acquired land in the Santa Ynez Valley. At the end of the gold rush, the great land holdings in the valley began to be broken up and subdivided into smaller parcels. This encouraged farming and orchards.

With two of his six sons, Hayne planted large olive orchards. They used the property at Montecito as a nursery. Hayne's second son, Arthur, went to the new University of California at Berkeley and studied viticulture. While there, he also learned much about olive trees and encouraged his family to plant more of them in the Santa Ynez Valley. The land contained much gravel, and the climate was dry and free of fog, discouraging the pests associated with the humid coastal areas.

It was at this point that the Haynes combined resources with W. R. Gould from New York and eventually planted thirteen thousand trees. The trees had to be transported over the San Marcos Pass from their nursery in Montecito, a heavy and arduous task. The Hayne's investments are said to have raised the value of the land from $20 per acre to over $200 per acre.

Harwood and Woodford (Ontario)

A P. Harwood filed an affidavit with the California Secretary of State for the design of the Harwood and Woodford olive oil bottle on May 5, 1891.

Hemet Packing Company (Hemet)

At one time, this company made oil. It was owned by a family called Nelson.

Irvin Henery (Oroville)

Irvin Henery's name appears in the lists of early olive growers and processors in Butte County. He was the brother-in-law of the owner of the Villa d'Oro Company.

Heredia Colony (Placer County)

This was another early olive-producing ranch. It is uncertain if olive oil was actually made on the premises.

G. F. Hooper (El Verano and Sonoma)

Hooper was producing olive oil in 1893. He registered the design of his bottles with the California Secretary of State on June 2, 1891.

J. F. Howland (Pomona)

The Howland brothers had huge olive nurseries in Riverside County. They also made olive oil and their bottles can still be seen today.

W. A. Hughes (Auburn)

Hughes had a ranch at Robie Point and was another of the early olive producers in Placer County.

David Kelsey (Napa)

David Kelsey died of smallpox in 1845, but his sons bought land in the Napa Valley and grew fruit. There is some hint that they also made olive oil, but that is very unclear.

Keystone Ranch (Auburn)

A Japanese man, M. Takashege, owned this ranch, buying part of the property of J. W. Hulbert in 1893. He produced olives and olive oil there. Takashege lived until the outbreak of World War II, when he was interned as an enemy alien. He died in the camp. His son, Louis, never came back to the ranch. There are some Keystone bottles in existence.

Dr. Edward Kusel (Oroville)

Edward Kusel, a doctor, came to Butte County in 1856 and opened a general store. His sons, C. E. and Emile, became important citizens, acting as mayor and trustees for the town of Oroville. C. E. and Emile planted an olive orchard on the Marysville Road in 1887, the same year as Judge Gray and E. W. Fogg planted theirs. They made olive oil in Butte County.

Lakeland Olive Ranch (Riverside)

A directory records this company as making olive oil in 1913.

La Mirada Ranch (La Mirada)

Ira Well bought the La Mirada Olive Company, which had been started in 1925, and moved the business to Corning. His wife's nephew is George Powell, former corporate secretary for Lindsay Ripe Olive Company. Ira Well took Powell on at La Mirada as a very young man; George learned all about the business during the stint with his uncle.

When Well's business was sold, Powell joined the Lindsay Ripe Olive Company. He made it a point to attend all the technical conferences of the California Olive Association and kept all the reports.

Frank La Notte Olive Oil Company (Fresno)

Starting in 1935, Frank La Notte made olive oil at 340 Tehama Avenue.

Lima Olive Oil Company (Palermo)
Only the name of the Lima company remains.

Lindsay Ripe Olive Company (Lindsay)
Formed in 1916 as a cooperative for canning pickled olives, Lindsay also produced olive oil for a brief period.

Livoti Olive Company (Roseville)
Charles Livoti was much respected in the olive world. When the California Olive Association formed a committee to help the oil makers fight a tax battle, Livoti was asked to participate.

Loma Olive Oil Company (Los Angeles)
The Loma Company made oil at 334 Mason Building during the early years of the twentieth century.

Lo Popolo (Fresno)
John Lo Popolo was first listed as a resident of a rural area near Fresno in 1917. His occupation was laborer. By 1920, he had moved to 924 Mariposa Avenue in Fresno. In 1939, the Lo Popolo Olive Oil factory was listed in the Fresno City Directory for the first time.

Lucca Olive Oil Company (Lindsay)
Anthony Bennetti and Jim Lanza owned the Lucca Olive Oil Company. Bennetti was born in Italy. The firm was active in the 1930s and later. John Ugaste, Sr., began to work for them when he was ten years old.

Lucchese Olive Oil Company (Roseville)
Only the name of the Lucchese company remains. It suggests the founders were from Lucca. Immigrants to California from the Tuscan city of Lucca were very numerous, and many had expert knowledge of olive oil.

David Martinelli (Napa)
David Martinelli made olive oil at his California Olive Oil Manufactory starting in the 1890s. He was still active in 1908 and 1909. It is not clear whether he was related to Serafino Martinelli or not. (See Serafino Martinelli below.) David Martinelli had learned to make olive oil in his native Lucca. He worked for a Mr. Fuller when he first came to the United States, but after eight years, saved enough money to buy over two hundred acres of prime valley land to start his own vineyard and olive orchard. Much of his land abutted the Crystal Springs, and he used the water to great advantage.

Serafino Martinelli (Madera)
Serafino Martinelli came from Italy in 1902 to work in the U. S. as a shoemaker. He managed to save enough money to buy a piece of land in Madera, and in 1904 he planted an olive orchard and vineyard. Serafino built a small olive oil mill in the orchard and pressed his own olive oil there. His son Adolph

later replaced the vineyard with olive trees, and built a larger oil plant in the town of Madera. He sold the olive oil under the S. Martinelli Olive Oil Company label.

Mrs. Della Martinelli, Adolph's widow, lived on the property until her death in 1998. She continued to raise olives. The trees had been grafted to produce the Manzanillo variety, better for canning. Even after her death the olive orchard remains in production. Della's son Adolph Jr. runs it under a crop share lease with Erickson Farming of Madera.

I still treasure my visit with Mrs. Martinelli, a truly sweet and gentle person. She showed me a privately printed testimonial volume entitled *Attivita Italiane in America,* which commemorates Italian immigrants to the United States and their achievements. The right-hand pages were printed in Italian and the left-hand in English. Her late husband, Adolph, was featured in the book, together with such luminaries as A. P. Giannini, founder of the Bank of America. Mrs. Martinelli was not able to find any connection in her husband's family to David Martinelli of Napa.

Charles Mastro Olive Company (Sylmar)
Only the name of this firm remains.

Mat-mor Olive Company (Lindsay)
The Morici family operated this olive oil mill. According to Jerry Padula, it operated during the Second World War.

Matranga Olive Company (Los Angeles)
This factory was located near the Italian immigrant district of Los Angeles in the late nineteenth and early twentieth century.

Maywood Packing Company (Corning)
Warren Woodson started this concern in 1906 with several other investors. For a time they made olive oil, but principally concentrated on other products, including canned olives. The company lasted until 1982 when it was bought by Bell-Carter Foods. A few of the managers remained in their positions under the new ownership. In April 1996, I spent a very delightful hour with Robert Swank of Corning, who at that time was eighty-six years old. He had been in charge at Maywood and ran the plant until he retired. Maywood was no longer making olive oil even when he began to work there over fifty years before. (See chapter 3.)

McNally (La Mirada)
Andrew McNally, president of Rand McNally and Company, owned the five hundred-acre Windermere Ranch in La Mirada. He had fifty thousand bearing olive trees and produced about ten to fifteen thousand gallons of olive oil a year. McNally advertised his oil in the publications of the College of Physicians in Philadelphia, emphasizing its purity, the cleanliness of his process, and the delicious flavor of his product. The business offices of the ranch were in Chicago.

Melba Olive Oil Company (Fresno)
Melba Olive Oil Company was at 550 Tehama Avenue in Fresno. The first entry was in 1939. Possibly it was named for Dame Nellie Melba, a world famous opera star who was at the height of her fame during that epoch.

Monteleone Olive Company (Sylmar)
Only the name Monteleone remains.

E. Montgomery and Son (Los Angeles)
Montgomery was in business at 1630 North Main Street in 1906.

Moreno Olive Company (Los Angeles)
Only the name Moreno remains.

Peter Motto Olive Company (Corning)
Only the name Peter Motto remains.

Nicolo Musco (Orland)
Nicolo Musco originally made a brand of olive oil called "La Chevre." He only did it for a few years.

Napa Valley Olive Oil Manufactory (St. Helena)
This was a family-owned enterprise that was still in business in 1968.

Neopolitan Olive Company (Los Angeles)
Only the name of this firm remains.

Nigro Olive Company (Ripon)
The Nigros suffered severe reverses when the price of olive oil plunged in 1946. They expanded very fast in the early 1950s but again suffered cruel losses when the price of olive oil plunged from $20 per gallon to $3 per gallon.

Old Mission Olive Oil Company (San Diego)
This was the continuation of Akerman and Tuffley's firm. There are still some Old Mission olive oil bottles with the labels on them. The plant was in the heart of old downtown San Diego.

Orsi Olive Company (Roseville)
Angelo Orsi started this company. He sold the oil in both bottles and cans. The can had a charming idealized view of California on the panels, with a green valley, bright blue sky, and two grizzly bears cavorting about.

Pala Grove Olive Company (San Jose)

A family named Gordon came from Minnesota and settled in Santa Clara County in the 1880s. Hamilton Gordon bought his ranch from the estate of Charles White, who had been killed in the explosion of the steamer *Jenny Lind* in 1853. Mrs. White inherited the very large estate and sold off portions of it over the years. The orchard on McKee Street that Mr. Gordon bought had one hundred olive trees in it.

Gordon pressed the olives in the oil mill on his property, and since that section of the town was known as Pala Land, he called the olive oil Pala Grove. There is evidence that Mrs. Gordon continued to run the business after his death. By the middle of the twentieth century, the land was gradually sold off in pieces and the olive orchard no longer exists. A few Pala Grove bottles are in private collections.

Pantaleo Olive Company (Reedley)

Frank Pantaleo sold his business in Reedley to John Ugaste, Sr. At one time, Pantaleo had worked at "California Olive Oil," presumably California Olive Growers in Los Angeles. He now lives in Delano and sells grapes.

Michael Pastore (Visalia)

Mr. Pastore came to California from Bari in Italy. He had learned about making olive oil there. In 1936, together with S. D. Crosina, he started his own very small firm in Farmersville. He produced Visalia Pride.

When Edward van Dellen and Richard Ball formed the Pacific Olive Company in 1940, it was Pastore who gave them that name. In 1964, Pacific Olive joined B. E. Glick and Sons and the Sunland Olive Company to form Early California Foods. This firm did all its olive canning in Visalia. Bill Leigh was their chemist. It was most unusual in those days for a food processing company to employ its own chemist.

(Bill Leigh is still active, a youthful septuagenarian, who runs a private chemistry laboratory in Lindsay that investigates agricultural problems arising from environmental hazards. When he was working in the olive industry, he was invited to spend several months in Israel to help them build up and modernize their olive industry. About a week after he accepted this invitation, he received another one from the Greek government. He told me he managed to do both, stopping in Greece for a week or two en route to Israel, and traveling around with some of the professors from the university at Athens.)

Prior Brothers Olive Company (Riverside County)

Only the name of this firm remains.

Dr. Joseph Prosek (Guerneville)

Dr. Prosek had olive orchards and a press out in Sonoma County. Prosek olive oil bottles are in private collections.

From 1875 to 1917, the year he died, Dr. Prosek practiced medicine in San Francisco. He was an assistant physician at the German Hospital. There was a mild scandal when it appeared that he might not actually have a medical degree because he refused to produce any documents. Some of his descendants are still physicians and dentists in San Francisco.

Rancho Chico (Oroville and Chico)

General John Bidwell's activities have been described elsewhere in this work. He was one of the most impressive early pioneers in California. In 1841, he led the first successful wagon train of emigrants over the Rockies and the Sierras into California, without losing a single person. When the gold rush started, he found a large amount of ore at Bidwell's Bar and was able to buy many acres of valuable land in Butte County. He named his property Rancho Chico. The town of Chico stands on this land.

Bidwell believed in the Jeffersonian agrarian philosophy, that a strong and successful country would be composed of free men each farming his own land. These men should take their part in the affairs of the community. He lived his life in consonance with this idea. Rancho Chico was a leading example of how agriculture should be conducted in the new state. Bidwell grew wheat, and had orchards. An offshoot of his orchard operation was the production of olive oil.

A Rancho Chico olive oil bottle with its label intact is a very rare artifact. Somehow the bottle underscores the remarkable qualities of John Bidwell: his ability to lead and to recognize the new direction agriculture would go are transmuted into such a mundane article. John Bidwell and Ellwood Cooper were friends and often corresponded about their olive oil. (See chapter 2.)

W. H. Reeve Olive Oil Company (Los Angeles)

Reeve was in business at 326 Temple Street in 1902.

Regina Olive Company (Terra Bella)

Regina was the former Southern Tulare Olive Marketing Association (STOMA).

Rincon Heights Olive Orchard (Santa Rosa)

This company belonged to a Swiss immigrant, Captain Guy Emmanuel Grosse, a countryman of John Sutter. He was born in Bern in 1839 and came to the United States in 1852. He worked as an errand boy in Pittsburgh, Pennsylvania. While in the United States, he visited California for six months but returned to Europe for several years. For some reason, he chose to return to the United States in 1861 and fight in the Civil War. Unlike Sutter, his military rank was earned legitimately.

It was not until 1876 that Grosse traveled overland to California. He went to Sonoma County and

entered the real estate business. The olive orchard was really an offshoot of this, but he prided himself on making a fine oil. The trees were planted before 1890. In 1897, Grosse won first prize for olive oil at the Cloverdale Citrus Fair. Rincon Heights olive oil bottles still exist.

Grosse's real estate business failed miserably, and he had to apply for bankruptcy in 1899. In spite of that, he managed to keep the olive orchard for a while, but eventually even that went to the bank. His last years were sad. He tried to sell real estate in small parcels from his home. He died in 1907 at the age of sixty-eight. In some ways, he resembled Sutter in his rising very high and then falling abruptly, even though it was for different reasons.

☙ RINCON HEIGHTS OLIVE OIL BOTTLE.

Robb Brothers Olive Company (Riverside)

The Robbs were making olive oil in 1893.

Emily Robeson (Placer)

Mrs. Robeson owned Olivina Ranch in the Edgwood district of Auburn. She had her own press and used a beam method. She displayed five varieties of olive oil and two of pickled olives at the 1892 Auburn Citrus Fair. In 1900, her crop failed, but she bought three thousand gallons of pickled olives from someone else and made over one thousand gallons of oil.

Roeding Olive Oil Company (Fresno)

The Roeding Fig and Olive Oil Company was an offshoot of George Roeding's Fancher Creek Nursery. He entered the firm in the Fresno City Directory every year from 1905 until the 1930s.

Dominic Rubino (Reedley)

The first time Rubino appeared in the Fresno City Directory was in 1933. Reedley is a small town about twenty miles south of Fresno, but it is still in Fresno's orbit. Rubino worked at 1020 H Street in Reedley.

Sacramento Olive Company (Sacramento)

This company started to make olive oil in 1895. The company secretary was a W. D. Lawton.

San Fernando Olive Company (San Fernando Valley)

Two realtors, J. Basket and Michael Powers, built this plant in 1946. They had been the brokers in the sale of Sylmar Packing Corporation.

Sanitarium Food Company (St. Helena)

The California Medical Missionary and Benevolent Association in San Francisco formed this company as an offshoot and sent patients to their own health resort in the Napa Valley at the turn of the century. Olive oil was one of their products, considered to be a health food.

    The resort started in 1878. There were a gym and a swimming pool, and it was advertised as "perfect in both winter and summer." The special foods were stocked by grocers in San Francisco and no doubt contributed to the profitability of the organization. The C.M.M. and B.A. did not hesitate to promote themselves in the most resounding manner. "To live long and well, ask your grocer for the famous Health Foods manufactured by the Sanitarium Food Company of St. Helena, California."

Scarlota (Manteca)

Jerry Padula recalled this olive oil firm in Manteca. Scarlota later switched to canning table olives.

❧ SANITARIUM FOOD COMPANY OLIVE OIL BOTTLE.

Scattaglia (Pacoima)
Only the name of Scattaglia remains.

Sciappatura and Abbotti (Oroville)
Sciappatura was on the FBI's "ten most wanted" list, and ended up being deported to Italy in 1947. (Maybe this was the place where machine guns turned up in a closet. See chapter 3.) They made olive oil during that period when the Second World War prevented imports from Europe.

Rose Schiavon (Fresno)
Starting in 1936, Mrs. Schiavon made olive oil at 3736 Tyler Street in Fresno.

Sciavoni (Lindsay)
No other information exists about Sciavoni apart from the name.

Theo Schwein (Oroville)
Schwein made oil at 527 Cherry Street in Oroville in the 1890s.

Ralph Selby (Ballard)
Selby was said to be a pioneer in growing olives in the Santa Ynez Valley, even before Hayne and Gould decided to do it.

Seville Olive Company (Strathmore)
The Seville Olive Company is quite old. Mr. A. Adams owns it and still makes olive oil today.

Petar Sliskovich (Rialto)
Petar Sliskovich was born in Yugoslavia in 1911 and immigrated to the United States. In the 1940s, he began to buy olive crops and prepare oil under the Dalmatia label. His son Vladimir is still in the olive oil business, as is his grandson Joseph.

Julius P. Smith (Livermore)
Julius Smith registered the design for his olive oil bottles on July 8, 1891.

Vincent R. Smith (Napa)
Smith was active from the 1890s until about 1910. He registered the design for his olive oil bottles on May 4, 1891. Smith was primarily a vintner and distiller, but Napa city directories of the time list him as an olive oil bottler. A few years later, during the 1920s, a Vincent Smith (possibly the same man), owned olive canning plants in Tulare County.

Soyotome Olive Oil Company (Healdsburg)
A record of this company's existence is noted in Betty Zumwalt's book, *Ketchup, Pickles, Sauces: Nineteenth Century Food in Glass*. It was the brand name for oil produced at P. H. Mothorn's ranch.

STOMA [Southern Tulare Olive Marketing Association] (Terra Bella)

This cooperative had its headquarters in Terra Bella. It was the sole plant in Terra Bella, but through sales and mergers, it changed its name twice. STOMA concentrated on canned olives, but it also made olive oil in the early days. As noted above, STOMA became Regina and later Sunland Olive Company after A. Adams, Jr., bought it. When B. Glick and Sons, Pacific Olive Company, and the Sunland Olive Company merged, the plant was managed by Edward van Dellen for four years, from 1970 to 1974. The brand name for its products was Rumano. It has since closed, and the premises are used for making plastics.

A. V. Stuart (San Jose)

Augustus Stuart made olive oil very early. Little is known about him.

Suni-cal Packing Company (Oroville)

In 1914, the Wolff brothers began the California Ripe Olive Company. In 1916, they changed the name to Suni-cal Packing Company, because they had broadened their scope to include other fruits and vegetables. In 1916, the Wyandotte Olive Growers began to send their products to Suni-cal to be packed but subsequently took over the packing company. The Berkeley Olive Growers Association also participated in this action. Some Suni-cal bottles still exist.

Supreme Olive Company (Sylmar)

Only the name Supreme remains.

Sylmar Packing Corporation (Sylmar)

This company was said to be the largest single producer of olives in the world at one point. In view of the size of the Spanish estates, that claim is probably doubtful. Sylmar Packing Corporation began as a result of a pamphlet written by Judge Robert M. Whitney, promoting the possibilities of making money from olives in California. A group of businessmen in Illinois decided to follow up and invested in the Los Angeles Olive Growers Association. This later changed its name to the Sylmar Packing Corporation. The association was doing business at 304 South Building at that time.

The group bought one thousand acres in Sylmar near Los Angeles. Later that was increased to two thousand acres. At the peak of their activities, they made 50,000 gallons of olive oil per year and 200,000 gallons of canned ripe olives.

The company began in 1887 and by 1895 was prospering. It remained in business until 1925. Several men who ended up with their own firms began by working at Sylmar. Bottles from Sylmar Packing Corporation are still in existence.

Termini Olive Oil Company (Fresno)

Termini Olive Oil Company, at 1820 Mary Street, first appeared in the Fresno City Directory in 1934.

Trafton Olive Company (Lindsay)

No other information about the Trafton firm exists.

John Ugaste (Reedley)
John Ugaste and his father still make olive oil in the time-honored way. John Ugaste, Sr., began to work in olive oil at the age of ten. After he had been at the Lucca Olive Oil Company in Lindsay for a few years, working for Anthony Bennetti, he decided to go into business for himself. He bought the California Olive Oil Company in Reedley from Frank Pantaleo in 1966. The Ugaste oil is sold under the brand name of Bari. The Ugastes sell it exclusively by mail order, not even using a catalog. Their market depends entirely on personal recommendation and word of mouth.

Saverio Verni (Clovis)
Verni made olive oil in wholesale quantities. He supplied olive oil to the Hain grocery firm, which bottled it under its own label.

Villa d'Oro Olive Oil Company (Oroville)
Villa d'Oro was not like the other firms, which prided themselves on carefully pressing the olives cold. The Villa d'Oro Olive Oil Company used solvents to rectify and extract oil. The Obertis bought it from the original owner's brother-in-law (and bookkeeper) after the owner was deported to Italy in the late 1940s. Oberti closed down the solvent extraction system, and the plant went to Tri Valley Growers when Oberti sold their business to them.

C. A. Washburn Olive Oil Company (Los Angeles)
This firm was listed as doing business in the Walton Building in 1906.

Wente Olive Oil (Manteca)
Wente Brothers is well known as a winery. More recently, they have begun to make estate olive oil using the trees planted among their vines.

Charles A. Wetmore (Livermore)
Charles Wetmore was very active on the State Board of Horticulture. He was a state official but cherished his olive orchards. On August 9, 1891, he registered the design of his olive oil bottles.

Whitney Ranch (Rocklin)
Only the name Whitney Ranch remains.

Wyandotte Olive Growers (Oroville)
The section of Butte County named Wyandotte was settled briefly during the gold rush by some Wyandotte Indians from Michigan. In 1887, olive trees were planted there for the first time. Judge Gray and E. Fogg, some of the original planters, were among the Oroville men who submitted California olive oil to the Paris Exposition in 1900, where it won the Grand Gold Medal. A few years later, this group formed the Wyandotte Olive Growers Association. It was a cooperative.

When olive oil became too difficult to sell because of competition in the early twentieth century, WOGA switched to canning table olives. In 1916, the group contracted with Suni-cal to process their olives. (See appendix C for more about the subsequent changes at WOGA.)

Appendix C

OLIVE PROCESSING COMPANIES (1895–PRESENT)

Over many years, a large number of firms have been in the olive processing, or canning, business. I list ninety-five of them below, each with as much story about them as I have been able to find. Some of them lasted such a short time that very little information remains about them.

Within this list are a few companies that were secondary packers and brokers, not primary canners as far as is known. The original list was started by the late Harold Schutt, once senior plant manager of the Lindsay Ripe Olive Company and a devoted local historian, and kept up by Ralph Fusano, who was employed at the Lindsay Ripe Olive Company in a variety of capacities and reported to Harold Schutt. I have added a few other names from searching old city directories. Most of the companies that have been described in some detail in the main text do not appear here.

A. Adams, Jr. Olive Company (Terra Bella)

Alfred Adams, Jr., went to California in 1906 or 1907. He worked as an olive processor for the American Olive Company in Los Angeles, which was later taken over by the Grogan Olive Company. Adams then went into business for himself, opening the Sunland Olive Company with his sons.

In 1935, Gordon K. Patterson (always known as "Pat") began to work for Sunland. He married one of Adams's daughters and joined the firm's management. Sunland bought the Southern Tulare Olive Marketing Association (STOMA) in 1954. Sunland was a pioneer in canning sliced olives, but until the rise in the consumption of pizza, these were not very popular. I learned about the company from "Pat" Patterson.

Mr. Patterson was very cordial and attentive when we met in Visalia in the summer of 1996, but he was in a considerable hurry. He was rushing to get ready to go to Spain as a consultant to a new joint venture in olive processing there. Theoretically he retired in 1988, but he was not ready to stop working after sixty-one years in the business.

Albers Olive Company (Riverside County)

The story of the Albers Company is noted in appendix B. J. V. E. Titus represented Albers at the California Olive Association. Albers began growing olives and pressing olive oil in Riverside County in the late 1880s. Later the firm switched to canning table olives.

Berkeley Olive Growers Association (Oroville)

The Berkeley group made oil and packed olives in its early years. The cannery lasted from 1922 to 1930. After that, the association confined itself to growing the fruit. They sent their crops to local canners to be made into oil or pickles. A. L. Chaffin represented this group at the California Olive Association.

Bolivar Packing Company (unknown)

Bolivar was in business for twenty years, from 1923 to 1943. H. A. Barraclough and Gilbert Thompson represented Bolivar at the California Olive Association. At one time, Bolivar made olive oil.

Burt Brothers (Palermo)

One of the Burt brothers represented this firm at early meetings of the California Olive Association. The Burts later joined the group of sixteen companies that made up the California Packing Company, subsequently known as Del Monte Foods. Del Monte was the first food packer to offer a guarantee of special quality if consumers bought their products by name. Its approach was radically new and different, and changed advertising practices in this country.

California Associated Olive Growers, Incorporated (San Francisco)

This company started in the same year as the Lindsay Ripe Olive Company (1916), but it failed after a few years because of unsophisticated business practices. The organizers did not understand business fundamentals. When a broker offered to take their first season's pack from them, he did not think of telling them that unused inventory gets returned to the manufacturer. He assumed they knew that fact of business life. The officers of the company believed that he would pay them for the whole pack and made their plans accordingly. They were shocked when he reported back the following year how much he had sold and how much was being returned. He also brought some criticisms from the wholesalers about the flavor and quality of their brand of olives.

Several growers who were well known at the time belonged to CAOGI, and they had worked hard to make it a success. Colonel Harris Weinstock, the California State Director of Markets, had tried to ensure its growth and help them to flourish, but he could not overcome the innate flaws in its practices.

There was no successor organization. We would have known almost nothing about CAOGI were it not for serendipity. One of the original organizers of the corporation, Mr. Livingston Crichton, had built the house in Corning now owned by Mr. and Mrs. Claude Craig. The house was inherited by Crichton's sister, Anna Pugsley. She in turn sold it to Loren Vinson, from whom the Craigs bought it. The Craigs found the former association's ledgers and receipt books in their garage when they bought the house and carefully preserved them. Without their actions, most of the information about the business would have been lost. The bindings have deteriorated badly but most of the pages can be deciphered.

Careful perusal of these records confirms the fact that the business ceased to operate because it lacked sufficient capital. It was not a cooperative like the Lindsay Ripe Olive Company, but a standard business corporation. The directors had very ambitious plans, building large canning plants in Lindsay and Oroville. They committed too many resources to this expansion at a time when sales were not secure.

Crichton had built his house in an established olive orchard. The Craigs continue to grow the olives and sell them for canning. Claude Craig recently retired from thirty-four years of work as a millwright for Crane Mills and can now devote much more of his time to the trees. He enjoys this labor, not finding it a chore.

The irrigation schedule tends to shape some of their activities in the summer, cutting short certain trips if the weather becomes excessively hot. At harvest time, they bring in crews to pick the fruit, putting them up in dormitories on the property.

California Canners and Growers (plant: Oroville; main office: San Francisco)
California Canners and Growers sent four men to attend the meetings of the California Olive Association in the 1960s. One, Stanley S. Scott, was a director of the organization. In the early 1970s, when the association was about to merge with the Canners' League, Bruno Filice from this firm was the president of the California Olive Association and facilitated the merger. The company had its main office in San Francisco, and the plant in Oroville. Mr. Filice worked from Richmond in the San Francisco Bay Area.

California Cooperative Canners (unknown)
The cooperative only functioned from 1922 to 1925.

California Growers Association (Los Angeles)
The association ran from 1920 to 1925, and then ceased operations. During its brief existence, E. W. Rickard attended the meetings of the California Olive Association.

California Olive Growers, Incorporated (Los Angeles)
The cannery began in 1920 but by 1928, it had become the California Olive Growers Exchange. Three officials from this company attended meetings at the California Olive Association: C. E. Weikert, A. M. Drew, and C. R. Cooper.

California Olive Packers, Incorporated (unknown)
The corporation began processing olives in 1940 and stayed in business until 1961.

California Packing Corporation (San Francisco)
This firm processed olives from 1914 to 1934. It had offices on California Street, San Francisco. Henri Bernier represented the firm at the 1920 meetings of the California Olive Association (the botulism period).

California Ripe Olive Company (Oroville)
Only the name of this firm remains.

California Sanitary Canning Company (Long Beach)
Only the name of this firm remains.

Caripo Olive Company (Oroville)
This name was used by the Wolff brothers, Carl and Henry, prominent citizens of Oroville, for their olive company. It functioned during the 1920s.

Carpenter Brothers (El Toro)

Carpenter Brothers, a firm which processed both table olives and olive oil, was active in the 1920s.

G. L. Chapman (Los Angeles)

Only the name of this firm remains.

Richard Codman (Fair Oaks)

Only the name of this firm remains.

Consolidated Olive Canners and Growers (Lindsay and Corning)

Consolidated had two plants, one in Lindsay and one in Corning. At first, Maxwell King, Jr., spoke for it at the California Olive Association, but in 1970, he was replaced by Earl Fox.

Corning Olive Company (Corning)

Corning Olive Company canned olives from 1929 to 1936. It merged with La Mirada, Olives Incorporated, and the Feather River Growers, but it was eventually incorporated into Bell-Carter Foods.

Corning Olive Growers Association (Corning)

The Corning Olive Growers Association only lasted four years as a canner, from 1934 to 1938.

George Craig Olive Company (Merced)

Only the name of this firm remains.

Curtis Corporation (Long Beach)

The president of this business, Alexander Stewart, was a founding member of the California Olive Association in 1915. Beginning in 1919, he published a monthly newsletter called *The Curtis Sandwich*. The stimulus for this came from the botulism epidemic. He wanted his customers to know that his olives were safe to eat. There were testimonials from physicians and pictures of the women employees packing the olives in hygienic conditions. Stewart noted that his company kept the various lots of processed olives separate, so it was easy to determine if any lot was contaminated and also to prevent the contamination from spreading to other lots.

In 1928, Curtis Corporation became Stewart Curtis Packing Corporation. Stewart Curtis Packing Corporation lasted for five years, from 1928 to 1933. From 1934 to 1935, it became the Western Canners, Incorporated, but in 1936, Alexander Stewart took it over again. It closed in 1942.

Fred Dietz Olive Company (Corning)

The Dietz family was very highly regarded in Corning. Fred Dietz was originally a nurseryman. He obtained his initial olive trees in Oroville. Many growers in the San Joaquin Valley bought Sevillano trees from him. Mr. Dietz processed olives throughout the war years, from 1939 to 1947. He had bought part of the old Heinz plant. After his only son died from bulbar poliomyelitis in 1950, he was too distressed to continue working and he went out of business.

Early California Foods (plant: Visalia; offices: Los Angeles)

Early California Foods took over the Pacific Olive Company in the late 1950s. In 1964, B. E. Glick and Sons and the Sunland Olive Company merged with Early California Foods. During this phase, the company had its business offices in Los Angeles and its plant in Visalia. In the early 1990s, the combined company was sold to the Vlasic Pickle Company, a subsidiary of Campbell's Soup. The most recent development was the 1998 sale of the Early California division to Musco Olive Products.

Ehmann Olive Company (Oroville)

Everyone credits Mrs. Ehmann with establishing the canned California ripe olive business. Her company in Oroville remained in the family from 1899 until the 1930s, although it merged with the Mount Ida Packing Company in 1929 and later became Olive Products. Her son-in-law, Charles W. Bolles, and later one of her grandsons, was in charge for many years. The company was in business as Olive Products until 1981. At one point, the manager was George Chaffin, a descendant of the original Berkeley group.

One of Mrs. Ehmann's granddaughters, Terry McShane, lives near San Diego. Mrs. McShane's daughter, Tracy Pisenti, lives and works in the East San Francisco Bay Area. These ladies were most helpful to me and could not have been more cordial or charming. Neither they nor their relatives are in the olive business. That connection is broken.

Fair Oaks Fruit Company (Fair Oaks)

Fair Oaks Fruit Company canned olives as well as made olive oil. A report in the *High School Advocate* of February 1903 indicates that over one hundred tons of olives were produced that season. An improved, larger cannery was added and operated from 1921 to 1946. W. W. Hinsey and E. L. Maddox attended meetings at the California Olive Association for this company in the 1920s. A descendant of Mr. Hinsey, Ralph, owned a large grocery store in Fair Oaks.

Feather River Growers (Butte)

This firm was active in the 1930s and 40s. In the 1950s, the Lindsay Ripe Olive Company bought it.

William H. Floyd Company (Corning)

William H. Floyd of Pasadena was a broker in canned olives and olive oil for over forty years. He bought a plant in Corning from Michael Pastore and ran it for a short time before selling it to Ira Well's Orinda Olive Company.

Cristo Fusano and Sons (Sylmar)

The Fusano family originally made olive oil but later began canning olives. These olives were made under the San Fernando label. They sold their business to Lindsay Ripe Olive Company in 1977.

C. M. Gifford and Son (San Diego)

Gifford processed olives by himself very early, and put them up in metal cans before Mrs. Ehmann. He too obtained advice from Professor Bioletti at the University of California. What he did not do was to establish a market for California ripe olives across the United States, a unique contribution of Mrs. Ehmann. He remained a local business. In 1960, Gifford's business was sold to Westgate Foods, but they only kept it going for four years. (For more about Gifford, see chapter 6 on olive oil.)

B. E. Glick and Sons (Corning)

The Glicks began in Corning in the 1920s. They lasted until 1965, when they sold their business to Lindsay Ripe Olive Company. (See chapter 6.) A large truck stop stands on the site of Glick's orchards, close to Highway 5. Its parking lot still has some old olive trees for shade.

Golden State Canneries (unknown)

Golden State Canneries lasted from 1920 to 1923. Allan Cutler represented the firm at meetings of the California Olive Association.

Golden State Olive Company (unknown)

Golden State Olive Company also had a brief existence, from 1952 to 1954.

B. A. Goodwin (Manteca)

Only the name of this firm remains.

C. C. Graber Olive Company (Ontario)

Clifford Graber was born in Clay City, Indiana, in 1873. He went to Ontario, San Bernardino County, with his brother in 1892. The Pomona Valley was noted for its citrus, but it was also known as the leading olive growing region in the 1880s and '90s. Graber began by growing oranges, but he enjoyed curing olives as a hobby. There were many old olive trees around the ranch. He turned to the University of California for an improved recipe, and his wife sold the cured olives in bulk directly from the vats. In 1894, he began to can the olives and by 1910 this aspect of his business had grown considerably.

Graber recognized the need for uniform sizing of the olives in each can and built a wooden grading machine very early. He also used tree-ripened fruit to make the cured olives softer with a milder flavor. It is more expensive to work this way since the hand picking must be done several times each season and not all at once. Picking must also be done more slowly and carefully because the ripe fruit is so easily damaged.

In succeeding years, Graber and his sons bought more land and planted more olive trees. Now the ranch is in the San Joaquin Valley. Clifford's son Bob, with his wife, Betty, and grandson Cliff C. are in charge of the whole business. In spite of its relatively small size, the company has a niche in the market and many devoted adherents.

Gregg Olive Company (Phoenix, Arizona)

There were so few olive processors in Arizona that they were allowed to join the California Olive Association as full members.

Charles P. Grogan Olive Company (Los Angeles)

Grogan worked in Los Angeles and had orchards both in the San Fernando Valley and near Lindsay. He started out making olive oil but added pickled olives to his product line in 1932. Grogan ceased operation in 1960. Grogan was at 1744 Albion Street, next door to the Leverton Olive Company at 1740 Albion Street in Los Angeles.

Harbor City Canning Company (Harbor City?)

Two years, from 1936 to 1938, was the entire life span of this company.

Hazen Canning Company (Corning)

Hazen lasted a very short time, from 1940 to 1942. Mr. Hazen originally worked for the Mayood Packing Company and represented that company at the California Olive Association.

Frank Hebert (San Francisco)

Only the name of this firm remains.

H. J. Heinz and Company (Corning)

H. J. Heinz began his business of canning fruit and vegetables in Pittsburgh, Pennsylvania, in 1888. He too rode the wave of improved methods of preserving fresh produce from California and other farm states. Heinz conceived of preserving and selling many types of fruits and vegetables. At the time, his fifty-seven different sorts of fruits and vegetables was a very large number. The success of his "57 Varieties" was complete.

After the First World War, and after the management was satisfied that there would be enough raw material on a regular basis, Heinz opened an olive canning factory in Corning. Heinz brought in its olives on flatbed cars from the San Joaquin Valley. The plant ran from 1920 to 1943 and is now part of the Bell-Carter complex.

H. J. Heinz also played its part in the affairs of the California Olive Association. It sent two men named Mason and Soper to represent them at the association's meetings.

Hemet Canning Company (Hemet)

Hemet Canning Company was owned by the Nelson family. They were in business for forty years, from 1922 to 1962.

George B. Henry (Fair Oaks)

George B. Henry was listed in a 1920 directory of the California Olive Association as producing both standard table olives and minced olives. A George J. Henry produced table olives only in San Francisco. They could have been connected, perhaps father and son.

Highland Olive Grove (unknown)

Highland Olive Grove processed olives from 1922 to 1925.

Hollister Canning Company (Hollister)

The Hollister Canning Company was in business for one year, 1933.

Hunn Packing Company (Long Beach and Woodlake)

Hunn operated from 1944 to 1945. Two years later, it was taken over by Woodlake Ranch.

Hunt Brothers (San Francisco)

No other information about the Hunt company exists.

Frank Kimball Olive Company (San Diego)

Frank Kimball started olive orchards in 1868 to make olive oil, but in 1926, a canning company by that name began work and went on until 1946. This Kimball was an early member of the California Olive Association.

Joseph Kimball (San Bernardino)

Only the name of Joseph Kimball's firm remains.

J. C. Kubias (Redlands)

Mr. Kubias was an active member of the California Olive Association soon after it began. His plant produced standard table olives, olive oil, and ethnic olives. He lived with his wife, Anna, at 457 Alta Street in Redlands. Their advertisements list the Bohemian Club brand of olive oil and table olives, in glass and tins, as well as the Arrowhead brand of olive oil. The latter was bottled for the Church of Jesus Christ of Latter-Day Saints.

At a later date, J. C. Kubias gave up his business and joined the California State Health Department. He became the director of the division of cannery inspection in the Los Angeles office and continued to work until 1943.

Lake Elsinore Ripe Olive Company (Elsinore)

Riverside County had many olive orchards and several small canneries such as this one. It only functioned for three years, from 1923 to 1926.

Leverton-California Corporation (Los Angeles)

This was another very short-lived firm, from 1935 to 1937. It had originally been the American Olive Company in Los Angeles. In 1937, it became the Spencer Olive Company.

La Mirada Olive Company (Corning)

La Mirada Olive Company, owned by Ira Well, ran from 1935 to 1954. At one time, it formed part of the Corning Olive Company. La Mirada then merged with the Feather River Growers, which in its turn was sold to the Lindsay Ripe Olive Company. Mr. Well processed the olives in Corning.

After selling the firm to the Feather River Growers, he reopened in Corning as the Ira Well Cannery, working from 1953 to 1962. That company was then sold to the Orinda Olive Company and ended up as part of Bell-Carter Foods. Ira Well died in 1993.

Well's nephew by marriage, George Powell, went to work for Lindsay Ripe Olive Company when La Mirada closed. George represented La Mirada at the California Olive Association in the 1950s.

Libby, McNeill, and Libby (Chicago)

The Libby firm began as a meat packing business in 1868. Arthur Libby took in his brother Charles and friend Archibald McNeill as partners. They expanded enormously at the end of the 1880s and added olives to their very diverse products. Libby, McNeill, and Libby had an olive processing plant in Sacramento and offices in San Francisco, among others. The firm was represented at early meetings of the California Olive Association by a man called Bellew. In the 1950s and 1960s, Clarence Hill was one of the Libby men at the California Olive Association, along with Jimmie Chung and Bob Ilse.

Libby no longer processes olives. Tri Valley Growers took it over.

Loma Ranch Company (Fallbrook)

This ranch is not the same one that Frank Capra owned, but no other information exists about it.

Dr. W. E. Mack (Paradise)

Dr. Mack made table olives and olive oil in Butte County in the 1920s.

Mat-Mor Olive Company (Lindsay)

The Mat-Mor Olive Company began in 1935. It was owned by the Morici family. The company ceased to be a separate entity in 1950. Three other companies took it over in quick succession, but the final one, Contadina Foods, gave up canning olives in 1956.

Mawer Gulden Annis, Incorporated

This company functioned from 1946 to 1950. Pat Grace and Henry Titus, son of J. V. E. Titus, represented it at the California Olive Association.

Maywood Packing Company (Corning)

Maywood Packing Company was another Warren Woodson enterprise in Corning. It started in 1906 to process fruit but quickly added olives to its products. It had gone out of independent existence when I met Robert Swank, manager of the plant for many years, in April 1996. He was already very old and sick but in spite of not feeling well, he spent time with me and gave me much useful information.

Mr. Swank was born in Indiana but came to California as a small child with his family. His father had been asthmatic and was told to try California because of the climate. The family traveled across the country in a car in 1923. His mother had a brother in Richfield, north of Corning, and so they settled there.

After Robert finished college in Chico, he started to work for Maywood. He never held another job. An accident as a child had left him with a useless left arm, but that did not hinder his career. It did make him very concerned about crippled children, and he was devoted to charities that helped them.

Mrs. Swank had been the secretary of the Stanley Roush Olive Company before her marriage, so she too was very well informed about the olive business. The Swanks told me that when they first went into the olive business, the fruit was harvested by poor migrants from Oklahoma, Texas, and Kansas. This group was followed by Filipino workers, and only later did Mexicans take over the task. Bell-Carter Foods acquired the Maywood plant in 1977 and kept on most of the staff.

McNally Ranch (South Los Angeles)

McNally Ranch was in business at the time of the founding of the California Olive Association in 1915. It ceased to operate in 1923. This ranch was owned by Andrew McNally of Rand McNally, the map company.

Ferdinand Mier (Fair Oaks)

The only mention of Ferdinand Mier was in the 1920 directory of the California Olive Association.

H. H. Moore and Son (Stockton)

H. H. Moore and Son was a firm of general merchants. Among their departments was a pharmacy, later to become a wholesale operation. At the end of the nineteenth century, olive oil was often a pharmaceutical. It is most likely that this company was not a producer of olive products but was a packager and wholesaler. Various members of the Moore family worked in the business for over forty years, from the 1890s to at least 1936, if not later.

W. J. Moore (Oroville)

Only the name of this firm remains.

Mor-Pak Preserve Company (unknown)

Mor-Pak was only active from 1927 to 1929.

M. B. Moulton (Stockton)

Moulton operated from 1923 to 1928, but it may have been a grocer rather than a primary canner.

Mount Ida Olive Company (Oroville)

This company was a very early business in Oroville. Judge John C. Gray began it in the 1890s. It subsequently merged with the Ehmann Olive Company and then with Olive Products. It was later reconstituted under the name of the Ehmann Olive Company, but the company no longer had any connection with Mrs. Ehmann's family. They simply used a well-known name.

James Mulryan (San Francisco)

Only the name of Mulryan remains.

Munson Brothers (Phoenix, Arizona)

Only the name of Munson remains.

Northern California Olive Corporation (Palermo)

Northern California Olive Corporation was in business from 1929 to 1933.

Ojai Olive Company (Ojai)

This company appeared to have a very brief life, from the time of the First World War to the 1920s.

Old Mission Canneries and Packing Company (San Diego)

This was the successor to Akerman and Tuffley's firm in San Diego. It has been described in some detail in the chapter on olive oil. E. W. Akerman and R. L. Tuffley started an olive oil factory and pickle business in the Old Town section of San Diego in 1901. They took the name "Old Mission Inn." In 1925, it went through a bankruptcy. The cannery was in existence from 1920 to 1980, when it was sold to Tri Valley Growers.

Old Ranchers Canning Company (Upland)

Old Ranchers Canning Company did not begin until after the Second World War (1946). It existed until 1981. The founder was one of Clifford Graber's sons.

Olives Incorporated (Corning)

This was the name of Stanley Roush's firm in Corning. He ran a relatively small canning factory. In the 1980s, he sold it to John Psyllos, who in turn sold it to Bell-Carter.

Olive Products (Oroville)

Olive Products began in 1916, the same year as the California Associated Olive Growers Association and one year before the Lindsay Ripe Olive Company. One of the initial investors was Joseph Cooper, Sr. His son only recently sold the family olive orchard in Butte County to Napa Valley Kitchens.

Ehmann Olive Company and the Mount Ida Olive Company merged in 1925 to form one company. This combined company subsequently merged with Olive Products. More than five hundred growers supplied fruit to this company. Beatrice Foods bought Olive Products in 1970. It then purchased the Wyandotte Olive Company in 1976, further reducing the number of plants in Oroville. For a time, Beatrice called this cannery Ehmann's Olive Company. By mid-1996, after several changes in ownership, the Oroville plant was closed. The premises went to a different company.

Orinda Olive Corporation (Corning)

Orinda Olive Corporation only lasted from 1960 to 1966, when it was sold to the Lindsay Ripe Olive Company. Ira Well set it up after he sold La Mirada Olive Company.

Pacific Olive Company (Visalia)

Edward van Dellen, a graduate food chemist, came to California from Iowa in 1935 and joined the Lindsay Ripe Olive Company. Van Dellen and Richard Ball founded the Pacific Olive Company in

1950 after they both left the Lindsay Ripe Olive Company. The two men originally bought a disused beet sugar factory in 1951 to start their plant. As the business grew, they purchased the premises of the Visalia Canning Company, still in use today, but now part of Musco Olive Products.

Pacific Olive Company was very successful and was taken over by Early California Foods in 1965. Gerald Murphy was in charge of the newly merged firm, although he kept his office in Los Angeles. In 1985, Murphy sold the company to Specialty Brands. That firm in turn sold it to the Vlasic Pickle Company, because Specialty Brands was involved in a quite different segment of the food industry. I visited the Vlasic plant in Visalia and chatted with Lubbert van Dellen, a senior executive and son of Edward van Dellen.

Vlasic is a subsidiary of Campbell's Soup, and the new organization did not work out. Olives were too small a product to command the attention of senior Campbell's officials and too unpredictable for their long-range planning. Campbell's no longer wished to pack olives.

Phoenix Brothers Olive Company (Phoenix, Arizona)

Phoenix Brothers Olive Company was one of the few olive companies in Arizona, but it was allowed to join the California Olive Association. It began in 1921 and closed in 1940.

F. A. Plagg (unknown)

F. A. Plagg worked intermittently for ten years from 1936 to 1946. The factory was then sold to the Scarlota Canning Company of Manteca.

Pratt Olive Company (Los Angeles)

Dr. Charles Pratt was a founding member of the California Olive Association.

Regina Olive Company (unknown)

The Regina Olive Company was the former South Tulare Olive Marketing Association (STOMA). It operated from 1943 to 1951.

Robertson and Sutton Company (unknown)

Robertson and Sutton were in business for five years from 1922 to 1927. In 1928, John Robertson took it over by himself but closed the company permanently in 1934.

Rocca Bella Olive Company (Calaveras County)

Rocca Bella was the name invented by Louis Sammis when he began his company in the foothills of Calaveras County. He thought it made sense to have an "Italian" name for an olive enterprise and the property was quite rocky. Sammis was a Connecticut Yankee who traveled across the country in 1916 by car, an interesting adventure in itself. He married a San Francisco woman whose family gave the young couple a piece of land in the foothills. There he planted additional olive trees and built a cannery that became a cooperative and stayed in business for many years, from 1922 until 1966, when it was sold to the Orinda Olive Company. The olive orchard is now in the possession of the Sciabica family of Modesto.

Roeding Fig and Olive Company (Fresno)

George Roeding had a famous nursery but also made olive oil for some time. He canned olives too, very briefly, in 1920.

Santa Cruz Fruit and Olive Company (Santa Cruz)

The Santa Cruz Fruit and Olive Company did business on Seabright Avenue in Santa Cruz.

V. R. Smith (Visalia)

V. R. Smith began canning olives in Visalia in 1920. The firm lasted until 1966 when it was sold to the Lindsay Ripe Olive Company.

Southern Tulare Olive Marketing Association [STOMA] (Terra Bella)

The Southern Tulare Olive Marketing Association began in 1911 as a solution to the problem of over-production and lack of an organized marketing program. The cooperative started processing olives in Terra Bella and ceased in 1946. The organization remained active for another few years as the Regina Olive Company before finally being bought by Sunland Olive Company.

Strathmore Olive Company (Strathmore)

A few growers got together to finance this plant. It was built by Leo Maselli and Leo Chrisafulli, but the firm only lasted from 1946 to 1947. The end of the Second World War led to a marked decline in the prices of canned olives.

Superior Olive Company (Visalia)

Superior ran from 1935 to 1945. It was owned by Michael Pastore.

Sylmar Packing Corporation (Sylmar)

Sylmar Packing Corporation grew out of the Los Angeles Olive Growers Association and has been described in some detail in the chapter on olive oil. The administrative offices were in Los Angeles. The company was started by a group of Illinois businessmen in 1887, and rapidly prospered. They built an extremely large plant, and everything was done on a heroic scale. Sylmar Packing Corporation ran until 1925.

Tehama Olive Company (Corning)

The Tehama Olive Company operated for three years, from 1943 to 1946.

Terra Bella Olive Association

Terra Bella Olive Association was only in existence for two years. It then became a part of the Southern Tulare Olive Marketing Association (STOMA).

Tri Valley Growers and Packing Corporation (Madera)

Tri Valley bought the Oberti Olive Company. It next bought the Libby olive operation and the S & W plant. As a result, Tri Valley developed a very large olive division. The main offices were in San Francisco. This all ended in 1999, after the harvest was processed. Tri Valley closed down its olive plant, but will continue some processing activity under an arrangement with Bell-Carter.

Virden Olive Company (Oroville)

Virden is mentioned in Harold Schutt's notes during the 1920s.

Wyandotte Olive Growers Association (Oroville)

This organization, a cooperative, grew out of the original effort to make and sell olive oil in Butte County (see appendix B). Once they switched to processing table olives, WOGA eventually took over the canning business of Suni-cal in Oroville. The "Berkeley" group in Oroville joined them in the enterprise. During the early phase, the 1920s, E. P. Hilborn and Fred Cornehl represented WOGA at the California Olive Association. WOGA remained in business until 1965.

The company was then sold to California Canners and Growers, and finally ended up as part of the Lindsay Ripe Olive Company. Once that company came to an end, no further olives were canned at the plant.

Appendix D

The attached list is a composite, created from several different sources. The principal ones are the inventory of the USDA National Clonal Germplasm Repository at Winters, California; the work of Byron M. Lelong, secretary of the State Board of Horticulture in the 1880s and '90s; and that of Hudson T. Hartmann, professor of pomology at the University of California at Davis, during the 1950s and '60s. A note such as "Hartmann only" means the cultivar was not recorded in other sources.

In some instances the origin of a particular cultivar was not available. The spelling of the names of the cultivars retains the idiosyncratic and variable character developed over many years. Quite often, the importer simply guessed at how a word in Italian or Spanish should be spelled.

ふ   ふ   ふ

Adrouppa (from Cyprus)

Ageezi Shami (from Egypt)

Aghizi

Amellau

Arbequina

Ascolana Dura (from Cyprus)

Ascolano 1

Ascolano 2

Ascolano Tenera

Ascoli

Asiolini

Atro-rubens

Atro-violacea

Attica (Lelong)

Azapa (from Chile)

Balady (from Egypt)

Barouni

Becca Ruffa

Bella de Spagna

Bellatudo (Lelong)

Belmonte

Bianchette (Lelong)

Bidh El Hamman (from Italy)

Black Italian (from Italy)

Bouchok (Hartmann only)

Bouquetier (from Italy)

Bouteillon

Cajon (Lelong only)

Calamata (Kalamata)

Calamignara (sold only by Meherin)

Carrasqueno (Lelong only)

Carydolia (Hartmann only)

Casalivo (Lelong only)

Cayon

Chalkidiki (from Greece)

Champion

Chemlali (from Tunisia)

Chetoui (Hartmann only)

Chitoni (Chetoui)

Colchonudo (Lelong only)

Columbaro (Lelong only)

Columella

Conditiva

Conservolia (from Greece)

Cordovil (from Italy)

Correggiolo

Criolla

Cucca (Cucce)

Cucci (from Argentina)

Cypress 31

Da Olio (sold only by Meherin)

Da Salare

Dalmatian (Obliza?)

Dolce de Napoli

Dolce del Maroco (from Morocco)

Doucette

Dwarf D

Edremit (Hartmann only)

Empeltre

Favoral (Lelong only)

Franklin

Frantoio (Frantoiano)

Frantoio (from Albania)

Gaidourelia (from Greece)

Galega

Gargnau (Lelong only)

Gentile (Lelong only)

Giaraffa

Gigante di Cerignola (from Italy)

Giogliaio (Lelong only)

Gordale

Gordo (Hartmann only)

Grantois

Grappolo

Gremignolo (Lelong only)

Grossa Di Spagna

Grossaio (Grossajo)

Grossane (from France)

Grossayo (Grossajo)

Grosse Aberkan

Hamid

Hervaza

Hispania

Huff's Spanish

Hurma (Hartmann only)

Infrantojo

Jalut (from Syria)

Javaluno (Lelong only)

K 18 (from Israel)

Kadesh

Kalamon

Karolia (from Greece)

Karydolia

Koroneiki (from Greece)

Laccio?

Lalvaguino (Lelong only)

Late Blanquette

Lavagnino

Lecci

Leccino

Leccino (from Yugoslavia)

Liguria

Lucca

Lucques

Macrocarpa

Madrileno (Lelong only)

Mammolese (Lelong only)

Manzanillo

Marcherito (Lelong only)

Maremanno (Lelong only)

Massabi (from Syria)

Mastoides Tsounati (from Greece)

Maurino

Mavrelia

Megaron (from Greece)

Memeli (from Turkey)

Menara

Merhavva

Meski (from Italy)

Meslale (Hartmann only)

Midx-elbasan (from Albania)

Mignolo

Mission 1

Mission 2

Mission 3

Mission 4

Mission Leiva (from Colombia)

Mission Modjeska (Whisler, from El Toro)

Mission Nieland

Monopolese (Lelong only)

Moraiolo

Morcal

Morchaia

Morinello

Mortinello (Lelong only)

Mortino (Lelong only)

Mostazal

Nab Tamri

Nabali

Nevadillo blanco

Nieland Banger

Nigerina

Nigretta (Lelong only)

Nikitskaya no.1 (from Russia)

No. 1 (from Cyprus)

No. 12 (from Cyprus)

No. 31 (from Cyprus)

No. 63 (from Cyprus)

No. 65a (from Cyprus)

Nocillara (Lelong only)

Nostralis (sold only by Stevens)

Nuevo di Sicrone

Qbliza

Obliza (from Croatia)

Oblonga

Occluino (Lelong only)

Ogliarola (Ogliaro?)

Oleastro (Lelong only)

Olivastro

Oliviere (sold only by Meherin)

Olivo A Prugno

Oriola (Oriolo?)

Ouslati (from Tunisia)

Palazzriolo

Palomino (Lelong only)

Palono (Lelong only)

Patronese (Lelong only)

Pecudo (Lelong only)

Pendoulier

Pendulina

Perugino (Lelong only)

Pesci Atino (Lelong only)

Phinicoti (Hartmann only)

Piangente

Picholine

Picholine du Languedoc

Picio (Lelong only)

Piconia

Picual

Pigale (sold only by Meherin)

Pignolo (Lelong only)

Pilloro (Lelong only)

Pleurer

Pocoma Peru (Whisler)

Polymorpha

Praecox

Prunara (from Italy)

Puntarolo (Lelong only)

Racemi (Lelong only); Racimal?

Racinoppe (Lelong only)

Radiola

Ragghio (Lelong only)

Ragialo (Lelong only)

Rapuina

Rastrellino (Lelong only)

Razzo

Redding Picholine

Redondillo de Lomgrona

Regalis

Rigali

Ronde du Languedoc

Ropades

Rosselina; Rosseldino?

Rouget

Rubra

Ruffa

Saiali Magloue

Salome

Salonica

Salvatico (Lelong only)

Sam (from Turkey)

San Francesco

Santa Caterina (Santa Catherina)

Saracena (not at USDA Winters)

Savillano (from Spain)

Sevillano

Sevillano Stralock

Sevillano-lovisone

Sevillano-tufts

Sigoise

Sir George Grey's Spanish (Nevadillo)

Souri

Sweet olive (Lelong only)

Syrogylolia (from Greece)

Taggiasco (Lelong only)

Thrombolea (from Greece)

Throumbolia (Whisler)

Tondo (Lelong only)

Touffahi (from Syria)

Trillo (Lelong only)

Uc 49-14 (Ascolano x Barouni)

Uc 52.24.1 (hybrid)

Uvaria

Varal blanco (Lelong only)

Vassilika (from Italy)

Verdale

Verdeal? (from Italy?)

Verdena (from Spain)

Verdugo (Lelong only)

Yuaca (from Peru)

Yullutt

Zarazi (Hartmann only)

Zitoum

Zoragi (from Tunisia)

❧   ❧   ❧

Appendix E

SYNONYMS OF SOME OLIVE CULTIVARS

The list that follows is compiled from several sources: The catalog at the USDA National Clonal Germplasm Repository in Winters, California; reports to the California State Board of Horticulture by USDA and UC Berkeley scientists; and reports and other documents left by nurserymen and olive growers. In spite of collating information from all these sources, a few gaps still remain.

৯৹   ৯৹   ৯৹

Standard Name and Synonyms	Country of Origin	Importer of Variety	Year Imported	Current Grower
Adrouppa (*grafted onto Mission*)	Cyprus	UC Department of Pomology	1950	USDA
Aghizi Shami	Egypt	Professor William Cruess	1940	USDA
Amellau, Amenlau, Amenlaou, Amellenque, Amandier, Amellaude, Amydalina, Olea sativa, Major oblonga, Angulosa, Amygdaliforma	France	Charles Wetmore		
Ascolano, White Olive of Ascoli	Italy		1885	
Ascolano dura (*grafted onto Mission*)	Cyprus	UC Department of Pomology	1949	USDA
Atrorubens, Saillern, Saillerne, Sagerne, Olea rotunda, Rubro-nigrians	France	John Rock	1885 or 1886	
Atroviolacea, Le Brun	Australia (Adelaide), but mentioned by Loop in 1890 as French	USDA	1920	USDA (in 1947)
Azapa (*grafted onto Mission*)	Chile	UC Department of Pomology	1950	USDA

Balady	Egypt	Professor William Cruess	1940	USDA
Barouni, Baruni	Tunisia	USDA	1905	
Bidh el Hamman	Tunisia	USDA	1875? 1922	USDA
Black Italian	Australia (Adelaide)	USDA	1920	USDA (in 1946)
Bouchok (grafted onto Mission)	Algeria	UC Department of Pomology	1947	
Bouquetier	Australia (Adelaide), originally from France	USDA	1920	USDA
Bouteillon	Australia (Adelaide)	USDA	1920	USDA
Carydolia	Greece	UC Department of Pomology	1947	
Chemlali	North Africa (Tunisia?)	USDA	1900s	USDA
Chetoni, Chitoni, Chetoui	Tunisia	UC Department of Pomology	1949	USDA
Columbella, Columella, Figaniere, Pasala, Loaime	France	John Rock	1880s	USDA, Michael Henwood
Cucco, Chietina, Coglioni di gallo, Francvillese, Francavinese, Lancianese, Oliva del mezzadro, Oliva tonda, Olivoce, Olivona/olivone, Testicolo di gallo	Italy		1895	
Dolce del Maroco	Italy (originally from Morocco)	USDA	1925	USDA

Edremit	Turkey	UC Department of Pomology	1948	
Empeltre	Spain			
Frantoio, Infrantoio, Infrantojo, Frantoiano, Raggio, Correggiolo (Hartmann), Piangente, Gentile, Larcianese, Laurino, Nostrato, Comune	Italy; there are 16 synoyms in total. Modern Italian authorities do not include Razzo as one of the synonyms, but the early California experts did so, as do today's French specialists.	Judge J. R. Logan, Santa Cruz	1885?	USDA; many others grow it now
Galaga, Trageola, Negral	Portugal	UC Department of Pomology	1950	USDA
Gigante di Ceragnola	Italy	UC Department of Pomology	1948	USDA
Gordale, Sevillano?	French Morocco	UC Department of Pomology	1950	USDA
Grappolo	Italy	USDA	1925	USDA
Grossa di Spagna	Italy	USDA	1925	USDA
Grossane (grafted onto Mission)	France	UC Department of Pomology	1948	USDA
Grosse Aberkan	Algeria (Mustafa)	USDA	1905	USDA
Hurma	Turkey	UC Department of Pomology	1948	None known. Said to be good for green olives only
Jahlut, Jallut, Jalut, Yullutt?	Syria	UC Department of Pomology	1949	USDA
Late Blanquette	Australia (Adelaide); originally from France	USDA	1920	USDA
Leccino, Leccio, Leccino di Belmonte, Leccino pesciatino, Premice, Silvestrone	Italy	USDA	1925	USDA?

Liguria (grafted onto Mission)	Chile	UC Department of Pomology	1950	USDA
Lucca	Australia (Adelaide)	USDA	1920	USDA
Lucques, Olive de Lucques, Lucquoise, Cornezuelo, Crescent	France	Charles Wetmore	1890	USDA
Macrocarpa	France	John Rock	1890?	USDA
Manzanillo, Rojal, Pomiformis, Ampoulleau, Mancanilha	Spain	F. Pohndorff; propagated by Juan Gallegos at San Jose	1870s	Many
Massabi	Syria	UC Department of Pomology	1949	USDA
Maurino, Maurino lucchese	Italy		1925	USDA
Menara	Morocco (Marrakech)	USDA	1930	USDA
Merhavy, Merhavva?	Palestine	UC Department of Pomology	1947	USDA
Meski	Tunisia (also said to have come from Italy)	UC Department of Pomology	1949	USDA
Meslala	French Morocco	UC Department of Pomology	1950	USDA
Meslale	Morocco (Marrakech)	USDA	1930	USDA (in 1946)
Mignolo, Gremignolo, Madregremignolo, Mignuolo, Minuto, Prugnolo, Rei dei mignoli	Italy		1880s?	
Mission, Cornicabra Cornezuelo (Tablada), Rostrata, Crisiomorpha, Cournaud, Plant de Salon, Plant de la Fane Cayon, Plant d'entrecasteaux, Rapunier, Olivier de Grasse	Spain	Franciscans (Marvin)	1775?	Many
Moraiolo, Morinello, Morino, Oliva tonda, Cimignolo, Cornico, Migno, Murajolo, Nerella, Oliva cornica, Oliva rotunda	Italy; there are 34 synonyms in total. The preceding is a selection. Spain	USDA	1925; perhaps previously in the 1880s	USDA (in 1946)

Morcal, Mollar?		USDA	1933	USDA
Mouraou, Olivier, Praecox, Acituna	Originally from Spain, but later brought to the U.S. from France? Italy?		1880s?	
Nabali	Palestine	UC Department of Pomology	1947	USDA
Nevadillo blanco, Moiral, Doncel zorzalena, Moradillo, Mourau and three variants, Sir George Grey's Spanish, Mourescale, Mouraoudo, Argentata, Praecox	Spain; in addition to these synonyms, one French authority considers this to be the same as Hoja blanca, a very widespread modern Spanish olive.	F. Pohndorff	1870s	Sciabica, USDA
Obliza, Oblitza, Oblica	Croatia (Dalmatia)	G. N. Milco	1892	USDA; L. Sammis grew it at Rocca Bella
Oblonga, Lucques, Lucquoise, Oliverolle, Oderante, Olea minor, Fructu oblongo, Incurro, Odorato, Ceratocarpa	France	John Rock	1880	USDA; many others
Ogliarola	Italy (Sicily); there are six main types, and a total of 103 syn.	UC Department of Pomology	1950	USDA
Olivo a prugno	Italy	UC Department of Pomology	1948	USDA
Ouslati	Tunisia	UC Department of Pomology	1949	USDA
Pendoulier (Pendulier), Corniale and three variants, Lucques batarde, Corniaou and three variants, Gournale, Plant de Salon, Courneaud and two variants, Oliva cornicabra (Tablada), Salonenque, Rostrata, Taggiasco	France (Marvin says all these identical with Mission?)	Albert Montpellier of Vacaville	1885	
Pendulina	France	John Rock	1880?	USDA
Phinocoti (grafted onto Mission)	Cyprus	UC Department of Pomology	1949	

Picholine (true Picholine) and two variants, Saurine, Sausen and two variants, Saurenque, Plant de Sauren (Saurine), Punchado, Lucques batarde, Pignola, Oblonga? (Hartmann), St. Chamas	France	B. B. Redding	1872	USDA
Pleurer, Caillet, Caye, Caillette, Cayette, Cayon, Nostrale, Olivier de Grasse	France	Dr. Hall (dentist), Carpinteria		
Polymorpha	France	John Rock	1885?	USDA
Praecox, Acituna	Spain (see Mouraou)	John T. Doyle	1880	
Prunara	Italy (Sicily)	UC Department of Pomology	1950	USDA
Racemi, Racinoppe, Oblonga (incorrect)	France? Italy?	(mentioned in Lelong)	1880s?	
Razzo, Alvaia, Oliva dolce: possibly the sweet olive, Ortana Pendaglio, Ragghio, Raggia, Raggiale, Raggiolo, Ragia, Razzillo	Italy; there are 19 synonyms in total. Authorities differ as to whether this is synonymous with Frantoio. The Italians do not think this, but French experts still mention it.	Judge J. R. Logan, Santa Cruz	1880	
Redding Picholine	France	B. B. Redding	1870s	Many
Ropades	Greece (Mytiline)	USDA?	1926	USDA
Rose	France	(Lelong)		
Rouget, Cayon, Rougette, Rousseoun, Merveilletto, Pigan, Vermillau, Caillose, Cayhonne, Rougealle, Olea rubicans	France			USDA
Rubra, Caillon?	France	John Rock	1880s?	USDA; Michael Henwood
Saiali Magroud	Tunisia	USDA	1905	USDA
Salome	Australia (Adelaide)	USDA	1920	USDA

Sam	Turkey	UC Department of Pomology	1948	USDA (said to be very good oil)
San Agostino (Sant' Agostino), Olivo di S. Agostino, Cazzarola, Oliva andresana, Oliva di andria, Oliva dolce di andria, Oliva grossa, Oliva grossa andrianese, Oliva pane, Oliva senza pane	Italy		1890?	USDA
San Francesco	Italy	UC Department of Pomology?	1948	USDA
Santa Caterina, Oliva di San Biagio, Oliva di San Giacomo, Oliva lucchese	Australia (Adelaide); originally from Italy	USDA	1920	USDA
Sevillano, Gordal, Sevillana, Sevilanha, Espagnole, Queen	Spain	F. Pohndorff	1885?	USDA, many others
Sigoise (grafted onto Mission), Zitoum	Algeria	UC Department of Pomology	1947	USDA
Souri	Palestine	UC Department of Pomology	1947	USDA (Note: said to be most widely used because of high oil content)
Tafahi, Tiffahi, Tefah, Tefahi	Egypt (Fedimine)	USDA?	1922	USDA (Note: it does not turn black when pickled)
Taggiasco (Taggiasca), Gentile, Oliva di Taggia, Pignola d'oneglia, Tagliasca, Tagliasco	Italy (Liguria)	(Marvin says this is the Mission olive)	1880s	
Touffahi	Syria	UC Department of Pomology	1949	USDA
Turilya	Turkey	UC Department of Pomology	1948	
Vassiliki, Vassilika	Greece (said to have come from Italy)	UC Department of Pomology	1947	USDA

Verdale, Verdaou and two variants, Aventurier, Classen, Olea viridula, Olea media, Rotunda viridia, Olivo verdago (Tablada)	France; also brought from Japan	UC Department of Pomology	1950	USDA
Yullutt	Syria	USDA	1934	USDA
Zarazi	Tunisia	UC Department of Pomology	1949	
Zitoum, Moroccan Picholine, Sigoise	French Morocco	UC Department of Pomology	1950	USDA

Appendix F

What follows is a listing of the early nurseries that sold olive trees in the last quarter of the nineteenth century and the early part of the twentieth century. If available, information about the owners is also given.

Sources for this information include Thomas Brown's *A List of California Nurseries and Their Catalogues: 1850 to 1900,* U. P. Hedrick's *A History of Horticulture in America to 1860,* and the work of Harry M. Butterfield, an agriculturist with the University of California's Agricultural Extension Service and a student of the history of California horticulture. Some nurseries not included in Brown's list are mentioned by Butterfield and Hedrick. Very few of the catalogs from these latter nurseries survived and the information concerning them is sketchy at best, but there are indications that they grew olive trees. The names appear below in brackets, to distinguish them from the ones which are certain. The reader should note that the spelling of foreign names was often completely idiosyncratic and not be confused by wild variation. I am quoting from original sources.

Armstrong Nursery, Ontario, Riverside County

John Armstrong came from Scotland and started the nursery in 1889. After his retirement, his son James took it over. James, in turn, handed the business on to his son John in 1970. The founder lived to be almost a hundred years old. At the time of the First World War, the elder Armstrong issued a pamphlet on growing olives intended to instruct the new generation. He concentrated on the table olive varieties and gave excellent advice about planting, culture, and the business opportunities offered by olives. Armstrong cited Clifford Graber's success as an example. (Graber had opened his olive business in Ontario in 1894.) Graber Olives are still a family concern, with their products available all over the country.

Eleven catalogs from Armstrong Nursery are in the Bailey Hortorium collection. Unfortunately the 1889/90 price list noted at the National Agricultural Library could not be found. The Bailey Hortorium pamphlets start in 1907. Armstrong sold Mission, Manzanillo, and Nevadillo types for several years, according to the catalog series that started in 1907. Armstrong may well have been selling them earlier, but we cannot know that. He noted that Graber used Manzanillos for his pickles. Small trees went for 30 cents each, or $2.50 for ten. Larger trees cost 50 cents. In 1913, Armstrong added the Ascolano and Sevillano varieties. In his 1914 catalog, he included a photograph of his nursery showing 75,000 young olive trees. That year he included the Chemlali, newly imported by the USDA. This tree was imported specifically for oil. The promotional pamphlet was probably written sometime about then, as it comments on data for 1912.

The Bancroft Library has one 1916 Armstrong catalog in its collection. In that year, Armstrong tried out a new marketing technique. For every $10 worth of olive trees purchased, the buyer would receive a can of Manzanillo olives. The catalog for 1921 still had a whole page devoted to olives, with five photographs. Armstrong offered Ascolano, Manzanillo, Mission, and Sevillano. In the cultural notes attached to the description of the stock, he inveighed against the practice of grafting all the new varieties onto Picholine rootstock.

Barren Hill Nursery, Nevada City

In 1886, Felix Gillet sold "imported" olive trees without specifying which type, though they were most likely French. Gillet did not list them in 1887. The 1888 and 1889 catalogs are missing. In 1890, Gillet once again offered olive trees, "large fruited from Provence" and grown "true from the root." Presumably these were seedlings and not grafted. This might have been Pendulina or the real Picholine. He charged from 50 cents to 75 cents each according to size. A catalog from 1892 in the Bancroft Library shows that he was still selling this limited stock. In spite of his foreign origin, Gillet quickly learned idiomatic English. On the inside cover page of the 1892 catalog, there is a paragraph headed "cheek and fraud of Eastern nurserymen." He complained about the theft of cuttings from his stock and their resale under new names. That was a real grievance, and Gillet took it to the American Nurserymen's Convention.

A. F. Boardman and Company, Auburn

A catalog from 1889 is in the National Agricultural Library. Boardman's list contained Nevadillo, Manzanilla, Mission, and "Picholene" (presumably Redding Picholine) trees, ranging from 25 cents to $1.00 each, according to size. He commented that some new kinds had been introduced of late. He wrote, "We have a few of them, but have not seen them fruiten [sic] enough to judge of their merits." All his cultivars, except for Mission, had only been in California for fifteen years, but that was ample time for them to be acclimatized. In another note, he pointed out that olive orchards at 1,800 to 2,000 feet elevation near his property in Auburn did very well.

Another Boardman catalog is in Special Collections at UC Davis. It dates from 1893/94, still only listing the well-known Mission, Nevadillo, Manzanillo, and Picholine trees. Evidently Boardman never felt it would be worthwhile to propagate the other types.

E. J. Bowen, San Francisco

There is only one catalog, dated 1883, for this company in the Bancroft Library. Bowen sold "olives," without further elaboration, for 75 cents apiece.

California Nursery Company, Niles

The man who became John Rock arrived in the United States in 1852 at the age of seventeen. He was born in Germany and had been named Johann Fels. Soon after arriving in the United States he anglicized his name. He later fought in the Civil War as an officer in the Fifth New York Regiment, but in 1865 he emigrated to California and started his nursery in San Jose.

John Rock was so intimately connected with the olive program at the University of California College of Agriculture that his later catalogs read like minor treatises. It was not always so. The transition began in the mid-1880s. In 1873, Rock sold "olives" without any other description. In 1880 and 1882, olives were still an afterthought. He listed them under "Miscellaneous fruits," offering "California or Mission" and "Italian or Picholine" at 50 cents and 75 cents each.

The expansion in olive trials under the auspices of the University of California coincided with that of the nursery. Originally Rock had started his own premises in 1865, but in 1884, he merged with R. D. Fox of Santa Clara to form the larger entity, California Nursery at Niles. Each man continued to manage his own acreage, but eventually Rock took over as chief.

The 1885 catalog was still under Rock's name. In this issue, he noted that he had been growing twelve new European varieties of olive trees for four years and could now offer them for sale. These were grafted and already very productive; they cost $2 each. For that period, $2 was expensive. The other varieties cost from 10 to 25 cents apiece. Rock listed each tree with a synonym:

Atro-violacea (Brun)
Oblonga (Figaniere)
Regalis (Ronde de languedoc)
Columbella (Figaniere)
Pendulina (Boussalu)
Rubra (Caillon)
Macrocarpa (Belgentier)
Polymorpha (Pleurer de Grasse)
Rufa (Beca)
Nigerina (Rapugon)
Praecox (Repugnier)
Uvaria (Rapugnier)

All of them came from France. He obtained them directly himself.

In 1891, the list was modified. Rock added Amellau, Atro-rubens, Attica, Columbaro, Correggiola, Conditiva, Cucco, Da Salare, Frantoio, Lechin (Huff's Spanish), Lucques, Marajola, Nigricans, Radiola, Rapuina, Razzo, Salonica, Taggiasco, and Verdale. Many of these now came from Italy, except for Attica, which was Greek. Attica was imported by Mr. Agapius Honcharenko, a very cultivated man of Russian birth who had grown up in Greece to become a scholar and poet.

Other trees from Italy that were good for oil were added to this list, together with their region of origin: Frantoio (Grossajo, Infrantoio) from Tuscany, Grantois from Lombardy, Leccino from Tuscany, Marajolo (Morinello) from Tuscany, Piangente from Tuscany, Radiola from Rapollo, Rapuina from San Remo, Razzo from Tuscany, and Taggiasco from Porto Mauricio. The synonyms are from the period, and not necessarily the ones acknowledged today.

The lists of olive trees stayed much the same for several years. Only George Roeding at Fancher Creek Nurseries had as many varieties. By the end of the nineteenth century, the change to table olives affected Rock's business. He had to drop the foreign cultivars and stick to the tried and true Mission, Manzanillo, Sevillano, and Picholine. Ultimately, George Roeding bought California Nursery, combining the two companies.

Other catalogs in the Bancroft Library are from the next decade. In 1908, the combined company of Fancher Creek and California Nursery still sold nineteen cultivars of olive, including two new ones, Calimignara and Bella di Spagna. Even in 1913, they still offered fifteen kinds of trees. It was not until about 1930 that they finally gave up hope, coming down to six varieties, but there was a small addendum on this page in which the owner noted that ". . . in addition to the above, we have stock trees of a great many other sorts, some very fine, but little known. Our collection is doubtless the most complete in America."

John Calkins, Pomona

Brown lists two of Calkins's price lists in the National Agricultural Library. They could not be found, nor could the one at UC Davis, but Calkins's 1894 *Olive Grower's Handbook* is still in Special Collections at Davis. There is also supposed to be a price list in the Bailey Hortorium, but it too could not be found. A price list on a pocket-sized card can be seen in Special Collections at the University of California at Los Angeles. The Huntington Library at San Marino has two price lists, 1890 and 1894.

Olives were Calkins's principal business. He only stocked a very few other types of plant. He offered fifty-nine varieties of olive tree, three still only designated by number because their names were "not yet positively known." At the time, this was a larger selection than either Rock's or Roeding's. He seems not to have known that Frantoio and Infrantoio were synonymous, listing them as two varieties.

Calkins's *Olive Grower's Handbook* was a sixteen-page document, with careful instructions about all aspects of growing and processing olives. Its tone was very much like that of George Roeding. The booklet was available free of charge to anyone who requested it. Calkins also wrote other papers and articles about olive growing.

Capital Nurseries, Sacramento

The proprietor, W. R. Strong, was very conservative. The nursery had been started in 1852, when it was "under the control of Mr. Williamson and his son." In 1891, Strong sold Mission, Picholine, Nevadillo blanco, and Manzanillo (which he called "Queen" olives). The notes state that Mission was an all-purpose tree and that Picholine was good for oil. The 1891 catalog is in the Sacramento Archive and Museum Collection.

The catalog for 1893/94, which is in the National Agricultural Library, comments, "There are a great many variety of olives now being propagated, most of them not yet thoroughly tested, and we only offer those varieties that have been tested and are known to be the most profitable." Strong's list of trees offered was the same as in 1891: Mission, Picholine, Nevadillo blanco, and Manzanillo. He also offered a fertilizer that was endorsed by Dean Eugene Hilgard and another professor at the UC College of Agriculture.

Central Avenue Nursery, Los Angeles

A.W. Eames owned this nursery. One very small pamphlet for 1891/92, now in the National Agricultural Library, survives. Eames listed sixteen cultivars of olives, "all cuttings from bearing trees." Besides Mission, Manzanillo, Nevadillo blanco, and Picholine, he had the newer French and Italian oil trees.

Chollas Valley Nurseries, San Diego

A catalog that survives at the National Agricultural Library records the fact that this nursery sold California, or Mission, olives and Picholine, "introduced from Italy ten years ago in 1890." The proprietors, L. E. Allen and J. H. Orcutt, were not the only ones who misunderstood the Picholine's origins.

Christensen and Huston, Los Angeles

A catalog for 1895 survives in the Bailey Hortorium at Cornell University. Fruit trees were relegated to the back cover, including "olives," with no other description. The olive industry was a major one in early Los Angeles and this skimpy offer is a little surprising.

[D. W. Clark, Santa Barbara]

A single catalog is at the Santa Barbara Historical Society. It shows that Clark grew olives together with bananas, guavas, dates, and cherimoyas in 1874, as well as citrus, which was his specialty.

[C. J. Couts, Vista]

Cave Johnson Couts grew olive trees at his ranch, the Old Adobe, in the 1850s, but it is unclear from Butterfield's notes if he also functioned as a nurseryman. The trees survived until 1936.

Thomas Cox Seed Company, San Francisco

The Bailey Hortorium at Cornell University has thirteen of Cox's catalogs, from 1894 to 1907. He was not very adventurous. He stocked Manzanillo, Mission, Nevadillo blanco, and Picholine as well as selections from the French and Italian imports: Atro-violacea, Columella, Oblonga, Pendulina, Rubra. He offered one Spanish variety, the Sevillano.

Fancher Creek Nursery, Fresno

George Roeding's father, Frederick, had come to Fresno from Germany as an early settler. He prospered, founding a bank and investing in property. Frederick Roeding started the nursery his son George later ran. He was very civic minded and philanthropic, giving land to the city. This piece of land is now named Roeding Park.

George was very energetic and skillful. His interest in figs led to many important findings about setting the fruit. Fancher Creek's 1886 catalog listed twenty-two kinds of figs and noted that he was working on another fifty. He pursued olives with the same thoroughness, cooperating with the university as a test site. Like the California Nursery at Niles, new olive varieties appeared in the mid-1880s. The 1887 catalog offered four varieties for "general planting": Mission, Manzanillo, Nevadillo blanco, and Picholine. In addition, there were eleven varieties for "experimental planting": Atro-violacea, Columella, Macrocarpa, Nigerina, Oblonga, Pendulina, Polymorpha, Praecox, Regalis, Rufa, and Uvaria.

By 1897, ten years later, the list had grown to forty-three types of olive trees. Among other things, Roeding distinguished between Manzanillo no. 1 and Manzanillo no. 2. He said that he received truncheons of Manzanillo no. 1 from Professor Pohndorff, the person who imported this variety from Spain, and that it was entirely different from Manzanillo no. 2. Unlike the other sources, the notes in this catalog show the differences. Manzanillo no. 1 was a straggling, upright type of tree. The fruit was very large, deep black when ripe, with small white specks on the surface. Manzanillo no. 2 also grew upright but in a dense and compact fashion. The fruit looked very similar but was slightly smaller. Roeding also said that no. 1 ripened in October and no. 2 much later. It is Manzanillo no. 1 that has become so widespread in California. Most of the horticultural expertise in Roeding's enterprise was supplied by his manager, Gustav Eisen, an authority who was consulted by the USDA about olives and grapes at a later date and who probably wrote these notes.

Roeding offered the following varieties almost as "standard," indicating that they had been in cultivation for a considerable length of time: Atro-rubens, Atro-violacea, Columella, Empeltre, Gordal (which he did not know was the same as Sevillano), Lucques, Macrocarpa, Manzanillo no. 1, Manzanillo no. 2, Mission, Nevadillo blanco, Nigerina, Obliza, Pendoulier, Pendulina, Polymorpha, Praecox, Redding Picholine, Regalis (which he said was synonymous with Columella), Rubra, Rufa, Salonica, and Uvaria.

Under the heading "Olives of recent introduction," Roeding listed Ascolano, Attica, Belmonte, Columbaro, Correggiolo, Cucco, Frantoio, Leccino, Moraiolo, Morinello, Piangente, Radiola, Rapuina, Razzo, San Agostino, Santa Caterina, and Taggiasco. "New Olives" were Picholine St. Chamas (the true Picholine) and Sevillano. Each cultivar had a few words of description, and even a brief cultural note or two. Roeding continued to carry more than forty types of olive trees up until 1903, charging from 25 to 40 cents each. He evidently did not think they had run their course.

The cover of the 1909 catalog sported, in naturalistic color, four different olives on their branches. That was the year Roeding ran a joint venture with Luther Burbank, licensing the latter's discoveries in fruit and flowers for sale. In 1913, he offered yet another new type of olive tree, the Chemlali (a new variety imported by the USDA from Tunisia). Finally, several years later, two catalogs from 1917 and 1919 show he understood that oil olives were no longer dominant.

Roeding's 1917 and 1919 catalogs are in the library at UC Davis. Both have four or five pages of closely spaced small type on the culture of the olive and illustrative photographs, but the text conveys the fact that olives were now being grown primarily for the pickling process. Gustav Eisen's name does not appear in these documents, but, as mentioned above, he was the horticulturist at Fancher Creek and probably made a large contribution to the content. The cultivars for sale at that time included Mission, Manzanillo, Lucques, Chemlali, Nevadillo blanco, Obliza, Ascolano, and Sevillano. Of these, only Chemlali and Nevadillo blanco are grown for their oil.

In 1922, Roeding reduced his inventory to four kinds of olive trees. He still featured the trees as an important commodity. His instructions were even more detailed and elaborate than they had been in earlier editions.

Bernard Fox, Santa Clara

Bernard Fox emigrated from Ireland in 1848, at the age of thirty-two, and worked in New York and Massachusetts initially. This was still during the famine period in Ireland. After five years, he crossed the country to California and, at the suggestion of Commander Stockton of Santa Clara, started a nursery. In the next seven years, he did very well, and by 1860, he claimed that he had a million fruit trees in his orchards as well as many fine ornamentals.

Like many men who escaped from the Irish famine, he never married. Instead, he brought a nephew over from Ireland, adopted him legally, and educated him at the new University of Santa

Clara. When Bernard Fox died in 1884, his nephew, R. D. Fox, inherited the nursery. The younger Fox did marry and had children. In 1884, he and John Rock merged their nurseries to form the larger California Nursery.

An undated Bernard Fox catalog at UC Davis lists simply "Olives" as a miscellaneous fruit tree. This was probably from an early date.

Fresno Nursery, Fresno

Messrs. Marshall and Wilson opened this nursery in competition with Fancher Creek. They used land east of Visalia for propagation. One catalog from 1884 in the Bancroft Library shows that no olives were sold that year. The Bailey Hortorium has many of their catalogs. In 1894, they had eleven types of olive trees: the standard ones plus Columella, Pendulina, Praecox, Regalis, Rubra, and Uvaria. At some point, they experimented with Ascolano, and Obliza, but by the 1920s they only sold Mission, Manzanillo, Sevillano, and Ascolano (the latter after proving successful in experiments).

[Edward Germain Nurseries, Los Angeles]

This company did not sell olive trees, but there was a vintner with the same name at the same time, at about the end of the nineteenth century. The latter advertised its own brand of olive oil together with the wine vintages, a very modern concept. Conceivably the nursery provided the source of the olive oil.

Kelsey Nursery, Oakland

The Bancroft Library has two catalogs, 1872 and 1874, from this company. In 1872, no olives were sold, but in 1874, Kelsey offered "olives," without further description, for 50 cents each.

Thomas Meherin, San Francisco

Meherin was a member of the board of directors and an agent for the California Nursery Company. He had no facilities for propagation in the city. Special Collections at the University of California at Davis has two of his catalogs, for 1876 and 1877. They offered "olive trees—two or three years old" for 75 cents each. No variety was listed.

A catalog from 1899/1900 survives at the National Agricultural Library. Apart from the now familiar cultivars above, Meherin also carried a few newer ones. Eight never previously seen types were now available: Calamignara (Sicily), Da Olio (Sicily), Giarraffa (Sicily), Picholine d'Aix (France), Oliviere (France), Pigale (France), Rouget (France), and Ronde de Languedoc (France). These were probably really new, except perhaps for Rouget, which had been brought in as Caillon earlier. They do not appear in my sources of synonyms.

Morris Nursery, San Bernardino

Morris entitled his 1895 catalog *Trees and Trees*. A copy is in the Bailey Hortorium at Cornell University. He sold Columella, Manianillo [sic], Mission, Nevadillo blanco, Oblonga, Pendulina, Praecox, Regalis, Rogga [sic], Rubra, and Uvaria. The list concluded with a testimonial from Mr. C. F. Eaton of Santa Barbara. Mr. Eaton had a three-year-old olive tree that produced ten gallons of berries. This fruit fetched 50 cents a gallon once pickled.

Napa Valley Nursery, Napa

This nursery was owned by Leonard Coates, an Englishman who came to California in 1876 for his health. His symptoms were not specified, but he apprenticed himself to Professor Heald, a leading horticulturist, and worked exceedingly hard at the craft of horticulture without any apparent difficulties. The nursery industry involves a lot of sheer physical labor. It appears that Coates could withstand this perfectly well.

After he went to several other nurseries in the state to gain greater skill, he returned to Napa and took over land offered by Heald. He eventually had an orchard with 150,000 fruit trees. Coates spent six months in Europe early in the twentieth century as an advocate for the California fruit growers, opening up markets. He did this in his capacity as a charter member of the California Horticultural Society.

The catalog for 1886, in the Bancroft Library, does not list olives. In Coates's 1893 catalog, he offered Mission and Manzanillo olives. Copies of this and a few other Napa Valley Nursery catalogs survive in both the National Agricultural Library and Special Collections at the University of California at Davis. He was not particularly adventurous with olive trees, though in 1896 he added Columella, Nevadillo blanco, Pendulina, Regalis, and Rubra to the list.

Orange County Nurseries, Fullerton

The Bailey Hortorium at Cornell University has nine of the Orange County Nurseries's catalogs. In 1894, P. A. Schumacher owned the nursery. He only offered Nevadillo blanco olives for the two years that followed. By 1896, he had added "All varieties." The 1898/99 catalog is in the National Agricultural Library. In that interval, from 1896 to 1898, Schumacher had sold the nursery to two men: E. S. Richman, who was responsible for the fruit trees, and S. Lenton, who was responsible for the flowers. Olives appear on page 4, once again with the enigmatic statement: "all varieties; prices on application." In the succeeding years, Orange County Nurseries restricted its list of olives to Columella, Mission, Nevadillo blanco, and Pendulina.

Pajaro Valley Nurseries, Watsonville

Three of these catalogs are in the Bailey Hortorium. The proprietor, James Waters, listed olives only in one of them, for the year 1900/01. That year he offered Alto-violacea [sic], Conditiva, "Doucette," Mission, Picholine, Regalis, and Rubra. ("Doucette" is a new name, one that I have not seen elsewhere. It may be a synonym.) Small trees, less than four feet tall, went for 18 cents each, or $1.75 for ten. The larger trees cost 25 cents.

Palm and Citrus Nursery, Santa Barbara

The National Agricultural Library has one of these catalogs for 1891. In spite of its name, the Palm and Citrus Nursery also sold fruit trees. Regarding olives, the proprietor, Kinton Stevens, wrote that he had "several thousand potted plants of the following varieties; cuttings taken from trees imported from Italy by Dr. Gould of Montecito. All are the best varieties of the oil Olive. See report of Prof. B. M. Lelong in the annual issue of the State Board of Horticulture for 1889." His trees were Cucco, Correggiolo, Frantoio, Morchiaio, Morinello, and Palazuolo. Morchiaio could be the same as Morchiaia and Palazuolo might be Palazzriolo. Correggiolo and Frantoio were probably one and the same.

In the next paragraph, Stevens offers "Common Varieties": Mission, Mansanillo [sic], Navadillo blanco [sic], Redding Picholine, Rubra, and Nostralis. The last one was said to be a very good type for both oil and pickles from the south of France. It is most likely a synonym, though I have not seen it elsewhere.

Poway Valley Nursery, Piermont (near San Diego)
This nursery was owned by Messrs. Chapin and Meeker. Catalogs for 1889 and 1890 are in the National Agricultural Library. Mission, Nevadillo blanco, Picholine, and Manzanillo olives were available. Poway Valley Nursery had a telephone very early.

Rancho Chico, Chico (property of John Bidwell)
Bidwell never involved himself in the new varieties. Catalogs from 1889 and 1893 at the National Agricultural Library show that he only sold Mission, Manzanillo, Nevadillo blanco, and Picholine ("Italian pickling") olives.

Santa Barbara Nursery and Floral Depot, Santa Barbara
A catalog from 1877 is in the Special Collections at the University of California at Davis. There is a brief entry, saying that *Olea europaea* is "supposed to have originally been a native of Greece. Proximity to the sea is favorable to it and hillsides are more eligible for its culture than the plains. There are many varieties. Baron von Muller describes 34." It is not clear what was available for sale. Santa Barbara was important in the revival of olive growing, since Ellwood Cooper began his epoch-making activities near there at Goleta.

Santa Rosa Nursery, Santa Rosa
This was Luther Burbank's nursery. In 1887/88, they sold Picholines at modest prices. Seedling olive trees from a "hardy Northern grown tree" cost a little more. "Small rooted cuttings of most of the new and rare kinds can be supplied at 20 to 50 cents each." Twelve years later they would try to unload these foreign varieties at a much reduced price.

J. Seulberger, Oakland
There are two of J. Seulberger's catalogs, 1890 and 1893, at the National Agricultural Library. Both of them offer Picholines as the sole representatives of olive trees. The catalogs are interesting because he listed his telephone number in them.

Sherwood Hall, San Francisco
A copy of the 1893 catalog survives in the Bailey Hortorium. The proprietor, Timothy Hopkins, offered seven types of olive tree: Amellau, Atro-rubens, Atro-violacea, Mission, Nevadillo blanco, Oblonga, and Polymorpha. An undated catalog is in the Bancroft Library. No olives were offered that year.

Shinn's Nurseries, Niles

The Shinn family played a long and very distinguished role in California's nursery trade. James Shinn was born in Ohio in 1807. He practiced horticulture in several western and southern states before coming to California in 1855. The last place he had lived before opening a nursery in Alameda County was Texas. He helped to found the California State Board of Horticulture and later became president of the California Nurseryman's Association.

His son Charles was also influential in horticulture, working at the University of California for a time. He collected some of the early history, which would otherwise have been lost, and wrote about it in a number of papers. Charles Shinn was an important horticultural journalist as well as an early environmentalist. Shinn's other son, Joseph, was less active in the field.

An undated catalog at the University of California at Davis, mentions only "olive trees of several sizes" without any other description. The Shinns devoted their energies to the fig.

C. M. Silva and Sons, Newcastle

Special Collections at the University of California at Davis has seven of Silva's catalogs, from 1878 to 1887. Olives, unspecified, were offered in 1879/80, 1881/82, 1882/83, 1883/84, and 1887. The National Agricultural Library has a catalog from 1894/95. Silva now distinguished between Mission and "Picholene" olive trees, selling them for 15 to 35 cents apiece, depending on their size. Five later catalogs, into the 1920s, are in the Bailey Hortorium at Cornell University. By now Silva had acquired a partner, Bergholdt. The 1918/19 catalog lists only four types of trees, all rooted on Picholine stock: Ascolano, Manzanillo, Mission, and Sevillano.

Silva wrote that large food processing companies such as Libby, McNeil, and Libby, and H. J. Heinz had invested a lot of capital in the olive business and had "vast selling facilities." He maintained that the Mission olive was the most profitable and the Sevillano the least, because it was "a shy bearer." It was Silva who considered the Picholine rootstock to be best.

Silver Gate Nurseries, San Diego

The proprietor, D. W. Parker, probably had an arrangement with John Rock. The 1889 catalog in the National Agricultural Library contains information on sixteen varieties with the comments verbatim from Rock's pamphlets.

[Lorenzo Soto, San Diego]

Soto grew olives on his ranch thirty miles out of San Diego, but it is unclear whether he was a nurseryman too. He had bought a rich claim in the southern mines, probably near Sonora, from a Señor Valdez back in 1848 and so became wealthy.

Southern California Acclimatizing Association, Santa Barbara

In May 1897, this nursery offered "all the leading varieties, both for pickling and for oil making; detailed lists and prices for large quantities furnished on request." One catalog is at the University of California at Davis. Harris Newmark mentions this association in his memoirs, *Sixty Years in Southern California: 1853 to 1913.*

[T. K. Stewart, near Sacramento]

In 1849 Stewart planted olive trees, together with figs, on his property. He later added oranges and had large orchards. It is not known whether he was a nurseryman too.

Stockton Nursery, Stockton

Stockton Nursery was owned by William B. West. One catalog, from 1880, is in the Special Collections at the University of California at Davis. Mr. West offered two cultivars of olive, Mission and Picholine, the latter "an Italian variety, very large and fine." West also contributed occasional articles about horticulture to contemporary magazines.

Sunset Nursery, San Francisco

There are three catalogs of this nursery (1894, 1896, and 1898) at the National Agricultural Library. The 1894 catalog shows an interest in olives, with eight new varieties, plus the standard Mission and Redding Picholine. In 1896, the owner sold Mission olives as a "sidewalk" tree, saying it withstood the inevitable neglect well. He added that "the fruit is not liable to be molested by small boys, at least not the second time." In the next sentence, he also noted that a good income could be had from the fruit. A four- to five-foot tree cost 25 cents. The catalog had a number of close-up photographs of olive branches heavy with fruit. Its cover was very artistic, with engravings of tropical palms. The olive trees were propagated and grown in the company's orchard at Menlo Park.

In another section, the owner elaborated on his stock, listing eighteen modern varieties as well as the Mission. He gave brief explanatory notes for each one. There were Atro-violacea, Columella, Lucques, Macrocarpa, Manzanillo, Nevadillo blanco, Nigerina, Oblonga, Picholine, Pendulina, Polymorpha, "Queen" (Sevillano), Razzo, Regalis, Rouget, Rubra, Uvaria, and Verdale.

By 1898, the selection had been reduced to ten cultivars, three of which were Mission, Manzanillo, and Nevadillo blanco. This suggests that the owner may have thought the trend was changing, away from the more exotic oil olives. Other nurseries of that epoch were also reducing their investment in these varieties, such as Burbank's attempt to get rid of them by reducing the price drastically.

R. J. Trumbull and Company (later known as Trumbull and Beebe), San Francisco

Trumbull's was a large, prosperous nursery. He specialized in lavish ornamental plants for such exacting customers as Governor Leland Stanford. The governor built his conservatory in 1876, and Trumbull supplied the contents. By 1897, the firm had added Beebe, to be known now as Trumbull and Beebe.

The catalogs in the National Agricultural Library date from 1884, 1897, and 1900. The list for 1884 simply offers "Olive," Mission and Italian, by which he may have meant Picholine. They cost from 25 to 75 cents each.

Once Trumbull joined with Beebe, the nursery added Columella ("Columballa"), Manzanillo, Nevadillo blanco, Rubra, and Uvaria—that is, three of the newer kinds and two more standard ones. Prices remained in the same range. They continued to offer this list in 1900 and again in 1905.

B. F. Wellington, San Francisco

An 1875 catalog survives in the Bancroft Library. Wellington sold olives without other description for 50 cents to $1.00 each, depending on size and age.

Western Nursery, San Francisco

Charles Abraham was a much-loved, slightly eccentric nurseryman in San Francisco. He came to California from Germany in 1877, having been trained as a gardener in Russia and Germany. Abraham started the Western Nursery at the corner of Franklin and Greenwich Streets in 1883 and ran it until he died in 1929. He imported many beautiful plants from Europe. In about 1885 he ordered five thousand olive trees from Italy, variety unknown, had them grafted onto Mission stock, and sold them throughout California. This was very unusual for him. His interests lay in ornamental plants, not fruit trees. The experiment with olive trees was not repeated.

W. M. Williams, Fresno

There is one catalog from this company in the Bancroft Library, but it has no date. Williams sold Mission olive trees for oil and Picholine for pickling.

Notes

Preface

1. Mary Hamalian Taylor, "Pioneers of Yettem," *Los Tulares, Quarterly Bulletin of the Tulare County Historical Society* 150 (December 1985): 1–5.

Introduction: The Olive in Ancient Times

1. Reay Tannahill, *Food in History* (New York: Stein and Day, 1974).
2. J. Robert Sallares, *The Ecology of the Ancient Greek World* (Ithaca, New York: Cornell University Press, 1991), 30.
3. P. Fiorino and F. Nizzi Griffi, "The Spread of Olive Farming," *Olivae* 44 (December 1992): 9–12.
4. Sallares, *The Ecology of the Ancient Greek World*, 17.

Chapter 1: How the Olive Came to California

1. Manuel de la Puente y Olea, *Los trabajos geograficos de la casa de contratacion* (Seville, Spain: Escuela Tipografica y Libreria Galesianos, 1900).
2. Father Zephyrin Charles Engelhardt, *Missions and Missionaries in California* (San Francisco: James H. Barry, 1908).
3. Clements Markham, *A History of Peru* (1892; reprint, New York: Greenwood Press, 1968). Sir Clements Markham knew something about stealing a contraband tree. In his youth as a clerk at the Board of Trade in London during the 1870s, he was sent on a secret and very hazardous mission to steal seeds and cuttings of the cinchona tree in South America. The bark of the cinchona tree is the source of quinine, at that time the only reliable treatment for malaria. The Brazilian and Bolivian governments had draconian penalties for anyone caught taking cinchona out of the country. Markham succeeded by using clever strategems.
4. Garci Ordonez de Montalvo, *Las Sergas de Esplandian* (Madrid, 1510).
5. Alexander Forbes, *A History of Upper and Lower California* (1839; reprint, with an introduction by Herbert Ingram Priestley, San Francisco: J. H. Nash, 1937).
6. Robert Archibald, *The Economic Aspects of the California Missions* (Washington, D.C.: Academy of American Franciscan History, 1978).
7. Edwin Bryant, *What I Saw in California* (1848; reprint, Marguerite Eyer Wilbur, ed., Santa Ana, California: Fine Arts Press, 1936).
8. Guadalupe Vallejo, "Ranch and Mission Days in Alta California," *Century Magazine*, December 1890.
9. G. M. Waseurtz af Sandels, *A Sojourn in California by the King's Orphan: The Travels and Sketches of G. M. Waseurtz af Sandels,* a Swedish gentleman who visited California in 1842–1843, with an introduction by Helen Putnam Van Sicklen (printed at the Grabhorn Press for the Book Club of California, in arrangement with the Society of California Pioneers, 1945).
10. William E. Brewer, *Up and Down California in 1860 to 1864* (Berkeley/Los Angeles: University of California Press, 1974).

Chapter 2: Development of a Market and an Industry

1. Marc Reisner, *Cadillac Desert: The American West and Its Disappearing Water* (Harmondsworth, England: Penguin Books, 1986, 1993).
2. General N. P. Chipman, "Fruit Versus Wheat" (paper presented to the California State Board of Horticulture, San Jose, Calif., November 15, 1892).
3. Ulysses P. Hedrick, *A History of Horticulture in America to 1860* (New York: Oxford University Press, 1950).
4. Harris Newmark, *Sixty Years in Southern California* (1915; reprint, Los Angeles: Zeitlin and Ver Brugge, 1970).
5. Viola Lockhart Warren, "Dr. John Griffith's Mail 1846–1853," *California State Historical Society Quarterly* 34 (1955): 21–41.
6. Eliza Farnham, *California In Doors and Out* (1856; reprint, with an introduction by Madeleine Stern, Nieuwkoop, The Netherlands: B. de Graaf, 1972).
7. California State Agriculture Society, *Transactions of 1858*, Report of the Visiting Committee (published 1859), 166 et seq.
8. Lansford Hastings, *The Emigrants' Guide to Oregon and California* (1845; reprint, New York: Da Capo Press, 1969).
9. Hans Christian Palmer, "Italian Immigration and the Development of California Agriculture" (Ph.D. diss., University of California at Berkeley, 1965). Dino Cinel, *From Italy to San Francisco: The Immigrant Experience* (Stanford, California: Stanford University Press, 1982).
10. P. C. Remondino, M.D., Proceedings of the State's First Olive Growers' Convention, July 1891.
11. Booth Tarkington, *The Magnificent Ambersons* (1918; reprint, Bloomington: Indiana University Press, 1989).

Chapter 3: Transition to the Modern Era

1. E. J. Wickson, *The California Fruits and How to Grow Them,* 9th ed. (San Francisco: Dewey and Company, 1889, 1926).
2. Louise Ferguson, G. Steven Sibbett, and George C. Martin, ed., *Olive Production Manual* (Oakland: University of California Division of Agriculture and Natural Resources Publication 3353, 1994).
3. *Alta California,* 29 January 1854.
4. *Alta California,* 4 December 1860.
5. Ferguson et al., *Olive Production Manual.*
6. Harold Schutt, "The Missions Planted Olives," "Early Olives at Lindsay," "The Beginning of Olives," "Lindsay Ripe Olive Company," *Los Tulares, Quarterly Bulletin of the Tulare County Historical Society* 47 (March 1961). The entire March 1961 issue of *Los Tulares* was devoted to Harold Schutt's history of olives in California.
7. Karl Opitz, "New Plantings," *California Olive Industry News* 24, September 1970.
8. The minutes of the California Olive Association are replete with entries about the outbreaks of botulism and what was done to prevent them during this critical period.
9. The Federal Marketing Order of December 1933 ceased in May 1937 when it was replaced by a State Marketing Order, known as the Olive Advisory Board. On October 2, 1965, this in its turn was superseded by the current Federal Marketing Order, administered by the California Olive Committee.

Chapter 4: Why Olive Growers Changed to New Kinds of Trees

1. Glauco Prevost, Giorgio Bartolino, and Carlo Messeri's *Cultivar Italiane di Olivo e Loro Sinonimi* (Florence Institute of the Department of Orthoflorofrutticoltura, 1993) is a standard monograph on this complex subject.
2. There was an extensive literature on the olive during this period of activity. The California Olive Growers' Association was formed in 1883, and the leadership was extremely diligent in spreading the word. The association held several annual meetings sponsored by the California State Board of Horticulture.

    The olive growers were active on the board and several of them were officers, such as Ellwood Cooper. Their deliberations are preserved in various documents, the annual and biennial reports of the board to the governor and the proceedings of the Olive Growers' Convention. These documents cover a period from 1880 to 1900. The University of California Agricultural Extension Service's Agricultural Experiment Stations also reported the results of their research in a series of papers put out by the university as bulletins, reports, and circulars over the same period.
3. Wickson, *The California Fruits and How to Grow Them.*
4. Federico Pohndorff. Letter to Eugene Hilgard, 20 November 1885. Bancroft Library, University of California at Berkeley.
5. Vincent Lamantia, "The Olive Culture and the Question of the Day: Can California Be Made the Olive Garden of the United States?" (Consular Report, Department of State, 1891). Signor Lamantia was the U.S. Consul in Sicily, and most assiduous in his duties. He wrote the report while living and working in New Orleans.
6. W. Harrison Bradley, "Olive Culture in the *Alpes Maritimes* (in response to a circular from the Department of State)" (U.S. Department of Commerce. Bureau of Foreign Commerce. Special Consular Reports, 6 December 1891). W. Harrison Bradley was the U.S. Consul in Marseilles. Consul Bradley, like Consul Lamantia, was very thorough and quite scholarly in his approach. He noted that twelve varieties of olive grew successfully in the Maritime Alps, and quoted from twenty-nine different French authorities in describing the culture, pests, and preservation of the olive in that area. Charles Trail (U.S. State Department Report, December 6, 1890) was another observant consul.

Chapter 5: Nurseries and the Dissemination of Olive Trees

1. Report to the California State Agriculture Commission, 1851.
2. A. Williams, "Agriculture in California," Report to the United States Patent Office, Washington, D.C., 1851.
3. A. Williams, "Agriculture in California," Report to the United States Patent Office, Washington, D.C., 1852.

Chapter 6: The Olive Oil Trade

1. Rafael Frankel, Shmuel Avitsur, and Etan Ayalon, *History and Technology of Olive Oil in the Holy Land* (Arlington, Virginia: Olearius Editions and Tel Aviv: Eretz Israel Museum, 1994).
2. Edward E. Goodrich, "Experiments and New Varieties," *Report of the Second Annual Olive Growers Convention,* California State Board of Horticulture, 1892.

Chapter 8: Botulism

1. Charles Jennings, Ernest Haass, and Alpheus F. Jennings, "An Outbreak of Botulism: Report of Cases," *Journal of the American Medical Association* 74, no. 2 (1920): 77–80.
2. Dwight Sisco, "An Outbreak of Botulism," *Journal of the American Medical Association* 74, no. 8 (1920): 516–21.
3. Charles Armstrong and Ernest Scott, "Botulism from Eating Canned Ripe Olives," *Public Health Reports* 34, no. 51 (1919): 2877–905.
4. G. G. De Bord, R. B. Edmondson, and Charles Thom, "Summary of the Bureau of Chemistry's Investigations of Poisoning Due to Ripe Olives," *Journal of the American Medical Association* 74, no. 18 (1920): 1220–21.
5. Stewart A. Koser, "A Bacteriological Study of Canned Ripe Olives," *Bureau of Chemistry Bulletin*, Washington, D.C., 1920.
6. William Vere Cruess at the University of California at Berkeley contributed significantly to the solution of this problem between 1921 and 1923 in papers such as "Olive Pickling and Sterilizing Experiments" (*California State Board of Health Monthly Bulletin*, 20 September 1920, 45–50).

Chapter 10: The University of California's Role in the Development of the Olive Industry

1. Anne Foley Scheuring, *Science and Service: A History of the Land-Grant University and Agriculture in California* (Oakland, California: University of California Division of Agriculture and Natural Resources Publications, 1995).
2. Dean Hilgard's work is to be found in the bulletins, reports, and circulars of the University of California's Agricultural Extension Service, Agricultural Experiment Station, and in the reports of the California State Board of Horticulture.
3. Comments made at the sixth annual Forty Niner Service award to William Vere Cruess, February 20, 1959, recorded in Professor Cruess's reminiscences in the University of California Oral History Project compiled by Ruth Teiser, 1966.
4. William Vere Cruess, "Olive Pickling and Sterilizing Experiments" (*California State Board of Health Monthly Bulletin*, 20 September 1920, 45–50) is only one of dozens of such papers.
5. Ferguson et al., *Olive Production Manual*.

Bibliography

"All about Oberti Olives." Promotional piece privately published by the Oberti Olive Company. n.d.

Aloi, A. "1890 Olive Oil Manufacture." *Annual Report of the State Board of Horticulture*. 190–232.

American Horticultural Annual 1867–71. New York: Orange Judd Yearbooks, n.d.

Archibald, Robert. *The Economic Aspects of the California Missions*. Washington, D.C.: Academy of American Franciscan History, 1978.

Armstrong, Charles and Ernest Scott. "Botulism from Eating Ripe Olives." *Public Health Reports* 34, no. 51 (1919): 2877–905.

Armstrong, John. "A Summary of Facts Pertaining to the Culture of the Olive." Ontario, CA: Privately published, n.d.

Attivita Italiane in America. Privately printed. San Francisco, 1931.

Baegert, S.J., Johann Jakob. *Observations in Lower California*. Translated from the original German with notes and an introduction by M. M. Brandenburg and Carl L. Baumann. Berkeley/Los Angeles: University of California Press, 1952.

Bancroft, Hubert Howe. *The Book of the Fair: An Historical and Descriptive Presentation of the World's Science, Art, and Industry—The Columbian Exposition at Chicago 1893*. San Francisco: The Bancroft Company, 1893.

_____. *California Pioneer Register and Index: 1542–1848*. Baltimore: Regional Publishing Company, 1964.

_____. *Chronicles of the Builders of the Commonwealth*. San Francisco: The History Company, 1890.

_____. *History of California*. 1888; reprint, Santa Barbara: Wallace Hebberd, 1970.

Banks, M. G. "History of the California Olive." Internal paper. Compiled from records at Consolidated Olive Growers. 1971.

Barker, Malcolm E., ed. *San Francisco Memoirs: 1835–1851*. San Francisco: Londonborn Publications, 1994.

_____. *More San Francisco Memoirs: 1852–1899—The Ripening Years*. San Francisco: Londonborn Publications, 1996.

Barton, Stephen. "Early History of Tulare County." *Visalia Times-Delta*, 28 July 1905.

Beck, Warren A., and David A. Williams. *California: A History of the Golden State*. Garden City, N.Y.: Doubleday, 1972.

Benjamin, Marcus. *John Bidwell, Pioneer: A Sketch of His Career.* Washington, D.C.: n.p., 1907.

Berg, Bill. "Olive Trees Serve as a Reminder of Badger Hill's Early History." *Visalia Times-Delta,* 29 October 1965.

Bernays, Lewis Adolphus. *The Olive and Its Products.* Brisbane, Australia: Government Printer, 1872.

Bioletti, Frederic, and George E. Colby. "Olives." *California Agriculture Experiment Station Bulletin* No. 123 (1899).

____ and W. V. Cruess. "Improvements in Methods of Pickling Olives." Agriculture Experiment Station Bulletin No. 298. University of California Agriculture Extension Service, 1917.

Bitting, K. D. "The Olive." Internal publication. Chicago Glass Container Association Research Laboratory. December 1936.

Bleasdale, John Ignatio. *The Olive and Its Products and the Suitability of the Soil of California for Its Extensive and Profitable Cultivation.* San Francisco: Dewey, 1881.

Bolles, Walter E., and Gertrude N. Bartley. "Freda Ehmann." *Diggin's: Butte County Historical Society* 23 (Fall/Winter 1979): 47–71.

Bolton, Herbert E. *Anza's California Expeditions.* Berkeley: University of California Press, 1930.

____. *The Colonization of North America.* 1920; reprint, New York: Macmillan, 1948.

____, ed. *Historical Memoirs of New California: Fray Francisco Palou.* Berkeley: University of California Press, 1926.

____. *History of the Americas: A Syllabus with Maps.* Boston/New York: Ginn and Company, 1935.

____. *The Mission as a Frontier Institution in the Spanish–American Colonies.* El Paso, Tex.: Texas Western College Press for Academic Reprints, 1960.

____. *Spanish Exploration in the Southwest: 1542–1706.* 1908; reprint, New York: Barnes and Noble, 1952.

Boynton, S. S. "Olive Culture in California." *Overland Monthly,* 2d ser., 14 (1889): 70–75.

____. "The Olive in America." *Overland Monthly,* 2d ser., 18 (1891): 420–27.

Brackett, F. P. *A Brief History of the San Jose Rancho and Its Subsequent Cities: Pomona, San Dimas, Claremont, LaVerne, and Spadra.* Privately published, 1920.

Bradley, W. Harrison. "Olive Culture in the *Alpes Maritimes.*" U.S. Department of Commerce. Bureau of Foreign Commerce. Special Consular Reports, 6 December 1891.

Brewer, William E. *Up and Down in California in 1860 to 1864.* Berkeley/Los Angeles: University of California Press, 1974.

Brown, John, and James Boyd. *History of San Bernardino and Riverside Counties.* N.p.: The Western Historical Association, 1922.

Brown, Thomas A. *A List of California Nurseries and Their Catalogues: 1850 to 1900*. Privately published. Petaluma, California, 1993.

Bryant, Edwin. *What I Saw in California*. 1848; reprint, Marguerite Eyer Wilbur, ed., Santa Ana, California: Fine Arts Press, 1936.

Burke, J. Henry. "Olive Industry in Lower California." *Foreign Agricultural Service Report No. 85.* Washington, D.C.: U.S. Department of Agriculture, 1955.

Burr, Charles J. "Leonard Coates Nurseries: The First Century 1878–1978. *Pacific Horticulture* 39, no. 1 (1978): 11–14.

Burrows, William. *Textbook of Microbiology*. Philadelphia/London/Toronto: W. B. Saunders, 1973.

Butterfield, Harry Morton. "Builders of California Horticulture: Past and Present." *Journal of the California Horticulture Society* 22, no. 1 (1961): 2–7.

____. "Builders of California Horticulture: Past and Present." *Journal of the California Horticulture Society* 22, no. 3 (1961): 102–107.

____. "The History of Ornamental Horticulture in California." *Journal of the California Horticulture Society* 26, no. 2 (1965): 47–50.

____. "A History of Subtropical Fruits and Nuts in California." University of California Division of Agricultural Sciences. Agricultural Extension Service. Agricultural Experiment Station. 21–26 September 1963.

____. "Introduction of Plants to California during Spanish and Mexican Periods." *Journal of the California Horticulture Society* 20, no. 3 (1959): 54–57.

____. "Nurseries in the Eastern United States: A Source of Ornamentals for Early California." *Journal of the California Horticulture Society* 27, no. 2 (1966): 42–56.

____. Papers. Special Collections. Shields Library. University of California at Davis.

____. "Some Pioneer Nurseries in California and Their Plants: Part 1." *Journal of the California Horticulture Society* 27, no. 3 (1966): 70–77.

____. "Some Pioneer Nurseries in California and Their Plants: Part 2." *Journal of the California Horticulture Society* 27, no. 4 (1966): 102–108.

____. "Some Pioneer Nurseries in California and Their Plants: Part 3." *Journal of the California Horticulture Society* 28, no. 1 (1967): 132–40.

Byers, S. H. M. "Olive Orchards of the Riviera." *Overland Monthly,* n.s., 5 (1885): 348–55.

Cain, Stanley A. *Foundations of Plant Geography*. New York: Hafner, 1971.

"Cairns Family." *Porterville Evening Recorder,* 25 October 1949.

California Cultivator, 22 January 1904. Newspaper with many advertisements for olive trees.

California Gazeteer and Business Directory. San Francisco: R. L. Polk, 1893.

California Olive Association archives. Papers. Special Collections. Shields Library. University of California at Davis.

California Olive Association Trade Journal. 1946–71.

"California Olive Crop: Increasing Importance." *California Cultivator,* 21 December 1911.

California Olive Industry News. 1946–71.

"California Olives." *Daily Democratic State Journal,* 9 July 1855.

California State Agriculture Society. *Transactions* of 1858. Report of the Visiting Committee (published 1859), 238–97.

Calkins, John. *The Olive Grower's Handbook.* Privately published. Pomona, Calif., 1896.

Calkins, John S. "Olive Culture in California." Business pamphlet. Pomona, Calif., 1900.

———. "The Olive in Southern California." *Land of Sunshine* 1 (20 June 1894).

Campbell, Robert C. "Review of the Olive Oil Industry." Typescript. 1979.

Capra, Frank. *The Name above the Title.* New York: Macmillan, 1971.

Caughey, John Walton. *Hubert Howe Bancroft: Historian of the West.* Berkeley: University of California Press, 1946.

Chan, Sucheng. *This Bittersweet Soil: The Chinese in California Agriculture 1860–1910.* Berkeley/Los Angeles/London: University of California Press, 1986.

Chapin, Earl. *The Canning Clan: A Pageant of Pioneering Americans.* New York: Macmillan, 1937.

Chapman, Charles Edward. *History of California: The Spanish Period.* New York: Macmillan, 1923.

Chazan-Gillig, Suzanne. "The Civilization of the Olive Tree and Cereals." *Olivae* 53 (1994): 14–22.

Chipman, General N. P. "Fruit versus Wheat." An address to the California State Board of Horticulture. San Jose, Calif.. 15 November 1892.

Cinel, Dino. *From Italy to San Francisco: The Immigrant Experience.* Stanford, Calif.: Stanford University Press, 1982.

Cleland, Robert Glass. *California in Our Time: 1900–1940.* New York: Alfred A. Knopf, 1947.

———. *California Pageant: The Story of Four Centuries.* New York: Alfred A. Knopf, 1946.

———. *From Wilderness to Empire: A History of California: 1542–1900.* New York: Alfred A. Knopf, 1944.

Clough, Charles W. "Madera." Pamphlet. Madera County Historical Society, 1983.

Colby, George. "Olive Varieties and Their Adaptation." University of California Agricultural Experiment Station Bulletin No. 123 (1899).

_____. "Analyses of California Olives." University of California Agricultural Experiment Station Report. March 1898.

Complete Business Directory of Los Angeles, Pasadena, Pomona, Santa Ana, and Santa Monica 1898–99. Los Angeles: Los Angeles Printing Company, 1899.

Comrie, B., ed. *The World's Major Languages.* New York: Oxford University Press, 1987.

Condit, Ira J. "Olive Culture in California." University of California Agricultural Experiment Station Circular No. 135. 1947.

_____. "Report on Olive Varieties for Oil Production." Typescript. n.d.

Cooper, Ellwood. "In His Own Words: Some Incidents in the Life of Ellwood Cooper." Reprinted in *Noticias: Quarterly Magazine of the Santa Barbara Historical Museum* 39, no. 2 (1993): 25–44.

_____. "The Olive in California." *California Illustrated Monthly* 12 (1892): 51–57.

_____. "A Treatise on Olive Growing." Pamphlet. San Francisco: Cupery and Company, 1882.

"Corning." *Californiana* 4, no. 1 (1970): 1–5.

"Corning: An Olive Town." Privately published. Corning Museum, n.d.

Costello, Julia Marvin. "Variability and Economic Change in the California Missions: An Historical and Archaeological Study." Ph.D. diss., University of California at Santa Barbara, 1990.

Coulmas, Florian. *The Writing Systems of the World.* Oxford, England: Blackwell, 1989.

Crider, F. J. "The Olive in Arizona." University of Arizona (Tucson) College of Agriculture. Agricultural Experiment Station Bulletin 94 (January 1922): 490–528.

Cronise, Titus Fey. *The Natural Wealth of California.* San Francisco: H. H. Bancroft, 1868.

Crosby, Harry W. *Antigua California.* Albuquerque: University of New Mexico Press, 1994.

_____. *The King's Highway in Baja California.* La Jolla, Calif.: Copley, 1969.

Cruess, William Vere. "Bacterial Decomposition of Olives during Pickling." University of California Agricultural Experiment Station Bulletin No. 368 (1923): 1–15.

_____. "A Half-Century in Food and Wine Technology." Typescript. Food Technology Department, University of California at Davis. Berkeley Regional Oral History Office. 1967.

_____. "Home Pickling of Olives." *California Cultivator,* 29 November 1918.

_____. "Methods of Refining Olive Oil in California." *Fig and Olive Journal* (October 1918): 5–7.

_____. "Observations on the Sterilization of Olives at 240°F." *Olive Journal* 57 (1921): 21.

____. "Olive Pickling and Sterilizing Experiments." California State Board of Health *Monthly Bulletin* (20 September 1920): 45–50.

____. "Olive Pickling in the Mediterranean Countries." University of California Agricultural Experiment Station Circular No. 278 (1924): 1–33.

____. "Pickling Green Olives." University of California Agricultural Experiment Station Circular (Supplement) No. 278 (1924).

____. "Some Factors Affecting the Quality of Ripe Olives Sterilized at High Temperatures." University of California Agricultural Experiment Station Bulletin No. 333 (October 1921): 221–31.

____. "Suggestions for Olive Oil Standards." *Pacific Rural Press,* 8 February 1941.

Culture of the Olive: Olive Oil. San Francisco: Roman and Company, 1871.

Cutter, Donald C. *California in 1792: A Spanish Naval Visit.* Norman, Okla./London, England: University of Oklahoma Press, 1990.

D'Aygalliers, P. *L'olivier et l'huile de l'olive.* Paris: J. B. Baillierre et Fils, 1900.

Dakin, Susanna Bryant. *A Scotch Paisano in Old Los Angeles.* Berkeley/Los Angeles/London: University of California Press, 1939.

Dana, Julian. *A. P. Giannini: Giant in the West.* New York: Prentice-Hall, 1947.

Daniel, Cletus E. *Bitter Harvest: A History of California Farmworkers 1870–1941.* Berkeley/Los Angeles/London: University of California Press, 1981.

Davidson, Winifred. "Olives of Endless Age." *California Garden,* Spring 1954.

Davis, W. Heath. *Seventy-Five Years in California.* San Francisco: John Howell, 1929.

De Bord, G. G., R. B. Edmondson, and Charles Thom. "Summary of Bureau of Chemistry's Investigations of Poisoning Due to Ripe Olives." *Journal of the American Medical Association* 74 (1920): 18, 1220–21.

De Candolle, Alphonse. *Origin of Cultivated Plants.* New York/London: Hafner, 1886 (reprinted 1967).

De Kruif, Paul. *The Microbe Hunters.* San Diego: Harcourt, Brace, Jovanovich, 1954.

De Lorgeril, M., S. Renaud, and N. Mamelle. "Effects of a Mediterranean Type of Diet on the Rate of Cardiovascular Complications in Patients with Coronary Artery Disease." *Journal of the American College of Cardiology* 28 (1996): 1103–1108.

Denny, J. O. and George C. Martin. "Freeze Damage and Cold Hardiness in Olives: Findings from the 1990 Freeze." *California Agriculture* 47, no. 1 (1993): n.p.

Dickson, Ernest, et al. Special botulism issue. California State Board of Health *Monthly Bulletin* 16, no. 3 (1920): 35–52.

Dictionary Catalogue of the National Agricultural Library: Holdings from 1862 to 1965. New York: Rowman and Littlefield, 1969.

Donno, Giacinto. *Bibliografia sistematica dell' olivo e dell' olio di oliva.* Rome: Ramo Editoriale degli Agricoltori, 1943.

Dudley, M. E. "The Olive Industry in California." *Sunset* 13 (1904): 559.

Dwinelle, John Whipple. *The Colonial History of the City of San Francisco.* San Francisco: Towne and Bacon, 1866.

Eakins, George. "Olive Culture." *Land of Sunshine* 8 (December 1897): 48–52.

Edlin, H. L. *Trees and Man.* New York: Columbia University Press, 1976.

Ehmann, Freda. "The California Ripe Olive." Typescript. n.d.

Elder, Robert. "First Olive Orchard," in *Auburn: A Century of Memories.* Auburn, Calif.: Placer County Historical Society. Privately printed. n.d.

Engelhardt, Fr. Zephyrin. *Missions and Missionaries in California.* San Francisco: James H. Barry, 1908.

Engels, Donald W. *Alexander the Great and the Logistics of the Macedonian Army.* Berkeley/Los Angeles/London: University of California Press, 1984.

Erdman, H. E. "The Development and Significance of California Cooperatives: 1900–1915." *Agricultural History* 32 (1958): 179–84.

"Extensive Process Required to Make Martinelli Olive Oil." *Madera Daily News-Tribune,* 24 September 1957.

Farnham, Eliza. *California In Doors and Out.* 1856; reprint, with an introduction by Madeleine Stern, Nieuwkoop, The Netherlands: B. de Graaf, 1972.

Ferguson, Louise, G. Steven Sibbett, and George C. Martin, ed. *Olive Production Manual.* Oakland: University of California Division of Agriculture and Natural Resources, 1994. Publication no. 3353.

Fernandez, Garrido, and M. J. Fernandez. *Table Olives: Production and Processing.* London: Weinheim, 1997.

Fink, Augusta. *Monterey County: The Dramatic Story of Its Past.* Santa Cruz, Calif.: Western Tanager Press, 1972.

Fiorino, P., and F. Nizzi Griffi. "The Spread of Olive Farming." *Olivae* 44 (December 1992): 9–12.

Flamant, Adolphe. "A Practical Treatise on Olive Culture, Oil Making, and Olive Pickling." Pamphlet. San Francisco: Louis Gregoire and Company, 1887.

_____. "The Olive: Picholine vs. Mission." Privately printed. Napa, Calif.. 1890.

Forbes, Alexander. *A History of Upper and Lower California.* 1839; reprint, with an introduction by Herbert Ingram Priestly, San Francisco: J.H. Nash, 1937.

Forbes, James G. *Sketches, Historical and Topographical, of the Floridas.* New York: n.p., 1821.

Foytik, Jerry. "Trends and Outlook [in the] California Olive Industry." University of California Agricultural Experiment Station Circular No. 492 (1960).

Frankel, Rafael, Shmuel Avitsur, and Etan Ayalon. *History and Technology of Olive Oil in the Holy Land.* Arlington, Va./Tel Aviv: Olearius Editions/Eretz Israel Museum, 1994.

Friedman, Nancy. "Some Like 'Em Green." *San Francisco,* December 1982, 80–84.

Fuller, Willard P., Jr., Judith Marvin, and Julia G. Costello. *Madame Felix's Gold: The Story of the Madame Felix Mining District—Calaveras County.* Murphys, Calif.: Calaveras County Historical Society/Foothill Resources, Ltd., 1996.

Galaup, Jean-François. *Life in a California Mission: Monterey in 1786.* Berkeley: Heyday Books, 1989.

Gates, Paul W. *The Farmer's Age: Agriculture 1815–1860.* New York: Rinehart and Wilson, 1960.

_____. *History of Public Land Law Development.* Washington, D.C.: U.S. Government Printing Office, 1968.

Geiger, O.F.M., Maynard. *Franciscan Missionaries in Hispanic California 1769–1848: A Biographical Dictionary.* San Marino, Calif.: The Huntington Library, 1969.

"George Ashlok: The Cherry Challenged Him." Pamphlet. *Food Packer,* April 1952.

Giovinco, Joseph. "The Ethnic Dimension of Calaveras County History." Paper completed under a grant to the Calaveras County Heritage Council (San Andreas) from the National Endowment for the Humanities. 1980.

Gist, Brooks DeWitt. *Empire Out of the Tules.* Tulare: n.p., 1976.

Gitin, Seymour. "Ekron of the Philistines, Part II: Olive Oil Suppliers to the World." *Biblical Archaeology Review* (March/April 1990): 33–42.

"Golden Eagle Olive Oil." *Farm Tribune,* 11 January 1962.

Goodrich, Edward E. "Experiments and New Varieties." *Report of the Second Annual Olive Growers Convention.* California State Board of Horticulture, 1892.

Gracey, Wilbur T. "Olive Growing in Spain." Report for U.S. Bureau of Foreign and Domestic Commerce. 1918.

Green, Peter. *Alexander of Macedon 356–323* B.C. Berkeley/Los Angeles/Oxford: University of California Press, 1991.

"A Growing Community of Beautiful Homes and Fruitful Orchards." Pomona Board of Trade promotional pamphlet. Circa 1900. Pomona, Calif..

Gudde, Erwin G. *1000 California Place Names.* Berkeley/Los Angeles/London: University of California Press, 1959.

Guest, Francis F. *Fermín Francisco Lasuén.* Washington, D.C.: Academy of American Franciscan History, 1973.

Guinn, J. M. *History of the State of California.* Chicago: Chapman, 1904.

Hager, Ed and Anna Marie Hager, ed. *The Zamorano Index to the History of California.* Los Angeles: University of Southern California, 1985.

Harlan, Jack R. *Crops and Man.* Madison, Wisc.: American Society of Agronomy, Inc., 1992.

Hartmann, Hudson T. "The Olive Industry in California." *Economic Botany* 2 (October/ December 1948): 341–62.

_____, and Karl Opitz. "Olive Production in California." University of California Agricultural Experiment Station Circular No. 540 (1966).

_____, and P. Papaioannou. "Olive Varieties in California." University of California Agricultural Experiment Station Bulletin No. 720 (1951).

_____. "Progress in California Olive Research." *California Olive Industry News* 32 (1948).

_____, and Karl Optiz. "Spray Thinning of Olives." *California Olive Industry News* 13, no. 1 (1958): 2–3.

_____. "'Swan': A New Ornamental Fruitless Olive for California." *California Agriculture* 21, no. 1 (1967): 4–5.

Haslam, Gerald W. *The Other California.* Santa Barbara: Capra Press/Joshua Odell Editions, 1990.

Hastings, Lansford. *The Emigrants' Guide to Oregon and California.* 1845; reprint, New York: Da Capo Press, 1969.

Haughton, Claire. *Green Immigrants: The Plants that Transformed America.* New York: Harcourt, Brace, Jovanovich, n.d.

Hayne, Arthur P. "California Olive Industry Proceedings of the Third State Convention of Olive Growers." Sacramento, Calif., 14 July 1893.

_____. "Investigations of California Olives and Olive Oil." University of California Agricultural Experiment Station Bulletin No. 104 (1894).

_____. "Olives and Olive Oils." Report of Work of the Agricultural Experiment Stations of the University of California for the Year 1892–93 and Part of 1894. Sacramento: A. J. Johnson, Supt. State Printing, 1894: 279–322.

_____. "Olives. Pickling Processes—Further Notes on Olive Varieties." Appendix to 1894–95 Report of the California State Board of Horticulture (1895).

_____. "Report on the Condition of Olive Culture in California." University of California Agricultural Experiment Station Bulletin No. 129 (1900).

Hedder, Jane. "Story of the California Olive Industry." *Overland Monthly* 65 (1915): 574–75.

Hedrick, Ulysses Prentiss. *A History of Horticulture in America to 1860.* New York: Oxford University Press, 1950.

Heizer, Robert F., and Alan J. Almquist. *The Other Californians.* Berkeley/Los Angeles/London: University of California Press, 1972.

Hendry, George W. "The Source Literature of Early Plant Introduction into Spanish America." *Agricultural History* 82 (1934): 64–71.

Higgins, F. Hal. "A Green Thumb '49er: Colonel Warren's Nursery Catalogues." *California Farmer* (1949).

Hilgard, Eugene Woldemar. "Notes on California Olives: Their Adaptations and Oils." University of California Agricultural Experiment Station Bulletin No. 92 (March 28, 1891).

____. *Soils.* New York: Macmillan, 1911.

Hill, Mary. *California Landscape: Origin and Evolution.* Berkeley/Los Angeles/London: University of California Press, 1984.

Hinckley, Edith P. "On the Banks of the Zanja: The Story of Redlands." Pamphlet. Claremont, Calif.: The Saunders Press, 1951.

Hirsch, Arthur H. "French Influence on American Agriculture in the Colonial Period with Special Reference to Southern Provinces." *Agricultural History* 4 (January 1930): 1–4.

"History of the Lindsay Ripe Olive Company." Stockholders' report, 1932.

Hittell, John. *Commerce and Industry of the Pacific Coast.* San Francisco: A. L. Bancroft and Company, 1882.

Holson, Laura. "No Deal: Finances, Waste Clean-up Killed Lindsay Olive Merger." *Fresno Bee,* 27 September 1992.

"Home Pickling of Olives." University of California. Division of Agricultural Sciences Leaflet 2758. 1980.

Hoskin, Beryl. *A History of the Santa Clara Mission Library.* Oakland: California Biobooks, 1961.

Houston, James D. "From El Dorado to the Pacific Rim: An Overview of Themes in California Fiction." California State Library Bulletin No. 54 (January 1996): 19.

Howland, John. "The Olive in California." Pamphlet. Pomona Nursery, 1892.

Hunt, Rockwell Dennis. *John Bidwell: Prince of California Pioneers.* Caldwell, Idaho: The Caxton Press, 1942.

Hutchinson, Claude B., ed. *California Agriculture.* Berkeley/Los Angeles: University of California Press, 1946.

Hutchinson, Sadie (Mrs. Arthur). "Brief History of Lindsay." Manuscript. Lindsay Public Library. n.d.

Impey, L. H. *A Handbook for South African Olive Growers.* Paarl, South Africa: South African Olive Growers Association, 1974.

Inventory. U.S. Department of Agriculture. Bureau of Plant Industry. List. 25 February 1909.

Isaac, John. "The Olive in Tulare County: A Production Manual." Pamphlet. Special Collections: California State University at Fresno. Harold Schutt papers. n.d.

Jackson, Helen Hunt. *Glimpses of California and the Mission.* Boston: Little, Brown, 1902.

Jefferson, Thomas. *The Garden and Farm Books.* Edited by Robert C. Brown. Golden, Colo.: Fulcrum, 1987.

Jelinek, Lawrence. *Harvest Empire: A History of California Agriculture.* San Francisco: Boyd and Fraser, 1973.

Jennings, Charles, Ernest Haass, and Alpheus F. Jennings. "An Outbreak of Botulism: Report of Cases." *Journal of the American Medical Association* 74, no. 2 (1920): 77–80.

Jesse, Edward V., and Aaron C. Johnson, Jr. "Effectiveness of Federal Marketing Orders for Fruits and Vegetables." Agricultural Economic Report No. 471 (1981). U.S. Department of Agriculture. National Economics Division. Economics and Statistical Service. Washington, D.C.

Jones, Helen Luken. "A Great American Olive Ranch." *World's Work* 3 (1902): 1751–56.

Kearney, Thomas H. "Dry-land Olive Culture in Northern Africa." U.S. Department of Agriculture. Bureau of Plant Industry Bulletin No. 125 (1908).

Keep, Rosalind. *Fourscore Years: A History of Mills College.* Oakland: Mills College, 1931.

Kimball, Frank. "How I Make Olive Oil." *Sunset* 13 (1904): 564–65.

King, Mitchel. "The History and Culture of the Olive." Anniversary address of the State Agricultural Society of South Carolina, 1846.

Kinman, C. F. "Olive Growing in the Southwestern United States." Farmer's Bulletin No. 1249 (1942) U.S. Department of Agriculture.

Kinnaird, Lawrence. *History of the Greater San Francisco Bay Region.* New York/West Palm Beach, Fla.: Lewis Historical Publishing Company, 1966.

Klee, Waldemar Gotriek. "Observations on Olive Varieties." University of California Agricultural Experiment Station Bulletin No. 85 (1890).

_____. "The Olive." University of California Agricultural Experiment Bulletin No. 41 (1885).

Klein, Jack. "Here and There with Jack Klein." *California Farmer* 191 (1949): 482.

Klein, Maggie. *The Feast of the Olive.* San Francisco: Chronicle Books, 1994.

Klinkenborg, Verlyn. "Amigo Cantisano's Organic Dream." *New York Times,* 10 March 1996.

Koser, Stewart Arment. "A Bacteriological Study of Canned Ripe Olives." Bureau of Chemistry Bulletin, Washington, D.C., 1920.

Kruckerberg, Henry. "Growth of the Olive Industry." *Pacific Rural Press* 83 (1912): 337.

Lamantia, Vincent. "The Olive Culture and the Question of the Day: Can California Be Made the Olive Garden of the United States?" Consular Report, Department of State. New Orleans: Privately published, 1891.

Landau, David Lewis. "The Olive in the Mediterranean and in California: A Study in Historical Development and Current Conditions." Master's thesis. San Francisco State University. 1985.

Langley, Henry G. *Pacific Coast Business Directory 1876–1878*. San Francisco: Henry G. Langley, 1879.

Larkey, Joann L., and Walter Shipley. *Yolo County: Land of Changing Patterns*. Northridge, Calif.: Windsory, 1987.

Larsen, Grace. "A Progressive in Agriculture: Harris Weinstock." *Agricultural History* 32 (1958): 187–93.

"Late Olive Industry Developments Reviewed." *Terra Bella News,* 9 April 1943.

Lelong, Byron Martin. "The Mission Olive." Annual Report to the California State Board of Horticulture (1890).

_____. "The Olive in California." Proceedings of the Tenth Annual Fruit Growers Convention, 20–23 November 1889. Sacramento: Government Printing Office, 1889.

Levy, Joanna. *They Saw the Elephant*. Norman, Okla.: University of Oklahoma Press, 1992.

Lewis, Donovan. *Pioneers of California*. San Francisco: Scottwall Associated, 1993.

Lewis, Oscar, ed. *Sketches of Early California*. Compiled by Donald De Nevi. San Francisco: Chronicle Books, 1971.

Locke, John. "Observations upon the Growth and Culture of Vines and Olives; the Production of Silk; the Preservation of Fruits." Pamphlet. London: W. Sandby, 1766.

Loussert, R. R., and G. Brousse. *L'olivier*. Paris: G. P. Maisonneuve et Larose, 1978.

"Marketing Agreement and License for California Ripe Olive Canning Industry." U.S. Department of Agriculture. Agricultural Adjustment Administration. 13 December 1933.

Markham, Sir Clements. *A History of Peru*. 1892; reprint, New York: Greenwood Press, 1968.

Marsico, Dante Floreal. *Olivocultura y Elayotechnica*. Barcelona: Salvat Editres, 1955.

Martinez, J. M., M. Ponsich, J. M. Rodriguez, and E. R. Almeida. "The Oil from Baetica." *Olivae* 35 (February 1991): 6–9.

Marvin, Arthur Tappan. *Olive: Its Culture in Theory and Practice*. San Francisco: Payot, Upham and Company, 1889.

Mason, Silas C. "Drought Resistance of the Olive in the Southwestern States." Bureau of Plant Industry Bulletin No. 192. Washington, D.C.: U.S. Department of Agriculture, 1911.

Masri, Allan, and Peter Abenheim. *The Golden Hills of California*. Fresno, Calif.: Valley Publishers, 1979.

Masten, Peter Dunne. *Pioneer Jesuits in Northern Mexico*. Berkeley: University of California Press, 1944.

Masumoto, David Mas. *Epitaph for a Peach: Four Seasons on My Family Farm*. San Francisco: Harper San Francisco, 1995.

McClatchy, V. S., and C. K. McClatchy. "Sacramento County and Its Resources." Pamphlet. 1895.

McGie, Joseph F. "A History of the Orange and Olive Industry in the Oroville-Palermo Area at the Period of 1913." *Diggin's: Butte County Historical Society* 16 (Winter 1972): 6–17.

McGowan, Joseph. *History of the Sacramento Valley*. New York: Lewis Historical Publishers, 1961.

McKevitt, S.J., Gerald. *The University of Santa Clara: A History 1851–1977*. Stanford, Calif.: Stanford University Press, 1980.

McKittrick, Myrtle M. *Vallejo: Son of California*. Portland, Ore.: Binsford and Mort, 1944.

Memorial and Biographical History of Northern California. Chicago: Lewis Publishing Company, 1891.

Michaels, Mark. "Woodson's Dream: A Brief History of Corning." *Chico News and Review,* 29 August 1991.

Mitchell, Annie. *The Way It Was: A History of Tulare County*. New York: Criterion, 1976.

Modern Olive Production. Rome: United Nations Development Program/Food and Agriculture Organization, 1977.

Morrisey, Richard J. "The Northwest Expansion of Cattle Ranching in New Spain 1550–1600." *Agricultural History* 25 (1951): 115–21.

Moses, Bernard. *The Establishment of Spanish Rule in America*. New York/London: G. P. Putnam's Sons, 1898.

"New Cooperative to Refine and Sell Olive Oil Organized Here." *Lindsay Gazette,* 14 August 1942.

"New Olive Plant Being Built." *Terra Bella News,* 25 February 1938.

Newmark, Harris. *Sixty Years in Southern California 1853–1913*. 1915; reprint, Los Angeles: Zeitlin and Ver Brugge, 1970.

The Nurseryman's Directory. Galena, Ill.: D. W. Scott, 1883.

"The Oberti Brothers." *Pacific Coast Review,* January 1965.

Odell, Ruth. *Helen Hunt Jackson*. New York/London: D. Applecroft-Century Company, 1939.

Ogden, Gerald. "Agricultural Land Use and Wildlife in the San Joaquin Valley 1769–1930." Report for the San Joaquin Valley Drainage Program. 1988.

Olea (olives) Inventory. 1997. U.S. Department of Agriculture list. National Clonal Germplasm Repository. Winters, California.

"Olive Association Sells Entire Crop to Grogan." *Terra Bella News,* 6 October 1922.

"Olive Firm Boosts Product, Town." *Visalia Times-Delta,* 17 December 1973.

"The Olive in Los Angeles County and Southern California" Los Angeles Chamber of Commerce pamphlet. 1897.

"Olive Number." *Santa Barbara Magazine,* June 1906.

"Olives." Two-part article. *Gourmet,* November 1969, 28; and December 1969, 42.

"Olives." *Tideways* 8 (1959): 11.

Olmo, H. P. "California." In *History of Fruit Growing and Handling in the United States and Canada 1860–1972,* D. V. Fisher and W. H. Uphall, ed. University Park, Penn.: American Pomological Society, 1976.

Opitz, Karl. "New Plantings." *California Olive Industry News* 24, September 1970.

____. "The Olive Industry of Mexico." Foreign Agriculture Report No. 85 (1961). Foreign Agricultural Service. U.S. Department of Agriculture.

____. "Olive Production and the Table Olive Industry in Spain." Foreign Agriculture Report No. 92 (1956). Foreign Agricultural Service. U.S. Department of Agriculture.

____. "Olive Production in Italy." Typescript (1957).

____. "Verticillium Wilt Control in Olives." *California Olive Industry News* 22, September 1968.

Ordonez de Montalvo, Garci. *Las Sergas de Esplandian.* Madrid: n.p., 1510.

Orsi, Richard. "A List of References for the History of Agriculture in California." Agriculture History Center. University of California at Davis, 1984.

Osio, Antonio Maria. *The History of California.* Translated and edited by Rose Marie Beebe and Robert M. Senkewicz. Madison, Wisc.: University of Wisconsin Press, 1996.

Pagnol, Jean. *L'Olivier.* Avignon, France: Aubanel, 1975.

Palmer, Hans Christian. "Italian Immigration and the Development of California Agriculture." Ph.D. diss., University of California at Berkeley, 1965.

Paparelli, Louis. "Pickling Olives." Agriculture Experiment Station Report No. 156 (1890). University of California Agriculture Extension Service.

Perry, May. "The Olive and Olive Industry in Placer County." *Placer Nuggets* 1 (October 1960): 4, 697.

Petersen, Edward. "Pierson Barton Reading: Shasta County Pioneer." Typescript. 1969.

Phillips, Irene. *Development of the Mission Olive Industry and Other South Bay Stories.* National City, Calif.: South Bay Press, 1960.

Pierce, Marjorie. *East of the Gabilans.* Santa Cruz, Calif.: Western Tanager Press, 1992.

Pierce, Newton B. "Olive Culture in the United States." *Yearbook of Agriculture 1896.*

Pierre, Frederick. "A Study of the California Olive Industry." Ph.D. diss., Stonier Graduate School of Banking, Rutgers University, 1960.

Pifer, Marcia MacLagan. "The C. C. Graber Company Since 1894." *Pomona Valley Historian* 83 (1972): 115–38.

Pinney, Thomas. *A History of Wine in America.* Berkeley/Los Angeles/London: University of California Press, 1989.

Pisani, Donald J. *From the Family Farm to Agribusiness: The Irrigation Crusade in California and the West 1850–1931.* Berkeley/Los Angeles/London: University of California Press, 1984.

Pohndorff, Federico. "A Memoir on Olive Growing." Pamphlet. San Francisco: Bosqui Engraving Company, 1884.

_____. Letter to Eugene Hilgard. 20 November 1885. Bancroft Library, University of California at Berkeley.

Powell, George. "The California Olive Industry." Pamphlet. *Northern California Review of Business and Economics* (Fall 1979).

_____ and Lee Smith. "An Evaluation of California Marketing Orders." Report to the Board of Directors of the California Olive Association. Typescript. June 1983.

"Premier Olive Mills in California." *Pacific Rural Press* (1893).

Prevost, Glauco, Giorgio Bartolini, and Carlo Messeri. "Cultivar italiane di olivo e loro sinonimi." Florence Institute of the Department of Orthoflorofrutticoltura. Universita degli Studi. 1993.

Puente y Olea, Manuel de la. *Los trabajos geograficos de la casa de contratacion.* Seville, Spain: Escuela Tipografica y Libreria Galesianos, 1900.

Ratekin, Mervyn Adair. "The West Indian Sugar Industry, 1493 to 1615." Master's thesis, University of California at Berkeley, September 1952.

Redding, Benjamin B. *The Olive in California.* 1878; reprint, San Francisco: California Academy of Sciences, 1978.

Reisner, Marc. *Cadillac Desert: The American West and Its Disappearing Water.* Harmondsworth, England: Penguin Books, 1986 (reissued 1993).

Renfrew, Colin. *Archaeology and Language.* London: Jonathan Capey, 1987.

Research Reports. *California Ripe Olives and Related Subjects Bibliography.* Compilation by California Olive Association. 1972.

Riondet, Alexis. *L'olivier.* Paris: Librairie Agricole de la Maison Rustique, 1867.

Rixford, G. P. "Olives: History." *Sacramento Valley Monthly* 46 (1914).

Robertson, James A. "Some Notes on the Transfer by Spain of Plants and Animals to the Colonies Overseas." *Studies in Hispanic-American History* 19, no. 2 (1927): 7–21.

Robinson, William Wilcox. "Land in California." San Diego Title Insurance Company, 1948.

_____. *Land in California: The Story of the Mission Lands.* Berkeley: University of California Press, 1948.

_____. "The Story of San Fernando Valley." Los Angeles Title Insurance and Trust Company, 1961.

_____. "The Story of Tulare County." Los Angeles Title Insurance and Trust Company, 1958.

_____. "The Story of Ventura County." Los Angeles Title Insurance and Trust Company, 1956.

Roeding, George Christian. "California Horticulture: The Fruit Growers' Guide." Pamphlet. Fresno: Fancher Creek Nurseries, 1909.

Rosenblum, Mort. *Olives: The Life and Lore of a Noble Fruit.* New York: North Point Press, 1996.

Rothstein, Morton. "The California Wheat Kings." Davis: Library Associates of the University of California, 1987. Keepsake number 11.

Russell, V. F. "The Olive and Its Oil in California." *Overland Monthly,* o.s., 9 (September 1872): 207–10.

Sale, Kirkpatrick. *The Conquest of Paradise: Christopher Columbus and the Columbian Legacy.* New York: Alfred A. Alfred A. Knopf, 1991.

Sallares, J. Robert. *The Ecology of the Ancient Greek World.* Ithaca, New York: Cornell University Press, 1991.

Samson, Karri. "Digging Up Placer County History." Privately published. California History Room, California State Library, Sacramento. 1987.

Sandels, G. M., Waseurtz af. *A Sojourn in California by the King's Orphan: The Travels and Sketches of G.M. Waseurtz af Sandels.* San Francisco: Grabhorn Press for the Book Club of San Francisco, in arrangement with the Society of California Pioneers, 1945.

Santos, Robert Leroy. *The Eucalyptus of California.* Denair, Calif.: California Alley-Cass Publications, 1997.

Schacht, Henry. "Present Problems of the Ancient Olive." *San Francisco Chronicle,* 24 October 1961.

Scheuer, Joan G. "Searching for the Phoenicians in Sardinia." *Biblical Archaeology Review* 16, no. 1 (January/February 1990): 53–60.

Scheuring, Anne Foley. *Science and Service: A History of the Land-Grant University and Agriculture in California.* Division of Agriculture and Natural Resources, Publication No. 3360. Oakland: University of California, 1995.

Schulte, William. "Starvation Prices Are Offered Again for the Current Crop of Olives." *Corning Observer,* 20 September 1960.

Schultz, John A. *Spain's Colonial Outpost.* San Francisco: Boyd and Fraser, 1985.

Schutt, Harold. "Dr. Samuel Gregg George." *Los Tulares: Quarterly Bulletin of the Tulare County Historical Society* 102 (June 1974).

———. "The Missions Planted Olives." *Los Tulares: Quarterly Bulletin of the Tulare County Historical Society* 47 (March 1961): 1–8.

———. "Pacific Sugar Company, Visalia." *Los Tulares: Quarterly Bulletin of the Tulare County Historical Society* 96 (January 1973).

———. Papers. Special Collections. Henry Madden Library. California State University at Fresno.

———. "Olives in Northern California." Paper presented at the Technical Conference of the California Olive Association. 16–18 June 1964.

———. "When the California Ripe Olive Industry Came of Age." Presentation at the fiftieth anniversary of the California Olive Association. 24 June 1970.

Severson, Thor. *Sacramento: An Illustrated History.* San Francisco: California Historical Society, 1973.

Shallit, Bob. *California: Triumph of the Entrepreneurial Spirit.* Northridge, Calif.: Windsory, 1989.

Shaw, G. W. "California Olive Oil Manufacture." University of California Agricultural Experiment Station Bulletin No. 158 (1904).

Shideler, James Jelinek Lawrence. "A Preliminary List of References for the History of Agriculture in California." Typescript. 1967.

Shinn, Charles, ed. *California Horticulturist and Floral Magazine.* 1871.

Shultis, Arthur. "California Olives: Situation and Outlook." Pamphlet. University of California at Davis Library. 1947.

Sibbett, G. Steven. "Olive Has an Extensive History." Report to the Tulare County Board of Agriculture. 1995.

———, and Joseph Connell. "Producing Olive Oil in California." Division of Agriculture and Natural Resources Leaflet No. 21516 (1994). University of California Cooperative Extension Division.

Simon, Margaret Fripp. "Warren N. Woodson Pursued a Vision from Childhood." *Corning Observer,* 5 March 1982.

Sinclair, Upton. *The Jungle.* New York: Bantam Classics, 1981.

Sisco, Dwight. "An Outbreak of Botulism." *Journal of the American Medical Association* 74, no. 8 (1920): 516–21.

"Sketch of Olive Industry at Corning." *P. G. & E. Progress,* 24 March 1947.

Smith, Bertha. "What Women Are Doing in the West: Freda Ehmann, Olive Grower, and Elizabeth Taylor, Fruit Canner." *Sunset,* June 1911, 640–44.

Smith, McCall A. *Modern History of Tulare County.* Visalia: Limited Editions, 1974.

Smith, Wallace. *Garden of the Sun.* 1939; reprint, Fresno: Max Hardison, 1960.

____. "This Land Was Ours: The Del Valles and Camulos." Pamphlet. Ventura County Historical Society, 1977.

Standish, Robert. *The First of Trees.* London: Phoenix House, 1960.

Starr, Kevin. *Americans and the California Dream: 1850–1915.* New York: Oxford University Press, 1973.

____. *Inventing the Dream.* New York: Oxford University Press, 1985.

Statistics of California Production: Commerce and Finance 1900–01. San Francisco: M. M. Barnet and J. O'Leary, 1902.

Stearns, Robert E. "In Memoriam: Benjamin B. Redding." Pamphlet, California Academy of Sciences. 4 September 1882.

Sternad, Frank. "Captain Guy Emmanuel Grosse." Privately printed. n.d. California Historical Society, San Francisco.

Stewart, Alexander. "Canned Food Poisons." *The Curtis Sandwich* 1 (November 1919). Internal pamphlet.

Stone, Irving. *Men to Match My Mountains.* Garden City, N.Y.: Doubleday, 1956.

Stott, Philip Anthony. *Historical Plant Geography.* London: Allen and Unwin, 1981.

Sunseri, Alvin R. "Agricultural Techniques in New Mexico at the Time of the Anglo-American Conquest." *Agricultural History* 47, no. 4 (1973): 329–37.

Tannahill, Reay. *Food in History.* New York: Stein and Day, 1974.

Tarkington, Booth. *The Magnificent Ambersons.* 1918; reprint, Bloomington/Indianapolis: Indiana University Press, 1989.

Taylor, Mary Hamalian. "Pioneers of Yettem." *Los Tulares: Quarterly Bulletin of the Tulare County Historical Society* 150 (December 1985): 1–5.

Tays, George. "Agriculture in Colonial California," Typescript for *California's Colonial Life.* n.p. 1941. Bancroft Library, University of California at Berkeley.

Thomas, Keith. "Remembering the Deacon." *California Olive Industry News* 14 (February 1960).

Thompson, Frances. "Corning: Warren Woodson." *Wagon Wheels,* 20 (February 1970): 17.

Thompson, Robert A. *Historical and Descriptive Sketch of Sonoma County.* Philadelphia: L. H. Everts and Company, 1877.

Thornburgh, Margaret. "Why Olives Are Supreme." *Westways,* 53 (November 1961): 18–20.

Tolman, Lucius, and Munson L. S. Moody. "Olive Oil and Its Substitutes." *Bureau of Chemistry Bulletin* 77 (1905): 47–62. U.S. Department of Agriculture.

Toussaint, Danielle. "Hard Times on the Olive Ranch." *Chico News and Review,* 29 August 1991.

Trail, Charles. "The Olive Tree in the South of France." Annual Report of the State Board of Horticulture (1890): 460–67.

"Tri Valley Growers: 50 Years of Survival and Growth." Pamphlet produced by Tri Valley Growers. 1983.

"Two Bids for Olive Co-op: Survival at Stake." *Valley Voice,* April 1992.

"Tulare County Leads State in Olive Acreage." *Woodlake Echo,* 24 March 1921.

United States Bureau of Foreign Commerce. "Fruit Culture in Foreign Countries." Reports from the Consuls of the United States, on Fruit Culture in Their Several Districts, in Answer to a Circular from the Department of State. General Printing Office (1890): 393–97.

Vallejo, Guadalupe. "Ranch and Mission Days in Alta California." *Century Magazine* (December 1890.)

Venegas, Miguel. *Juan Maria de Salvatierra.* Translated by Marguerite Eyer Wilbur. Cleveland: Arthur H. Clark, 1921.

"Viewing Victorian Vistas—San Diego." Save Our Heritage Organization. n.d.

von Blon, John L. "The Olive's Royal Swartness Speaks an Ancient Spanish Line." *Westways,* March 1934.

Wallace, Berkeley. "A Glimpse of a California Olive Ranch." *Overland Monthly,* 2d ser., 21 (1893): 278–85.

Warren, Viola Lockhart. "Dr. John Griffin's Mail 1846–1853." *California Historical Society Quarterly* 34 (1955): 21–41.

Webb, Edith Buckland. *Indian Life at the Old Missions.* Los Angeles: Warren F. Lewis, 1952.

Webster, Robert, and Hudson T. Hartmann. "Results of Processing Tests with Several Minor Olive Varieties." *California Olive Industry News* 41 (1949).

Weinstock, Harris. "A Message to California Olive Growers." Pamphlet. Sacramento: State Printing Office, 1916.

Wellman, H. R. "Olives." University of California Agricultural Experiment Bulletin No. 510 (1931).

Wells, A. J. "Gold Mines atop the Ground: The Olive Growing Industry of California and Its Promising Future." *Sunset,* 6 (1900): 97–100.

"What the California Olive Association Is Doing." Pamphlet. 1920. Lindsay Public Library.

Whitaker, Arthur P. "The Spanish Contribution to American Agriculture." *Agricultural History* 3 (1929): 1–14.

Wickes, William. "The Renaissance of the Olive." *Outwest,* n.s., 5 (March/April 1913): 159–64.

Wickson, E. J. *The California Fruits and How to Grow Them.* San Francisco: Dewey and Company, 1889, 1926.

Wilford, John Noble. "Ekron: A Key Vassal of a Great Mercantile Empire." *New York Times,* 23 July 1996.

Williams, A. "Agriculture in California." Report to the U.S. Patent Office (1851). Washington, D.C.

____. "Agriculture in California." Report to the U.S. Patent Office (1852). Washington, D.C.

Wilson, Iris Higbie. *William Wolfskill: Frontier Trapper to California Ranchero.* Glendale, Calif.: Arthur H. Clark, 1965.

Winchell, Lilbourne Alsip. *History of Fresno and Madera Counties.* Fresno, Calif.: A. H. Cawton, 1933.

Woodson, Warren N. ". . . and the Olive Tree Reigned Kindly over Corning." Promotional article, n.d. Corning Chamber of Commerce.

____. "The Story of the Immortal Olive." *Telefood,* January 1940.

____. "The Trail of the Trail Blazers." Pamphlet, 1935. Rotary Club of Corning, California.

Woodward, Lucinda, and Jesse M. Smith, ed. *History of the Lower American River.* Vol. 1. Sacramento: Sacramento Museum and History Commission/County of Sacramento Department of Parks and Recreation, 1977.

"World's Largest Olive Plant." *Lindsay Gazette,* 3 November 1949.

Young, Stanley. *The Missions of California.* San Francisco: Chronicle Books, 1988.

Zohary, Daniel, and M. Hopf. *Domestication of Plants in the Old World.* Oxford, England: Clarendon Press, 1988.

Zumwalt, Betty. *Ketchup, Pickles, Sauces: Nineteenth Century Food in Glass.* Privately published. n.d.

Image Credits

Chapter 2: Development of a Market and an Industry

Page 28   Photograph reproduced with permission of the Butte County Historical Society.
Page 33   Photograph reproduced with permission of the California Historical Society, FN-25323.
Page 36   Photograph reproduced with permission of the Butte County Historical Society.
Page 37   Photograph reproduced with permission of Randall Taylor.
Page 42   Photograph reproduced with permission of the Santa Barbara Historical Society.
Page 45   Photograph from *Illustrated History of the University of California,* by William Carey Jones, 1901. Reproduced with permission of the Bancroft Library, University of California at Berkeley.
Page 47   Photograph reproduced with permission of the California History Room, California State Library, Sacramento, California.
Page 52   Photograph reproduced with permission of the Butte County Historical Society.

Chapter 3: Transition to the Modern Era

Page 56   Photograph reproduced with permission of the California History Room, California State Library, Sacramento, California.
Page 58   Photograph reproduced with permission of the Bancroft Library, University of California at Berkeley.
Page 65   Reproduced with permission of the City of Corning Museum.
Page 71   Photograph reproduced with permission of the California History Room, California State Library, Sacramento, California.
Page 74   Photograph from the College of Agriculture, University of California, reproduced with permission of the USDA National Clonal Germplasm Repository, Winters, California.
Page 77   Photograph by Robert Holmes, used with permission.

Chapter 4: Why Olive Growers Changed to New Kinds of Tress

Page 78   Photograph reproduced with permission of the California History Room, California State Library, Sacramento, California.
Page 83   Photograph from the College of Agriculture, University of California, reproduced with permission of the USDA National Clonal Germplasm Repository, Winters, California.
Page 92   Photograph from the College of Agriculture, University of California, reproduced with permission of the USDA National Clonal Germplasm Repository, Winters, California.

Chapter 5: Nurseries and the Dissemination of Olive Trees

Page 94   Diagram from Arthur Tappan Marvin, *The Olive.* San Francisco: Payot, Upham and Company, 1888.
Page 103   Reproduced with permission of Special Collections, Shields Library, University of California at Davis.
Page 108   Reproduced with permission of Special Collections, Shields Library, University of California at Davis.
Page 109   Reproduced with permission of Special Collections, Shields Library, University of California at Davis.
Page 110   Reproduced with permission of Special Collections, Shields Library, University of California at Davis.

Chapter 9: The California Olive Association

Page 176   Logo reproduced with permission of the California Olive Association.

Page 180   Conference cover sheet reproduced with permission of the California Olive Association.

Page 181   Photograph reproduced with permission of the California History Room, California State Library, Sacramento, California.

Chapter 10: The University of California's Role in the Development of the Olive Industry

Page 200   Photograph reproduced with the permission of the Bancroft Library, University of California at Berkeley.

Page 202   Photograph from *Illustrated History of the University of California,* by William Carey Jones, 1901. Reproduced with permission of the Bancroft Library, University of California at Berkeley.

Page 204   Photographs from *Illustrated History of the University of California,* by William Carey Jones, 1901. Reproduced with permission of the Bancroft Library, University of California at Berkeley.

Page 205   Photograph reproduced with permission of the Bancroft Library, University of California at Berkeley.

Page 206   Photograph reproduced with permission of Mrs. Hazel Hartmann.

Appendix B: Olive Oil Makers in California (1869–1996)

Page 218   Photograph reproduced with permission of Annette O'Connell.

Page 219   Photograph reproduced with permission of Annette O'Connell.

Page 220   Photograph reproduced with permission of Annette O'Connell.

Page 222   Photograph reproduced with permission of Annette O'Connell.

Page 223   Photograph reproduced with permission of Annette O'Connell.

Page 229   Photograph reproduced with permission of Annette O'Connell.

Page 230   Photograph reproduced with permission of Annette O'Connell.

Acknowledgments

The journeys I undertook in doing research for this book gave me the great privilege of talking to experienced men and women whose stories aroused the most profound admiration. Where possible, I asked them to speak into my tape recorder as a way of backing up my notes. In fact, it turned out that I hardly needed the tapes as what they said remains very clear in my mind.

Darrell Corti, whose name was the first I had received, turned out to be a most unusual and knowledgeable man. He refers to himself as a "grocer," but that is not really an appropriate designation. Dan Sciabica's description was apt. Darrell Corti has made a profound study of the fundamentals of wine, olive oil, and lately teas, as well as many other foods, with extraordinary results. He can offer insight after insight into all sorts of things connected with food and drink.

I visited him at his headquarters in Sacramento. He roosts in the cluttered office that technically still belongs to his father but which he has long since overrun and colonized. Piles of paper vie with decorative bottles and cans, and everything has spilled over onto the floor. It is impossible to see how he ever finds any of the material he has accumulated.

We talked about the beginnings of California agriculture. The Spanish Franciscan missionaries brought the olive trees to California. Darrell helped me to understand the Franciscan hierarchy, their table of organization, and their liturgical activities and priorities, all of which was essential information.

Darrell recommended I get a new book from the University of California, the *Olive Production Manual,* written and compiled by three members of the university faculty: Louise Ferguson, G. Steven Sibbett, and George Martin. It had just been reissued, an update of an older manual that the university puts out from time to time. He also suggested I try the Ag Access bookshop in Davis as an additional source of material.

I knew that Davis was the University of California's agricultural campus, and that it was about eighty miles away from my home. My husband and I had passed it on our way to visit friends at Lake Tahoe the previous summer. The journey along Interstate 80 had been long and seemed featureless at the time—just so many boring miles to cover until we got into the foothills and the gold country. Now I had to visit Davis to learn how I might proceed with the research for this book.

This time I paid much more attention to where I was going. As I left the San Francisco Bay Area and dropped down from the hills into the Sacramento Valley, I noticed the extensive horizon, the orchards and fields on either side of the road, and the small towns placed at intervals. The Sierras loomed in the distance. There was snow on their peaks till late in April.

There is a sober beauty in the neat rows of fruit trees stretching for many miles. The median divider on the freeway contains massive oleander hedges of an almost sculptural quality with flowers in pink, red, white, and cream for mile after mile. My eyes were opening, and I was beginning actually to see the Central Valley.

Driving into Davis was surprising. I was not prepared for a gracious, mature town with interesting old houses and tree-lined avenues. Many of those trees are old olive trees, laid out along First Street and Russell Boulevard. Somehow I had imagined Davis would be a raw, agricultural town with ugly industrial processing plants and warehouses. Ag Access, the bookshop, turned out to be a charming old house that had only been minimally modified to contain Karen van Eppen's stock. She could not have been more helpful.

I told her of my quixotic notion about writing a book on the olive in California, and she took it very seriously. She felt that this was a niche that could be filled by someone, although she thought that maybe one or two experts might be planning to write such a book. To help me with my research, we looked through her shelves and found one book from the United Nations' Food and Agriculture Organization devoted to olives. My visit to Ag Access was extremely satisfying.

I decided to contact the editors of the *Olive Production Manual* and see if they could help me continue the study. I still only had rather an indefinite notion in my head when I met with Professor Louise Ferguson at her office at UC Davis on a cold, dank December day. Now that I know how extraordinarily busy she is—she works with university outreach programs covering citrus, figs, and pistachios as well as olives, and teaches in the Department of Pomology—I am even more grateful for the time she took to clarify my thinking and tell me what I could do to get my arms around the subject. Her responsibilities force her to commute regularly between the UC Extension Station at Parlier in the San Joaquin Valley and Davis in the Sacramento Valley, more than two hundred miles each way. Slim and elegant in her crisp white shirt, blue jeans, and comfy hiking boots, Louise is a very impressive woman.

Louise gave me many useful names, addresses, and phone numbers, and confirmed that a book of this sort would be valuable. She told me that a great deal of material existed, but it was very widely scattered. It deserved to be collected together and preserved.

We talked about my visiting the older growers. Much of what they knew would disappear with their deaths. Louise and I also found a common interest in the works of John McPhee, one of her favorite authors. She gently warned me not to dwell too much on the "romance of the tree," even though it had been the route that brought me to her.

Before I went much further, I met the two other principal editors of the *Olive Production Manual*, Professor George C. Martin and G. Steven Sibbett. George Martin had just retired from the Department of Pomology and was enjoying his increased leisure. Unfortunately, while riding his bicycle, he had an unpleasant fall and fractured his hip. I met him when he began to walk again, slowly with crutches. He too considered the idea of a comprehensive history very useful and brought out many documents he had been collecting about olive history just for his own edification. I made notes of everything he mentioned, even though I did not know what they meant or to whom he referred. Now it has all fallen into place.

Arranging to see Steve Sibbett took a bit of planning. He is the farm adviser for Tulare County and had been to Argentina for a sabbatical leave to study the olive industry in South America. It is interesting how the farm advisers I met all seem to care so strongly about olives, even though they have responsibilities for all the crops within their territories.

After these initial interviews, I began to explore the Central Valley more fully. Louise Ferguson had given me the names and phone numbers of the relevant country farm advisers, and I started with them. They in turn introduced me to members of their communities. Meeting the Sciabica family on my own had been fortuitous. When I called someone new, it was helpful to be able to say that I had already met that highly regarded family. The *Olive Production Manual* identified the counties that represented the present-day olive belt. I could start to meet growers and processors in each of them.

This activity was delightful, taking me from one end of the Central Valley to another. I traveled to towns that are important in the agricultural sphere but not among the coastal centers of sophistication. My friends are not in the habit of visiting Visalia, Madera, Lindsay, Modesto, Fresno, Porterville, Exeter, Orland, or Corning. I also went to Santa Clara, Oroville, and Chico, towns that have other attributes besides an agricultural heritage. I was no longer just covering boring miles but looking around and observing as I drove.

Many, many other people helped me in person and in other ways. As I spoke to one, another was suggested. It was a living version of a chain letter without the sinister implications.

Some of the people seemed surprised that I should want to know about their life history. They had worked exceedingly hard, very far from the public eye, at mundane tasks. I wanted to know how, and in some instances why, they started to work in the olive business. I wanted to know when they came to it and what it had meant to them. Where had they gotten their trees? Who were their business associates, suppliers, and dealers? Who else was in the business when they were starting out? They answered all these questions, and more, graciously sharing their knowledge and their lives with me.

Turning then to archival work, I called the Bancroft Library at UC Berkeley and made the acquaintance of Walter Brem, chief of the Latin American division. He prepared a brief list of relevant titles for me, including aspects of agricultural history that once again were new to me. Lawrence Jelinek's *Harvest Empire* provided me with new insights.

Darrell Corti had also recommended I consult Axel Borg at UC Davis. Axel is the state enological librarian and archivist. He had prepared a bibliography of the holdings at UC Davis on the subject of olives for Darrell and shared it with me.

Another boon from which I benefited at UC Davis was being allowed to browse in the stacks. The stimulus to the imagination of seeing books that have peripheral and tangential connections to the topic at hand is enormous. Whole realms of new thought arise as a result.

A reference librarian at UC Davis sent me to find John Skarstad, the director of the Special Collections department. All his suggestions were helpful. I followed his advice to go to the California History Room of the California State Library at Sacramento where I was received enthusiastically by Sybille Zemitis, the doyenne of reference librarians. She pointed me to the old card catalog, which is still the best and easiest way to browse, and then skillfully decoded the antique notations describing newspapers from the 1850s and obscure magazine articles in *World's Work, Wagon Wheels, Overland Monthly,* and other publications engendered by the railroads' desire to attract population to the state. If only microfilm were easier to work with!

My debt of gratitude to all librarians, and California librarians in particular, cannot be measured. In the first place, there is the huge base of quiet, unsung work in which armies of their predecessors had annotated, cataloged, and made sure that nothing was missed in the accumulated holdings of the institutions. That would usually be classed by most of us as pure and unalloyed drudgery. Every issue of every newspaper had been analyzed and the contents sorted by subject. Without that foundation, work such as mine would be impossible. If ever there were a case to be made for card catalogs, this is part of it. Theoretically, it should be feasible to locate these data in a computer catalog, but the thoroughness of the cross indexing in the old manual system still needs to be perfected in computer reference databases.

A further characteristic of librarians is their selfless enthusiasm. I am sure they have healthy egos like everyone else, but there never seemed to be any hint that I might be infringing on someone's turf, or that they were withholding information to prevent me from competing with anyone.

Reading the reports of the State Board of Horticulture from the 1880s and '90s made me realize that nurserymen had played a major role in importing, growing, and propagating new varieties of olive trees at the height of the expansion period. The names that had intrigued me in E. J. Wickson's book on California fruits almost all turned out to be owners of nurseries. This made sense. The nurseries had space, skilled assistance, and the experience to distinguish good results from bad. John Skarstad was particularly helpful in this nursery quest. He told me about Thomas Brown of Petaluma, a landscape historian, and showed me Mr. Brown's list of all known nursery catalogs and brochures from 1850 to 1900 that had survived and where they are kept. Through Brown I found the work of Harry M. Butterfield, horticultural historian par excellence. There were nurseries that propagated nothing but olives at the height of the craze.

The nurserymen did not do this unaided. As part of my obsessive thinking about olive history, I wondered how the Californian of 1875 or 1880 had actually obtained the plants. Did they send an order and get the plant through the mail? Did someone go to Spain or Italy and buy them, and then bring them back with them on the ship? It would be several months later that I found Butterfield's notes and learned just how early the nursery trade began in California. His work made it possible to answer some of these questions.

I interviewed many of the present executives of large olive processing companies and quite a few of the recently retired ones, in addition to family farmers and growers. Some of the companies had historical records of varying types. Jud Carter, of Bell-Carter in Corning, gave me the book about California entrepreneurs that had the story of his grandfather and the origin of his company. He also referred me to George Powell, a former employee, whom I would subsequently visit.

From all these contacts I learned about the existence of the California Olive Association. It seemed to me that here would be a wonderful source of material. I wanted to see their archives. I was a little surprised, when I asked to see old minutes, reports, and other essential documents needed to maintain an organization, that nothing could be found at the office in Sacramento. Bill Grigg, director of the association, referred me to the Special Collections department at UC Davis. Unfortunately, these boxes turned out to be quite disappointing! They contained a hodgepodge of old financial records, odd correspondence, and individual research articles that had found their way into the files but no minutes, resolutions, or other materials of consequence. Some private individuals had more complete sets of material.

The current members of the California Olive Association have been very helpful. I was privileged to meet G. K. "Pat" Patterson for an hour or two in the summer of 1996, just before he set off for Spain as a consultant to a new olive enterprise there. Pat has to be in his eighties, but he could only spare me a few minutes because of the press of business. He was on the board of the COA for many years, and president in 1954. We had a stimulating chat and he recalled the names of many firms which no longer exist.

I was very lucky to meet another descendant of an early olive processor. Louis B. Sammis was active in the association almost from its beginning and was president in 1949. He is no longer alive, but his grandson, Ian Sammis, lives in Marin County. He practices law in San Rafael.

Ralph Fusano is one of the dedicated men who has saved extensive records. His father, Cristo, ran the Sylmar Olive Company with the aid of his sons. Ralph later went to work for the Lindsay Ripe Olive Company. He stayed there until it went out of business and was bought by Bell-Carter. He and his friend George Powell, who spent the larger part of his working life at Lindsay Ripe Olive before retiring to Monterey, felt a compulsion to keep all the records they could, perhaps because they thought they might write a book about it all one day.

In another wonderful instance of serendipity, I found correspondence in Ralph's papers dating to 1983 from Annette O'Connell in Redwood City. She is a collector of olive oil bottles and used to deal in them. She had been asking Ralph about the history of olive oil companies in the state, based on her findings from the bottles. He made her a list from memory with about seventy-five entries. Now I could understand some of the names thrown out by Joseph and Daniel Sciabica in an offhanded way but which did not mean much to me at the time. This list was another treasure I was welcome to use. I wrote to Mrs. O'Connell, and she shared a great deal more of her work with me, including a set of pictures of the bottles. Now I could correlate Ralph's notes with her list.

Mrs. O'Connell also suggested another resource, Betty Zumwalt's *Ketchup, Pickles, Sauces: Nineteenth Century Food in Glass,* a self-published compilation of facts, again gleaned from studying the bottles in which these items were packed. Mrs. O'Connell had found more companies than Betty Zumwalt, but I was in the best position of all with three sources to review. More recently, I met another collector of bottles, Dr. Thomas Jacobs, in San Francisco, who has extensive knowledge of early olive oil makers. Chasing down the full names and information about the companies that Ralph could only sketch in lightly took me to old city directories and archives in Sacramento, and to the Sutro Library in San Francisco. This was the fourth and final source for now defunct olive oil companies and olive processors.

Official "olivedom" is defined by four main organizations. Apart from the California Olive Association, which represents the large olive processing companies, there is the California Olive Committee. Its former director, Dave Daniels, also had a considerable amount of information available and shared much of it with me. The council, based in Fresno, was formed to administer the various marketing orders from the state and federal government.

Then there is the Olive Growers' Committee, headquartered in Visalia. Adin Hester is executive director and runs the committee, which acts to protect the growers' interests when they are dealing with the large processing companies. He was charming and helpful, passing me on to several town and county historians who later took me under their wing. The Tulare County farm adviser, G. Steven Sibbett, based in Visalia, completed this process. He told me about the "queen" of local historians, Annie Mitchell, a remarkable woman in her nineties who is still very active in following and codifying Tulare history.

Ora Kay Peterson, former president of the Tulare County Historical Society, introduced me to Annie Mitchell. Mrs. Mitchell had known Harold Schutt, a noted local historian and someone whose work was very important for me. He had traced the history of the olive very carefully and had written several useful articles in the society's journal, *Los Tulares.* Mrs.

Mitchell told me that some of his papers had been given to the California State University at Fresno after his death. It is possible that he intended to write a book, but none was found.

The newest organization in the field is the California Olive Oil Council, formerly the Northern California Olive Oil Council. I joined this group to be able to find out more of what was happening. Its members are redefining California's olive oil industry, from a mere fragment based on rejected fruit to a growing future in a special niche. The members mainly live and work in Napa and Sonoma counties. Some are vintners, some are professional farmers; others are dedicated amateurs who want to do something valuable with their time and money, the latter often obtained from altogether different businesses. Take Ed Stolman, for example. Ed retired to a handsome property in Glen Ellen, built a villa in the Italian style, and planted a thousand Leccino and Frantoio trees. He welcomed me very warmly to the society.

A most unexpected member of the California Olive Oil Council turned out to be a retired industrial oil chemist in Arlington, Virginia. Carter Litchfield is an authority on antique olive oil mills and runs a small press called Olearius, which is Latin for "oil maker." He publishes detailed monographs on such mills. I wrote to the press to buy one of the books and told him what I planned to do, asking for help and advice. The response was as if Vesuvius had erupted. The most amazing torrent of articles, suggestions, directions, advice, and general warm encouragement has followed since then. This was all done by mail and on the phone.

I did not get to meet Carter Litchfield for six months until he came to California to present a paper to the Society for Industrial Archaeology in Sacramento. We then had dinner together, joined by his wife, Carol, a microbiologist, and my husband. People listen to me politely when I tell them what I am doing, but Carter really understood the finer points of my progress.

When everything was collected together and put into a whole, Dr. Kevin Starr, California State Librarian and noted historian of California, very graciously provided me with the foreword, linking the small world of the olive trees to the larger one of California itself. I am grateful to him for his confidence in the work and encouragement to continue.

The owner of Ten Speed Press, Phil Wood, and his stalwart staff with Holly Taines White as my project editor, showed unfailing courtesy and support through a long, drawn-out process. Jean Blomquist, copyeditor, has been a model of her profession. Without Tom Southern's acquisitions assistance, I would not have found the press.

It is my husband, Irvin, who has been the most long-suffering. Without any complaints, he has sailed through all those times I had to travel around and leave him to fend for himself. This included the times when he had to entertain out-of-town guests whose visits coincided with appointments I had had great difficulty in setting up and therefore hesitated to break. I say truly that he made it all possible.

At this point, I want to acknowledge the many people who have assisted me in preparing this book. I am deeply grateful to all of them.

James Aguiar, olive grower (Orland)
Lawrence Aguiar, olive grower (Orland)
Louis Aguiar, former field man (Bell-Carter Foods)
J. S. "Pat" Akin, olive grower (Tulare County)
Father Virgilio Biasiol, librarian (Mission Santa Barbara)
Peter Blodgett, research associate (The Huntington Library, San Marino)
Jean M. Blomquist, copyeditor (Albuquerque, NM)
Axel Borg, wine bibliographer (Shields Library, UC Davis)
Walter Brem, chief of Latin American section (Bancroft Library, UC Berkeley)
Thomas Brown, expert on historical horticulture (Petaluma)
Dennis Burreson, manager (Musco Olive Products, Orland)
Robert "Amigo" Cantisano, organic farmer, olive grower,
    producer of olive oil and ethnic olives (Colfax)
Jud Carter, owner (Bell-Carter Foods, Corning)
Kevin Caskey, Tulare County Historical Society (Visalia)
Kathy Chambers, librarian (Shields Library, UC Davis)
Jean Coffee, archivist (Special Collections, Henry Madden Library,
    California State University at Fresno)
Joseph Connell, farm adviser (UC Extension Service, Butte County)
Carol Cooper (UC Davis Department of Food Technology, Cruess Hall)
Joseph Cooper, retired olive grower (Butte County)
Darrell Corti, food and wine consultant (Corti Brothers, Sacramento)
Frank Corti, co-founder and co-owner (Corti Brothers, Sacramento)
Julia G. Costello, archaeologist of the California missions (Mokelumne Hill)
Claude Craig, olive grower (Corning)
Marjorie Craig, olive grower (Corning)
David Daniels, former executive director (California Olive Committee)
Darlene Dickison, city official (Corning)
Louise Ferguson, extension specialist (Department of Pomology, UC Davis)
Ralph Fusano, olive grower and authority on olive history (Lindsay)
Marino Garbis, producer of olive oil and ethnic olives (West Coast Products, Orland)
Howard Gerson (USDA National Clonal Germplasm Repository, Winters)
Beth Graham, assistant librarian (California Historical Society Library, San Francisco)
William Grigg, executive director (California Olive Association, Sacramento)
Joan Hall (Riverside County Historical Society, Riverside)

Hazel Hartmann, widow of Professor Hudson T. Hartmann (Davis)

William Heintz, historian of the Napa Valley wine industry (Napa)

Margaret and Michael Henwood, olive oil makers (Marysville)

Adin Hester, executive director (Olive Growers Association, Visalia)

Clarence Hill, retired olive industry executive (Visalia)

Thomas Jacobs, DDS, collector of olive oil bottles (San Francisco)

Patricia Keates, director (California Historical Society Library, San Francisco)

Donald Koball, olive grower (Corning)

Matthew Koball, olive grower (Corning)

Norma Kobzina, librarian (Biosciences Library, UC Berkeley)

Everett Krackov, olive grower (Tulare County)

William Krueger, farm adviser (UC Extension Service, Glenn and Tehama counties)

Kurt Kuss, archivist (formerly at National Agricultural Library, College Park, Maryland)

Tammy Lau, director (Special Collections, Henry Madden Library,
   California State University at Fresno)

William Leigh, Ph.D. (Pentavate Laboratories, Lindsay)

Carter Litchfield, Ph.D. (Olearius Editions, Arlington, Virginia)

George C. Martin, Ph.D., retired (Department of Pomology, UC Davis)

Marvin Martin, former manager (Oberti Olive Company, Madera)

Della Martinelli, olive grower (Madera)

Judith Marvin, historian (Murphys, Calaveras County)

Nan McEvoy, olive grower and producer of olive oil (Petaluma, Sonoma County)

Jack McFarland, olive grower (Corning)

Anne McMahon, archivist (Santa Clara University, Santa Clara)

Terry McShane, author, consultant, and granddaughter of Freda Ehmann (Bend, Oregon)

Martin Miller, retired (Department of Food Technology, UC Davis)

Annie Mitchell, author and historian (Tulare County)

Therese Muranaka, formerly curator (Junípero Serra Museum, San Diego)

Doris Muscatine, author and San Francisco historian (Berkeley)

Felix Musco (Musco Olive Products, Tracy)

Nick Musco, owner (Musco Olive Products, Tracy)

Jan Nelson, executive director (California Olive Committee, Fresno)

Charlene Noyes, archivist (Sacramento City Museum and Archives, Sacramento)

Gary Oberti, former executive (Oberti Olive Company, Madera)

Annette O'Connell, collector of olive oil bottles (Redwood City)

Karl Opitz, former farm adviser (UC Extension Service, Tulare County)

Jerry Padula (Golden Eagle Olive Oil Company, Porterville)

Gordon K. "Pat" Patterson, consultant and former olive company executive (Visalia)

Maurice Penna, olive grower and processor (Orland)
Ora Kay Peterson (Tulare County Historical Society, Visalia)
Tracy Pisenti, Freda Ehmann's great-granddaughter (Danville)
George Powell, retired executive (Lindsay Ripe Olive Company, Monterey)
Martin Ridge, historian (The Huntington Library, San Marino)
William Roberts, archivist (UC Berkeley)
Ian Sammis, attorney and grandson of Louis Sammis,
   Rocca Bella Olive Company (San Rafael)
Daniel Sciabica (Nick Sciabica and Sons, Modesto)
Joseph Sciabica, owner (Nick Sciabica and Sons, Modesto)
Nick Sciabica (Nick Sciabica and Sons, Modesto)
G. Steven Sibbett, farm adviser (UC Extension Service, Visalia, Tulare County)
Robert Singletary, manager (Napa Valley Kitchens, Corning)
John Skarstad, director (Special Collections, Shields Library, UC Davis)
Tom Southern, acquisitions (Ten Speed Press, Berkeley)
Robert Swank, former manager (Maywood Packing Company, Corning)
Hugh B. Taylor, author's son, digital imaging assistance (Santa Monica)
Gail Terry, olive grower (Orland)
MaryAnn Terstegge, librarian (Annie Mitchell Room, Tulare County Library, Visalia)
Lucy Tolmach, director of horticulture (Filoli, Woodside)
John Ugaste, Sr., olive oil maker (Reedley)
John Ugaste, Jr., olive oil maker (Reedley)
Lubbert van Dellen, executive (Early California Foods, Visalia)
Karen van Eppen, owner (Ag Access Bookstore, Davis)
Sherry Vance, research associate (Bailey Hortorium, Cornell University)
Sam Vanella, olive grower (Corning)
Francois-Laurent Vitrac, olive grower (Calaveras County)
Paul Vossen, farm adviser (UC Extension Service, Sonoma County)
D. G. Voyiatsis, professor of horticulture (Thessaloniki University, Greece)
John Whisler, former assistant (Department of Pomology, UC Davis)
George White, Ph.D., director (USDA National Clonal Germplasm Repository, Winters)
Holly Taines White, project editor (Ten Speed Press, Berkeley)
Lewis Whitendale (UC Cooperative Extension Service, Lindcove)
Sybille Zemitis, librarian (California History Room, California State Library, Sacramento)

Index